Pen, Ink, & Evidence

Pen, Ink, & Evidence

A Study of Writing and Writing Materials for the Penman, Collector, and Document Detective

JOE NICKELL

Foreword by Charles Hamilton

Photographs from the author's collection by
Robert H. van Outer

Forensic assistance from John F. Fischer

THE UNIVERSITY PRESS OF KENTUCKY

To my mother,
ELLA T. NICKELL,
this book is lovingly dedicated

Copyright © 1990 by The University Press of Kentucky

Scholarly publisher for the Commonwealth,
serving Bellarmine College, Berea College, Centre
College of Kentucky, Eastern Kentucky University,
The Filson Club, Georgetown College, Kentucky
Historical Society, Kentucky State University,
Morehead State University, Murray State University,
Northern Kentucky University, Transylvania University,
University of Kentucky, University of Louisville,
and Western Kentucky University.

Editorial and Sales Offices: Lexington, Kentucky 40508

Library of Congress Cataloging-in-Publication Data

Nickell, Joe.
    Pen, ink, and evidence : a study of writing and writing materials
for the penman, collector, and document detective / Joe Nickell ;
with photographs from the author's collection by Robert H. van Outer;
and forensic assistance from John F. Fischer.
        p.   cm.
    Includes bibliographical references and index.
    ISBN 0-8131-1719-4 :
    1. Writing—History.   2. Writing—Materials and instruments
—History.   3. Manuscript dating.   4. Paleography.   I. Title.
Z40.N53   1990
652′.1—dc20   90-38544

Contents

Foreword

As I ventured into the pages of this history of handwriting, I was dazzled by the vast amount of information Joe Nickell has brought together in one volume. To accomplish this feat, the author explored innumerable written works, many of them rare and long out of print, and added his own experiences, including laboratory experiments. The result of all this research is a dramatic record of every aspect of handwriting. Nickell's comments are punctuated by drawings and photographs that chronicle the history of pens, paper, and ink.

A valuable reference work, it is also a perfect bedside or traveling companion. Do pens and ink intrigue you? Maybe not, but they will when you read what Joe Nickell has to say about them. Did you know, for instance, that the left wing feathers of the bird were preferred for quill pens or that nutgalls from the oak tree, an essential ingredient in the ink used by Shakespeare and Napoleon, were actually created by female wasps? And were you aware that rubber erasers like the one on the end of your pencil may soon be replaced by laser beams?

Without pen, ink, and paper, there would, of course, be no permanently recorded history, literature, music, or science. But the significance of this book goes far beyond the obvious. Aside from its appeal to the general reader, it is sure to intrigue and benefit calligraphers, those true devotees of the pen who enjoy turning every letter they write into a thing of beauty; philographers, or collectors and students of old and rare manuscripts and letters; graphologists and graphoanalysts; archivists and librarians; paleographers; forensic document examiners; criminologists and crime buffs; and collectors of the quaint and rare.

As for myself, I can only aver that had I owned this volume sixty years ago, it would have enormously eased my entry into the manuscript world and spared me countless hours of trial and error in deciphering old scripts and identifying forgeries, as well as adding a more polished background to my court testimony as an expert in forensic documents.

Charles Hamilton

Acknowledgments

In addition to those friends whose names deservedly grace the title page of this book—Charles Hamilton (the world's greatest signature sleuth), Robert H. van Outer (photographer extraordinaire), and John F. Fischer (a microanalyst of macro-brilliance)—I am supremely indebted to John T. Shawcross, distinguished scholar and professor of English at the University of Kentucky, for his example, encouragement, guidance, and friendship.

I am also grateful to the University of Kentucky faculty members who served on the committee for my doctoral dissertation (portions of which are scattered among the pages that follow): R. Gerald Alvey, John Greenway, Michael Harris, Jerome Meckier, and Rupert Pickens. I also wish to express my gratitude to Joseph Gardner, Kevin Kiernan, Guy Davenport, John Cawelti, and Robert Cazden for their encouragement. And to Joseph A. Bryant, Jr.—who believed in this book before ever a word of it was written—I extend my heartfelt thanks.

In addition, I appreciate the many antique dealers who helped me track down the treasures pictured herein. They are too many to list individually, but they include those who display their wares at the antique shows, the shops, and antique malls in the central Kentucky area. I do owe a special debt to Jerome Redfearn and Duane Yeager of Georgetown, and Scarlett and Steve Armstrong of Lexington who—time and again—squirreled away items earmarked for my collection and then presented them to me as gifts.

And finally, I am grateful for the repeated assistance I received from the staffs of the Margaret I. King Library at the University of Kentucky and the John F. Kennedy Memorial Library in West Liberty, Kentucky.

Without the contributions of all those who helped in some way, my task—which lasted more than a decade—would have been even greater and the results would have been much diminished.

PART 1

Writing Instruments

I rejoice that you have learnt
to write for another reason: for
as that is done with a goose quill,
now you know the value of a goose.

—Thomas Jefferson
to his granddaughter
1808

1

The Quill

Much ancient writing was done without benefit of the pen: The Babylonians impressed their cuneiform characters in clay tablets with a wedge-shaped instrument; the Greeks and Romans chiseled inscriptions on stone monuments and wrote with a stylus on wax-coated tablets; and the Chinese used the brush for their calligraphy, as did the Egyptians for their early hieroglyphics.

The same rush stem which the Egyptians frayed to make a brush, however, was later fashioned into a crisply cut writing instrument. This reed pen was used with a soot-and-glue ink, first on a writing material made from another type of reed, called papyrus, and subsequently (in Greece and Rome) on parchment.[1]

Because it was more readily available in western Europe, the quill eventually displaced the reed pen (although the latter survived for certain specific uses, such as large lettering).[2] According to one authority, "It appears safe to assume that the quill pen came into gradual use with the establishment of Roman formal capital letters, of graduated thick and thin strokes, and the supplanting of papyrus by vellum [parchment] about 190 B.C."[3]

Nevertheless, certain reference to the quill is not found before the early seventh century, when a specific passage occurs in the writings of Saint Isidore of Seville. Dated 624, it refers to *penna avis* (bird feather) used for *Instrumenta scribae* (scribes' implements). Indeed, the Latin for "feather," *penna*, is the source for our English word "pen." The equivalent terms for this writing instrument in France and Germany have a similar derivation, being *plume* and *feder*, respectively.[4]

Quill Selection

The feathers of choice were typically those of the goose, the most common of domestic fowls. Holland was a major European supplier, and—since it was often claimed the best quills came from the coldest climates—bales of them were imported into England during the eighteenth and nineteenth centuries from such additional countries as Norway, Iceland, and Greenland. Black goose quills from Hudson Bay were prized for over a century, and Ireland was also a supplier of quills, as shown by a *Kentucky Gazette* advertisement of 1818 announcing for sale "A few Thousand Superior Irish Quills."[5]

In England itself, quality quills from the county of Lincolnshire were especially plentiful. As Isaac Taylor wrote in 1823 in his *Scenes of British Wealth*, great flocks of up to ten thousand were driven from Lincolnshire to London. "But we have not done with the pens and the geese there. Their feathers and quills are so valuable that the avarice of man has put aside his better feelings; the geese do not live in peace until they die, and know nothing more about it; but, about the end of March, they have their quill [i.e., wing] feathers pulled out to make pens, and their other feathers also."[6]

In addition to geese, however, swans and turkeys also supplied feathers for pens, as did, occasionally, pheasants and ravens. In medieval times mention was even made of pelican and peacock quills.[7] Crow quills were often preferred for fine pen drawing as well as for the tiny handwriting sometimes affected by ladies (fig. 1.1). In fact, as an 1846 tract on penmanship summed up, in couplet form: "From the great Eagle to the Wren, / We may pluck quills that make a pen."[8]

Quill collecting usually took place at moulting time, with each wing producing five or more usable quills. The fresh feathers were naturally covered with a thin, tough skin which, after it had dried for a considerable time, peeled off easily. More often, to remove the skin the quills were baked for about an hour in hot sand (a process called "dutching" because it originated in Holland). They would usually then be dipped in a boiling alum solution for a final cleansing, and tied up in bundles for sale.[9] An 1836 watercolor depicts a bundle of quills and a penknife on the desk of a schoolmaster, one of whose duties it was to furnish pens for his

Figure 1.2. QUILLS AND ACCESSORIES. Displayed on a quill-written indenture of 1791 are (*from left*) a Victorian lady's writing kit, an assortment of quills with their box, a small redware inkwell, and a quill penknife. The writing kit includes (*from top*) two quills; a bookmark embroidered "Mother Dear"; an ivory paper knife; an ivory mechanical pencil, made by S. Mordan and Company; an unidentified bone implement (wafer tongs?); a chunk of rubber, for erasures; and a pouch for wafers (paste disks used to seal letters). The kit has a pocket for stationery.

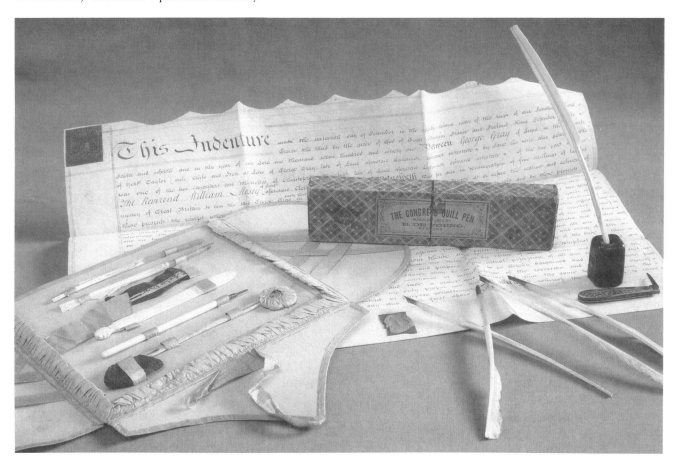

students. And Charles Dickens's 1853 novel *Bleak House* contains a reference to the "thin red cord that they tie up pens with." Later, when boxes became commonly used for packaging goods, they were utilized for sharpened quills as well. For example, T. and J. Smith's quill pens—sold in London about 1840—came in rigid, rounded-end cardboard boxes decorated with printed and handcolored floral designs (fig. 1.2).[10]

Quills from the left wing of the bird commanded a higher price because they were preferred by right-handed writers (as left-handed persons desired right-wing quills).[11] One author states this was "so that growth whorls, being opposite to the pull of the pen as it was being used, could provide additional strength and longer life to the pen."[12] Others explain that the preference was simply due to the curvature of the quill; Donald Jackson says, "the left wing feather curves comfortably around the knuckle of a right-handed person's hand."[13] The issue is quite old, as indicated by Giovanni Battista Palatino in his *Libro nuovo d'imparare a scrivere* (1540). Writing of quills plucked from the domestic goose, he states: "It does not matter from which wing they are taken, though some writers draw a great distinction here; those which are taken from the right wing should be broken off or bent above the barrel so that they do not twist when held in the hand; which is a serious impediment to rapid, even writing."[14]

Quill Cutting

How quills were to be cut depended on the fashion in writing at the time. The square-cut "broad pen" of the

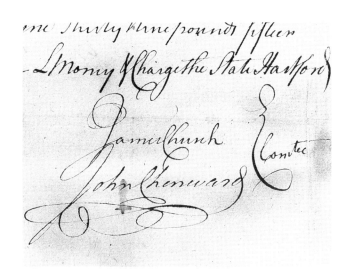

Figure 1.3. QUILL-WRITTEN SCRIPT, as in this Revolutionary War document of 1778, is characterized by thin upstrokes and heavy or "shaded" downstrokes, in which pressure caused the points of the split pen to separate. Light and responsive to the touch, the pointed quill could move swiftly and facilitated cursive and fluid styles of penmanship.

Middle Ages was suited to such styles of lettering as Gothic and italic, but it yielded to the pointed shape of the Renaissance pen, which made possible the engraving-like script known as round hand (fig. 1.3).[15]

Quills were cut with a special knife, the form of which varied over the centuries. The ancient ones had fixed iron blades and shaped handles (the length of which was about the width of the hand) made of wood, bone, ivory, or even leather. Penknives with very decorative handles—made of silver, gold, agate, or tor-

Figure 1.4. QUILL PENKNIVES include three (*at left*) probably dating from the late eighteenth century and five (*right*) from the nineteenth century. Note the narrow blades.

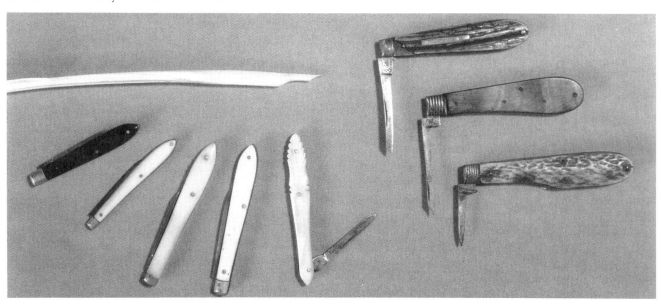

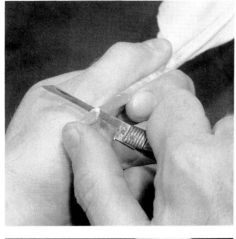
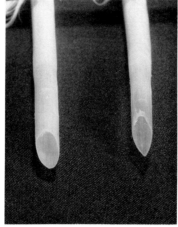

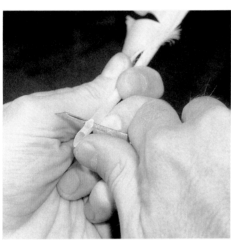

Figures 1.5-1.9. CUTTING A QUILL.

1.5 (*top left*). After removing barbs from the lower end and scraping the shaft, slice off tip at an angle. Remove internal pith.

1.6 (*top center*). Sharpen the resulting cut-off end (*left*) by paring from each side to shape pen to a point (*right*).

1.7 (*top right*). Cut the slit as shown, using a firm surface for support.

1.8 (*bottom left*). Begin another cut at an angle, like the first cut, and a short distance behind it, but slice down only about halfway; then, turning knife, cut toward yourself, horizontally, until piece is cut free.

1.9 (*bottom center*). Examine quill and, if desired, thin point by carefully shaving upper side of tip.

toiseshell, and sometimes inlaid with jewels—date from about the seventeenth century. They had fine steel blades, which were fixed or folding or perhaps even sliding, and a cutting edge that might be straight or concave or convex. By this time the knife blades had become quite narrow, perhaps as little as one-eighth of an inch wide.[16] Common eighteenth- and nineteenth-century penknives are shown in figure 1.4. The blades remain narrow, and most are flat on one side but rounded on the other (the underside when used by a right-handed person)—features that facilitated the blade's ability to turn easily when making the requisite curved slices. The two at the upper left of figure 1.4 are similar to one used by George Washington.[17]

As it fell into disuse with the advent of the steel pen in the first part of the nineteenth century, the penknife evolved into a small, folding pocketknife. Typically, one small blade is the so-called pen blade, although it is considerably wider than its ancestral form and used for a variety of purposes such as cutting string and sharpening pencils.[18] Modernists wishing to try their hand at quill-cutting often use surgical scalpels, budding or pedicure knives, or the like.[19]

Figure 1.10. QUILL TEST SHEET is a page from a notebook (1829-46) on which the writer has tried out his newly cut pens.

Figure 1.11. A QUILL NEEDING MENDING produced ragged writing and ink spattering in the first few lines of an 1843 power of attorney. The remaining text is problem free, indicating that the pen was mended with a knife.

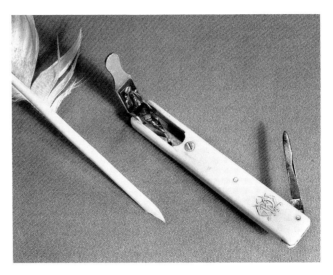

Figure 1.12. This QUILL CUTTER of the folding, pocket variety is made of ivory and monogrammed. The lever was raised, the quill inserted in the hole in the end, and the point was formed and slit by dies when the lever was pressed. Because quills are tubular, two points resulted—one at the upper and one at the lower side of the shaft; one of the points was removed with the knife.

Although directions for cutting a quill varied according to individual preference and fashion in writing, typical instructions for cutting the pointed quill were given by Nathaniel Dearborn in 1846:

> Cut off quarter of an inch in length in a slanting direction from the back of the quill; scrape the centre back of it to clear off all hoops and scurf; turn it over and cut off one inch in length in a slant or champ to the depth of one half the quill; turn it over and place your thumb on the back of the quill, as far as you intend to split it; then split the quill with the knife where it is scraped, observing that the thinner the quill, the shorter the split; turn it over and shave the two parts down to a tapering point, cutting the outer surface of the quill away, rather more than the inner, leaving the shoulders about one-third the distance from the point of the pen to the upper cut of the quill; lay the nibs of the pen on your thumb nail, and cut them off in a slant, with the handle of the knife a little farther from you than the blade; the right nib, as you write, will be the longest, as it should be, as that nib makes the fine hair lines.[20]

The sequence of the cuts can vary. Compare Dearborn's instructions, for example, with my simplified method of cutting a quill shown in figures 1.5 to 1.9.

Quill Problems

After being cut, quills were commonly tested to see if they worked properly (fig. 1.10), and there could be problems, as noted by the pencutter John Wilkes at the end of the eighteenth century: "Those who make their own pens have a great advantage providing they keep their knives in the best order possible, otherwise they can never make a good pen, for unless the knife cuts exceeding smooth, the pen will make a ragged stroke."[21] For an instance of writing produced by a faulty quill, see figure 1.11.

Although scribes and scriveners cut their own pens, professional quill cutters were available for those who wished to have the chore done for them. The pencutters would "station" themselves on local streets—hence the terms *stationer* and *stationery* for the seller and for his pens and other writing supplies.[22] There were other remedies for the person unwilling or unable to master the art of quill cutting. As James Fenimore Cooper confessed in 1843: "Although few living now have written more than myself—such as it is—I neither make nor mend a pen; a circumstance that may, in a degree, account for a handwriting that is as unequal as the spirits of a hypochondriac. A fortunate French invention enables me to cut quills into a form that enables me to scribble, but for which, and the steel pens, it is probable the world would have been spared many heavy inflictions from my hand."[23] The "French invention" Cooper referred to was the quill cutter. It existed in a variety of forms (French-made and otherwise), ranging from an elaborate stand-up model that dates from the eighteenth century to the more common folding pocket model shown in figure 1.12.[24]

Even after a quill had been successfully cut, it could continue to present problems. As Palatino cautioned in his 1540 treatise: "Quills should be kept clean of any ink

Figure 1.13. A GLASS QUILL HOLDER with a shaped depression held a quill and kept it from drying out or fraying if filled with a little water.

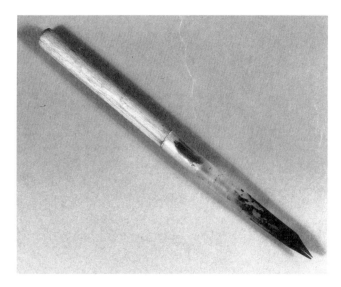

Figure 1.14. A QUILL NIB mounted on wooden holder is a transitional item. The one shown, probably a late version, was found in a pencil box of about 1870.

which remains after writing, because old ink interferes with the flow of fresh ink. They should invariably be kept in a vessel with just enough water to cover the part which has been cut to form the nib. A quill must never be allowed to dry out, because this makes your letters ragged and feeble, and it is extremely difficult to write with such quills." [25] To prevent quills from drying and fraying, a solid glass holder with a pen-shaped depression (fig. 1.13) was sometimes used, as were inkstands with quill holes. [26]

Another problem was that quills needed frequent sharpening, resulting in their often being whittled down to within a few inches of the tip. Sometimes quill points were even gilded for durability. In 1809, however, Joseph Bramah patented a machine that cut the quill into separate nibs, and subsequently, by 1827, S. Mordan and Company of London sold silver holders for such "Portable Quill Pens," which they advertised were "of great value, from their compact portability, as fifty or one hundred may be carried in a small box, fit for the waistcoat pocket." Thus the need for cutting or sharpening quills was potentially eliminated. [27] A late version of the quill nib on a wooden holder is illustrated in figure 1.14.

Quill problems and their solutions eventually led to the development of metal pens which effectively displaced the quill by about the mid-nineteenth century. [28] Interestingly, although soon superseded by the modern type of nib, the earliest steel pens were fashioned as tubes—their shape deriving from the centuries-old quill from which they had evolved.

SELECT BIBLIOGRAPHY

Ball, Berenice. "Writing Tools and Treasures." Part 2. *National Antiques Review*, September 1973. A brief look at quills and associated items.

Bishop, William. "Pens, Pencils, Brushes and Knives." In *The Calligrapher's Handbook*, 2d ed., ed. C.M. Lamb, 15-43. New York: Pentalic, 1968. Historical background on pens, with instructions on cutting a quill.

Carlisle, Lilian Baker. "How to Make a Quill Pen." *Antiques Journal*, September 1973.

Johnston, Edward. *Writing and Illuminating and Lettering*. 1906; rpt.: London: Pitman, 1979.

Mason, Philip. "The Lost Art of Quill Pen Making." *Early American Life*, April 1975, 40-41.

Encyclopaedia Britannica. 1910-11 ed. s.v. "pen."

2

Durable Pens

The Steel Pen

When, in the Old Testament, Job speaks of an "iron pen" (Job 19:24), the context demonstrates the reference is only figurative, an allusion to metal tools with which his words might be "graven" (i.e., chiseled) and so remain "in the rock for ever!"

Yet metal pens were, in fact, known in ancient times, a bronze pen being found, for example, at Pompeii.[1] The Roman experimental pens of metal had "shaft, barrel, nib and slit, all in one piece, similar in shape to a quill," states William Bishop. He concludes that the design proves the Romans "were well acquainted with the quill pen as a writing instrument (150 B.C.)," although it should be noted the reed pen was also of that form.[2]

Until the end of the eighteenth century there are isolated references to metallic pens. For example, in 1465, in the colophon of their first printed book, Gutenberg's former partners refer to both "quill" and "brazen reed."[3] Again, in 1595 it is recorded that the prize in a contest was to be a golden pen.[4] But it is difficult to know whether such references are more than figurative, or whether trophy or presentation pens were actually intended to be written with.

In 1700 Roger North stated in a letter to his sister: "You will hardly tell by what you see that I write with a steel pen. It is a device come out of France. . . . When they get the knack of making them exactly, I do not doubt but the government of the goose quill is near an end, for none that can have them will use other."[5] Ignorant of this prior invention, in 1748 a Prussian magistrate of Aix-la-Chapelle, Johann Jantssen, felt he might "without boasting, claim the honour of having invented new pens. It is, perhaps, not an accident that God should have inspired me at the present time with the idea of making steel pens." Having sold his entire stock of pens to visitors at a diplomatic congress, Jantssen added: "They are now sent into every corner of the world as a rare thing, to Spain, France, and England.

Others will no doubt make imitations of my pens, but I am the man who first invented and made them."[6] Indeed, according to one authority, steel pens were produced in the same year in France, but they were unpopular due to their stiffness and price.[7]

The steel pen was reintroduced in England in 1780 by Samuel Harrison, a manufacturer in Birmingham, who is known to have made such pens for Dr. Joseph Priestly, the clergyman and chemist, in that year. (Apparently it was Harrison's pen that led Julius Grant to give, erroneously, 1780 as the date steel pens were "invented.")[8] As Harrison's pen has been described, "a sheet of steel was rolled in the form of a tube. One end was cut and trimmed to a point after the manner of the quill, the seam where both edges of the tube met forming the slit of the pen."[9] Similarly fashioned pens were manufactured in London in 1803 by a man named Wise, who sold them for about five shillings each. They were quite stiff and unsatisfactory, however, and consequently in little demand.[10] The first patent for metal pens was awarded to Bryan Donkin in 1808, and about 1822 John Mitchell introduced machine-made pens.[11]

The Englishman James Perry is believed the first to have made steel "slip" pens; until then, sometime in the 1820s, the pen and holder were one piece.[12] Such tubular nibs were similar to the quill ones produced by Joseph Bramah in 1809 (fig. 2.1). They were used on wooden holders or slipped onto the end of uncut quills; some threaded into metal holders.

In 1824, Perry began making pens on a large scale.[13] In 1828 Josiah Mason, a former associate of Samuel Harrison, became associated with Perry after conceiving ways both to improve and to cheapen the manufacturing process, and he began to make barrel pens for him at that time as well as slip pens the following year.[14]

In 1830 Perry obtained a patent on a more flexible pen. It had a central hole punched above the slit, plus one or more extra slits on either side of the main one. As he announced later that year: "till about 6 months ago

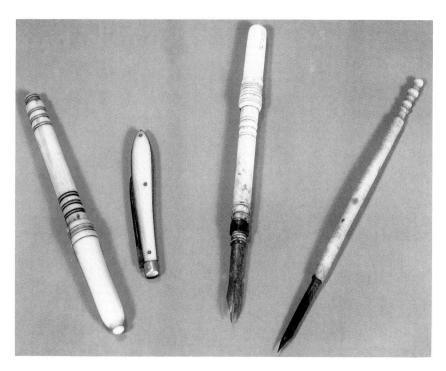

Figure 2.1. TRANSITIONAL NIBS. The early nineteenth century saw the quill cut into separate pen nibs, and these were followed by the manufacture of tubular, quill-like steel pens. Both fit on holders. Those shown here are bone, turned on a lathe. The holder at left is missing its pen, although it was probably a quill pen, since it was discovered with the accompanying penknife.

the public had heard little of metallic pens. At present, it would seem that comparatively few of any *other* kind are in the hands of any class of the community. This sudden transition may clearly be traced to the announcement of the patent Perryian Pens in various periodicals about 6 months ago."[15] The successful pen prompted the poet Thomas Hood to write:

> O! Patent, Pen-inventing Perrian Perry!
> Friend of the Goose and Gander,
> That now unplucked of their quill-feathers wander,
> Cackling, and Gabbling, Dabbling, making merry,
> About the happy Fen,
> Untroubled for one penny-worth of pen.
> . . . .
> In times bygone, when each man cut his quill,
> With little Perryan skill,
> What horrid, awkward, bungling tools of trade
> Appear'd the writing implements home-made!
> . . . .
> Not so thy Perryan Pens!
> True to their M's and N's,
> They do not with a wizzing zig-zag split,
> Straddle, turn up their noses, sulk and spit. . . .
> Pleasant they are to feel!
> So firm! so flexible! composed of steel.[16]

Eventually, the enterprising Englishman promoted his own Perryian system of education—which in turn promoted his pen—and sold such related items as a special "Perryian Limpid Ink" and the patented porcelain inkstand shown in figure 2.2.[17]

Many others contributed to the development of the steel pen, notably Joseph Gillott who began, fittingly,

as a maker of penknives but turned to manufacturing steel pens in the 1820s.[18] He patented an improvement, "which consisted in forming elongated points on the nibs of the pens."[19] Gillott's manufactory was in Birmingham—termed "the first home of the steel-pen industry."[20] From October 1838 to October 1839 the company manufactured 44,654,702 pens, and in 1840 Gillott was named "Steel Pen Maker to the Queen."[21]

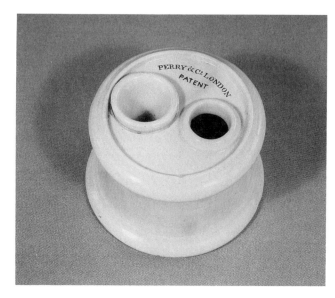

Figure 2.2. PERRY INKSTAND. James Perry, a major figure in the development of steel pens, also sold his own variety of ink as well as this patented blue-glazed pottery inkstand (3¼ in. in dia. by 2³⁄₁₆ in. high). It has a funnel-type well and separate vent hole (to aid in filling).

Figure 2.3. This ESTERBROOK PEN ASSORTMENT of about 1925 was only a representative selection from the world's largest manufacturer of steel pens.

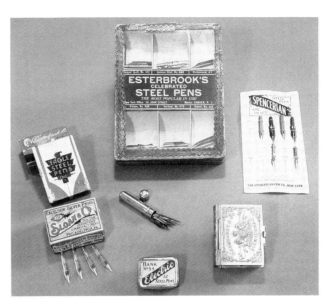

Figure 2.4 STEEL PENS were packaged in various ways for sale. *Counterclockwise from top:* an Esterbrook store-display box, a group of cardboard-boxed pens, a metal box of "bank" pens, a decorative book-effect metal pen box ("D. Leonardt & Co's / Birmingham"), and a card-mounted assortment of Spencerian-brand pens. The cartridge-type metal container in the center is probably from a pencil box.

Figure 2.5. STEEL-PEN ADVERTISEMENTS are featured on these envelopes of the 1880s. That of W.T. Rightmyer (*left*) states its special nib design was patented January 6, 1880. A penned notation records that a sample pen was received on March 1, 1883.

Gillott is credited with developing the modern method of pen making: shaping them not from tubes but from blanks stamped out of flat sheets of rolled metal. A skilled fly-press operator could cut as many as 28,000 blanks in one day.[22] The blanks were marked with the maker's name, then pierced, annealed, raised (rounded between dies into the semicylindrical form of a pen), hardened and tempered, scoured in acid, hand ground on a wheel, slit, polished, tinted (by heating to desired color), varnished or laquered (to prevent rusting), and inspected. The process has been documented in a series of photographs by the Spencerian Pen Company.[23]

Among a few American developments, the first patent for a "metallic writing pen" was issued to Peregrine Williamson of Baltimore on November 22, 1809, and a Shaker named Isaac Youngs of New Lebanon, New York, apparently invented machinery for manufacturing silver pens in 1819.[24] Still, the first steel-pen company in the United States was not established until 1858, when Richard Esterbrook, Jr., founded his company at Camden, New Jersey. Esterbrook began by selling English pens, but in early 1861, having brought

from Birmingham five craftsmen who had worked for John Mitchell, he began manufacturing his own Esterbrook nibs. Eventually Esterbrook became the world's largest steel-pen producer, and after other companies were established in the vicinity, the center of manufacturing steel pens shifted from Birmingham to Camden (figs. 2.3-2.5).[25]

Such success would never have been anticipated by Joseph Emerson. In his *Useful Penman* (1826) he stated, "As there is no probability, that metallic pens will ever

Figure 2.6. NIB TRACKS result from steel pens. The points of the split pen separate under pressure on the downstrokes and dig into the paper, creating furrows that fill with extra ink. The tracks are particularly evident in this example, which was blotted.

Figure 2.7. The STUB PEN produced writing with a distinctive line quality as shown in this handwriting dated 1908. The stub pen was rare in the 1870s but by 1927 represented about one-third of the total pen consumption.

Figure 2.8. The DOUBLE-LINE PEN is shown with the distinctive writing such a pen produced on a postcard of about 1910. The pen was sold by Esterbrook as a "Double Line Ruling Pen" (see fig. 2.3), and Hunt made a similar "Two Line Pen."

supersede those in common use, it will always be desirable, that every writer should be a penmaker." [26] But metal pens did triumph. As E. Kay Kirkham observes: "In America the first patent for a steel-type pen was in 1810 [actually 1809] but they were not common until 1820-1830 and not fully accepted as a writing instrument until about 1845. The next time you read an original microfilm copy of an 1800 or 1810 census of the United States you can say that in all probability it was written with a quill pen. With the 1850 census you can say that it was probably written with a steel pen." [27] The use of the steel pen in writing can be readily discerned by examining the pen strokes under magnification. In contrast to the quill, it is distinguished by

the presence of "nib tracks" (fig. 2.6). [28] Special types of steel pens produce distinctive line quality in writing. These include the "stub" (fig. 2.7), the "double-line" pen (fig. 2.8), and marking pens (fig. 2.9). [29]

Gold Pens

The gilding of quills to increase durability foreshadowed the gold pen. In 1818 Charles Watt patented a method of giving quills a metallic cast by dipping them in a solution of nitromuriate of gold. [30] Although gold was particularly suited to pens because it resisted the corrosion caused by acidic inks then in use, it lacked sufficient hardness for the points, which wore quickly. In the early nineteenth century the problem was attacked by adding to the tip a bit of hard substance such as rhodium. Lord Byron used such a pen in 1810, and "Doughty's Rhodium Pens" were sold in the late 1820s. [31]

Subsequently, iridium was employed. A tiny piece was fused to the tip of a pointed gold blank by means of a blowpipe. The blank was then further rolled and hammered to thin the metal, and the pen was again cut, stamped, raised, slit, ground, and polished in the standard manner. [32] Such pens are shown in figure 2.10.

Gold pens were made at Birmingham, and a major American manufacturer was John Holland. Holland was a watchmaker who founded a gold pen manufactory in Cincinnati in 1842. By the 1870s the John Holland Pen Company had contracted to supply gold pens to the United States Treasury Department and was even shipping them to Europe. [33] John Holland gold pens and penholders are highly collectible, some being among those illustrated in figure 2.11.

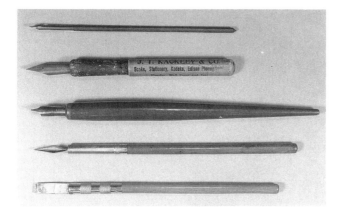

Figure 2.9. NIB CHOICE naturally affected line quality in writing. Fine and medium lines would result from the first two pens (*top to bottom*), bolder writing (see fig. 2.7) from the "stub" pen. The last two are, respectively, a "marking" pen (patented Sept. 30, 1890) shown in side view, and a "shading pen," identical to the marking pen except for slots cut about one-third the width; this allows a heavier flow of ink on one side and thus produces a graduated, or "shaded," line.

E. S. Johnson's 14-K Gold Pens.

The name of the maker is sufficient guarantee for these goods. Every Pen is warranted perfect. They are made of solid 14-K gold and have iridium points. The cuts are actual size.

No. 3. Given for one new name. Price, 90 cts.
No. 4. Given for one new name, and 10 cts. additional. Price, $1.
No. 5. Given for one new name, and 25 cts. additional. Price, $1.25.
No. 6. Given for one new name, and 40 cts. additional. Price, $1.50.
No. 7. Given for two new names. Price, $1.75.
No. 8. Given for two new names, and 15 cts. additional. Price, $2.

Postage and packing, 6 cts. additional for each Pen, when sent as a premium or purchased.

Figure 2.10. GOLD NIBS, tipped with iridium for hardness, are shown here actual size. From an advertisement in *The Youth's Companion*, October 28, 1886.

Glass Pens

Among the many materials experimented with in the making of pens—including horn and tortoiseshell, tipped with pieces of diamond or ruby or overlapped with sheet gold—glass is one of the most unusual.[34] Glass pens are known from at least as early as 1850. A later United States patent (no. 435,969), dated September 9, 1890, describes "a pen formed of a piece of round glass drawn out to a point and having grooves running spirally down the sloping sides and meeting at the point"(figs. 2.12 and 2.13).

A glass-pointed pen (fig. 2.13) was sold by F. Spors and Company, Minnesota, about 1928-29, and was advertised for its smooth writing.[35] A 1941 novelty catalog advertised another glass fountain pen which

Figure 2.11. GOLD PENS WITH HOLDERS, some with mechanisms to retract nibs, were common in the last half of the nineteenth century. Mother-of-pearl penholders predominate, two with velvet cases. At left center is a John Holland telescoping pen and a similar pen, closed. Above it are three slide-type holders, one topped with a carnelian. The two-piece penholder at right, in a leather case, is similar to one Robert E. Lee used at Appomattox. Beneath it are a penholder/letter opener and a bone-handled holder.

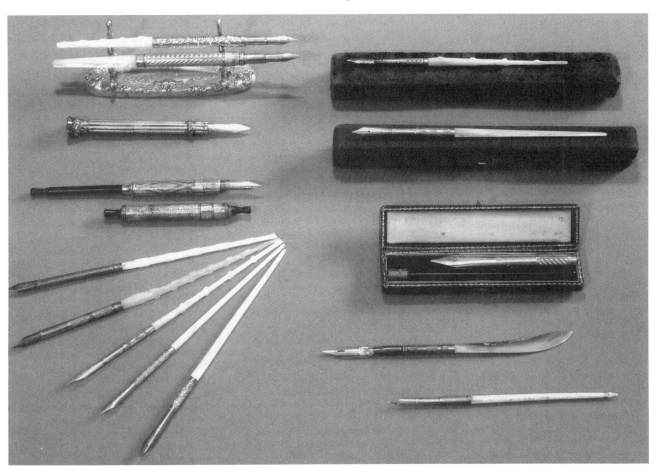

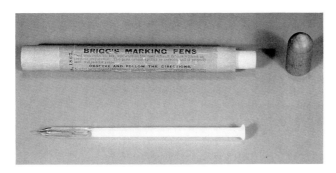

Figure 2.12. This EARLY GLASS PEN with its wooden case was sold as a marking pen to be used with indelible ink on fabric. Its shaft is milk glass and its point is clear glass. The label gives a patented date of January 15, 1867.

was said to "write almost like a pencil" and thus to be "ideal for carbon copy work."[36] Never very plentiful, and rendered less so by their fragile nature, glass pens make unique, interesting, and, since they are often of brilliantly colored glass, most attractive collectibles.

Penholders

Holders, first for quill nibs then for metal ones, were made from a wide variety of materials: cheaper ones were of common woods or bone; more expensive ones were made of silver, gold, ivory, mother-of-pearl, or ebony. Celluloid was employed after it was patented in 1868 (just as other plastics became common in the twentieth century). Later-nineteenth-century penholders often had a ferrule (a band at the lower, pen end). This might be of metal, textured to provide a sure grip, or, still later, rubber or cork (figs. 2.14 and 2.15).

Among the interesting mechanical forms were "spring penholders" from about the 1830s. According to a contemporary description, the spring action gave "a soft and easy motion to the pen, relieving the writer's hand from cramp, &c."[37] There were also "telescopic" and "slide" penholders which had means of withdrawing the pen inside for protection (fig. 2.11). With ordinary holders, schoolchildren often removed the pen and replaced it point first into the holder to protect it when it was not in use. Some types had caps for the same purpose (fig. 2.1). Also, many penholders were combined with mechanical pencils (frequently called "pencil cases"). Thus, among the models featured in a jewelers' catalog for 1889 were simple "Pearl Holders" and "Glory Desk Holders," as well as "Telescopic Desk Holders," "Black Celluloid Combination Slide Pen and Pencil Cases," "Gold-plated Telescopic Pen and Pencil Cases," and "Gold-plated and Pearl Slide Holders."[38]

"Peep show" penholders were among the more unique types (fig. 2.16), and, at the other end of the spectrum, penholders could even be improvised: I have been told of an old Kentucky storekeeper who made do with a pen nib tied by strong thread to a "penny pencil."[39]

Figure 2.13. This array of GLASS PENS includes (*top to bottom*) a Spors fountain pen (ca. 1929); three all-glass "dip" pens (one with a paper advertising insert), probably from the last quarter of the nineteenth century; and a glass pen in a wooden holder.

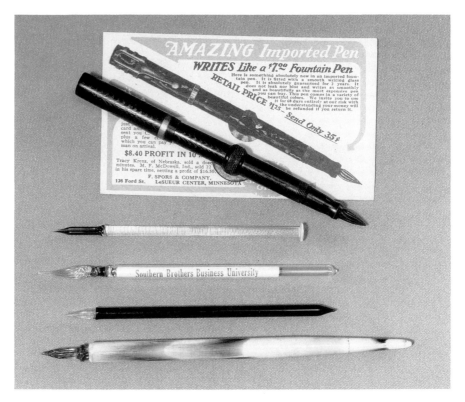

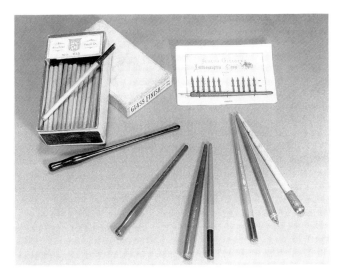

Figure 2.14 (*left*). PENHOLDERS. Boxed holders manufactured by the American Pencil Company and Gillott "crow quill" steel pens with holder date from the 1890s. In the foreground are common twentieth-century holders by pencil manufacturers: American Pencil Company, Dixon, Eberhard Faber, and Eagle Pencil Company.

Figure 2.15. HOLDERS FOR STEEL PENS came in various styles and materials—including wood, metal, celluloid, ivory, and porcelain. The jumbo penholder was a 1933 World's Fair novelty. At the left are wooden holders, including (*from top*) a hand-carved cedar holder with finger and thumb recesses, two advertising holders, a holder with cork grip, and two wood-and-metal holders. At right are penholders of hand-painted porcelain, celluloid disks, molded plastic (Zaner-Bloser), black hard rubber (John Holland), nickel-plated brass, and ivory. The latter is a Victorian holder with nib stamped "SETTEN & DURWARD/BIRMINGHAM/CRITERION."

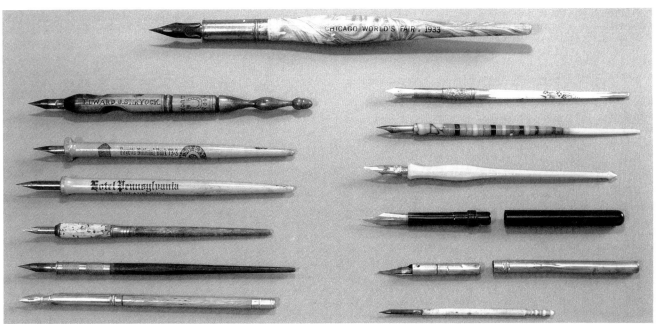

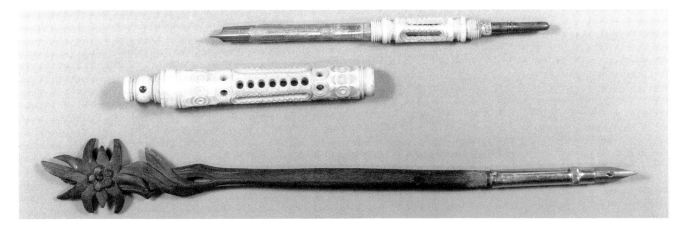

Figure 2.16. "PEEP SHOW" PENS, like similar novelty items, contained a "microscopic view" sandwiched between a tiny glass and a lens. Held to the eye and turned to the light, the image could be viewed: portraits of Columbus, Washington, and Grant in the ivory pen/pencil (ca. 1890s) and a view of "Interlaken" (Swiss resort) in the wooden holder.

Figure 2.17. HOMEMADE PENWIPERS include a scrap of gingham (with a pen, found in a late-nineteenth-century lap desk) and two hand-sewn penwipers with leaves of cloth, including the green-felt lady's hat at lower left.

Figure 2.18. DESK PENWIPERS include (*clockwise from top*) bristle brush inset in inkstand; two leather-covered felt assemblages; an Esterbrook blotter across which a pen was wiped; and a combined penwiper ("On my hat wipe your pen"), blotter, and calender.

Penwipers

Dried ink clogged pens and thus interfered with writing. Still, Palatino in 1540 cautioned users of quill pens to "be careful not to rub quills with a cloth," insisting instead that the nib should be covered with water. There were also quill cleaners—containers of silver, porcelain, or other material, some containing lead shot, bristles, or other means to help clean the inserted pen.[40]

Steel pens, on the other hand, were corroded by the acidic ink then in use, and storage in water would only have rusted them. The penwiper thus came into common use. In its simplest form it might have been a scrap of gingham cloth kept in a lap desk (fig. 2.17). But during the last half of the nineteenth century penwipers were among the common items of needlework, illustrated with directions in such periodicals as *Peterson's Magazine*. They were pieces of cloth gathered up and stitched into various forms: *Peterson's* 1865 selections included a "Braided Pen-wiper," a "Mouse Pen-wiper" (a seamed and stuffed "rodent" mounted on the penwiper proper, "which may be made of black and scarlet cloth"), and a "strawberry" model complete with beaded leaves and a stuffed, crocheted berry.[41] *Godey's Lady's Book* also featured penwipers such as its "Parasol" of 1874.[42]

For early twentieth-century penwipers, "felt was often used, cut into the shape of apples, strawberries, circles, squares, and the like. Sometimes five or six

Figure 2.19. PEN RETAINERS include (*left*) two pen trays and a pressed-glass "pen block"; also shown (*right*) are three cast-iron racks, including a wire-spiral "Star" pen rack, and at center front is a sterling silver pen rest with an engraved monogram.

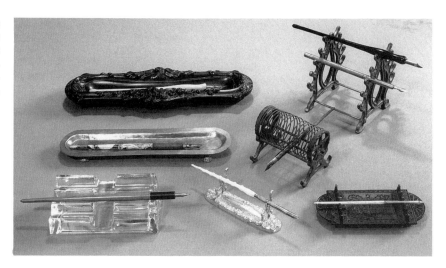

Figure 2.20. PEN RECEPTACLES. Desk holders for dip pens were relatively uncommon. Most similar receptacles were made for fountain pens of matching material. Note that the one on the left has an additional pen groove across the front of the base; it would be used for momentarily putting down the pen during writing, and before wiping and replacing it in its receptacle.

Figure 2.21. PENHOLDER DISPLAY RACK. This rack and its Faber-brand pens came from an old general store. It probably dates from the first quarter of this century.

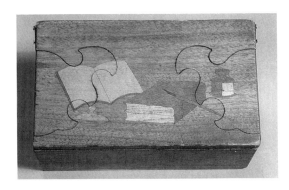

Figure 2.22. PEN RACK/DESK BOX. This unique box has inlaid-wood pictures of writing tools and opens to form a rack for pens.

pieces of felt were held together with an embroidered 'cover,' or several layers of felt circles were pinked and fastened tightly together in the center with a button so that the layers curled upward to form a half-sphere. These were gay little gifts for schoolchildren, who also found them easy to make."[43] Other types of penwipers, such as might appear on a desk, are displayed in figure 2.18.

Pen Rests

Whereas quill pens were typically stood in holders or in "quill holes" in inkstands, the combined steel-pen and holder was more practically and protectively stored by resting it on its side. Pens were laid in pen trays, which often matched other desk items, or perched on pen racks or pen rests (fig. 2.19). Pen recesses, racks, ledges, and rests that are part of inkstands and other containers will be discussed in chapter 6. Pen receptacles on bases, such as those shown in figure 2.20, were less common for dip pens than for reservoir pens. A store display rack is also shown, as is a unique

box/rack (figs. 2.21 and 2.22).

Problems such as pen cleaning and stowage had obvious solutions. Less easily solved was another problem—one as significant as that of durability: how to replenish the pen with ink without the need for repeated and frequent dipping. As we shall see, the solution required much ingenuity and technical development, which took more than a century and a half.

SELECT BIBLIOGRAPHY

Bodmer, Rudolph J., ed. *The Book of Wonders*. New York: Presbrey Syndicate, 1915, 15-17. Relates the history of the early steel pen; illustrates steps in the manufacture of nibs.

Jackson, Donald. *The Story of Writing*. New York: Taplinger, 1981. Chapter 9. Discusses the evolution of the steel pen.

Chambers's Encyclopedia. 1967. s.v. "pen."

Walker, Judith. "Collecting Glass Dip Pens." *Pen World*, summer 1989, 28-29.

Whalley, Joyce Irene. *Writing Implements and Accessories: From the Roman Stylus to the Typewriter*. Detroit: Gale Research, 1975.

3

Reservoir Pens

Fountain Pens

As one wrote with the quill or other dip pen, the nib gradually began to run out of ink and had to be recharged by dipping it again into the inkwell. This repeated activity shows itself in the writing thus produced as series of words graduated in intensity from dark to light and dark again (fig. 3.1). Sometimes the pen would run completely out of ink so that separate nib marks would become visible (fig. 3.2). "Ink failure" is the term document examiners give to this feature.[1]

The necessity of constantly interrupting writing to dip the pen was a problem that plagued writers from ancient times. And as early as the tenth century a solution was reportedly found. An Islamic leader, Caliph al-Mu'izz (d.975), is said to have requested a pen "capable of carrying its own supply of ink, where the ink would flow only when the pen was used for writing. So at other times it could safely be carried in his sleeve without fear of soiling his clothes." According to the story, the caliph's craftsmen succeeded in fulfilling the task and presented him with the desired pen, wrought in gold.[2]

If the account is true, and not mere legend, it is the first mention of a reservoir pen, although it is doubtful such an instrument could have worked very well. In 1663 Samuel Pepys recorded that he had a reservoir pen, but it was not until the following century (in 1723) that we find a detailed description of a pen containing its own ink supply.[3] The pen consisted of three pieces (of brass, silver, or other suitable material): a hollow tube having a pen at one end, a screw-on cover (to protect the point), and a cap for the opposite end, without which air pressure would "cause the ink to run out at once."[4]

Such was the basic concept of later self-contained pens, but until those were perfected, various attempts were made to increase the ink-holding capacity of the

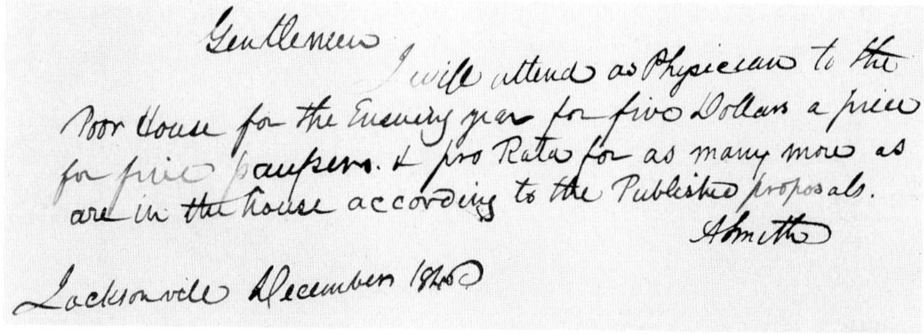

Figure 3.1. DIP-PEN WRITING is characteristically graduated from dark, when the pen is dipped, to light, as the ink is depleted, to dark again.

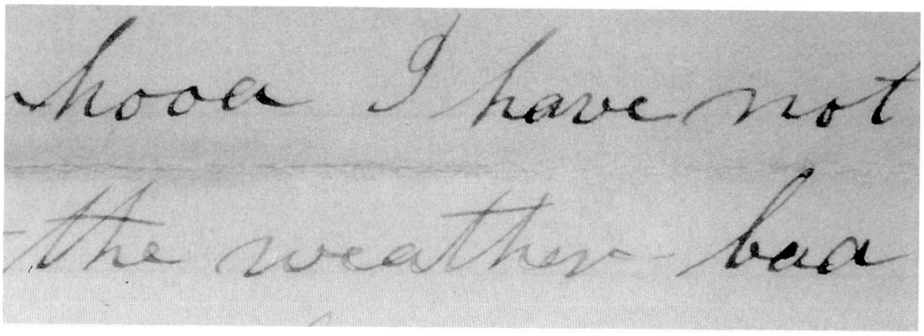

Figure 3.2. INK FAILURE (as document examiners term it) occurs when the pen runs out of ink, typically showing separate nib marks at the point of final exhaustion.

Figure 3.3. RESERVOIR NIB ATTACHMENTS such as this "Ink Spoon" were intended to hold extra ink and thus provide increased writing capacity with each dip of the pen.

Figure 3.4. "SOLID-INK" PENS held a rod of concentrated ink which supplied the nib when it was dipped in water. This undated advertisement is from the later 1860s or 1870s.

common dip pen. For example, Edward Johnston, in his classic treatise *Writing and Illuminating and Lettering* (1906), describes an S-shaped spring that could be inserted in the end of a quill causing it to hold more ink, although he gives no indication of when such a device might have been used.[5]

For steel pens, an early attempt to improve ink-retention was made by punching out a small orifice at the upper end of the slit.[6] This was followed by other methods: stamping a recess in the top of the nib; providing flanges that folded under the nib, thus forming a reservoir; and by employing separate devices (fig. 3.3) that adjoined the nib and enlarged the ink capacity. Such solutions were apparently common, as shown by English patents in the 1880s and 1890s, and have continued in use (e.g., for calligraphy pens) ever since.[7]

Yet another solution to the problem of ink supply was the "Solid-Ink Fountain" pen. It held a stick of concentrated ink which supplied the pen whenever it was dipped in water. "A single dip will write a page," promised an advertisement (fig. 3.4). Such pens were available by the 1870s, possibly even earlier.[8]

The ideal solution, however, was to store a quantity of ink inside the penholder as a means of supplying the nib (like the model described in 1723). This rendered the pen both portable and usable over a considerable period of time. The first two English patents for such pens were awarded in 1809, and a third was issued ten years later to John Scheffer.[9] With the latter, termed a "'Penographic' Fountain Pen," "the flow of ink to the nib was started, and had to be periodically refreshed by pressure on a lever in the side of the pen. The lever pressed upon a quill tube covered with layers of sheep gut, and as a cork made the ink reservoir air-tight this pressure forced ink through the aperture to the nib. The sheep gut was simply a device for making a suit-

able bond between the flexible quill reservoir and the solid metal of the pen structure. When the gut was swollen by contact with the ink this bond became very firm."[10] This "penograph" was intended for use with either a quill or steel nib, but by the mid-1820s the metal nib had become standard. Various additional fountain pens were patented over subsequent decades, and by the early 1870s magazines were regularly carrying advertisements for such devices as "Prince's Improved Fountain Pen. . . . The handle contains the ink."[11] Another was "The Darling Self-Supplying Penholder" which wrote "2,000 words with one dip of the pen."[12] Yet another advertisement read: "Hawkes' patent and only perfect fountain pen writes 10 hours, saves ⅓ time, handy as the ordinary pencil, holder fits any pen—$2, $3.50, $4."[13]

About this time the so-called "stylographic" pen became popular. Julius Grant states it was invented in 1878, but models date back to at least 1873, and patents include an "ink pencil" of 1849.[14] Instead of a holder with the usual pen nib, the stylographic pen consisted

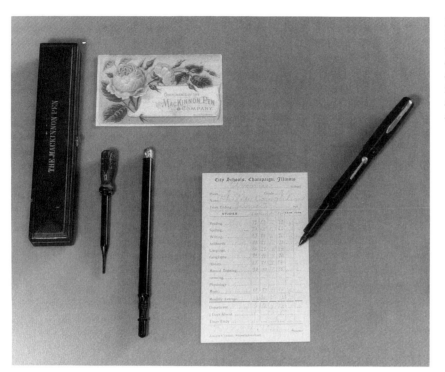

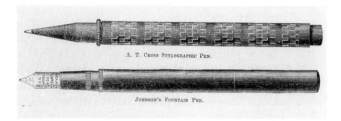

Figure 3.6. The STYLOGRAPHIC TIP is contrasted with
the standard fountain-pen nib in this advertisement in *The
Youth's Companion*, October 28, 1886.

Figure 3.7. STYLOGRAPHIC-PEN WRITING is
characterized by strokes of uniform diameter. Such line
quality is useful to draftsmen and graphic artists, and a
Rapidograph-brand stylographic pen (with interchangeable
points of varying diameters) is available today.

of a cylinder tapered to a point from which projected a
needlelike plunger; this was pushed back when the pen
was pressed to paper, allowing the ink to flow out (figs.
3.5-3.7).

Still, it remained for Lewis E. Waterman (1837-1901)
to market the first truly successful fountain pen in 1884.
Waterman was an American shorthand teacher turned
insurance agent who claimed his invention was inspired by an incident with a prospective customer in
New York. Glen Bowen tells the story:

> Up to that time Waterman had used a little non-spilla-
> ble ink bottle about the size of his thumb and carried it
> tied to a button on his waistcoat. But fountain pens had
> just come into the market. Waterman thought it would
> look good to have one of these new pens. On his way to
> the stagecoach to go uptown he bought one in order to
> try it out.
>
> The insurance agent met his prospect, on whom he
> had been working for months. He presented the ap-
> plication blank and then the new fountain pen. The
> prospect put his foot on a rock and laid the blank on his
> knee. As he touched the paper with the pen—blot! He
> tried again—blot! He tried a third time—the pen was
> empty!

The superstitious man refused Waterman's offer of his
ordinary pen, and the account was lost. Angered, Waterman was reportedly motivated to solve the problem
which had beset previous inventors, that of creating an
effective "feed" (allowing just enough air into the barrel to cause only the desired amount of ink to flow

Figure 3.8. FILLER MECHANISMS for fountain pens included (*from left*) the eyedropper; a built-in rubber sac; a plunger (Parker Vacuumatic); three mechanisms to press air out of a rubber bladder (crescent, hatchet, and lever); and an ink cartridge. The Jumbo pen at top is actually a novelty ballpoint (concealed under the nib of the "fountain" pen).

out).[15] After Waterman's improvement, "millions of fountain pens were sold each year."[16]

Further improvements were made by George S. Parker (1863-1937), a teacher of telegraphy and an agent for the John Holland fountain pen. Convinced he could make a better pen, Parker set to work, established his own company in 1888, and the following year obtained the first of several patents on ink-feed design. Over the years, Parker patented his famous Lucky Curve feed (1894), a slip-fit outer cap (1898), and the jointless pen (1899), which helped eliminate leakage. Still further inventions followed, and by the end of the thirties Parker had become the leading American fountain pen manufacturer.[17]

The early fountain pens were manually filled, using a common eyedropper (fig. 3.5). But in one of the many methods of producing a "self-filling" pen (a type that was first mentioned in an English patent of 1832), the bulb of the dropper, in effect, was encased in the barrel.[18] A mechanism was used to press air out of this rubber bladder (or ink sac), which could fill with ink when the mechanism was returned to its original position. Among such mechanisms was one invented by Parker in 1904, and it was followed by the now standard lever-filler invented by W.A. Sheaffer in 1907.[19]

Other filler mechanisms had pump, plunger, or vacuum-type actions; and cartridge pens (originally glass vials) were patented in 1890, marketed by Waterman in 1936, and popularized by Sheaffer in 1955 (figs. 3.8, 3.9-3.11, and 3.12).[20]

Fountain-pen collecting has become a growing, specialized hobby with its own important magazines, col-

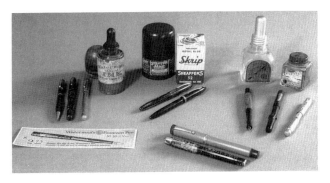

Figure 3.9. FOUNTAIN PENS & INKS. This assortment includes products by Waterman (*left*), Sheaffer (*center rear*), Parker (*foreground*), and other brands (*right*). Dropper bottles were for filling early fountain pens; wooden bottle cases were for travel.

Waterman pens include matching pencil and pen as well as engraved sterling silver pen. Sheaffer's Skrip ink was formulated in 1922; the bottle with the top-well feature has been made since 1933; the pens are Sheaffer's Lifetime White Dot. Of the Parker pens the uppermost is a 1920s Duofold with a button filler, and the other a 1940 Vacuumatic. Other items at right include a Carter's Fountain Pen Ink bottle, a Fre-flo ink bottle, an unidentified early pen, a Conklin pen with a crescent filler, and a Moore "safety" pen. A safety pen's nib retracts into the barrel and thus acts as a stopper to prevent leakage.

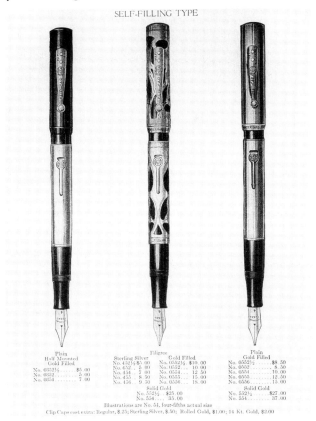

Figure 3.10. WATERMAN PENS are among the most desirable of collectible vintage fountain pens. This is a page from a 1920s Waterman catalog.

Figure 3.11. DESK FOUNTAIN PENS typically had lever fillers and ball-and-socket receptacles. They were common during the 1920s and 1930s.

Figure 3.12. FOUNTAIN-PEN WRITING is characterized by a line of continuous (rather than graduated) intensity, since the ink flow is unimpeded. There is also a contrast between upstrokes and heavier downstrokes, though less so than with the steel pen, which was usually more flexible.

lector's guides, and restoration facilities.[21] As a rule, pens from the big four—Waterman, Parker, Sheaffer, Wahl-Eversharp—are the most desirable and valuable, especially pens with gold nibs, fourteen carats or greater. Defects, such as bent levers, nib damage, sprung clips, and chew marks or cracks, can greatly lower their value.[22]

Ballpoint Pens

Although fountain pens continued in a great profusion of styles and patented features, they were largely displaced in the late 1940s by the ballpoint pen. Such a device had been invented long before. In 1888, John J. Loud of Weymouth, Massachusetts (who had patented earlier that year a "firecracker cannon"), obtained a patent on a uniquely new reservoir pen with a rotatable ball. Intended to be used for marking cartons and the like, it was described as a "fountain pen" with "a tube having a contracted mouth, in combination with a marking-sphere, a screw, a spring, and a centrally guided rod provided with suitable end bearings, whereby the marking-sphere may be closed tightly into the contracted mouth."[23] A commercial version of such a pen was marketed in 1895.[24]

Still, it remained for two Czechoslovakians—Frank Klimes (an inventor) and Paul V. Eisner (a manufacturer)—to begin producing a modern type of ballpoint, named Rolpen, in 1935 in Prague.[25] Apparently independently, two Hungarian brothers, Ladislao and George Biro, developed a rotatable-ball pen in 1938. During World War II Klimes was imprisoned in a concentration camp, but the Biro brothers moved to Argentina and began to manufacture their pen. The

Eberhard Faber Company obtained rights to it, and, when the United States Army revealed an interest in 10,000 nonleak pens for its air force, Sheaffer outbid both Parker and Eversharp to share American rights with Faber.

Enter then the Barnum of the pen industry, a sometime-millionaire, sometime-bankrupt businessman named Milton Reynolds. He saw the Biro pen in an arcade in Buenos Aires in April 1945 and by the end of October had marketed and sold some 25,000 ball pens through Gimbel's department store in New York. When the Reynolds pen was claimed capable of writing under water, a competitor countered satirically by advertising a nonexistent "rocket" pen that could "spotweld, melt locks, etch letters in solid concrete [and] remove superfluous hair." Nevertheless, Reynolds even advertised his writing instrument as the "Most Imitated Pen in the World," a bold assertion, since he had himself pirated it! Suits and countersuits were ineffectual, since the invention had been Loud's after all. But the comparative success of Biro and Reynolds was due to the development of a suitable ballpoint ink—a viscous variety more akin to printing ink than to ordinary writing fluids.[26]

Nevertheless, the early pens were troublesome, in large part because of the ink, which was basically a dye solution in an oily base. While the oils helped provide a smooth flow, they were slow drying and smudged, and many were not lightfast.[27] Many pens blobbed and skipped (fig. 3.13). The deficiencies were soon largely remedied, however. Figure 3.14 shows one of Reynolds's pens together with two other famous ball pens.

One was Parker's first ballpoint, introduced in 1954 and described here by Glen Bowen: "It was called the Jotter and it was different. It had an oversize cartridge which wrote five times as long as ordinary ball pens. Moreover, the cartridge rotated each time the button was pressed, assuring even, longer wear. The pen was made entirely of stainless steel and nylon, tough and handsome. A 400-pound man could stand on the twin-walled barrel without denting it. A further difference of the Jotter was that, for the first time, a ball pen offered a variety of point sizes to suit the individual hand."[28]

The remaining ball pen illustrated in figure 3.14 is the so-called Liquid Lead Pencil introduced by Parker in 1955. It was a ball-type pen but its ink contained "lead-pencil graphite in a new liquefied form"; an eraser was even provided so mistakes could be rubbed out, pencil-like. Despite its features, it failed to gain sufficient acceptance, and it was phased out during the early 1960s.[29]

Subsequently, a ballpoint with an easily erasable ink—the Eraser Mate pen, a product of the Paper Mate Division of the Gillette Company—was marketed in April 1979. It soon captured a significant portion of the market.[30]

Also a variety of ball pen termed "roller ball" or "floating-ball" has been widely sold. Instead of the oil-based ballpoint ink, which produces a distinctive line quality due to its viscosity and roller application, these roller pens have a free-flowing ink similar to fountain-pen ink. Thus, they produce "a mark that falls somewhere between the ball-point and the fountain pen."[31]

Porous-Tip Pens

Competing with the ballpoint is the porous-point pen; its nib is composed of fibrous or other porous material and its ink supply is contained in a cartridge or wick. Storing the ink in an absorbent, spongy material is one method of controlling ink flow, by regulating the rate of capillary attraction.[32]

Such a pen, first manufactured in the early 1940s and sold as a refillable "brush pen," was originally a cumbersome, oversized affair. In the early 1950s these devices became known as "markers," since their primary use was for marking rough wood, cellophane, or other material in industrial use, although artists quickly adapted them for poster and other bold work.[33]

In 1951, the canister-type marker, an airtight leak-proof barrel with a felt wick, was introduced. The felt nib of these markers was usually wedge-shaped and could thus produce both thin and broad lines in the manner of the ancient chisel-edged reed or quill, and again artists quickly took them up.[34]

A fiber-tip pen, fine-pointed and intended to be used for writing, was marketed successfully in Japan and the United States in 1964. This pen had a synthetic (nylon-

Figure 3.13. EARLY BALLPOINT WRITING was often marred by blotting and skipping, as in this example from 1947.

Figure 3.14. BALLPOINT PENS. At top is the Reynolds International Ball Point Pen, the first of its kind marketed successfully in America (1945). The boxed set by Parker features its famous Jotter ball pen and its so-called Liquid Lead Pencil, which wrote with an erasable graphite ink.

acrylic) point and paved the way for the use of such other materials as plastic, Dacron, rayon, and the like.

The black or colored inks for porous-point pens are loosely divided into "washable" (water-based) and "permanent" (petroleum-based, with benzene or naptha generally used as solvents). The latter will mark on such materials as glass, wet negatives, or other problematical surfaces.[35] When the ink is depleted, most porous-point pens are intended to be discarded, but a few have replaceable ink cartridges or nib-and-reservoir units.[36]

SELECT BIBLIOGRAPHY

Bowen, Glen. *Collectible Fountain Pens*. Glenview, Ill.: Glen Bowen Communications, 1982. Features four major brands: Waterman, Sheaffer, Parker, Wahl-Eversharp.

Lawrence, Cliff. *Official P.F.C. Pen Guide*. Dunedin, Fla.: Pen Fancier's Club, 1982. Identifies many vintage fountain pens, including early stylographic pens.

Maginnis, James P. *Reservoir, Stylographic, and Fountain Pens.* Cantor Lectures, Society for the Encouragement of Arts, Manufactures and Commerce. London: William Trounce, 1905. Definitive text on the early history of reservoir pens.

New Standard Encyclopedia. 1982. s.v. "pen." Includes a discussion of porous-tip pens.

Wharton, Don. "Mighty Battle of the Pens." *Nation's Business*, November 1946. Story of the origin of the ballpoint pen.

4

The Pencil

Wooden Pencils

Manufacturers of other writing instruments have frequently drawn comparisons between their product and the pencil: Of the "Solid Ink" pen it was said, "It requires no more room than an ordinary pocket pencil"; the Laughlin Manufacturing Company called its stylographic pen the "Ink Pencil"; the Hawkes Patent Fountain Pen was "handy as the ordinary pencil"; ballpoints were said to be capable of making "as many carbons as a pencil"; and the Parker Pen Company even devised a ball pen with a graphite ink which it termed a "Liquid Lead Pencil." On the other hand, a 1903 advertisement asked, "Ever find your pencil notes blurred? Use a 'Parker Pen' and avoid this annoyance."[1]

Such comparisons reflect the qualities—portability, self-containment, practicality, even its very impermanence—that have ensured the pencil's survival over four centuries. Its antecedents, of course, are much more ancient.

In the sense of being a stick of blackish material that produces marks for writing or drawing by means of abrasion, the earliest antecedent of the pencil might have been a charred stick such as was doubtless used for prehistoric drawing. Certainly the Romans used lead disks for ruling lines on papyrus scrolls, and they, as well as medieval scribes, used a small brush called a *pencillus* (Latin for "little tail") for some fine work—hence our word "pencil."[2] The later Renaissance artists used a silverpoint tool (i.e., a silver stylus) to draw on specially coated parchment or paper, or a small rod of lead or lead alloy to mark directly on the natural surfaces.[3] As the fifteenth-century Florentine artist Cennini described it in his classic arts-and-crafts treatise, *Il Libro dell'arte*, this would be "a style [i.e., stylus] made of two parts lead and one part tin, well beaten with a hammer." He added: "On paper you may draw with the aforesaid lead. . . . And if you ever make a slip, so that you want to remove some stroke made by

this little lead, take a bit of the crumb of some bread, and rub it over the paper, and you will remove whatever you wish."[4]

According to tradition, the true "lead" pencil was made possible by a freak event that occurred in the town of Borrowdale, Cumberland, England, in 1564. A fierce rainstorm uprooted an immense oak tree and in the cavity was discovered a deposit of graphite that proved to be of an unusual purity and in vast supply. The Borrowdale mine supplied the world with graphite for many generations.[5]

Originally the mineral was called *plumbeus*, "lead," of which it was thought to be a variety. In 1779 it was recognized as, in actuality, a form of carbon, and in 1789 Abraham G. Werner named it graphite, after the Greek *graphien*, "to write."[6]

That term was fitting because the properties of the Borrowdale "lead" were appreciated immediately. At first, rough chunks were used as "marking stones," but later, square sticks were sawed from sheets of graphite. They were spirally wrapped with string (to protect the soft material and at the same time to keep the fingers clean), and this was unwound as needed.[7] As early as 1565, only one year after the mine's discovery, a German-Swiss naturalist named Konrad von Gesner described what may have been the world's first wooden pencil. As Gesner reported in his treatise on fossils, he was using an instrument to make notes and sketches that consisted of a piece of graphite inserted into a wooden holder.[8]

While the Borrowdale graphite could be used without further treatment, as supplies began to dwindle experiments were made to bind graphite dust with adhesives and mold them into sticks. Such a graphite composition pencil was made in 1662 in Nuremberg, Germany. In the later eighteenth century, when war cut off French imports, Napoleon commissioned Nicolas Jacques Conté (1755-1805) to develop a replacement for imported pencils. Conté's process—the forerunner of the modern one—involved mixing graphite with clay and water, pressing the paste into grooves in wooden molds, and, after the leads were dry, firing them in a kiln. About the same time, a Viennese experimenter, Joseph Hardtmuth, developed essentially the same process and discovered that by varying the proportion of clay he could regulate the hardness of the leads.[9]

In the meantime, in 1761, at Stein, near Nuremberg, Kaspar Faber (d. 1784) founded a great pencil-making dynasty, with generation after generation of Fabers manufacturing pencils there. The business was inherited by Kaspar's son Anton Wilhelm (d. 1819); then the A.W. Faber Company passed to Georg Leonhard Faber (d. 1839) and then on to Johann Lothar von Faber (1817-96), Kaspar Faber's great grandson. Lothar expanded the twenty-worker facility into a modern factory with plants in London, Paris, Berlin, and New York and with agencies elsewhere, and in 1856 he secured exclusive control of graphite from the mines of eastern Siberia. Faber also began to manufacture such other supplies as slate pencils, artists' paints, ink, mechanical drawing instruments, and the like. Following the death of Faber's widow in 1903, the business was inherited by his granddaughter, Countess Otile von Faber-Castell, but eventually passed out of family control.[10]

In the mid-nineteenth century, however, Johann Lothar von Faber's younger brother, John Eberhard Faber (1822-79) had immigrated to America, taking up residence in New York City in 1849 and, in 1861, establishing there his own lead-pencil business. This was the first large-scale American pencil manufactory, the previous United States market having been largely supplied by his brother's European business, although a small factory that made thin, square-leaded pencils

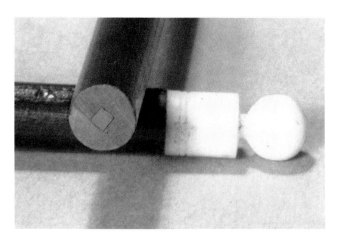

Figure 4.1. A.W. FABER PENCILS like these of the late 1860s were distinctively thin, square-leaded, capped with an ivory ornament, painted black, and stamped "A.W.F."

had been established by William Monroe of Concord, Massachusetts, in mid-1812 (fig. 4.1). Still, even after Eberhard's death his enterprise remained tied to the parent company. But in 1898 the Eberhard Faber Pencil Company was incorporated in the United States, and its name has since marked countless pencils, penholders (fig. 2.21), and other products.[11]

In 1985, Eberhard Faber IV discussed the company's most illustrious product, the classic Eberhard Faber yellow Mongol No. 2, first manufactured in 1900, when it sold for a nickel. Of its distinctive black-and-gold eraser fastener, Faber stated: "It costs a lot of money for that ferrule. We've been tempted to change it, but we think it's the best looking ferrule in the industry. It's a trademark we're not going to change."

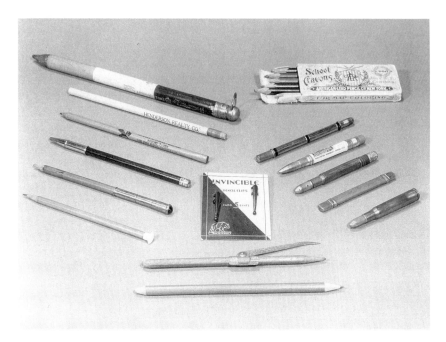

Figure 4.2. WOODEN PENCILS. Surrounding the pencil clips are common pencils (*at left*), boxed colored pencils of the 1880s and "pocket pencils" (*right*), and "penny pencils" (*bottom*).

The jumbo novelty pencil, made by the American Pencil Co., is eleven inches long. Beneath it are two advertising pencils, one with an eraser end; a pencil with a metal point protector; a pencil with an "amethyst"-topped brass pencil extender; and A.W. Faber's Stenographie pencil with a bone roll-resistant end. The lowermost "pocket pencil" at right is made from a rifle cartridge. One of the "penny pencils" shown at the bottom has a compass attached; note the characteristic sharpened white-eraser end.

Faber said of the future of pencils, which make up some 25 percent of the company's business (an additional 34 percent being represented by pens and markers and 27 percent by erasers): "People have been predicting the demise of the pencil for ages, but it hasn't happened. First, it was the typewriter, then the ballpoint pen. Now it's the computer. But we don't feel the computer is going to put the pencil out of business. The paperless office is not paperless. Over the last decade, the pencil market has been growing by smaller percentages. But the market isn't shrinking." And, yes, Mr. Faber does have a son named Eberhard.[12]

The basic pencil-making process has changed little from Kaspar Faber's day except for automation and some specific technical developments. In brief, the process, which includes some forty discrete, automated steps, involves extruding the graphite-and-clay dough into strands which are then cut to pencil length, dried, kiln-fired, wax-impregnated, and surface-cleaned. The leads are then sandwiched between cedar slats that have matching parallel grooves to receive them, and the resulting block is pressed until the adhesive sets. Finally, the blocks are machine cut into nine separate pencils which are rounded (or hexagonally shaped, etc.), sanded, varnished or painted, stamped with the maker's name or other identification, and tipped with a ferrule and eraser.[13]

Over the years wooden pencils manufactured in this fashion have included a wide variety intended for special uses, including drawing pencils (in hard, "H," and soft, "B," grades) and especially writing pencils (graded no. 1, very soft; no. 2, soft; no. 2½, medium soft; no. 3, hard; no. 4, very hard). There have also been flat carpenters' pencils, and additional varieties with

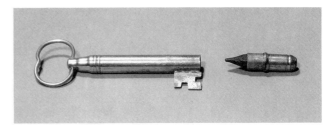

Figure 4.3. A NOVEL PENCIL, suitable for the pocket with its point safely tucked away, masqueraded as a common house key.

features that supposedly made them desirable for stenographers, editors, and others. The Eagle Pencil Company, for example, made a "Reporter" model that was sharpened on both ends, and Eberhard Faber sold a "Marking" pencil with a "thick black, soft weatherproof lead." Large-diameter pencils have traditionally been made for primary use, since they can be grasped more confidently by small hands (figs. 4.2 and 4.3).[14]

Pencil leads containing dyestuffs are not kiln-fired but are simply dried. Among these are the so-called indelible pencils that were patented in 1866 and in use until the advent of the ballpoint. They contained methyl-violet, graphite, and binder. Wetting converted the writing to a permanent inklike form; hence such pencils were sometimes called "ink pencils," a term once used for stylographic pens.[15] "Copying" pencils contained pigment and were first made in 1857. Slate pencils (fig. 4.4) were shaped from the natural material (like the earliest graphite pencils) and were not an extruded product. And paper-wrapped pencils, invented by Frederick Blaisdell and patented in 1895, continue to be marketed.[16]

Figure 4.4. SLATE PENCILS, CHALK, SLATES. Slate pencils were used for writing on school slates, including the folding one (*rear*) and a multipage clothbound "book slate." Chalk was used for blackboard writing. At right are a salesman's blackboard sample—resting against a wooden chalk box—as well as a metal and a cardboard chalk box.

Figure 4.5.
CRANK PENCIL SHARPENER, shown here in a quaint form of about 1925, was said to be "automatic," but the truly automatic sharpeners are the electric-powered ones.

THE DANDY

Pencil Accessories

Among pencil accessories, the simple eraser has a notable history. In 1770 the great British chemist Joseph Priestly announced that it was no longer necessary to employ bread crumbs for erasures; a solidified vegetable gum known as caoutchouc could instead be used for rubbing out mistakes. He thus applied the name "rubber" to the material which—after the vulcanizing process was discovered in 1839—made "India rubber" practical for erasers and many other products.[17] (A crude chunk of rubber, intended for erasures, is included in the antique writing kit shown in fig. 1.2.) Credit for placing a rubber eraser on the end of a pencil is usually given to Hyman L. Lipman of Philadelphia, but Lipman's 1858 patent seems to acknowledge that such an integrated writing instrument was already in existence. The patent reads: "I do not claim the use of a lead-pencil with a piece of india-rubber or other erasing material attached at one end for the purpose of erasing marks." Instead, Lipman wrote:

> What I do claim as my invention, and desire to secure by Letters Patent, is—
> The combination of the lead and india-rubber or other erasing substance in the holder of a drawing-pencil, the whole being constructed and arranged substantially in the manner and for the purposes set forth.

As he explained: "I make a lead-pencil in the usual manner, reserving about one-fourth of the length, in which I make a groove of suitable size, A, and insert . . . a piece of prepared india-rubber . . . secured . . . by being glued. . . . The pencil is then finished . . . so that on cutting one end thereof you have the lead B, and on cutting the other end you expose a small piece of india-rubber, C, ready for use." Therefore, as Lipman's patent drawings make perfectly clear, his was the prototype, not for the pencil with eraser affixed by a ferrule, but for the "penny pencil" (see fig. 4.2).[18]

In addition to erasers, other accessories include pencil sharpeners (figs. 4.5 and 4.6). The small, hand-held sharpener with a fixed blade is known from at least as early as 1857 (fig. 4.6).[19] Among the early crank-type sharpeners was one having a wheel-and-belt mecha-

Figure 4.6. PENCIL SHARPENERS—in one form or another—have been necessary as long as the wooden pencil has been used. The oldest of those shown, the "bell" at front center, dates from 1857.

Clockwise from lower left: a Remington pocketknife, which belonged to my father, shown with a "penny pencil"; a crank-type sharpener, familiar from schoolrooms; and simple fixed-blade sharpeners in various guises: the "telephone" and "desk" are contemporary; the "globes" have a metal base, made about 1900, and a plastic base, made in the 1950s; the "bell" was patented in the United States on September 22, 1857; and the "horn" was patented on November 8, 1870.

CARRITHERS & COMPANY   223 W. MADISON ST., CHICAGO

Pencil Point Protectors and Lengtheners

Figure 4.7. PENCIL PROTECTORS and LENGTHENERS were once common, as illustrated by this advertisement from an office-equipment catalog of about 1925.

nism, patented in 1869.[20] The penknife, of course, is obviously the first such sharpener, adapted from its original purpose of cutting quill pens.

A "pencil-clasp," namely "a device to hold a pencil to the lappel [*sic*] or breast of the coat" is known from at least 1875. Other accessories include metal "point protectors" (in the 1920s, boxes of six pencils often included one of these) and "pencil lengtheners," intended to be used with the remaining bit of a much-used pencil (fig. 4.7).[21]

Figure 4.8. "SCHOLARS' COMPANION" was an early name for a pencil box such as the cloth-covered one of about 1860 at the upper left. All are wooden boxes from the late nineteenth and early twentieth centuries. The double-tiered box has a swivel feature; the box behind is stenciled "Scholars Companion"; the one at the right has a chromolithographed label. The long box in the center has a slide top and a ruler-marked base; other slide-top boxes have a schoolboy's name penciled atop (*left*) and "Peters Weatherbird Shoes for Girls and Boys."

Figure 4.9. PENCIL BOXES made of cardboard and having snap fasteners replaced the earlier wooden boxes. Pencil companies such as Eagle and American sold them stocked with an assortment of their products. The giant "pencil" is a plastic pencil case of about the 1950s; the eraser is a removable stopper.

Pencil boxes were used by schoolchildren to carry not only pencils but other accessories. The early boxes were called "scholars' companions"; they and subsequent pencil boxes were typically of wood (fig. 4.8) until well into the twentieth century.[22] In the 1870s, for example, one might find a beautifully finished walnut box complete with engraved brass nameplate on top, built-in lock, and key.[23] Metal boxes were atypical.

Later pencil boxes were of cardboard—such as, apparently, the "fancy box" used for a "Schooldays Assortment" manufactured by the Eagle Pencil Company and advertised in 1921. The compartmented box contained four pencils with erasers and one each of the following: indelible pencil, cork-handled penholder, disk pencil-and-ink eraser, a metal box of pens, a metal pencil-point protector, and a drinking cup.[24] Cardboard pencil boxes with snap fasteners (fig. 4.9) were common from about the 1930s through the 1950s. Plastic boxes subsequently began to dominate.

Mechanical Pencils

Known variously as "propelling" or "screw" or even simply "metal" pencils, mechanically operated holders for pencil leads originated late in the first quarter of the nineteenth century. As noted in an 1837 issue of *Mechanics Magazine:* "It is not generally known that Mr. John Isaac Hawkins, Civil Engineer, of Hampstead, in the year 1822, invented that useful and now well known pocket appendage, the *patent ever-pointed pencil*, and the leads for the same, the right of making which was purchased from him by Gabriel Riddle and Sampson Mordan, under the well-known firm of S. Mordan & Co."[25] An early 1827 advertisement for "S. Mordan & Co's Patent Ever-Pointed Pencils" informed readers that they were "upon a principle entirely new, and which combines utility with simplicity of construction. The Black Lead is not inclosed in wood, as usual, but in a SMALL Silver Tube, to which there is attached a mechanical contrivance for propelling the Lead as it is worn. The diameter of the Black Lead is so nicely proportioned as NOT TO REQUIRE EVER TO BE CUT OR POINTED, either for fine Writing, Outline, or Shading. The Cases for the Drawing Table or Writing Desk are of Ebony, Ivory, &c.; and for the Pocket, there are Silver or Gold Sliding Cases, varying in taste and elegance." That the pencil worked on the screw principle is clear from the instructions: "Hold the two milled edges between the finger and thumb of the left hand. Turn the case with the other hand to the right, and the lead will be propelled as it is required for use; but if, in exhibiting the case, or accidentally, the lead should be propelled too far out, turn the case the reverse way, and press in the point."[26] One of S. Mordan's mechanical pencils is included in the writing kit shown in figure 1.2.

Mordan's advertisement noted that the company's pocket models were "slide" operated; that is, not only

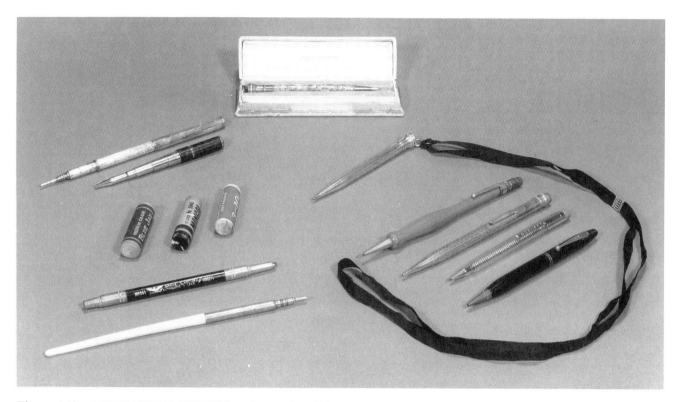

Figure 4.10. MECHANICAL PENCILS are known from 1822. At lower left is an early Victorian ivory-handled ever-pointed pencil. Other common pencils and lead containers are shown. The boxed pencil and the one with the "ribbon guard" are famous Eversharp models of the early 1920s.

Left, from top: two telescoping pencils, one with a leather covering; wooden boxes of leads; an Eagle Automatic pencil with spring-loaded jaws, and marked on barrel, "With copying lead/patd. Jun. 26, 77/ May 20, 79"; an early Victorian mechanical pencil with ivory handle. *Top center:* Wahl-Eversharp pencil in original box, 1922. *Right:* a Wahl-Eversharp pencil with ribbon, about 1921; a pencil with a blue plastic handle resembling a penholder, made by Zaner-Bloser, the penmanship instructors; a mechanical pencil with red lead, made by Simon H. Steiner of New York and Germany; the popular Scripto pencil of amber plastic, marked "U.S. Senate"; and a Parker Parkette, with eraser under cap, of about 1930.

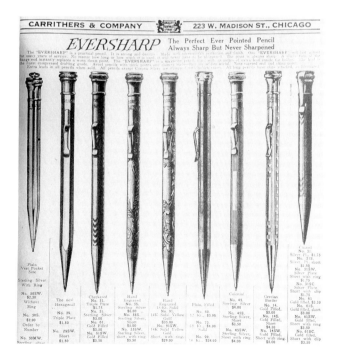

could the lead be retracted inside the point but that portion could itself be withdrawn inside the barrel of the holder for compactness. Any such retractable models were known as "magic pencils," such as one in the form of a silver peanut.[27] Another hideaway principle was employed in 1837 for Lownds's combination "Ever-pointed Pencil and Pen-case," which was also able "to carry two extra steel pens with perfect convenience."[28] Other mechanical pencils followed, such as one made by Alonzo T. Cross in 1868.[29]

A mechanical pencil capable of holding a large lead by means of spring-loaded jaws (opened by pushing on the top of the holder) was patented June 26, 1877 (fig. 4.10). This type came to be preferred by draftsmen in the second half of the twentieth century.[30]

Popular mechanical pencils in America in the period between the two world wars were those manufactured

Figure 4.11. EVERSHARP PENCILS were popular mechanical (or "ever-pointed") pencils. Here is a selection from about 1925.

by the Wahl Company and known by the brand name Eversharp. Some had pocket clips; others had rings for ladies' "ribbon guards" or men's watch chains (see fig. 4.11).

As common as pencils have been for more than two centuries (for example, Thomas Jefferson purchased one about the time he was drafting the Declaration of Independence), because they produce writing that can smear and become hazy they were eschewed even for some transient purposes.[31] Although Jefferson's drafts of the Declaration are in ink, he may have made notes or even preliminary drafts in pencil which have not survived.[32] Because pencil marks could be erased—the very quality that made pencils desirable for certain purposes, such as drawing guidelines for penmanship, or for making calculations—pencils could not be used for legal documents or other permanent records. More-over, rules of etiquette precluded their use for correspondence.[33] For all such purposes, ink, troublesome as it was, was required.

SELECT BIBLIOGRAPHY

Bodmer, Rudolph J., ed. *The Book of Wonders*. New York: Presbrey Syndicate, 1915. History and manufacture of wooden pencils.

De Bono, Edward, ed. *Eureka! An Illustrated History of Inventions from the Wheel to the Computer*. London: Thames and Hudson, 1974. s.v. "pencil." Includes a brief history of pencils, with illustration of Gesner's early pencil, 1565.

Encyclopaedia Britannica. 1973. s.v. "pencil."

"Invention of the Ever-pointed Pencil." *Mechanics' Magazine* 27 (1837): 32.

"Manufacture of Lead Pencils." *Mechanics' Magazine* 31 (1839): 174-75.

PART 2

Ink

But words are things, and a small drop of ink,

Falling like dew upon a thought, produces

That which makes thousands, perhaps millions, think.

—Lord Byron
Don Juan (canto 3)
1821

5

Writing Fluids

Carbon Ink

Ancient methods of writing, such as inscribing stone or impressing characters into clay tablets, were rendered, with the development of a suitable writing surface, quite literally more fluid: they were written with ink.

The exact origins of ink are obscured by time, but it appears that at least as far back as the third millennium B.C. the Egyptians were writing with a reed brush on papyrus using a black ink. Their simple writing fluid consisted of lampblack (probably prepared by burning resinous wood and collecting the soot) mixed with a solution of gum or glue.[1] This was made into cakes; however, "remains found in inkstands would seem to confirm that it was available in fluid form also."[2]

The ancient Chinese had a similar ink. In one tenth-century recipe, it consisted of ten parts of pine soot to three parts of powdered jade and one of gum.[3] It was pressed and dried into sticks, to be reconstituted as needed by grinding it with water on a hollowed-out stone slab (fig. 5.1).[4]

The Egyptian and Chinese inks differed little from the ink used today by draftsmen and artists, commonly termed india (or Indian) ink. Such inks, being made of carbon, which is extremely stable and consequently impervious to light and other effects of age or even to strong chemicals, remain black for centuries, while other inks may discolor and fade. Thus, as one expert notes, "the absolute permanence of the carbon inks can be approached by few other substances."[5]

There was one problem, however. A carbon-and-gum ink remains largely upon the surface of the writing material, where it is subject to removal by washing, rubbing, scraping, or similar process. While this allowed for easy erasure (whole pages could even be wiped clean and reused, such recycled sheets being termed "palimpsests"), abrasion could take an unwanted toll. Hence, with much handling over time, writing could be rubbed off its papyrus or parchment foundation.[6]

Iron-Gall Inks

The problem of abrasion was eliminated by the development of a later ink. Indeed, the very term is from the Old French *enque*, probably shortened (via the Latin) from the Greek *encauston*, meaning "burned-in or corroded." This acidic ink actually "bit in" to the surface of the paper and was consequently rendered more durable.[7] In extreme cases the ink has "burned" right through the paper, as shown in figure 5.2.

Inks of this type—an aqueous decoction of tannin and iron—may have been in use as early as the second century on Greek parchments.[8] Mention of such an ink is found in the seventh-century writings of Bishop Isidore of Seville (who was cited in chap. 1 as having made the first-known reference to the quill pen).[9] It is in a later, eleventh-century treatise, *De diversis artibus* ("On Divers Arts"), however, that we find detailed directions for the manufacture of an iron-tannate ink.

The author, an artist-monk named Theophilus, tells how to prepare a dried extract of "thorn wood" (hawthorne) bark, which is to be kept in parchment bags and used for making ink: "Whenever you want, take some of the dry material, temper it with wine over

Figure 5.1. CHINESE STICK INK dates from ancient times but has remained relatively unchanged, as in this nineteenth-century example entwined with a dragon. Such sticks were made by mixing soot with gum and forming in molds. For use, the stick was ground with water on a hollowed-out stone slab.

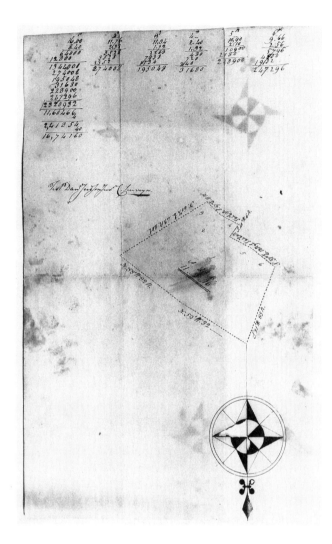

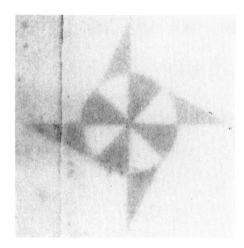

Figure 5.2. INK CORROSION has destroyed portions of this survey document's compass rose, where the iron-gall ink was applied heavily. Note at upper right (and in detail, *above*) a scorchlike image of the rose resulting from contact over time as the 1790 document was folded.

the fire, add a little green vitriol and write. If it happens through carelessness that the ink is not black enough, take a piece of iron a finger thick, put it into the fire, let it get red-hot, and immediately throw it into the ink." It is understood that the resulting ink "would be composed mostly of iron tannate or gallate."[10]

More often, however, gallic and gallotannic acids were obtained for the purpose from a quite different source—thanks to the female gall wasp. That insect deposits its eggs on certain species of oak, producing excrescences in the form of small, round, nutlike swellings known variously as galls, gallnuts, oak galls, and, in England, oak apples.[11] As one authority explains: "These gall-nuts contain tannic and gallic acids which can be soaked out of dried galls with water. The solution is clear and substantially colourless; but if it is mixed with a solution of an iron salt, a purplish-black compound is produced at once, and the ink becomes still blacker with age. Some of the salts produced by this mixture are colourless, but turn black upon oxida-

tion. . . . To bind this black colour securely some gum arabic was added to the ink."[12]

The "iron salt" used in this process was "sulfate of iron" (i.e., hydrated ferrous sulfate, $FeSO_4.7 H_2O$), which, because its greenish color suggested oxidized copper, was known as "copperas" or, alternatively, "green vitriol."[13] The gallnuts were often of a specified type—such as "the best blue galls" or "Aleppo galls" (after the name of the Syrian city famous for them)—commercial galls having been imported from Persia (Iran), Cyprus, Asia Minor, Syria, Italy, and elsewhere.[14] "Gum arabic" refers to the vegetable gum obtained from the acacia tree.

Those three ingredients were the essential ones, and an Italian rhyme of 1660 specified the ratio: *"Una due tre e trenta, / A far la bona tenta"* (one part gum, two of copperas, and three of galls in thirty parts of water).[15]

Some recipes were quite detailed, however, and contained other ingredients, as in this recipe from Edward Cocker's *The Pen's Triumph*, 1658:

Take three Ounces of Galls which are small and heavy and crisp, put them in a vessell of three pints of Wine, or of Rain-water, which is much better, letting it stand so infusing in the Sun for one or two dayes; Then take two Ounces of Coppris, or of Roman Vitrial, well colour'd and beaten small, stirring it well with a stick, which being put in, set it again in the Sun for one or two dayes more. Stir all together, adding two Ounces of Gum Arabique of the clearest and most shining, being well beaten. And to make your Ink shine and lustrous, add certain pieces of the Barque of Pomgranat, or a small quantity of double-refin'd Sugar, boyling it a little over a gentle fire. Lastly, pour it out, and keep it in a vessell of Glasse, or of Lead well covered.[16]

A more recent recipe, of about the 1830s, illustrating how the basic formula persisted over time, is shown in figure 5.3. Note the addition of indigo. Such an iron gallotannate ink did not reach its full depth of blackness until it had oxidized for some time upon the page, and so from time to time various coloring agents were added: in the Middle Ages carbon ink was sometimes mixed with it; in the eighteenth and nineteenth centuries such dyes as logwood and indigo were employed.[17] Over time, however, continued oxidation of iron-gall ink resulted in the ink's fading from black to the brown color commonly seen in old documents.[18]

As the notebook entry suggests, many people made their own ink—a simple process, shown in figures 5.4-5.7. Just as medieval texts (like Theophilus's) and later penmanship manuals (such as Cocker's) provided recipes, so did nineteenth-century magazines and books.[19] Galls could be sought in oak forests, or perhaps they could be purchased with copperas and indigo—dyestuffs stocked by general stores—and even gum arabic might be available or a substitute could be found.[20] Alternately—as at a frontier Kentucky printing office in the 1780s—one could purchase "ink

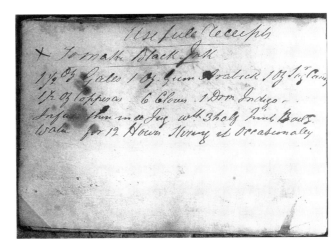

Figure 5.3. This RECIPE FOR INK was penned with a quill in a notebook kept from the 1830s and 1840s that also included instructions for making gunpowder. The page is headed *"Useful Receipts."* The recipe reads: *"To Make Black Ink / 1½ oz. Galls 1 oz. Gum Arabick 1 oz. Sug^r Candy / 1½ oz. Copperas 6 Cloves 1 Drm. Indigo. / Infuse these in a Jug wth 3 half pints Boilg. Water for 12 Hours, stir[r]ing it occasionally."* The sugar candy would make the ink glossy, the cloves would prevent molding, and the indigo was a provisional colorant.

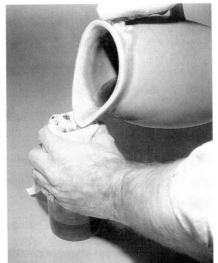

Figures 5.4-5.7. MAKING INK.

5.4 (*top left*). Crush oak galls with mortar and pestle and soak in rainwater to extract tannic and gallic acids.

5.5 (*top center*). Strain resulting tealike solution through cloth to remove unwanted particles of galls.

5.6 (*top right*). Add "copperas" (hydrated ferrous sulfate), which instantly reacts with the chemicals in solution to color it black. Add gum arabic (acacia gum) to increase viscosity and act as a binder.

5.7 (*left*). Pour the finished product into clean bottles (shown are actual antique ones), seal with corks, and add labels.

Figure 5.8. INK MAKER'S ADVERTISEMENT. This little girl has gotten more ink on herself than on the sign, which nevertheless promotes Whitmore's Ink on this chromolithographed trade card of the nineteenth century.

powder" along with inkstands to mix it in.[21] In this instance the powdered ink was probably simply a mixture of the three necessary ingredients.[22]

Inkmaking as a specific trade dates back several centuries, one early example being a mention, by the English lexicographer John Florio in 1598, of an "inkemaker."[23] Itinerant ink sellers were familiar in eighteenth- and early-nineteenth-century English towns. One is depicted in a wood engraving in a children's book of 1815, which shows casks of his liquid commodity hung on either side of his trusty donkey. Accompanying the drawing is a rhyme: "Through many a street and many a town / The Ink-man shapes his way; / The trusty Ass keeps plodding on, / His master to obey."[24]

Much ink was made by apothecaries who found they could easily prepare the fluid in quantity and pour it into standard bottles, which they sold with their own labels affixed.[25] According to William E. Covill, Jr., in his *Ink Bottles and Inkwells:* "There were literally hundreds of these shops that made and sold ink on a local basis. Later these shops died out due to the formation of large ink manufacturing firms, such as Carter's, etc. Ink was sold in many bookstores and carried only the label of the bookseller. The ink was no doubt made by the local apothecary shop or chemist."[26] An advertisement for one of the small ink manufacturers is shown in figure 5.8.

With the large firms came automation (fig. 5.9). A 1919 publication by the Carter Ink Company (established 1858) described "A Trip through Inkland"— that is, through "Carter Inx" main factory in Boston. It explained how bottles were taken from a storehouse to automatic washing machines, then on conveyors to the bottling floor "to await the ink":

> On the top floor the pure nut-gall solution is mixed with the iron salt and other ingredients in great tanks holding 3,600 gallons each. This nut-gall solution is the very purest obtainable, a super-U.S.P. Standard, so to speak, actually more refined than the grade of Tannin used in medicine. Of course, the purer the Tannin (Gall Solution) the better the ink. From here gravity takes the product to the big storage vats on the third floor, which have a total capacity of about 60,000 gallons. One of these vats alone contains enough ink to give each man in the regular army of the United States two desk bottles of Carter's Writing Fluid.

The account continued:

> After the ink has remained here long enough to settle out all sediment, the finished product is transferred by gravity to the automatic filling machines. It is also really fascinating to watch the labelling machines reach up with their mechanical hands, take down and gum the labels and fasten them to the bottles, in a marvellously smooth and secure manner. One of these machines alone labels 100 gross of bottles in a day, and the whole battery about 100,000 bottles.

Finally:

> After the ink bottles are filled, corked and labelled they are ready to be packed in boxes. The final act on this floor is nailing the cover on the boxes with automatic nailing machines. Placing the cover on the box by hand, a man slides it under the nailing machine, presses a lever, and the cover is nailed down securely with two blows. It is then slid on to another conveyor which lets the box down to the stock and shipping floor below. By means of trucks these boxes are then loaded on the freight cars which are left on a siding directly in front of the shipping platform.

From the shipping platform the ink went "to all quarters of the globe from Spain to China, and from Iceland to the Fiji Islands," Carter's at that time being "the largest manufacturers in our lines in the world."[27] An assortment of bulk-ink containers is shown in figure 5.10.

Later Common Writing Inks

Iron-gall ink was admirably suited for use with the quill pen, but its corrosive properties attacked the later steel nibs. Therefore, as the latter began to grow in popularity during the second quarter of the nineteenth century, so did inks advertised as especially formulated for them.

In 1834, Henry Stephens, a onetime roommate of the poet John Keats, set up a new ink factory in London and soon was offering to the public a selection of such inks.[28] These included his original patented Writing Fluid, which was a "distinct blue colour when first written with" but subsequently acquired a "superior blackness."[29] Such a "blue-black" ink (as this type is called) is an iron-gall ink so pure that the solution is at first colorless but turns black upon oxidation.[30] If a blue dye (such as indigo, used by Stephens) is added to the colorless solution, the result is an ink that writes blue but that will develop a deep black which will eventually obscure the blue color.[31] The ink would still be corrosive but proportionally less so due to the addition of the dye. Others later made similar blue-black inks, as shown by the Arnold advertisement of figure 5.11.

Figure 5.9. An INK FACTORY, about 1919. The illustration shows automated ink production with final bottling and corking of large "master" ink bottles.

By at least 1838 Stephens was advertising "a Carbonaceous Black Writing Fluid," whose name indicates it was carbon based, as does the claim it was "proof against every known chemical agent." He also advertised two unchangeable blue inks (one dark, one light, "which is a cheaper composition of the same character"), "a Brilliant Red Writing Fluid," and, later, "an Instantaneous Black Ink"—all advertised as "COMPOSITIONS, which have so remarkably extended the use of the STEEL PEN."[32]

Figure 5.10. BULK INK CONTAINERS include glass and stoneware "master inks" (as collectors term the large bottles)—many with pour lips or spouts—and a "Carter Inx" wooden shipping crate.

Left rear: Sheaffer's popular Skrip master ink with plastic pour spout; Levison's American Carmine Ink bottle of Levison and Blythe Manufacturing Company, St. Louis.

Middle left: an unidentified master ink embossed "IGCO"; an aqua glass bottle embossed "CARTER'S FULL PINT," with "PAT. FEB. 14, -99" on bottom.

Left front: embossed "DIAMOND INKS" bottle; Thaddeus Davids's cobalt-blue glass master ink, labeled "DAVIDS EXCELSIOR VIOLET INK."

Right (in front of box): stoneware bottle made by "J. Bourne & Son" for "P. & J. Arnold. London."; an aqua glass bottle with pour lip, embossed "STAFFORD INK"; a quart bottle containing blue-black MacMay Safety Ink, Columbus, Ohio. Bottles with original labels are highly desirable.

Figure 5.11. BLUE-BLACK INK is an iron-based variety that writes blue but changes to black due to oxidation. This 1888 advertisement is of P. and J. Arnold, London, which sold ink in stoneware bottles, like the one in figure 5.10.

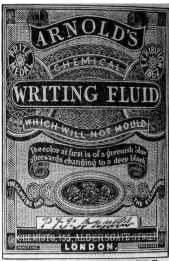

Figure 5.12. INK ASSORTMENT of Thomas's Inks, Chicago, about the turn of the century, includes black, crimson, and white ink, fountain-pen ink in dropper bottles, and such special items as "Hektograph" ink and ink eradicator.

Perry and Company, the steel-pen makers, countered with their own Perryian Limpid Ink, which they claimed "does not corrode Metallic Pens as other Inks."[33] Subsequent writing fluids which were not of the corrosive iron-gall variety included a potassium chromate type of logwood ink (ca. 1848), a synthetic indigo (1861), and certain other colored inks (made possible by the discovery of aniline dyes in 1856), as well as nigrosine ink (first produced commercially in 1867), and vanadium ink.[34] At least as early as the first part of the twentieth century, possibly earlier, common household laundry bluing doubled as a sometime writing fluid; indeed, the label of Mrs. Stewart's Liquid Bluing bore a drawing of a tiny fountain pen and urged, "USE IT FOR INK."

Special fountain-pen inks were formulated, including Sheaffer's popular Skrip (the "successor to ink," as it was advertised) in 1922, and a blue "washable" ink was developed in the 1930s.[35]

Other Inks

Although carbon and iron-gall inks were dominant, other inks were employed by the ancients. The Byzantines, for example, may have used semiliquid bitumen (a natural petroleum substance).[36] Colored inks were prepared from many natural materials. Animal-derived inks included sepia from the cuttlefish, and Tyrian purple from the Murex mollusk—both used by the Romans (the latter for the signatures of emperors).[37] Another was "Lombard gold" (fish bile), a medieval recipe for which reads: "Take the gall of a large fish and break it on a marble stone, and add a little chalk or calcined nitre and a little good vinegar and grind it on the marble to the consistency of rubric.

Write whatever you please with this on parchment and let it dry."[38]

The above-mentioned "rubric" refers to a red ink—used for initial letters, headings, or the like.[39] And here the terminology becomes somewhat blurred, since medieval colored "inks" were thick and rather paintlike, used less for writing than for "illuminating" (decorating or embellishing) text in manuscripts.[40] Among the common reds were vermilion (cinnabar), and red ocher (red iron oxide).[41] These were mineral pigments that were ground, levigated (placed in water so the heavier particles would sink and the finer, suspended ones could be drawn off), and mixed with glair (beaten egg white) or other binder such as gum arabic, natural gelatin, or diluted egg yolk.[42] This paint could be thinned to an "ink" by the addition of water and thus used with reed or quill pen for rubrication. Or it could be applied with a fine brush in coloring, for example, the embellishments making up an ornate initial letter. Other mineral pigments used in illumination were orpiment (yellow), limonite (yellow ocher), realgar

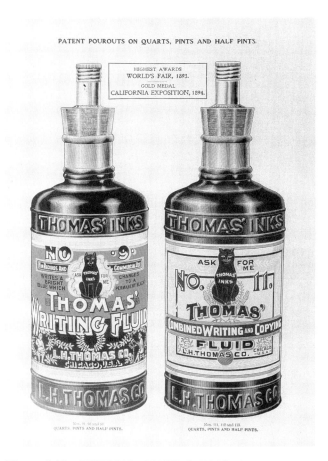

HIGHEST AWARDS
WORLD'S FAIR, 1893.
GOLD MEDAL
CALIFORNIA EXPOSITION, 1894.

THOMAS' INKS

NO. 91
FOR RECORDS AND COMMERCIAL USE
ASK THOMAS FOR ME
WRITES A BRIGHT BLUE WHICH CHANGES TO A PERMANENT BLACK
THOMAS' WRITING FLUID
L.H.THOMAS CO.
CHICAGO, U.S.A.
L.H.THOMAS CO

THOMAS' INKS

ASK FOR ME
NO. 111.
THOMAS INKS
THOMAS' COMBINED WRITING AND COPYING
FLUID
L.H.THOMAS CO. CHICAGO U.S.A.
L.H.THOMAS CO

Nos. 91, 92 and 93
QUARTS, PINTS AND HALF PINTS.

Nos. 111, 112 and 113.
QUARTS, PINTS AND HALF PINTS.

Figure 5.13. THOMAS "MASTER INKS" featured "patent pourouts" and held blue-black ink (*left*) or a "combined writing and copying fluid" (*right*).

(orange), malachite (green), lapis lazuli (ultramarine), and various earth colors (browns).[43]

In addition to animal and mineral substances employed in medieval illumination, plant materials were also common. These included brazil wood (red), indigo (blue), buckthorn berries ("sap green"), and saffron (yellow), among many additional vegetable extracts.[44] Berry inks were doubtless experimented with at varying times, including pokeberry ink, which was reportedly used on the American frontier.[45]

Over the ages, inks were also formulated for a wide variety of special purposes—for marking cloth or other problem materials (recall the marker ink, described in chap. 3, that is capable of writing on cellophane), for use with rubber stamps, and for additional specific functions. An assortment of Thomas' inks for writing and other uses is illustrated in figures 5.12 and 5.13. Represented along with common black and crimson inks are fountain-pen, stamping, and hectograph, or duplicator inks, as well as an opaque white ink intended for writing on dark surfaces, such as the black construction paper of old photograph-album pages. Not illustrated, but likewise used for decorative purposes was a "gold" ink, actually a suspension of bronze powder, sold by various manufacturers.[46]

Indelible inks were used to mark fabrics (laundry, for example) and were very much in evidence throughout the nineteenth and early twentieth centuries. Instructions for making such ink in 1823 read: "Pour a little nitric acid (aqua fortis) into a cup or glass, and add to it a small piece of pure silver; when the

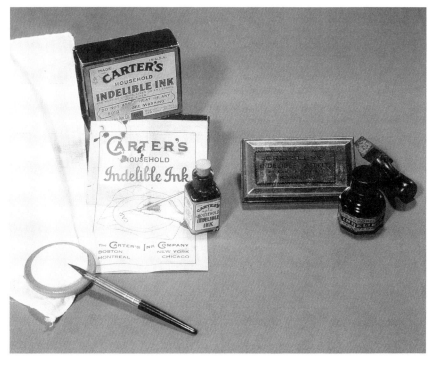

CARTER'S
HOUSEHOLD
INDELIBLE INK
DO NOT APPLY HEAT OF ANY KIND BEFORE WASHING

CARTER'S
HOUSEHOLD
Indelible Ink
THE CARTER'S INK COMPANY
BOSTON   NEW YORK
MONTREAL   CHICAGO

Figure 5.14. INDELIBLE INK was used for permanently marking fabric. Shown are a Carter's kit (complete with disk-and-ring stretcher), Cressler's stamp pad, and Sanford's Indelible Ink for pen or stamp.

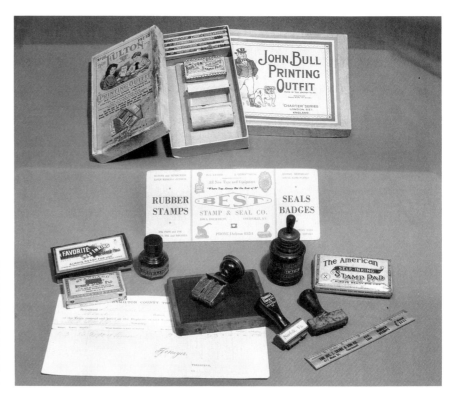

Figure 5.15. STAMPING INKS are shown with an assortment of pads and stamps, a stamp-advertising ruler and blotter, a stamp printing outfit, and a document with a rubber-stamped signature. The old changeable-date stamp is similar to ones still sold; an earlier version had revolving metal type wheels and received United States patent no. 18,249, September 22, 1857.

effervescence ceases, filter the solution through a piece of blotting paper, and put it in a small phial; then add to it a little gum arabic, and a little of the paint called sap green. After the whole is perfectly combined, it is then fit for use."[47] An 1867 recipe was brief: "Take 1 inch of stick nitrate of silver and dissolve it in a little water, and then stir it into a gallon of water, which will make a first-rate ink for cloth."[48] A patented indelible ink of 1872 was a composition of "silver, soda, gum, honey, tinctorial matter, ammonia, and water."[49] Indelible-ink kits, like those shown in figure 5.14, were also sold.

Copying inks, as their name indicates, were used in making "letterpress copies"—a process that involved dampening the original document and using a press to transfer onto tissue paper an impression which could be read from the opposite side.[50] Although "synthetic dye" inks were manufactured for the purpose, it was also true that copying inks could be "prepared by adding sugar, gum or glycerine to ordinary writing inks," and recipes were published for iron-gall-based writing inks with an increased proportion of gum.[51]

Packers' inks were used for marking crates, cartons, bales, and the like. They could be made simply by combining a suitable pigment—such as lampblack or ultramarine blue—with turpentine, mixed thinly enough to flow from a brush.[52]

Printing, canceling, and stamping inks were also often made of lampblack—reminiscent of the most ancient inks, except they were oil-based.[53] Modern rubber-stamp inks are usually solutions of dyes—for example, soluble blue, acid violet, nigrosine (for black) or magenta (for red)—in a base of glycerine or glycol and water (fig. 5.15).[54]

In marked contrast, literally, are so-called "sympathetic" inks that are invisible when written or drawn with but appear when desired. In the mid-nineteenth century, for example, they were employed "in coloring drawings made for parlor amusement, or the diversion of children and youth. As, for instance, a landscape drawn in ordinary colors with a wintry aspect, cloudy or sombre sky, snow on the ground, and leafless trees, if properly touched with sympathetic inks, will, at any time, when brought near a fire . . . change to the hues of summer." That is, it would if certain chemicals were used (cobalt chloride for the blue sky, for instance), "the whole disappearing as the picture grows cold."[55]

Other "sympathetic" writing fluids are the "secret" inks of diplomats and spies (reportedly first used by them in 1776) or of schoolchildren playing at the same. Sympathetic inks are known from as early as the third century B.C.[56] Such fluids may be written with a common "dip" pen and are rendered visible by some special treatment: lemon juice by heating with an iron, potassium ferrocyanide by sponging with a solution of iron sulfate, certain other solutions by exposure to chemical fumes or by viewing under ultraviolet light.[57]

Additional special-purpose inks are too numerous to allow an exhaustive list, even excluding such nonwriting concoctions as a greasy ink employed in lithographic printing, an 1890s "ink for zinc labels," and today's magnetic inks that can be read by computers.[58] More directly relevant to writing, because they are used for documents, are mimeograph and typewriter-ribbon inks, as well as other preparations.[59]

Inks made for the graphic arts range from a "show card," or poster-lettering ink, made by the Thaddeus Davids Company, a major nineteenth-century ink manufacturer, to today's waterproof drawing inks (india or colored inks containing shellac) used by some calligraphers and a special pale-blue nonreproducible, or "drop-out" ink that is invisible to photographic film.[60] One use for nonreproducible ink is in handwritten instructions to the printer that are not to appear on the finished plate.

Even an ink intended for ordinary writing could fall into the "special" category if there were something unique about its composition. Such would be the case, for example, with certain nineteenth-century formulations, including a "perfumed" and a "frost-proof" ink, as well as a *blue* writing fluid that was "Warranted to resist any eradicator." [61] One might also include "ink tablets," although their only unique feature would presumably be their distinctive marketing form, and even the novelty "vanishing ink" that is really a nonink, intended for practical jokes.[62] Its quality of disappearing stands in marked contrast to real ink, which, as we shall soon see, can be a very real and even troublesome presence.

SELECT BIBLIOGRAPHY

Fisher, M. Therese. "Ink." In *The Calligrapher's Handbook*, ed. C.M. Lamb, 65-74. New York: Pentalic, 1968. History of ink, with recipes.

The History of Ink, Including Its Etymology, Chemistry, and Bibliography. New York: Thaddeus Davids and Co. (ca. 1856-60).

Mitchell, C.A. "Section on Writing, Stamping, Typing, and Marking Inks." In *Allen's Commercial Organic Analysis*, by Alfred Henry Allen, 5:205-44. 1927. Revised ed. Philadelphia: Blakiston, 1948.

Rhodes, Henry T.F. "The Oxidation of Ferrous Iron in Iron Gall Ink." *Chemistry and Industry* 59 (1940): 143-45.

"A Trip through Inkland." In *The Story Your Ink Bottle Tells*. Boston: Carter Ink Co., 1919. Reprinted in *Pen Fancier's Magazine*, February 1984, 26-27.

6

Ink Containers

Recipes for ink—like those for cider, blacking, or tincture of cinnamon—presumed a quantity to be made greater than that immediately needed.[1] It was often about as easy to mix several ounces of a concoction as one, and so the liquid measure specified in the old ink "receipts" ranged from several barrels down to a few half-pints.[2] Such quantities naturally required storage until the ink could be used or sold.

As shown by the twelfth-century instructions of the monk Theophilus (given in chap. 5), ink in earlier times might well be stored in powdered form. Some five centuries later (1690) the *London Gazette* advertised "Holman's London Ink-Powder, . . . being the best Ingredients for making the strongest and best black Writing Ink," and the following century (1788) "ink powder" was being sold on the American frontier.[3] It was probably dispensed in small packets then as it definitely was later: for example, a Kentucky general-store ledger of the early 1830s lists (along with "1 paper blacking" and "1 paper lamp black") "1 paper ink powder."[4] In the meantime, Elija Bemiss, in his early-nineteenth-century treatise *The Dyer's Companion*, gave a recipe for making "an excellent Black Ink Powder" (a dry mix of powdered galls, copperas, alum, and gum), and in more recent times powdered ink was sold in cans for use in schools.[5]

The advantages of such an ink are readily apparent: it could be mixed to a consistency to suit individual preference; it would not mold; it could be transported more easily, since it was lighter than the liquid product and less fragile than bottles of ink; and it could be stored much more compactly.

Of course ink in the liquid form—whether it was made fresh or was constituted from ink powder or was simply bought, dispensed from the cask of an ink-seller—had to be placed in a suitable container for use. The ancient term for a vessel into which one dipped a pen is known from late-medieval English references to "an enkhorn" (in 1382), "inkehorne" (ca. 1440), and "a pener and a ynkorne" (1463)—a *penner* being a pen case

to which a small inkhorn was attached by a cord and carried at the waist, as in a reference of 1474: "On his gurdel a penner and an ynk-horn."[6] Similar small portable ink containers—still made of horn but in a bottlelike form with threaded cap—are known from as recently as about 1790-1810.[7]

The original form, however, was undoubtedly the container's namesake, a small horn of ox or cow (rather like a frontiersman's powderhorn but open at the opposite, wider end). Such an inkhorn dates far back in antiquity and is known, for instance, in a tenth-century French ivory carving, now in a Viennese museum.[8] A detail from the carving (which served as the model for the drawing in fig. 6.1) clearly illustrates the use of this ancient ink vessel. Often, since a horn's shape did not readily permit it to be stood on a desk, a hole was provided for the purpose.[9]

Later inkhorns were short segments of horn (thus tapering slightly toward the top), which were tooled with decorative lines; or they were imitative of those in

Figure 6.1. An INKHORN was the common container for ink during the Middle Ages, as shown in this drawing representing a detail from a tenth-century French ivory carving.

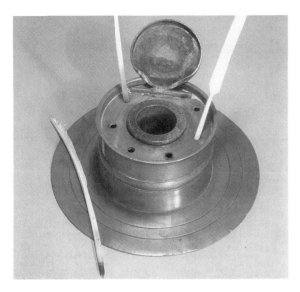

Figure 6.2. The PEWTER "COUNTINGHOUSE" INK-STAND in its basic form dates back to the sixteenth century. The disk base was added the following century. This later inkstand has six quill holes, a hinged lid, and a removable blue-glazed porcelain ink cup; its base measures 9⅜ inches across. A similar (but smaller) one stands today on Jefferson's revolving desk at Monticello.

shape but fashioned of hard leather, embossed, perhaps, with figures of saints; or they might be made of metal but, to prevent corrosion from ink, had inner containers of horn, pottery, or glass.[10]

Although the term "inkhorn" persisted into the late nineteenth century, it was rivaled by a variety of other terms (the dates following not necessarily being the earliest instances of use): "ynke pot" (1553), "ink-box" (1640), "ink glasses" (1680), "ink-holders" (1703), and "ink-well" (1875, when it was defined as "an ink-cup adapted to occupy a hole in a desk").[11] Eventually the latter term became common.

A more elaborate, composite container came to the fore as the province of writing expanded from that of the professional scribe or scrivener to include princes, men of letters, gentlemen, and merchants. For such writers it was convenient to have a sort of writing caddy that housed an inkpot, one or more pen receptacles, and possibly a pounce container, or "sander." Having a perforated top, this container was originally a dispenser of a powder used in preparing parchment or paper for writing; it later held "writing sand," which was used to "blot" wet ink prior to the advent of blotting paper. Sanders will be discussed in more detail in the following chapter.[12]

From at least as early as 1474 came references to such a composite item, termed a "standisshe" (later given as "standyshe," "stand-dish," even "standidge"—possibly simply a combined form of *stand* and *dish*, although there is no actual evidence for the assumption). A

reference to one, dated 1688, described some of its accoutrements: "This fashion of Horne . . . is now converted into Lead, and hath the denomination of a standish: or of tyn and soe haue both Inke place, sand box, candlestick and a long box to lay wax, pens and knife in: all fixt togather."[13] In its most simple form, a standish might consist of a base, or "stand," with a single inkwell, possibly in the form of a removable porcelain cup, and with a means of holding pens, as by holes for quills arranged around the well. Such forms include one traditionally made of pewter, having the same basic shape of the late horn or leather inkhorns described earlier. Later referred to as the "counting-house" type, these standishes originated in the sixteenth century and in the following century acquired a flat circular base (see fig. 6.2 for one dating from a later period.)[14]

By the late eighteenth century the term "standish" had begun to be transformed (by way of "ink-stand-ish") to "ink-stand," an early reference to which is dated 1773.[15] Today, "inkstand," "inkwell," and "ink bottle" represent the major divisions of ink containers, although there is much confusion as to terminology. One may commonly find, for example, in an antique shop, an old ink bottle that is labeled an "inkwell," or an inkwell termed "inkstand." Matters were not helped by some of the designations provided by early manufacturers of these containers. One 1880 glassware catalog, for instance, captioned its fancier ink bottles "ink stands," even though they were sold by the gross and were obviously intended to be filled and resold by ink makers just like other bottles.[16] Worse, some dictionaries, reflecting common usage, acknowledge the relative interchangeability of "inkwell" and "inkstand."[17]

It is true that some items defy easy pigeonholing, but we can clarify the term "ink bottle" as a bottle in which ink was sold or intended to be sold; "inkwell" can be reserved for permanent ink containers (sold without ink and intended to be filled and refilled) having the well feature only; and "inkstand" can be understood to refer to an inkwell combined with one or more additional features (another well, a pen rest, etc.). Of course there will still be items that are difficult to classify, and reasonable people may not always reach identical conclusions. The pages that follow do represent an attempt to adjudicate such matters.

A few special containers—cans of ink powder and barrels of ink as examples—lie outside the three divisions. Nevertheless, the distinctions are practical ones—for the serious collector as well as the interested reader—and serve to govern the following discussion of the great variety of ink containers that once so familiarly graced writing desks but which are now becoming increasingly scarce.

Figure 6.3. This CORAL-ENCRUSTED POTTERY INK (about 1⅛ in. in dia. by 2⅞ in. high) is believed to have been salvaged from an old shipwreck, dating from possibly as late as the Civil War, when such small earthenware ink bottles were still common.

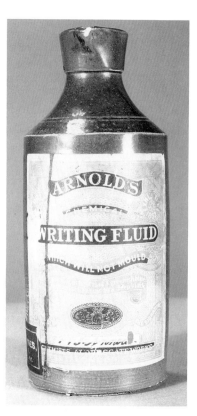

Figure 6.4. ARNOLD'S STONEWARE INK, a large or "master" ink bottle (6⅛ in. high), contained blue-black "Chemical Writing Fluid." The bottle is impressed with a pottery mark reading "VITREOUS STONE BOTTLES" and indicating it was made for P. & J. Arnold, London, by J. Bourne & Son. The Bournes operated the Denby Pottery and made bottles for Arnold's for many years. The label on the back touts awards won by Arnold's from 1862 to 1907 and shows how recently such bottles were sold. Another, smaller, label is that of the Richmond, Kentucky, druggist who sold the ink.

Figure 6.5. POTTERY INK CONTAINERS were common from the eighteenth century to the early part of the twentieth century. Collectors should beware of look-alikes: the wide-mouthed jar next to Sanford's crock held *blacking*, not ink, as some sources assert; the bottle at the opposite end of that row is of uncertain use. Most of the larger ones have pour lips, which assure their identification.

The large "master inks" with pour lips were used for filling inkwells and were often found in classrooms. The tall ("32 oz") one at the left rear is especially common and is impressed "VITREOUS STONE BOTTLES, / J. BOURNE & SON LTD / PATENTEES / DENBY POTTERY. / NEAR DENBY"; beneath is the name of the ink manufacturer, "P. & J. ARNOLD LTD / LONDON, / ENGLAND." Next to it is a stoppered bottle with a tattered label of "[HENRY C.] STEPHENS / [BL]UE BLACK / [W]RITING FLUID / . . . THE BEST INK FOR ALL FOUNTAIN PENS / . . . Aldersgate Street, London, E. C."

Small bottles, like the three at the right front, were common during the Civil War, and the large "Sanford's" crock advertising "Inks" and "Pastes" in blue letters is from this century. The wide-mouth blacking jar is impressed "DOULTON / 20 LAMBETH." Other embossed ones include those of "Stephens Inks" (*right rear*), "Lovatt & / Lovatt LTD" (the pair of brown bottles, *middle row*), "Carter's Inks" ("Stiff & Sons / London, / England"; the stoppered "white" glaze bottle, *middle row*). Two other "Doulton" bottles are also shown (*left front, and rear, second from right*).

Figure 6.6. PONTIL-MARKED INKS. A jagged scar on the bottom of a bottle (resulting from the attachment of a pontil rod after the bottle was blown and while the lip was being shaped) indicates it was probably made before about 1860. Maynard and Noyes (*second bottle from the left*) established the first significant ink manufactory in America in 1816.

The bottle at the left was blown in an open mold and measures about 1¾ inches square by 1¾ inches high. The tall bottle (2⁵⁄₁₆ in. high by 1⅜ in. in dia.), dating from the 1840s and bearing the label of Maynard and Noyes, Boston, is of so-called black, actually dark-olive, glass. Its label states: "This ink, however light it may appear when first opened, will always turn perfectly black soon after it is written with or by exposure to air in the inkstand." This indicates an iron-gall ink, confirmed by tests of residue. At the right are two common "umbrella" inks, so termed because of their paneled shape.

Ink Bottles

Just how far back in time the first ordinary bottle was pressed into service for ink storage cannot now be determined, but there is a reference as early as 1583 to an "inke-bottell" which may have been intended for dipping a pen into.[18]

Most ink bottles, including English ones shipped to the American colonies, were made in ceramic (i.e., were pottery bottles fired in a kiln) until the nineteenth century.[19] And pottery bottles made for such English ink makers as P. and J. Arnold, as well as for other English and American companies, continued into the twentieth century (figs. 6.3-6.5).

In 1772, however, there appeared in a newspaper what is probably the earliest advertisement for glass ink bottles, made by the Manheim Glass Factory. It was one of three such manufactories established by Henry William Stiegel (1729-85), who founded Manheim, Pennsylvania, in 1765.[20] The advertisement merely listed "Inkes of all sorts"—"inks" referring to the empty bottles which would have been sold, for example, to druggists to be filled with their own brand of writing fluid.[21]

The first American ink manufactories, as such, were the Maynard and Noyes Company, Boston, established in 1816, and the Thaddeus Davids Ink Company, which began making ink in 1825.[22] Still later was the inkworks of Apollus W. Harrison of Philadelphia, "without a doubt the largest ink maker of his day." For his Harrison's Columbian Ink, he "probably used more sizes and styles of bottles than any other maker of the period" (figs. 6.6 and 6.7).[23]

Figure 6.7. HARRISON'S COLUMBIAN INK. Apollus W. Harrison of Philadelphia was one of the major inkmakers of the mid-nineteenth century and used a wide variety of bottles for his "Columbian" (i.e., "American") product. Note the large pontil scar and the reversed *N* in "INK." The bottle has a diameter (measured from the "corners") of 2 inches and is 3⅝ inches high.

The early bottles were blown from a blob of molten glass gathered on the end of a long blowpipe—either free blown, or blown in molds. Both the free-blown bottles and those blown in "open" (i.e., one-piece) molds lack the seams exhibited by bottles formed in two- and three-piece molds. Until about 1860, when the newly formed but still hot and pliable bottle was ready to be disengaged from the blowpipe, the glassblower's assistant attached the end of a long, iron "pontil" rod to the opposite (bottom) end by means of a dab of molten glass.[24] When the bottle was thus securely fused to the pontil, the blowpipe could be removed. One early method was to cut the soft bottle neck with shears;

another was to weaken the glass by wetting it and then break off the blowpipe, afterward fire-polishing the lip. From about 1840 to 1900, an "applied lip," in the form of a collar of glass around the uppermost part of the neck, was occasionally added.

After the bottle was finished it was broken off the pontil, leaving a circular, jagged "pontil scar" centered on the bottom of the bottle. On bottles of a high quality this was removed by grinding, but on cheap bottles, like inks, the scar was left. Today such a pontil scar serves as a useful indicator of a bottle's age (fig. 6.6).[25]

Another indication of age is embossed lettering, which began to be common about 1869 (fig. 6.8).[26] The lettering was cut into the mold, leaving it in relief on the ink bottle. The fact that the lettering had to be cut in mirror image (so it would read correctly on the bottle) no doubt accounts for occasional errors such as the backward *N* in the Harrison's bottle in figure 6.7.

A very useful age indicator is the mold seam that runs up either side of the common two-piece mold bottles. As one authority states:

It is true that the mold seams can be used like a thermometer to determine the approximate age of a bottle. The closer to the top of the bottle the seams extend, the more recent was the production of the bottle.

Bottles of the early nineteenth century will have mold seams which end low on the necks or perhaps down on the shoulders of the bottles.

Between 1860 and 1880 the seam will stop below the mouth of the bottle, and it will be easy to observe that the lip was formed separately. After 1880, there was noticeable advancement in the art of mold making.

Utilizing improvements such as air vent holes, bottle molds were designed to shape the whole vessel, including the lips. The glass had to be severed from the blowpipe and just the ridge smoothed off by hand. After 1900, utilizing the bottle-making machine, the seam will extend clear to the top.[27]

The bottle machine had a marked (albeit delayed) effect on ink-bottle stoppers, another useful dating feature. Before about 1880, the fact that the bottle's neck extended from the mold, and thus had to be shaped by hand, meant a frequently off-round mouth best fitted by a compressible cork. Later improvements meant other closures could be employed, but they were generally too expensive for inks. Exceptions were perfumed and carmine inks that—due to an evaporation problem—required tight-fitting glass stoppers. The bottle machine made screw-on caps more practical than they had previously been, although they did not become really common until 1924, when bottle threads were standardized by the glass industry.[28]

An ink bottle's most noticeable feature, of course, is its shape, which serves not only as yet another indicator but also represents one of the attractions the ink bottle holds for collectors. The variety of unique, interesting, and decorative shapes (shown by two of the standard books on the subject) is truly impressive.[29]

Most inks can be roughly sorted into three basic shapes: square or rectangular; conical or pyramidal; and cylindrical, including the so-called "turtle" shape. Some are paneled (or "fluted," as the old bottle makers said), like the paneled cone or "umbrella" inks that were popular from the 1820s to the 1880s.[30] That does not disguise the primary form, however (fig. 6.9).

Figure 6.8. EMBOSSED INK BOTTLES began to be common by 1869. Impressions formed in the bottle mold resulted in the raised lettering. Shown are bottles of (*front row, left to right*) Thaddeus Davids; J. Field; the Diamond Ink Company (on bottom: "PAT. 12-1-03"); (*rear*) Sanford Manufacturing Company (entwined "SMCo."); and L.E. Waterman, maker of the famous fountain pen. All were made by an automatic bottle machine except the Davids bottle, which was blown in a mold.

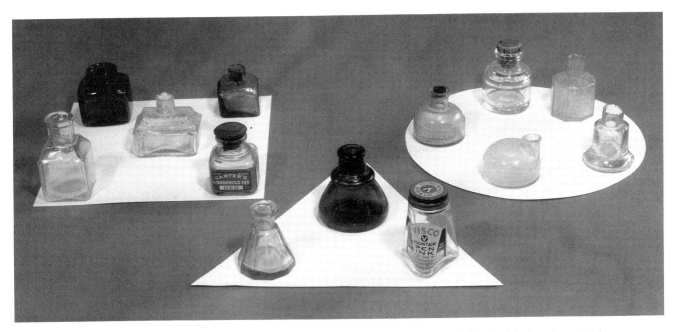

Figure 6.9. INK-BOTTLE SHAPES can generally be classified as square (or rectangular), cylindrical, and conical (or pyramidal).

Square bottles include (*rear*) two of blue glass—one of deep blue and made in an automatic bottle machine and the other of light blue and blown in a mold; (*center*) a rectangular ink with pen ledges; (*front*) a square ink blown in a mold and embossed on the bottom, "W.T. & Co." (Whitall, Tatum and Co.); and a square ink made by an automatic bottle machine, with a wood-and-cork stopper, labeled "Carter's Household Ink / Red."

Cylindrical bottles include (*clockwise from rear*) an aqua blown-in-mold bottle, embossed on the bottom "STANFORD'S," with wood-and-cork stopper; an octagonal ink, blown in a mold and embossed "HYDE / LONDON"; a bell-shaped, blown-in-mold ink, embossed on the bottom, "H.C. STEPHENS / LONDON"; a domed, offset-neck, or "turtle," ink, a type known since 1865; a domed, central-neck bottle, blown in a "key" mold and embossed "J.J. BUTLER / CINCINNATI," with cork.

Conical bottles include (*rear*) a blown-in-mold ink of brown glass, embossed "CARTER" on the bottom; (*front*) a ten-paneled "umbrella" ink, blown in a "key" mold; a triangular-base bottle with screw-on metal cap, made in an automatic bottle machine, labeled "Visco Fountain Pen Ink or for Ink Wells."

Inks in figural shapes date at least as far back as 1840, when log-cabin-shaped inks were specially made for the "Log Cabin and Hard Cider" presidential campaign of William Henry Harrison and John Tyler.[31] Another log-cabin ink was patented in 1884, and a "cottage ink bottle" received a design patent on March 14, 1871.[32] Other figural inks are barrels (from 1840 to 1900, including one patented in 1864 for Bailey's Anti-corrosive Ink), a locomotive (for Lochman's Locomotive Ink, patented Oct. 13, 1874), and shoes (most common from about 1870 to 1890).[33] All figural inks are highly collectible—even the Carter Ink Company's "cathedral" master ink (about 1920), a quasi-figural bottle.[34] It is of beautiful cobalt-blue glass with embossed panels suggestive of its name.[35] Rarely seen with their original paper labels, the bottles held Carter's Ryto permanent blue-black ink (fig. 6.10).[36]

Other distinctively shaped ink bottles include ones having pen ledges. Since they have often been termed "inkwells," even sold as "inkstands," they are discussed in the following section.[37]

Figure 6.10. CARTER'S "CATHEDRAL" INK is a quasi-figural bottle so-named from its embossed panels. A quart-size "master" ink of cobalt-blue glass, dating from about 1920, it held Carter's Ryto blue-black ink.

Figure 6.11. STONE INKWELL. Carved of dark-gray soapstone, this two-inch square rustic inkwell is of a type common to New England about 1740-1800.

Figure 6.12. QUILL-ERA INKSTANDS and WELLS. Prior to the advent of the steel pen, ink-stands like these often had holes for standing quill pens. Also shown are two "pocket" inkwells (*left front*) and a small "redware" inkwell (*right*). The group of wooden inkstands and inkwells on the left have glass ink receptacles. They were made by the S. Silliman Company, about the middle of the nineteenth century. Right of center is a gray-glazed earthenware inkstand, about 3¼ inches in diameter by 1⅜ inches high, probably American and from the early 1800s. At the far right is a red earthenware or "redware" inkwell. It is similar to a blue-glazed one made in Ohio and "used by schoolchildren"; it is shown closed with a wooden plug in Harold F. Guilland's *Early American Folk Pottery* (Philadelphia: Chilton, 1971), 189.

Inkwells and Inkstands

Like ink bottles, inkwells and inkstands are much-sought-after collectibles. Outside museums, very few are available from before the seventeenth century, but from then and especially the subsequent three centuries, interesting and elegant and otherwise desirable specimens may be obtained, if not always easily afforded.

Inkwells exist as either entirely separate entities or as containers designed as part of an inkstand, or made to insert in a desk, or the like. Examples of the former would be the simple stone inkwells of the late eighteenth and early nineteenth centuries. A few were cut from marble or limestone, but most were fashioned from easily workable soapstone, such as the typical one shown in figure 6.11, or another in my collection, a later, figural traveling trunk. Other simple wells were made of lead or pottery, such as the "redware" well included in figure 6.12.[38]

Inkwells that are part of inkstands include those of the quill era, which are typically surrounded by an array of holes in which the pens were stood (fig. 6.12). Such stands were common until about the middle of the nineteenth century, by which time the steel pen had largely replaced the quill.

Later inkstands were frequently designed to accommodate steel pens, whose heavy holders might have damaged their points had they been stood upright. Instead, the later stands often had racks or rests which held the pens and holders horizontally. In some of these the wells were integral to the stands, whereas in others the wells could be removed. Indeed some types of ink-wells were made to be sold both individually and with inkstands (fig. 6.13).[39]

Some other inkwells were shaped so as to fit into holes in desks, such as those illustrated in figure 6.14. The Sengbusch Company even made "countersunk" inkwells that could "set into round hole in desk or in bases" (i.e., inkstand bases having recesses made to receive the inkwells).[40]

An interesting variety of inkwell is the "pocket" or traveling type, which was an answer to an old problem. As it was expressed in a letter to the editor of *Mechanics' Magazine* in 1828: "No doubt hundreds of your readers must have felt the inconvenience of taking dimensions out of doors, as notes in surveying, &c. &c.: the common way of fixing an ink-bottle to the button-hole of the coat, is in many respects troublesome."[41]

Carried in pocket, portable desk, or saddlebag, traveling inkwells were made as early as the eighteenth century, perhaps earlier, and were common throughout

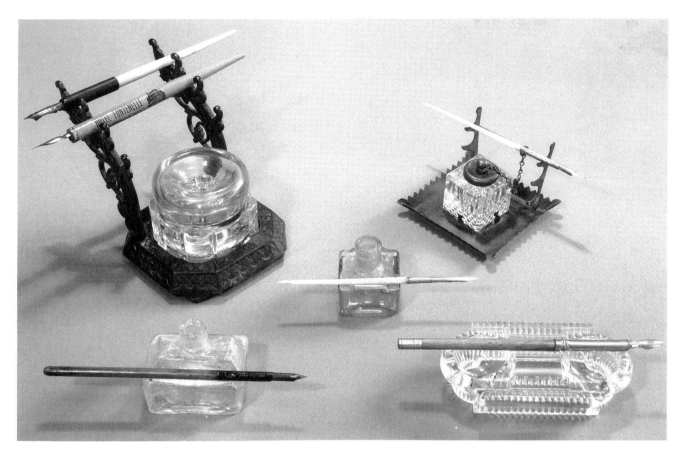

Figure 6.13. PEN-REST "INKWELLS" and STANDS. Many post-quill-era inkstands and bottles (often termed "inkwells" and even sold as "inkstands") were provided with racks or ledges for penholders. At the upper left is a cast-iron stand with a "safety" inkwell of pressed glass; its funnel-type opening made it resist spills if it were tipped over. The stand on the right is made of sheet brass, holds a pressed-glass well, and features a brass cover with a chain attaching it to the pen rack. At the center and lower left are two blown-in-mold ink bottles, each with two pen ledges, and at the lower right is a pressed-glass double-well inkstand, embossed "RIPLEY & CO / PITTSBURGH / PENN. USA," and having a central pen rest.

Figure 6.14. DESK-HOLE INKWELLS. The porcelain inkwell and this group of glass inkwells were made to fit a hole in a desk. The three at right were used for school desks. The porcelain inkwell (*left*) may be from the late nineteenth century. The glass well shown second from left is embossed on the bottom "FOR A HOLE 1¾ IN." and has a black cap with an attached cork stopper embossed "INK" twice. The three wells at the right have Bakelite tops, one with a small opening, the others with swivel closures. The second well from the right is marked "AMERICAN SEATING CO. / NO. 60." The one at the right is marked "HENRY S. WOLKINS CO. / BAKELITE / BOSTON, MASS." Not shown is one of silver plate, similar in shape to the porcelain.

Figure 6.16. FIGURAL TRAVELING WELLS, such as this brass barrel and painted-metal bottle (embossed on the shoulder "JOHANN HOFF / BERLIN" and on the bottom "MADE IN AUSTRIA"), are highly desirable collectibles. They both have push-button locks, and the barrel has a second closure inside. The bottle is about 2¹⁵⁄₁₆ inches high.

the nineteenth century in a variety of forms. Small wooden ones having either screw caps or "bayonet catches" and containing bottlelike inserts were manufactured by S. Silliman and Company of Chester, Connecticut, in the mid-1800s. These were typically of rosewood or boxwood and had a spring underneath the

glass container that helped form a tight seal when the lid was fastened. The Silliman price list labeled these "pocket inkstands" and many were carried by soldiers in the Civil War.[42] Other typical traveling inkwells were of leather-covered metal (again with tiny bottle-like inserts) and had push-button locks. Many of these had an additional, inner closure for double security against leakage (figs. 6.15 and 6.16).

Another important class is the patented inkwell, the first American one dating from May 13, 1813.[43] Such wells fall into two basic categories (following the two types of United States patents). There were those patented simply for their appearance (*design* patents, originating in 1842, including figurals like Edward Finney's "Liberty Bell" inkwell, patented July 27, 1875).[44] And there were those patented for their unique function (*mechanical* patents). The latter include revolving wells known to collectors as "snails" because of their shape. They could be tipped forward from their closed position so they could be dipped into. Many of the cast-iron inkstands into which they are incorporated (there being one-, two-, and three-well models) are marked "Pat. Jan. 14. 79," or "Patd. Nov. 25. 1879," some carrying both dates.[45]

The "self-closing" inkwell is another important type of functional inkwell, probably the most common being the mechanism patented in 1903 by the Sengbusch Company (fig. 6.17). Another is the spring-and-float "New Action Automatic Ink Stand" (i.e., inkwell) of the Davis Company, patented in 1889.[46] At a touch of the pen, a plunger was depressed, and when the pen was removed, the access hole was again automatically sealed.

Still other patented inkwell features included a fountain-supplied "pen dip cup," which "gauges accurately a panful of ink and insures cleanliness"—the whole being invented in 1887 by Samuel Darling and sold as Darling's Patent Pen Gauge Inkstand.[47] And there were countless other patented mechanisms relating to inkwells and flourishing from about 1850 through the turn of the century.[48]

Apart from considerations of design and function, inkwells and inkstands are usually classed by the type of materials and workmanship used in their manufacture. A major category, for example, comprises those made of silver and gold—ink containers, certainly, fit for kings. As Betty and Ted Rivera state in their authoritative *Inkstands and Inkwells:* "Previous to the sixteenth century, it was considered undignified for an aristocrat to do his own writing. Scriveners fulfilled the duties of correspondents, and thus the inkstand—or standish, as it was called—was not in great demand as an ornament. By the end of the sixteenth century in England, the silver inkstands were made in the shape of a box, which contained an inkpot, wafer box (to hold paste wafers for sealing letters), and a sander. . . . The box was also fitted with a drawer for quills and sealing wax."[49] Few of these survive. More common are silver standishes of the eighteenth and nineteenth centuries. Typically, these are stylish, oblong trays supported by small feet, the trays containing an inkwell and sander, or two inkwells, and, between those two items, usually another: either a taperstick or wafer box, or a bell, used to call a servant to post a letter. Still, a later king might prefer a simple silver inkpot like that shown in figure 6.18. Other items in this category would be sterling-

Figure 6.17. PATENT "INKSTAND." The "Sengbusch Self-Closing Inkstand Company" received a United States patent on its inkwell on April 21, 1903, and another on April 23, 1904. The pen was provided with "a uniform dip at all times," and when it was withdrawn the patented mechanism closed the opening automatically. For a photograph, see figure 6.21. (From the 1925 office supply catalog of Carrithers and Company, Chicago.)

silver inkwells or gold- or silver-plated Victorian inkstands with glass wells (fig. 6.19).[50]

Inkwells and stands have also long been made of pottery, which is basically of two types. *Earthenware* has a soft base which is porous until it receives its fired-on glaze. Varieties include rustic redware (fig. 6.12); creamware (or queensware), perfected by Josiah Wedgwood in the 1760s; and delftware, which has a white

Figure 6.18. A ROYAL SILVER INKPOT is shown in use, in an old-fashioned cylinder-top desk, by His Majesty King George V (1865-1936), grandfather of Queen Elizabeth II.

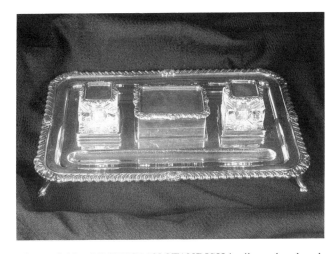

Figure 6.19. VICTORIAN STANDISH is silver-plated and features two glass inkwells, two pen rests, and a wafer box.

Figure 6.20. POTTERY INKWELLS and STANDS often graced ladies' writing tables. *From left*: two Staffordshire figural wells of the late nineteenth century, and two porcelain inkstands: the French "pump" type of about 1840 and one with a matching well and sander, about 1850. The "pump" inkstand's brass control knob turned a reverse screw which lowered or raised a plunger, causing ink to well up in founts or flow back into a reservoir. Embossed on the knob is "MEDAILLE D' ARGENT [silver medal] 1839" and "ENCRIER BOQUET INVENTEUR . . . PARIS." It measures about 6 inches in diameter by 7⅛ inches high and has three quill rests arrayed around the inside rim of the bowl.

Figure 6.21. UTILITY GLASS WELLS and STAND. Surrounding the "fountain" inkwell are, *left,* a group of inkwells with various patented closures, including a Sengbusch "self-closing inkstand" (with large black top); *rear,* a double-well inkstand with metal swivel covers; and *right,* a group of utility wells with lift-off glass covers. All are pressed glass except the fountain well, which was blown in a mold.

The Sengbusch "inkstand" was patented in 1903; see the text and figure 6.17. The inkwell at left front has a screw-on metal cover with a slide-type closure; the bottom of the well is embossed "JACOBUS PAT. NOV. 10 '96." So-called "fountain" inkwells, like the one at the center, were common during the mid-to-late nineteenth century and had some type of cover over the mouth.

opaque surface that could be printed with colorful designs and then refired, also known as *faience* (from France) and *majolica* (from Spain and Portugal, as well as Italy).[51]

Stoneware, or ceramic, is a heavy, nonporous pottery, partially vitrified by firing. Varieties range from common salt-glazed stoneware (in gray, brown, or white) to the thin, white, hard but lightweight varieties of porcelain (including china).

All types of pottery were used for inkwells and inkstands (figs. 6.12 and 6.20). As early as 1809 in America, Clarkson Crolius of New York offered for sale at his factory his assortment of "Stone Ware," which included "Fountain and common Ink Stands equal to glass."[52] Porcelain ones range from a set of "Mr. and Mrs. Carter Inx" (colorful little ceramic figures, patented for Carter's and dating from the period 1914-16) to inkstands resembling—and even rivaling in prestige—those of silver.[53]

Although extant in ancient times, glass inkwells existed in profusion from the late eighteenth century until the end of the dip-pen era. In America they were made by the Boston and Sandwich Glass Company (which made several types from 1825 to the company's closing in 1888) and the New England Glass Company—neither of which is thought to have made ink bottles—as well as other glasshouses.[54]

Glass wells were either blown like bottles (free blown or blown in molds) or they were "pressed," that is, the

Figure 6.22. POST OFFICE GLASS WELL. These substantial, pressed-glass inkwells (embossed on their bottoms as shown) were similar to the utility wells in figure 6.21. By official order on June 13, 1957, they and their accompanying dip pens were replaced by ballpoint pens, which were attached to the counters by thin chains. The discarded inkwells measured 2⅞ inches square by 2 9/16 inches high.

Figure 6.23. This DOUBLE-WELL GLASS INKSTAND is embossed "Made in England." It is similar to the utility wells shown in figure 6.21, except for its distinctive twin-cup feature. This allowed a choice of two inks—such as black and red, or blue-black and "copying"—and was thus appropriate for an office. The stand is of pressed glass and measures 2 by 4 inches by 2⅛ inches high.

Figure 6.24. DECORATIVE HINGED-TOP WELLS were especially common from about 1870 until after the turn of the century. Except for two—second and third from left, one encased in brass with a semiprecious stone atop, and one with an art nouveau–style metal top—all are of cut glass with prismatic glass lids and metal fixtures, including a blue-glass well at the far left. Miniature inkwells in a brilliant cut-glass stand are only 1 inch square by 1½ inches high, among the smallest of their type known. The stand was a gift from the poet Jonathan Green, who inherited it from his grandmother.

molten glass was mechanically forced into a mold (figs. 6.21-6.23). A "cut glass" well originated as one of those two types and was then decoratively cut in a separate process; the result was a sharply patterned and sparkling appearance.[55] Many inkwells of cut or pressed glass had hinged lids of glass, silver, or brass (fig. 6.24).

Among the blown-type wells were those of swirled and ribbed glass known as "Pitkin type" after one of the primary manufacturers of them, the Pitkin Glass Works (1783-1830) of East Manchester, Connecticut.[56] Inkwells of pressed (and often cut) glass include those with hinged lids of glass, silver, or brass (fig. 6.24). Typically, inkwells protected by mechanical patents (like those made by Sengbusch) were of pressed glass, as were certain common glass inkstands (like one shown earlier in fig. 2.19).

Many additional materials were employed in the manufacture of inkwells and inkstands. These include brass (fig. 6.25), wood (fig. 6.26), molded plaster over wood (see the figural inkstand in fig. 6.27), and even leather (as in the unusual inkstand in fig. 6.28). Also used have been papier-mâché, gutta-percha, bronze, nickel silver, and others, including seashells.[57]

Dating inkwells and inkstands is not always easy but some of the dates and time frames already given should provide assistance. Experience will teach one to recognize certain stylistic features of the Victorian era, for example, or the free-flowing forms of art nouveau and the contrastingly geometric shapes of the art deco period. If one can point to a specific date for the close of the inkwell era it would be this: "On June 13, 1957, the U.S. Post Office Department notified its branches that their scratchy old straight pens and messy inkwells, retained long after most people had switched to newer writing intruments, would be replaced by ball-points. The retired inkwells were offered to local schools and

Figure 6.25. This BRASS and GLASS INKSTAND features a domed-top inkwell with milk-glass insert (which was used with blue ink). The well is mounted on a black cut-glass base having a single pen groove.

other institutions, but most were discarded. After 4,500 years of use in literate nations, inkwells had vanished from daily life." [58]

Other Ink Containers

Mentioned earlier were such additional containers as the casks of early inksellers, the wooden crates used for master ink bottles (fig. 5.10), and the "papers" and tins used for powdered ink. There was also an "ink bottle box" (cylindrical, of paper-covered cardboard) marked on the base "Patented January 30, 1855. By E.

Figure 6.26. The WOODEN INKSTANDS shown range from the small, log-segment one, ca. 1945 (*lower right*) to three more substantial models, all probably dating from the end of the nineteenth century. The larger models include an inkstand base with a brass handle and glass well (*lower left*), and two large desk boxes (*back row*). Having multiple wells covered by hinged lids plus pen troughs, the latter were suitable for offices. The largest box has wells for "Copying," "Red," and "Black" ink, as well as a drawer for accessories. It measures about 5½ by 10½ inches by 4 inches high.

Figure 6.27. This FIGURAL INKSTAND of about the 1880s, is representative of an interesting class of inkwells and stands made of many materials—in this case molded plaster over wood. The stand measures about 3¼ by 6 inches by 5⅞ inches high overall.

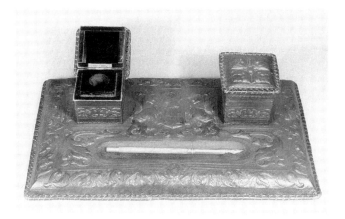

Figure 6.28. This LEATHER INKSTAND features tooled and laced dark red leather over a wooden base. Of relatively recent (twentieth-century) vintage, it nevertheless recalls the embossed leather "inkhorns" of the late medieval era.

Waters Troy N.Y." [59] And of course more recent ink bottles, like the Skrip well-top bottle, came in ordinary squarish boxes for ease both in packing and in stacking on store shelves.

To all these can be added the stoneware beer bottles and whiskey jugs in which ink was sold prior to potters' production of special ink bottles. The latter usually had a pouring lip to facilitate their use in filling inkwells.[60]

A sort of transient ink container was the tin or copper ink pourer, a small pitcher roughly 3½ inches in diameter by about 4½ inches high, complete with handle and oversized spout. States one authority: "The ink pourers were used to dispense ink in schoolhouses and in commercial offices. These were filled from large master ink bottles ranging from a pint up to a gallon in size. The use of ink pourers declined rapidly in the early 20th century as by that time most of the master ink bottles had closures which allowed the pouring of the ink directly from the bottle" (for such special closures or "patent pourouts," see fig. 5.13).[61] Pourers and pouring spouts represented more than simple convenience when it came to the dispensing of ink, for that was a serious activity, as we shall see presently.

SELECT BIBLIOGRAPHY

Covill, William E., Jr. *Ink Bottles and Inkwells*. Taunton, Mass.: William S. Sullwold, 1971.

"Inkwells: Practical Elegance for Writing Desks." *The Encyclopedia of Collectibles*. Alexandria, Va.: Time-Life Books, 1979.

Kolbe, Tim. "Collecting Inkstands & Inkwells." *Antique Trader Price Guide to Antiques and Collectors' Items* 20 (August 1989): 92-97.

Munsey, Cecil. *The Illustrated Guide to Collecting Bottles*. New York: Elsevier-Dutton, 1970. Includes information on early ink bottles, bottle manufacturing, collecting.

Nelson, Lavinia, and Martha Hurley. *Old Inks*. Salem, Ore.: Old Time Bottle Publishing Co., 1967. Guide to ink bottles, illustrated with line drawings.

Rivera, Betty, and Ted Rivera. *Inkstands and Inkwells: A Collector's Guide*. New York: Crown, 1973.

Whalley, Joyce Ircne. *Writing Implements and Accessories: From the Roman Stylus to the Typewriter*. Detroit: Gale Research, 1975.

7

Ink Problems

Spilled Ink

A nineteenth-century cartoon (a humorous little wood engraving actually) portrays a thoroughly dejected man. At his elbow, clutching a quill pen in his small fist, is what appears to be at once a grandchild and the originator of the disaster. For there on the table is the overturned inkwell, its contents spilling over the map or chart the man had been working on, running like a black river, the branching rivulets becoming tributaries across the white expanse of paper. Beneath the drawing is the wry caption: "Source of the Niger," that is, the great African river whose Latinate name means "black" and whose source was then uncertain.[1]

Tipped over, an inkwell could indeed seem a fount of great capacity, all the more so because its very nature meant its staining properties were intense. In fact one old method of staining wood was to brush on first a solution of nutgalls followed by "strong copperas water"—the major ingredients, in other words, of ink.[2]

Even if ink were kept safe from juvenile offenders, there could still be accidents involving freshly written papers—as in a mention of 1645 that "the secretary pour'd the Ink-box all over the Writings."[3] Perhaps the secretary did not cause a *spill* but simply made an error: a source of 1806 mentioned the possibility of "Emptying the ink-glass (by mistake for the sand-glass) on a paper which you have just written out fairly."[4]

In any event, other casualties of ink were the tops and interiors of what Charles Dickens referred to (in *Nicholas Nickleby*) as "old, rickety desks, cut and notched, and inked."[5] The greater and lesser blots and spills, as well as the rings left by the inky bottoms of bottles or wells often remain vivid for centuries. In addition, floors, rugs, clothing—all could be marred by the penetrating stain.

The essential antidote to spills was the proverbial ounce of prevention. Therefore, early on, ink containers were so designed as to minimize their being tipped over—hence the characteristically squat appearance of ink bottles, and the typically weighty bottoms and base members of inkwells and inkstands.[6] Safety inkwells became popular for their ability to minimize spills, even when knocked over (fig. 6.13).[7]

Nevertheless, spills occurred, and the first course of action was to attempt to soak up the ink with whatever was available—a paper blotter, of course, being well suited to the purpose.[8] Then one of the old "receipts" for removing ink stains could be consulted.

Most of the treatments, however, simply involved application of an acid to bleach the stains. For example, in 1819 it was said, "Lemon-juice [citric acid], and the juice of sorrel [containing oxalic acid] will also remove ink-stains."[9] In 1853, in *Bleak House*, Dickens described the use of vinegar (acetic acid) for that purpose: "She would not sit down, but stood by the fire, dipping her inky middle finger in the egg-cup, which contained vinegar, and smearing it over the ink stains on her face."[10] Again, in an 1894 compendium, under "Useful Recipes and Trade Secrets," one reads:

> *Ink spots and recent iron moulds* [e.g., rust stains, "mould" being a corruption of *mole*, "stain"], on washable fabrics, may be removed by dropping on the part a little melted tallow from a common candle, before washing the articles; or by the application of a little lemon juice, or of a little powdered cream of tartar [acid potassium tartrate] made into a paste with hot water. Old ink spots and iron moulds will be found to yield almost immediately to a very little powdered oxalic acid, which must be well rubbed into the spot previously moistened with boiling water, and kept hot over a basin filled with the same.

The instructions went on to note, "Very frequently, when logwood has been used in manufacturing ink, a reddish stain still remains after the use of oxalic acid. . . . To remove it, procure a solution of the chloride of lime [i.e., chlorinated lime: bleaching powder] and apply it in the same manner."[11]

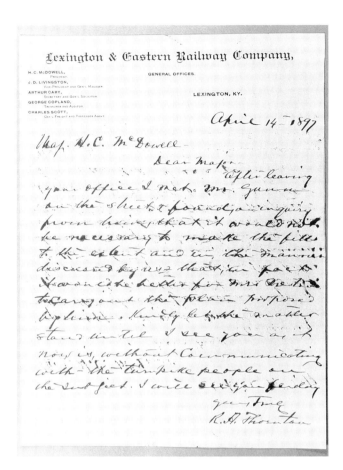

Figure 7.2. DOCUMENTS, BOX, and SANDER. Papers from the early 1840s were kept in this hide-covered document chest that belonged to the superintendent of Indian Affairs, Iowa Territory. An opened document—the ink of which was blotted with sand—is shown with a sander of the early 1800s.

Figure 7.1. A SMUDGED LETTER resulted from hasty folding. To prevent ink from offsetting like this, fresh writings were often blotted—with either writing sand or blotting paper.

Blotting

Ink did not have to be spilled to create a mess. When freshly penned it could easily smear, since it took time to dry, especially in the heavier strokes of the writing. (Because the points of the split pen separated under pressure on the downstrokes, extra ink flowed out, producing strokes that were not only wider but proportionally more heavily deposited. There the ink pooled until dry.) If a letter or other writing were folded too soon, the result could resemble that shown in figure 7.1.

For that reason, fresh writings were blotted by some means or, preferably, were allowed to dry before folding or further handling. The latter approach was that of Franklin D. Roosevelt, as shown by an incident that occurred on the day of his death. A visitor, a woman painter, arrived not long before he was stricken. She described Mr. Roosevelt as sitting at a card table and signing numerous papers. His secretary, who stood by, did not blot the signatures but instead spread them out, here and there, to dry. The president jokingly referred to the array of white sheets as his "laundry."[12]

Figure 7.3. WRITING SAND is embedded in this magnified script from the document in figure 7.2. Microscopic examination by John F. Fischer revealed it was common water-worn quartz sand, probably from the locale where the document originated. Sometimes a signature or other bit of writing at the end of a document has a speckled appearance, as if once sprinkled with writing sand which has subsequently sloughed off.

Medieval scribes had no need to blot their slowly and carefully wrought parchments, but for some later writings blotting was convenient. Entries in account books, for example, were frequently posted in haste, and blotting eliminated the need for the book to be left open until the ink dried. In fact, the book could simply be closed upon the insertion of a piece of blotting paper, the earliest known pieces of which are those found among the pages of fifteenth-century English accounts.[13]

Figure 7.4 (*far left*). This TINWARE SANDER, used to dust writing sand on wet ink, is of a utilitarian type common in the early nineteenth century. Note the concave top, which allowed excess sand to be returned to the container.

Figure 7.5 (*near left*). This BRASS SANDER once graced a writing desk in the first half of the nineteenth century. As with most sanders, the only means of filling it were through the holes in its recessed top.

Nevertheless, although it appears the use of blotting paper may have been the earliest method of drying ink, it also seems to have been largely superseded (until about 1800) by another technique: dusting the wet writing with fine sand. Possibly the earliest mention of sandboxes occurs in Richard Huloet's *Abecedarium* (considered the first English dictionary) in 1552.[14]

As experimentation readily shows, the sand does have a notable absorbing/drying effect even though the grains of sand themselves are nonabsorbent. By capillary attraction the ink is dispersed upwardly, honeycomblike throughout the spaces in the coating of sand—which immediately gives the effect of coagulating the ink and preventing its running. And by thus increasing the surface area of ink that is exposed to the air, the sand enables it to dry rapidly. Ink that has adhered to the uppermost granules is carried away with the sand as the excess is shaken off the paper. Some sand may become embedded in the ink, where it may long remain. Figures 7.2 and 7.3 show a document from the 1840s and an enlarged pen stroke from the same, revealing the clustered granules of writing sand.

Although chalk has reportedly been used for the purpose, sand was the usual substance employed. In a source of about 1655, "Calis-sand" was specified; this was a fine white sand imported from Calais, France.[15] In the nineteenth century several varieties of sand were sold, typically packaged in paper parcels that rather resembled miniature (about 3-inch long) sacks of flour. A gold-colored sand so parceled and labeled "California Gold Writing Sand. A New Article. Manufactured wholesale and retail by G.S. Allen, Pittsfield, Mass." was probably inspired by the California gold rush. Another package was labeled "8 ounces, superior black writing sand. Prepared and put up, by L.W. Leach & Son, Durham, Conn." Yet another parcel contained "round style black writing sand."[16] Most often, the common black writing sand was powdered biotite (a form of mica).[17]

Sandboxes—or sand casters, sand dredgers, or simply "sanders"—were common by the mid-sixteenth century, as their listing in Huloet's *Abecedarium* demonstrates. Such a container can be traced back to the "pounce pots" of medieval scribes. These contained powdered pumice or sandarac (a translucent resin), or other material, such as pulverized cuttlefish, that was used to prepare parchment for writing. Later, when paper began to replace parchment, sandarac was rubbed into the surface of unsized paper, or paper roughened by erasure, to prevent the writing from soaking in and leaving a frazzled, spangled appearance. Still later, the availability of good writing paper rendered the pounce pot all but obsolete, and it became a container for writing sand instead.[18] Some eighteenth-century inkstands even held a pounce pot *and* a sander.[19]

Sanders are distinguished from other types of shakers (such as pepper shakers) by their recessed—often concave—top, which allowed excess sand to be poured back into the container. Collectors should carefully scrutinize shakers which are purported to be sanders yet lack this feature.

The oldest-known English silver standish, dated 1630, has a cylindrical sander that matches the accompanying inkpot, which is usually the case when both items are included in an inkstand or writing box. Hence there is the possibility of mistaking one for the other, as mentioned earlier. Like the inkwells they frequently resemble, sanders are found in a variety of materials: pottery (including white salt-glaze stoneware, blue and white Staffordshire, and porcelain), glass (often having screw-on pewter caps and found in Victorian "lap" desks with matching wells), wood (e.g., maple, cherry, rosewood, lignum vitae), metal (e.g., brass, tinware, pewter, silver), and other materials, such as horn and vulcanized rubber (see figs. 7.2 and 7.4-7.6 for a variety of sanders from my collection).[20] Although sanders continued to be made in the latter half of the nineteenth century, their use declined as that of blotting paper increased.[21]

The earliest known mention of blotting paper in English is dated 1465, and in a text of 1519 is the following reference: "Blotting paper serveth to drye wette wryttynge, lest there be made blottis or blurris."[22] Still another reference is in Huloet's *Abecedarium* which cited (along with the sandbox) blotting paper as a means "to dry a writing."[23]

As mentioned earlier, sand displaced paper over subsequent centuries until about 1800, according to Julius Grant's chronological "Dating Evidence from Ink and Other Sources." At that time, states Grant, blotting paper was "in general use in England, following an accidental rediscovery at Hagbourne, Berkshire."[24]

Be that as it may, nearly a decade before, in America, it appears blotting paper was already well known. In the old records of the Moravian religious community of North Carolina is found this entry, made following the establishment of their new paper mill: "April 29, 1791, blotting paper will be made this week."[25] That was two months before they made writing paper, blotting paper being a simpler and cheaper variety that lacked sizing and could consequently absorb ink readily.[26]

Figure 7.6. TRAVELING INKWELL and SANDER. This pocket writing kit of the mid-nineteenth-century consists of a glass inkwell, a metal sander, quill holes (for standing the pen when in use), and a pen ledge (for resting the pen when the box is closed). Spring-type closures in the lid prevented ink and sand from spilling. The kit measures only 1½ by 2⁹⁄₁₆ inches by 1⅜ inches high.

Figure 7.7. LEDGER BLOTTERS. Large sheets of blotting paper, printed on both sides with advertisements, were made for use with hotel registers or ledgers. The one on the left (10 by 15½ inches) was patented December 5, 1866; the blotter on the right (11½ by 18 inches), of about 1890, is printed in red and black.

Figure 7.8. "ADVERTISING BLOTTERS" include one (*left center*) with that heading. Others are calendar blotters, a "Little Signature Blotter" (*lower left*), and a set of colored blotters with a celluloid cover (*bottom center*). Those of known dates range from 1913 to 1960. *Left column from top:* 1913 calendar; Esterbrook pens advertisement; "Advertising Blotters"; ruler blotter; "Little Signature Blotter" (about 2½ by 4½ inches). *Center column:* 1946 pinup calendar; die-cut florist's ad; political advertisement, "Blake for clerk"; celluloid-covered gray, pink, and blue blotters. *Right column:* 1960 advertisement for Coca-Cola; 1927 calendar.

References to both blotting paper and sand are found in subsequent years in both England and America. In his *Pickwick Papers* (1837), Charles Dickens told how Mr. Pickwick had concluded making entries in his journal and "carefully rubbed the last page on the blotting paper," yet in Dickens's 1853 *Bleak House* a "Little sand-box" is mentioned.[27] The American novelist Herman Melville wrote in *Moby Dick* in 1851: "Nantucket! Take out your map and look at it. There is more sand there than you would use in twenty years as a substitute for blotting paper."[28]

By about this time, sanders appear to have been effectively supplanted, and American blotting paper began to be made on a large scale by means of the Fourdrinier paper machine. This was begun in 1856 by the Joseph Parker and Son Company at the West Rock Paper Mill in New Haven, Connecticut, and eventually spread to other mills.[29] The process allowed the paper to be produced in continuous rolls rather than individual handmade sheets. By 1866, a contributor to the

Figure 7.9. ROCKER BLOTTERS were popular desk accessories because they were easy to use. Shown are blotters of brass (*top row*), painted wood (*center*), natural wood (*lower left*), and sterling silver (*lower right*).

Figure 7.10. This ROLLER BLOTTER of unique design features a "marble" top and knob with rollers of blotting paper. It is about 2¾ by 4½ inches by 3³⁄₁₆ inches high, overall. A more common type of roller blotter was a simple brayer, its roller covered with blotting paper and its handle made of stag horn, sterling silver, or other material.

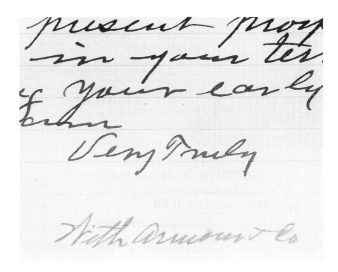

Figure 7.11. BLOTTED WRITING exhibits progressive dimming, since the freshest ink is more readily taken up by the blotter than that which has partially or completely dried.

English *Notes and Queries* could write that blotting paper had superseded the sandbox "almost in the present generation."[30]

Advertising blotters now became common, as shown in figure 7.7. One such blotter was published by the National Advertising Hotel Register Company and patented December 5, 1866; it has advertisements for New Hampshire apothecaries, a photographer, a carriage smith, an undertaker, and others. Also illustrated is a similar blotter of about 1890. These blotters were intended to be used with ledgers, which could be closed upon them.[31] An improvement in blotting paper featured a smooth surface on the reverse side and was patented September 3, 1872.[32] Blotters of this basic form were used as advertising giveaways until the end of the blotter era (fig. 7.8).

In addition to plain blotting paper, desk-blotter holders with leather corners ("desk pads") and small holders of similar designs that served as compartment lids in writing boxes came on the market.[33] Portfolios made of leather (or velvet or other materials) and known as "blotting cases" began to be sold in the 1880s. Many of the more elaborate ones were hand painted with floral designs or had metal corner mounts and ornaments, and one from Japan was inlaid with mother-of-pearl. Blotting books and pads were also sold.[34] Rocker blotters like those shown in figure 7.9 became extremely common and were often made to match other items in a desk set, such as the inkwell, letter opener, and stamp box. Rocker blotters were sometimes sold as "roller blotters," but that term is best restricted to the unique model pictured in figure 7.10.

The use of blotters progressively dwindled in the 1950s as they became casualties of the ballpoint pen.

The most recent blotter in my collection is a common advertising one having calendars for 1962 through 1964. Its blotting side is unused.

One should not lament the demise of the blotter. It removed much of the coloring matter from the ink, causing it to fade sooner. The use of the blotter on a piece of writing can be recognized from a progressive dimming of coloring, the last-written portion being lightest because the ink was least absorbed by the paper before blotting (fig. 7.11).[35] Although the application of sand likewise removed some ink, it also often left some black behind in recompense.

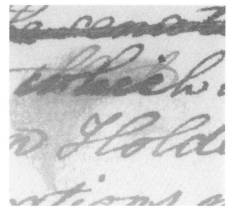

Figure 7.12. WIPE ERASURES (like the three shown here and in the above detail) were made by rubbing over the ink with a finger while the ink was wet; the space was then written over. Words that have been "inked out" are shown at the upper left. This document dates from 1819.

Ink Erasures

Another frequent problem with ink arose whenever mistakes were made, since—unlike pencil writing—errors in ink could be difficult to erase. Hence words were commonly stricken out with one or many marks of the pen. Another approach was frequently employed in the quill-pen era, however, and that was simply to wipe off the ink. Once again, Dickens provides a contemporary description in *The Pickwick Papers* (1837) as he tells of a writer who "had unconsciously been a full hour and a half writing words in small text, smearing out wrong letters with his little finger, and putting in new ones which required going over very often to render them visible through the old blots."[36] A document in which precisely that method was employed is shown in figure 7.12. Such a fast, simple technique would have had an added legal advantage, since it would be obvious the

erasure had been done at the time of writing and not subsequent to a document's being signed.

Errors discovered after ink had dried could be removed with a sharp knife, the method that was used alike by medieval scribes lettering on parchment and by later penmen writing on paper. Medieval illustrations, such as one in a twelfth-century manuscript that shows other steps in the process of producing a handmade book, depict a scribe at work with his knife, scraping off an error.[37] The results of a more recent (1876) knife-erasure on paper are illustrated in figure 7.13, wherein backlighting reveals the scrape marks. Often the roughened area would be smoothed by rubbing firmly with another piece of paper.[38]

The knives used for the purpose are known by many names, including steel erasers, steel scrapers, ink erasers, and ink knives (fig. 7.14).[39] Such knives are often misidentified by antique dealers and amateur collec-

Figure 7.13. KNIFE ERASURES are revealed by backlighting, which shows the resultant thinning of paper and scrape marks from the blade. Writing over the roughened spot has caused "feathering" (spreading of ink into paper fibers) because of the removal of sizing. This is from a business letter written in New York, August 26, 1876.

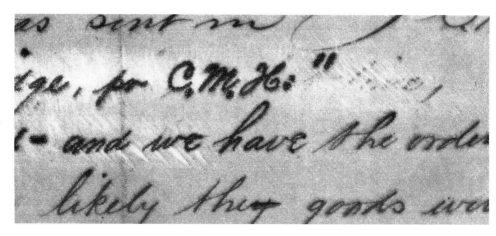

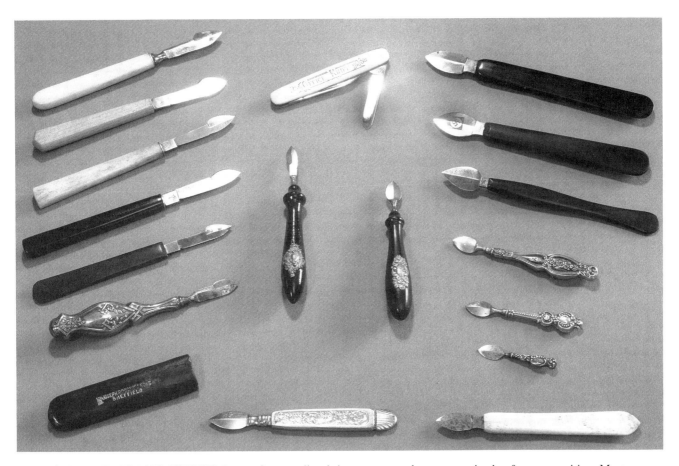

Figure 7.14. INK-ERASER KNIVES, known from medieval times, were used to scrape mistakes from pen writing. Most handles, as with these nineteenth- and early-twentieth-century specimens were of wood, bone, or sterling silver. A small sheath (like the one at the lower left) often protected the sharp blade. Sometimes misidentified as a "bleeder," or even a scalpel, the knife exists in two major blade styles: symmetrical and asymmetrical.

Right: knives with symmetrical, spade-shaped blades. At the lower right is a bone-handled one stamped "ERASER" at the base of the blade. Above it is a tiny sterling knife only 2¹/₁₆ inches long. A German one in the group has a swastika imprinted on the blade. *Bottom center:* the handle of this symmetrical-blade knife is embossed with a carrier pigeon clasping a letter in its beak, thus demonstrating the knife is indeed a writing implement. *Top center:* this celluloid-handled "Office Knife" has one blade also considered an "eraser." *Left:* knives with asymmetrical blades.

tors (particularly collectors of Civil War memorabilia) as "bleeders" or "veiners" or even "scalpels." An identification aid, figure 7.15, is taken from an old office-equipment catalog.[40] It illustrates the two major blade types of these collectible "erasers."

Of course the term "ink eraser" would today be understood to refer to the rubber variety, sold as early as 1867 by A.W. Faber. Unlike the softer pencil eraser, ink erasers are of a coarse, gray, hard type once known as "sand rubber."[41] They have sometimes been sold as a separate oblong block with beveled ends; as a combination (similarly shaped) having a pencil eraser forming one half; or in other forms, such as the "Sanitary O.K. Eraser" that consisted of a metal holder, refillable with erasers "for pencil" or "for typewriter or ink" Typewriter erasers are essentially just alternate forms of ink erasers.[42]

Yet another type of abrasive eraser was advertised about 1925 as "The Beegee Perfect Ink Eraser." It was described as "a brush of extreme delicacy but infinite hardness, made from scientifically prepared fibers encased in a heavy nickeled solid brass holder, four inches in length and the thickness of a pencil. The brush is adjustable."[43]

Chemical "ink erasers," or so-called ink eradicators, actually neither erased nor eradicated. Instead they were bleaching solutions which took the color out of ink (although not carbon varieties) yet left the ink ingredients on the paper in an invisible form.[44] The usual procedure involved two solutions such as described in the following 1894 instructions headed "Erasing-Fluid": "Recently written matter may be completely removed by a solution of chlorine gas in water. Wash the written paper repeatedly with this, and afterward

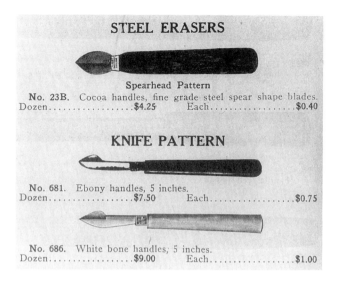

STEEL ERASERS

Spearhead Pattern

No. 23B. Cocoa handles, fine grade steel spear shape blades.
Dozen..................$4.25   Each..................$0.40

KNIFE PATTERN

No. 681. Ebony handles, 5 inches.
Dozen..................$7.50   Each..................$0.75

No. 686. White bone handles, 5 inches.
Dozen..................$9.00   Each..................$1.00

Figure 7.15. "STEEL ERASER" TYPES were twofold, as shown in this advertisement from Carrithers office-supply catalog (about 1925): the "Spearhead Pattern" (often having a handle fashioned so as to double as a paper knife) and the asymmetrical "Knife Pattern."

Figure 7.16. INK ERADICATOR—or as Carter's once termed its product (*second from left*), "Inky Racer"—rivaled the eraser knife after the late nineteenth century. In cardboard boxes or, later, metal canisters, two-bottle kits were standard.

wash it with lime-water [solution of calcium hydroxide], to neutralize any acid which may be left. The writing will thus be removed."[45]

Two-solution kits were sold by such major ink manufacturers as Sanford and Carter. During the 1920s and 1930s Carter's labeled its product "Inky Racer" and provided an illustration of a black runner to complete the pun.[46] Typically such solutions were intended not only for writing but for ink blots on paper, cloth, and elsewhere; they were applied by glass rods affixed to the bottle stoppers (fig. 7.16). In a pinch, ordinary Chlorox-brand bleach was used.[47]

More recently, Pen & Ink Correction Fluid has been marketed by the Liquid Paper Corporation of Boston, which earlier had developed a similar fluid for typewriting errors. Formulated especially for "Handwritten Corrections," the fluid is an opaque-white, brush-applied solution that covers various inks without "bleed-through," dries quickly, and permits overwriting.

The latest advance in corrections, a successor to the electrically powered rubber or vinyl eraser, would appear to be the "laser eraser"—a pulsed laser beam that is absorbed by the ink, which is vaporized and burned away, while the paper is uninjured.[48]

Other Ink Problems

In addition to ink spills, the need to blot wet ink, and the necessity of correcting mistakes, there were many

other ink problems, including the tendency of common iron-gall ink to fade, to corrode the pen, and to "burn" through the page (discussed in chap. 5). An advertisement for the Sengbusch Self-Closing Inkstand, insisting that it was "air tight—dustproof—non-evaporating," points to further ink problems.[49] For if ink were not kept "in a vessell of Glasse, or of Lead well covered," as Edward Cocker instructed in 1658, dust would settle on the surface and the ink would evaporate and thicken.[50] The latter problem could be remedied by carefully adding a little water from an ink pourer and stirring.

Because of the evaporation problem, ink required storage in a stoppered bottle or an inkwell with a cover—or at least a well with a very small access hole, no larger than necessary for dipping a pen. Collectors should be wary of any wide-mouthed but coverless inkwell, an indication that it may not be complete. Many nonattached covers have been lost or broken, and inkwells without them are considerably less valuable.

On the other hand, covered or not, ink could become moldly, as noted in many sources. For instance, in 1733 one lady confided in a letter, "Two days ago I washed the mould out of my inkhorn, put fresh ink into it."[51] Or as a correspondent to *Mechanics' Magazine* wrote in 1831: "I shall . . . be thankful to any one who will acquaint me with a certain way to prevent ink from moulding; I have tried cloves, and find they are not effectual."[52] The use of cloves was a standard early preventative, as shown earlier in the recipe in fig. 5.3. The editor replied, "A drop or two of oil of lavender prevents moulding effectually."[53] A source of 1815 advocated "a little salt," and another recommendation was published in 1894: "A small quantity of carbolic acid added to paste, mucilage or ink will prevent mould."[54] Of course powdered ink, which could be mixed fresh daily, represented a different solution to the problem.[55]

At least one writer found a "comforting thought" in the fact that in England, because of its moderate climate, "ink does not freeze in fountain-pens and ink bottles."[56] In parts of America, however, measures to prevent ink from freezing were necessary and fell into two categories. The first, as was given, for instance, in an 1815 text, was to add "a little spirits of any kind"— alcohol, in other words, such as the wine used in some iron-gall "receipts."[57] Alcohol was probably also the secret behind the "frost-proof" ink sold by a Washington, D.C., firm about the end of the last century.[58] The other solution was one provided by S. Silliman and Company, whose wooden inkstands contained glass wells (fig. 6.12). As stated in a mid-nineteenth-century Silliman price list, "the Ink Wells are surrounded with an Air Chamber, so that the ink is not liable to freeze in cold weather."[59]

Such problems did not deter the use of a commodity so essential to the work of the literate. Problems were meant to be solved, then as now, and by a bit of trial and perhaps a bit more error, and with some Yankee ingenuity thrown in for good measure, solutions were invariably found.

SELECT BIBLIOGRAPHY

The Shorter Oxford English Dictionary on Historical Principles, 1973, s.v. "blotter."

Covill, William E., Jr. *Ink Bottles and Inkwells.* Taunton, Mass.: William S. Sullwold, 1971. Includes photographs of antique sanders.

"Pounce Boxes and Sand Shakers." *Antiques,* July 1947, 36-37.

Whalley, Joyce Irene. *Writing Implements and Accessories: From the Roman Stylus to the Typewriter.* Detroit: Gale Research, 1975. Discussion of ink and some of its problems; illustrations of blotting cases, blotting books.

PART 3

Paper

RAGS make paper,

PAPER makes money,

MONEY makes banks,

BANKS make loans,

LOANS make beggars,

BEGGARS make

                    RAGS.

      —Anonymous
        ca. eighteenth century

8

Papermaking

Paper's Antecedents

The original precursor of paper was the ancient product from which it took its name: papyrus. This was developed by the Egyptians, and later used by the Greeks and Romans, to replace such materials as soapstone, which was scribed with an iron stylus.[1]

Written on with ink and a brush or pen fashioned from a reed, papyrus was itself made from a water plant. Of the genus *Cyperus*, the papyrus plant *(C. papyrus)* is tall (four to eight feet), stout-stemmed, and topped with a rosette of drooping leaves. It was native to the marshy shores of Egypt, Palestine, and the Persian Gulf.[2]

To produce the writing material, the plant's pithlike tissues were sliced into thin strips, which were united by slightly overlapping the edges and then covered by a similar arrangement of strips placed at right angles. The two layers were bonded by pounding and then drying under pressure, utilizing the plant's own juice as an adhesive. Finally, the side of the sheet that was to be used for writing was polished smooth (fig. 8.1). Individual sheets were glued end-to-end to form huge papyrus rolls, an early form of the book.[3]

From late Hellenistic times the rolls, or scrolls, began to be made of a more durable and more flexible material than the rather brittle papyrus. This new material was a thin, prepared animal hide; because it could be creased without breaking, it prompted the development of the modern type of bound book, or codex, which gradually displaced the roll between the first and fourth centuries A.D. The codex allowed one to turn to a central page directly, without the troublesome unwinding required by the roll form.[4]

Figure 8.1. PAPYRUS was made by the ancient Egyptians from crisscrossed strips of a water plant. From its name, the term "paper" derived.

Figure 8.2. PARCHMENT, made from specially prepared animal hides, began to be used instead of papyrus in Greco-Roman times. As shown in this late-medieval choral page, the "hair" (as opposed to "flesh") side is easily identifiable by a rough, yellow appearance, and even hair follicles.

The new material was parchment, the name of which (Greek, *pergamene;* Latin, *charta pergamena;* German, *Pergament;* French, *parchemin*) derives from the ancient Greek city of Pergamum. According to long-standing tradition, development of an improved method of preparing the skin—which allowed both sides to be used—can be credited to Eumenes II of Pergamum, 197-158 B.C.[5] Parchment was made from the skins of sheep, primarily, but also from calves, goats, and other animals. The term "vellum," technically applicable only to calf skin, is today loosely used to refer to any fine parchment made from the skin of young animals (calves, kids, lambs).[6] Increasingly, the term is losing its meaning and becoming synonymous with parchment.[7]

Parchment is prepared by washing the skin, steeping it in lime, removing the hair, scraping the skin with a convex blade, washing it again, stretching it over a frame and scraping it a second time, dusting it with chalk (to remove fattiness), and rubbing it with powdered pumice. The method has changed little from ancient times.[8]

The "hair" side of parchment is yellow, rough, and marked with recognizable hair follicles (fig. 8.2); the opposite, or "flesh," side is smoother and whiter. Whenever manuscript books were made, the sheets were folded and placed so that like sides were facing and thus a mismatched appearance was avoided wherever the book was opened.[9]

Invention and Spread of Paper

It appears that paper—essentially thin sheets produced from macerated rags, wood pulp, or other fibrous material—was first made by the Chinese during the Han dynasty (206 B.C.-A.D. 221). According to legend, this was accomplished by one Ts'ai Lun at the beginning (A.D. 105) of the reign of Yuan Hsing, his paper supposedly being made from a mixture of tree bark and hemp, old rags, and fishnets. Later, Ts'ai Lun became one of the chiefs of the imperial palace but suffered disgrace from involvement in a factional dispute; and so, "after bathing and dressing himself in his finest and most elaborate robes, he drank poison."[10]

From its Chinese origins, paper spread elsewhere, beginning in the middle of the eighth century. In 751, the Chinese attacked the Arabs who occupied Samarkand, but they were repulsed and among the captives taken were some who were skilled in papermaking. Thus were sown the seeds of Arabian paper manufacture, which soon spread throughout the Arab dominions. As a result many Arabic paper manuscripts exist from the ninth century.[11]

Early in the twelfth century, trade with Asia brought Egyptian and Syrian paper to Europe, chiefly via Constantinople. The oldest recorded European paper document is a deed of King Roger of Sicily, dated 1102.[12] Paper mills were subsequently established in Spain (by 1150), Italy (first mentioned in 1276), France (1348),

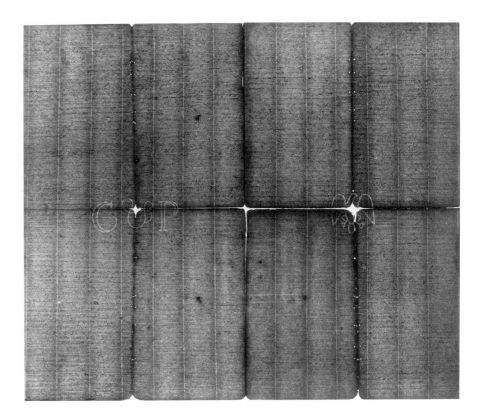

Figure 8.3. HANDMADE PAPER. This full sheet, reconstructed from four small, sewn-together pages of a sermon, shows the chain and laid lines resulting from the wires of the paper mold. The "C & P" watermark identifies it as Craig, Parkers, and Company, which in 1793 produced the first paper made on America's western frontier. A different Craig, Parkers watermark is shown in figure 9.6.

and Germany (1390).[13] Paper was first used in England in 1309 and soon became common, although it was not made there until 1495, when John Tate built the first English paper mill in Hertfordshire.[14] With the beginning of book printing (by Gutenberg in Germany, ca. 1450), paper began to be used on an increasingly larger scale and by the end of the century had superseded parchment.[15]

England, of course, supplied paper to the American colonies, as did Holland, which became a major papermaking country (giving to the world the Hollander, a machine for macerating materials into paper pulp, invented in 1680).[16] In fact, it was an Amsterdam-trained papermaker, German-born William Rittenhouse, who founded the first American paper mill, near Germantown, Pennsylvania, in 1690.[17] Additional states soon obtained paper mills, but the industry did not really flourish until Revolutionary War shortages prompted the establishment of more American mills. The largest concentration remained in Pennsylvania, where there were about sixty in 1810, far more than in any other state.[18] Thus it was largely Pennsylvania mills in the latter part of the eighteenth century that supplied paper to the western frontier, it being taken overland with other goods by wagons to Fort Pitt (Pittsburg), placed on flatboats, and carried down the Ohio River. The goods were dropped off at various settlements, such as Louisville, from whence they could be disbursed to interior settlements.[19]

The first paper mill in the early frontier—that is, west of the Alleghenies—was completed in 1793 in central Kentucky at a settlement named for President Washington, Georgetown. It was established by the Reverend Elijah Craig in partnership with James and Alexander Parker, brothers whose store in Lexington, Kentucky, advertised for sale "bearskins, dry hides, and butter" and no doubt served as one convenient market for "Writing & wrapping paper . . . by the ream." Craig, Parkers and Company had two different watermarks but both included the initials "C & P" (fig. 8.3).[20]

The second frontier paper mill was established in western Pennsylvania, in 1796-97. Built on Redstone Creek in Fayette County by two Quakers, Samuel Jackson and Jonathan Sharpless, it was in operation by June 1797. In his treatise *Papermaking*, Dard Hunter wrote of the Craig, Parkers and the Jackson and Sharpless mills: "These two pioneer mills supplied much of the paper used in western Pennsylvania, Kentucky, Ohio, Indiana, Illinois, and even Missouri during the late eighteenth and early nineteenth centuries; both establishments played a very considerable part in the opening of the West." [21]

By the mid-1830s machine-made paper had become relatively common, and the United States was the world's dominant paper-producing country.[22] Handmade paper was still common also, but in only a decade and a half "the Census of 1850 reported four hundred

Figure 8.4. CONFEDERATE PAPER SHORTAGE. Not only is this South Carolina paper astonishingly thin, but the one-dollar notes have been printed on the blank back of a recycled sheet of four-dollar bills.

and forty-three paper mills in the country, with an average of fifteen employees each. Virtually all paper was machine made."[23]

During the Civil War, the Confederacy experienced a chronic paper shortage caused by numerous factors, one of which was the South's sudden need to originate its own paper currency, postage stamps, military forms, and so on. In addition, "at this period it was not possible to procure woven wire or felting in the South, and as these materials were essential to the operation of a paper-machine, it was necessary to smuggle them through the Union lines."[24] As a result, in comparison with Revolutionary War paper, "the paper available in Southern states during the Civil War was of even poorer quality—wood pulp was at a premium, and such substitutes as cornhusks had to be found—and was so thin and fragile that it rapidly crumbles and deteriorates unless it is kept under careful conditions, including the proper degree of temperature and humidity" (fig. 8.4).[25]

By the end of the war "all papermaking by hand had ceased on the North American continent."[26] A reunited America remained number one in world paper production, and technological improvements continued steadily. By the mid-twentieth century, modern high-speed machines were capable of turning out continuous sheets at the rate of 3,000 feet per minute.[27]

Hand Papermaking

Briefly described, the production of handmade paper consisted of dipping a sievelike *mold* (a rectangular frame covered with a wire screen) into a vat of *stock* (macerated rag fibers suspended in warm water); after the water drained off, the resulting deposit of matted fibers represented a rudimentary sheet of paper that would be pressed, dried, and (if intended for writing) later dipped in *size* to inhibit absorption of ink. In actual practice, however, the process was much more complicated and required considerable skill and experience.

The essential tool of papermaking is, of course, the mold. From ancient times this consisted of a rectangular wooden frame (with numerous parallel crossbars, or "ribs," for strength), covered with a screen that was formed into a "laid" pattern. The screen was of heavy, widely spaced "chain" wires (each placed over one of the frame's ribs), crossed at right angles by fine, closely spaced laid wires. Brass wire was

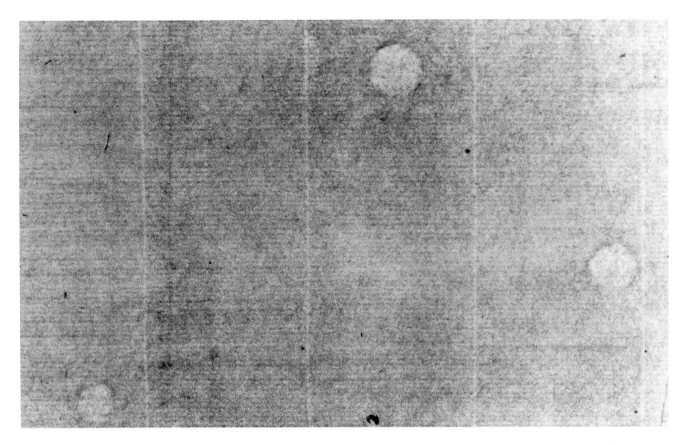

Figure 8.5. WATER (DRIP) MARKS were made by drops of water falling from the vatman's hands onto the freshly dipped sheet of handmade paper.

The stock for papermaking consisted of fibrous material suspended in water in a heated vat. Unlike papyrus, bark, or other writing material, true paper is made of material first broken down into individual fibers.[31] Thus papyrus could be so treated to form papyrus paper, just as hemp, flax, jute, and other plant materials have been used; but when made of crisscrossed strips as the Egyptians did, it cannot be called paper.

The traditional material for handmade paper was macerated rags—especially linen and cotton, which were high in cellulose and very durable. Demand for paper consistently exceeded the supply of rags, largely because of the increased use of paper for printing, occasionally with notable consequences. For instance, in England in 1666 Parliament issued a decree intended to assist papermakers as well as wool producers; only wool was allowed to be used for burying the dead, thus saving some 200,000 pounds of cotton and linen in a single year.[32]

In 1769, the *Boston News Letter* carried an article announcing that "the bell cart will go through Boston before the end of next month to collect rags for the paper mills at Milton, when all the people that will encourage the paper manufactory may dispose of

used in Europe for both the heavy and fine strands, but the Chinese employed, respectively, bamboo splints and horsehair.[28]

The only other pattern of mold-covering is that designated as "wove." As its name implies it was formed of uniformly fine wires woven like cloth on a loom (and thus similar to ordinary window-screening). The wove mold originated in England about 1755, apparently produced at the behest of John Baskerville, the famed printer who designed the "Baskerville" typeface.[29]

Quite often, an emblematic device or lettering was bent to shape from wire and sewn to the laid or wove mold covering. With or without such a "watermark" device, the mold screen patterns left their impressions in the paper they formed. Therefore, since the thickness of the wire resulted in thin spots in the paper, a sheet can be easily identified as laid or wove paper by holding it to the light. (An exception is an *imitation* laid, a pattern impressed into some machine-made wove paper, which will be discussed later in this chapter.) A portion of a sheet of handmade laid paper is shown in figure 8.5, bearing the accidental marks of water that dripped from the papermaker's hands. These are occasionally found in old paper, usually in the corner of a sheet.[30]

them."[33] Similarly, in 1795 Elijah Craig gave notice "that my Rag stage will attend the first day of every Fayette and Bourbon court, near the courthouses, where the person who attends will . . . exchange writing paper for clean linen rags."[34] About 1797 a Massachusetts mill actually watermarked its paper with the slogan, "save rags."[35]

To be made into stock, rags were first dusted, sorted into grades (depending on the quality of the paper to be made, undyed linen being most desirable), cleaned, cut into small pieces, and placed in heaps to ferment. After sufficient decomposition, the rags were washed and then beaten to a pulp with wooden mallets or pestles. The mill's waterwheel turned an axle bearing a series of cams that caused the hammers to rise and fall in rag-troughs. After its invention about 1860, the Hollander cutting machine was used to macerate rags more effectively while using less power.[36]

To make paper, a workman kept the dilute stock, or pulp, in the vat stirred, to prevent it from settling to the bottom. The "vatman," or master papermaker, placed onto the mold a loose frame of the same size, called a *deckle*, which he held firmly with his thumbs. Without the deckle, which operated as a sort of fence, the stock would simply flow over the edges of the mold. The vatman dipped the mold into the stock and—as the water drained back into the vat, trapping a layer of fibers on the mold's wire screen—he gave the mold a shake in different directions to mesh the fibers.

Removing the deckle, the vatman passed the mold to a coworker known as a "coucher" (after the Old French verb *coucher*, "to lay down"). He turned the mold over and deftly transferred the nascent sheet of fragile wet paper onto a piece of felt. While he was doing this, the vatman used a duplicate mold to dip up another sheet. The pair worked in this alternating fashion, with the coucher interleaving sheets of paper with sheets of felt until a certain-sized stack, or "post," was reached (usually six quires, or 144 sheets).

When the post was ready for pressing, a bell was rung or a horn was blown to summon other workmen to assist. The post was placed in a large screw press and half a dozen men pushed down on the long lever to squeeze excess water from the sheets. The sheets were then separated from the felts—the job of the "layman," or "layboy"—and restacked and pressed again.

The paper was next dried in "spurs," or groups of four or five sheets. This prevented the wrinkling and curling that would have occurred if the sheets were dried separately. The spurs were draped across heavy ropes that were stretched throughout the mill loft. The usual oriental method was to allow the individual, wet sheets to adhere to smooth walls in the sun; they would fall loose when dry.

If the paper was intended for writing, the dried sheets were dipped in "size" to reduce absorbency. This was usually a solution of starch or hot gelatin. In 1794 Elijah Craig advertised for various dried animal scraps "as we need them in the prosecution of the business of making paper." The scraps would be boiled to yield collagen, or natural gelatin.[37] After sizing, the sheets were dried again, then polished—either by hand, using an agate burnisher, or by mechanical means. Finally the paper was stacked and wrapped in coarse gray paper; this bore the mill's label, specimens of which are known from the sixteenth century. (Figs.8.6-8.8 depict the process of small-scale hand papermaking; see fig. 8.9 for a finished sheet.)[38]

With relatively minor regional and temporal variations, these processes continued—from the advent of paper in Europe in the twelfth century until the middle of the nineteenth century. By then the paper machine had reached the ascendant, and it began to have ramifications on the raw ingredients and structure of paper as well as a direct influence on printing processes.

Machine Papermaking

With the increasing use of mechanisms in paper-making—for pulp beating, vat stirring, and paper polishing—it was inevitable that attempts would be made to develop a machine for forming sheets of paper. Impetus was also reportedly given by the chronic discord among workers at the eighteenth-century French paper mill of François Didot. There a young inspector of personnel with a mechanical bent, Nicholas-Louis Robert (1761-1828), began experiments in mechanizing paper manufacture. His first attempts (1797) were failures, but on January 18, 1789, he secured a patent. Ultimately, however, little was accomplished with the machine in France, and Robert never profited from his important invention.[39]

Robert's contribution lay in having devised the essential method of forming a continuous sheet of paper. For this he employed a woven-wire belt—an endless paper mold, in other words. A cylinder was fitted with little buckets which dipped into the liquid pulp and filled a reservoir that then poured continuously upon the wire belt. As excess water drained off, the material ran under a felt-covered roller and came out as damp paper ready for pressing.[40]

A different method employed a woven-wire cylinder revolving in a vat of paper stock, and having an internal vacuum that caused the pulp to adhere to it. This "cylinder" machine was developed at the Hertfordshire, England, mill of John Dickinson, and was oper-

Figures 8.6-8.8. HAND PAPERMAKING.

8.6 (*top left*). With screws and waterproof glue, assemble two matching wooden frames of ¾-inch stock, the inside dimensions representing the size of the paper to be made. Make one frame into a mold by covering it with 30- or 40-mesh screen wire, stapling it in place, trimming it flush with the outer edge, and covering the front and outer sides of the frame with duct tape as shown. The second frame is the deckle.

8.7 (*top right*). Place the deckle on the upper (screen) side of the mold and clamp with thumbs. Dip nearly vertically into a vat of "stock" (easily made by pulping waste paper with a kitchen blender); turn horizontally and lift up, trapping a layer of fibers on the screen. Shake from front to back and side to side to mesh fibers and remove excess water.

8.8 (*lower right*). Remove the deckle and turn the mold completely upside down onto a piece of damp felt. If necessary, use a sponge on the back of the screen to help release the paper, and gently lift away the mold. (If the sheet tears, set it aside to be repulped.) Press by placing a stack of interleaved sheets of paper and felt between two pieces of plywood and then standing on the top or weighting it with concrete blocks. Dry as described in text.

Figure 8.9. A DECKLE EDGE is the natural margin of handmade paper, caused by the pulp running slightly between the deckle and the mold frame. Machine-made paper is often given a fake deckle edge to impart an appearance of handmade quality.

Figures 8.10-8.12. MACHINE-MADE PAPER. From *The Story of Paper-Making* (Chicago: J.W. Butler Paper Co., 1901).

8.10 (*top left*). As illustrated in this turn-of-the-century photograph, women wearing bonnets to protect their hair from dust worked in "the sorting and shredding room" of a large paper mill. There began the process of converting rags into paper.

8.11 (*top right*). After a cleaning in scalding limewater, the rags were reduced, by "the washers and beaters" shown here, into pulp for paper.

8.12 (*lower left*). A watery stream of filtered pulp was deposited on the Fourdrinier paper machine's endless wire-screen belt. As water drained through the screen, the layer of trapped fibers passed between various rollers that impressed watermarks, squeezed out more water, dried, and "calendered" (polished) the paper.

ative in 1809.[41] America's first "endless-paper-making" machine, developed by Thomas Gilpin in Delaware in 1816 (and in operation the following year), was of the cylinder type.[42]

A problem with the early machines was that the paper had to be wound while wet and fragile, cut into lengths, and hung up to dry in the centuries-old manner. This problem was solved by Thomas Bonsor Crompton, who patented heated "drying cylinders" in England, November 1, 1820, along with the first cutting device placed on a paper machine.[43]

The machine that is the basis of modern papermaking (figs. 8.10-8.12) is known as the Fourdrinier machine—named for two brothers, Henry and Sealy Fourdrinier, London stationers, who financed the development. The machine was based, not on the cylinder, but on Robert's original wire-belt concept, yet it contained patented improvements. It was not perfected until about 1810 and was not in fully commercial use until the beginning of 1812, when it is said to have caused riots by angry papermakers outside a Hertfordshire mill.[44]

For smoothing the surface of machine-made paper, a series of rollers was employed as early as 1830.[45] These were called "calenders" (a corruption of the Latin word *cylindrus*, "cylinder"). For writing paper, the web of paper was passed through a "size tub" to give it the necessary gelatin coating.[46]

The earliest machine-made paper was necessarily a wove type, lacking any watermark, except an occasional accidental one in the form of stitch marks where the ends of the continuous wire-screen belt were fastened together (fig. 8.13). On January 11, 1825—or about thirteen years after the first practical paper machine began operating in England—John and Christopher Phipps patented a device subsequently known as a dandy roll. This was a cylinder affixed to the paper machine and capable of impressing a pseudo–laid pattern—and/or a watermark—into the tender, freshly formed wove paper.[47] Such paper can, nevertheless, be distinguished from true handmade laid paper, as discussed in appendix 3.

The success of the paper machine reverberated through other industries—printing and publishing, for

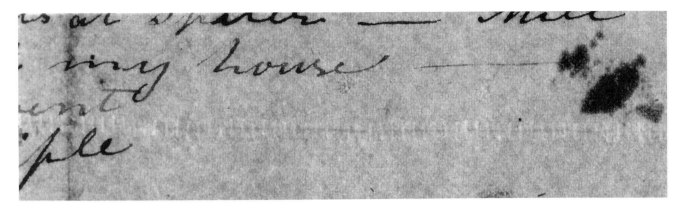

Figure 8.13. MACHINE STITCH MARKS are a form of "accidental watermark" seen in some early machine-made paper when it is held to the light. They were caused by the seam in the wire-screen belt, which impressed itself into the continuous web of paper at every revolution. When the paper was later cut into sheets, some bore these distinctive markings.

example, since "its continuous web of paper later suggested and made possible the invention of the rotary press."[48] The paper machine also profoundly affected the lumber industry, because its increased productive capacity exacerbated the ever-ominous shortage of rags and prompted the development of a suitable substitute.[49]

This was ultimately found in wood pulp. The concept can be traced to 1719, when the French naturalist René-Antoine Ferchault de Réaumer (1683-1757) suggested it should be possible for man to duplicate the capabilities of the common wasp, whose wood-filament nest represented a kind of paper. More than a century passed, however, before his suggestion was taken up.

In 1765 experimental paper was made from straw, and straw paper was produced commercially at Chambersburg, Pennsylvania, in 1829. Still later, esparto grass was introduced for papermaking in England in 1857 and in the United States in 1869. Ground-wood

paper was first produced commercially in 1847 in Saxony, but not until 1867 in Curtisville, Massachusetts, did successful commercial production take place in North America.

A serious problem with ground-wood (or "mechanical" wood) pulp is the presence of extraneous materials, primarily lignin, the material that naturally binds wood fibers together. Such materials are destructive of the cellulosic material in paper (fig. 8.14), and so other ("chemical") wood-pulp processes were developed to eliminate them, the first being a soda process used in England in 1851. Despite these methods, machine-made, wood-pulp paper—as compared with the old handmade rag variety—generally represents a sacrifice of quality and durability to cheapness and speed.[50]

Many special techniques have been applied to the manufacture of paper, whether hand- or machine-made. Among them are coloring (1687, in Europe), machine ruling of lines (ca. 1770, in England), bleach-

Figure 8.14. WOOD-PULP PAPER, unless chemically treated, contains lignin, which has a degradative effect. Here is the scorchlike imprint of a wood-pulp postcard upon one made of better-quality paper. Note the blank areas in the imprint where a postage stamp (*lower left*) and printed words blocked the corrosive effect.

Figure 8.15. EMBOSSED PAPER was formed by engraved dies in a process first patented in 1796. It became common during the middle of the nineteenth century, as in this embossed invitation and envelope of 1853.

ing (1792, in England), embossing (1796, in England; see fig. 8.15), rosin sizing (ca. 1800, in Europe), "loading" with filler material (1807, in Europe), and hot-pressing (1809, in the United States).[51] The embossing process was commonly used to impress identifying paper-mill crests and designs into the corners of sheets of writing paper from about the 1840s to the end of the century (fig. 8.16). Another method of identifying paper mills, of course, consists of watermark designs, as discussed in the following chapter.

SELECT BIBLIOGRAPHY

"The Age-Old Craft of Papermaking." *Decorating and Craft Ideas*, August 1983. Shows a simple way of making paper by hand.

Gravell, Thomas L., and George Miller. *A Catalog of American Watermarks, 1690-1835.* New York: Garland, 1979. Contains much data on early American papermaking.

Hodgson, Margaret L. "Skins, Paper, Pounces." *The Calligrapher's Handbook*, 2d ed., ed. C.M. Lamb, 75-95. New York: Pentalic, 1968. Information on manufacture, selection, and preparation of paper and parchment.

Hunter, Dard. *Papermaking: The History and Technique of an Ancient Craft.* 2d ed., 1947. Reprint. New York: Dover, 1978. Standard treatise on all aspects of paper and papermaking.

The Story of Paper-Making. Chicago: J.W. Butler Paper Co., 1901. Illustrated description of machine papermaking at the turn of the twentieth century.

Figure 8.16. PAPER-MILL EMBOSSMENTS were common from about the 1840s to the end of the century. Impressed into the upper-left corner of prefolded sheets of writing paper, they were crests or other designs of paper manufacturers (or possibly wholesale stationers) such as these of Eagle Mills and the Vantic Paper Company (*second and third from left*).

Left to right: the embossments of Superfine Laid Paper, 1858 letter; Eagle Mills, 1863; Vantic Paper Company, 1869; unidentified, with ship, 1870; and unidentified, with United States Capitol, 1871.

9

Watermarks

According to one authority, "It is not generally realized that in a sense most papers are watermarked even if they do not contain a definite design, letter or name." That is because the overall patterns of the wove and the laid and chain lines are impressed into the paper during its early formation, "these markings being really watermarks."[1] In a rather loose sense that is so, and we have earlier seen some "accidental watermarks"—the marks of water drops from the papermaker's hands (fig. 8.5), and the stitch marks of the belt seam from the old papermaking machines (fig. 8.13). Learning to recognize the various markings impressed in paper is important to anyone with an interest in old documents— whether the interest is that of a collector, genealogist, archivist, or document examiner.

The very early handmade paper was not only of the laid variety but exhibited what is known as the "antique" pattern, that is, a significant darkening along the heavy chain lines, observable if the paper is held to the light (fig. 9.1). Because the chain wires were sewn directly to the mold's wooden ribs, the pulp lay more heavily along them and resulted in the darkening. Beginning about the late eighteenth century this feature was gradually eliminated in favor of the uniform "modern" pattern.[2]

Machine-made "laid" paper (fig. 9.2) naturally lacks the rib, or "bar shadows."[3] Such laid patterns are

Figure 9.1. ANTIQUE LAID PAPER exhibits a striped appearance due to darkening along the chain lines (the white vertical lines). This is caused by the chain wires being sewn to the mold's ribs with the result that the paper pulp lies more heavily along them. Note also the right-hand deckle edge.

Figure 9.2. This MACHINE-MADE "LAID" PAPER, exhibiting a date watermark, is identifiable as such on close inspection. In the white linear spaces a fine, wire-mesh or wove pattern is observable that would be lacking in true laid paper. Machine-made paper is naturally wove, although a laid pattern can be impressed into it by the dandy roll just after the sheet has been formed.

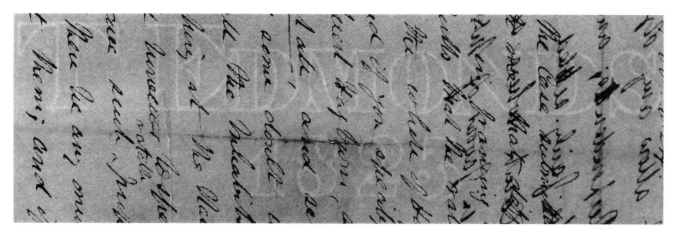

Figure 9.3. WOVE PAPER (exhibiting another date watermark) lacks the laid and chain lines of handmade laid paper. Instead it has the appearance of finely woven cloth, although this is sometimes barely perceptible.

more appropriately termed pseudo-laid, since, as Hunter correctly insists, "paper formed on a machine is naturally of the 'wove' variety and any 'laid-line' watermarking applied by use of a 'dandy-roll' is an imitation."[4]

The early wove paper (first produced about 1755) likewise had the "shadows" of the mold ribs, since the wire covering was sewn to them. As Dard Hunter states, "these imperfections appeared in paper until about 1800, when they were eliminated by placing a coarsely woven metal screen under the top 'wove' covering."[5] Machine-made wove and the late handmade wove paper are similar in appearance but can be differentiated, as explained in appendix 3 (see fig. 9.3).

Apart from overall wove and laid patterns and the "accidental watermarks" mentioned earlier, the term "watermark" strictly applies to "semitransparent letters, figures, or an emblem, seen in paper when it is held to the light; produced in the process of manufacture. Sometimes called Papermark."[6] That definition by the Committee on Library Terminology of the American Library Association, like the similar one in the *Oxford English Dictionary*, is sufficiently limiting to characterize watermarks in the usual sense of the term, yet is broad enough to allow both those produced by the papermold and by the paper machine's dandy roll, even if purists might regard the latter watermarks as imitations.[7]

The original method of making watermark devices involved fashioning them of brass wire like that used for the chain lines. Whereas the latter were uniformly straight (due to the use of a special implement called a "straightening board"),[8] watermark designs were typically bent into curvilinear shapes with pliers. These were then affixed to the mold screen by sewing with fine brass wire. Soldering seems not to have been used until the early nineteenth century.[9]

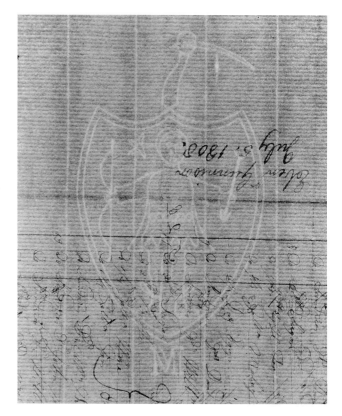

Figure 9.4. A WATERMARK is produced by a device made of brass wire, twisted into the desired form and affixed to the mold's wire screen. The wires result in thin spots which are noticeable when the paper is held to the light.

The thickness of the wire of the watermark device resulted in thin spots in the paper (like those caused by laid and chain wires, or even, to a lesser extent, the fine mesh of a wove mold). In a sense then, a sheet of paper is a casting, made from pulp, of the texture of the wire covering of the *mold*—which thus clarifies the use of that term (fig. 9.4).

The History of Watermarks

It is thought that the idea of putting a characteristic mark in paper originated in Fabriano, Italy, where a celebrated paper mill was in operation by 1276. At least, the earliest known watermark comes from there, dated 1282 and consisting of two crossed lines with a circle at the juncture and an additional, smaller circle at the end of each arm (i.e., a form of Greek pommée cross).[10] Another early (about 1286) Italian watermark consisted of two small circles connected by a short bar (rather like a dumbbell).[11] Additional early watermarks were the fleur-de-lis and the ram's horn, introduced in 1285 and 1330, respectively.[12]

Referring to theories of the meaning of the early papermarks—for example, that they might have religious or mystic symbolism—Dard Hunter states:

> It is not entirely out of the way to suggest that the old watermarks were perhaps nothing more than a mere fancy with the papermakers, who may have formed the designs or emblems to satisfy their own artistic natures. In the entire craft of papermaking there is no part more interesting or fascinating than to couch a sheet of paper upon the felting and watch the impressed mark become clear and distinct as the water slowly evaporates. Another supposition regarding the use of the early papermarks is that since many of the workmen could not read, it was necessary to appeal to them by means of pictures. Simply to have marked a mould with letters or figures would have meant little to the artisans of the fourteenth and fifteenth centuries; it was essential to convey the meaning to them by the aid of illustrations. For the same reason the old signboards of inns and shops were always of a pictorial nature; the mere name of the tavern lettered upon the swinging sign, or of the commodity sold by the tradesmen, would not have been sufficient.[13]

In any event, Gaskell states that watermarks "first appeared in the thirteenth century as the personal or trade marks of individual paper-makers and mills."[14]

Indeed, about 1285 or soon thereafter, watermarks began to contain the initials of the papermakers (fig. 9.5), and names began to appear by 1307.[15] According to Gaskell, "in the early days of paper-making the marks had been placed almost anywhere on the surface of the mould, but by the fifteenth century they were normally put in the center of one half of the oblong, so that when a sheet of paper was folded in half (as in a folio) the watermark appeared in the centre of one of the two leaves."[16]

As early as 1500 some mills began to use watermark designs to indicate the quality of paper, and the early sixteenth century saw an increasing correlation between the watermark and the size of the sheet. During

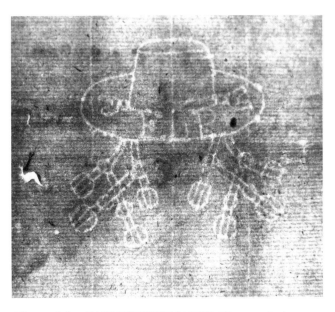

Figure 9.5. EARLY WATERMARKS. Watermarks in paper are known from 1282, and by about 1285 began to contain papermakers' initials. Note the "E.P." on the brim of this cardinal's hat watermark of circa 1650.

the following century international conventions began to be adopted, and, during the eighteenth century, watermarks that indicated quality and size replaced the old trade watermarks.[17] In the meantime, beginning in the sixteenth century, as the trade significance of the marks declined, many mills added to the mold a secondary, private trademark (e.g., initials or other design). Called a "countermark," it was centered on the other half of the mold.[18] Thus a postman's horn indicated "post" size writing paper (15¼ by 19 inches); a tankard denoted "pott paper" (12½ by 15 inches); a regal crown meant "crown" size (15 by 20 inches); a hand with a star meant "Royal-hand" (20 by 25 inches); and so on. There were many variations, depending on such factors as the time, the country where the paper was made, and whether it was writing or printing paper.[19]

Another mark was the so-called fool's cap, denoting "foolscap" paper, which varied in size but was about 13 by 16 or 17 inches. Actually a profile of a jester, the mark exists in numerous variants over a considerable time period, tracing back to 1479, but was especially common in the sixteenth and seventeenth centuries.[20] According to a persistent legend, the fool's cap watermark was "originally a crown which Cromwell changed to a jester's cap or to the figure of a jester's head" after the overthrow and execution in 1649 of King Charles I; it was supposedly not until after the Restoration (the return of the monarchy in 1660 in the person of Charles II) that it was "altered to the familiar Britannia figure" (i.e., the female symbol of Britain).[21]

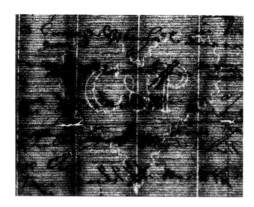

Figure 9.6. The "C & P" WATERMARK is one of two used by Craig, Parkers, and Company, who erected the first paper mill in the western frontier at Georgetown, Kentucky, in 1792-93. This watermark featuring a "rugged heart" is found in papers of about 1812-13. An earlier "C & P" watermark with an eagle is shown in figure 8.3.

Figure 9.7. The "REDSTONE" WATERMARK is only partially visible at the edge of this paper (while the full sheet would have also borne a "J & S"), but it is sufficient to identify it as made by Samuel Jackson and Jonathan Sharpless. Their paper mill on Redstone Creek in western Pennsylvania was in operation in 1797 and was the second one in the early West.

According to the authoritative *Oxford English Dictionary,* however, "There is no foundation for the oft-repeated story that the Rump Parliament [during part of Cromwell's dictatorship] ordered a fool's cap to be substituted for the royal arms in the watermark of the paper used for the journals of the House."[22] (For illustrations of the fool's cap and other early marks, turn to figure 15.4.)

In America, there seems to have been little relationship between sheet size and watermarks except of course in paper imported from Europe. The bulk of that was from Britain, but some came from Holland as, for example, a sheet in my collection. Dated 1770, and recording "sales of 5 half Barrels of gun Powder" in "York money," it bears the watermarked name of L.V. Gerevink. He was a prominent Dutch papermaker of the period, and it may be his "LVG" in some of the paper Thomas Jefferson used. Jefferson used other Dutch paper for drafting the Declaration of Independence, and printed copies of the Declaration are watermarked "J. Honig & Zoonen," papermakers of Zaandyk, Holland.[23]

Not surprisingly, the first American paper mill, established by William Rittenhouse in 1690 (as discussed in the previous chapter), produced the first American watermark. It bore the single word "Company" (apparently referring to the partnership that established the mill) and was crudely made.[24] Before and after the Revolution many molds were imported, and the English papermark designs were often left on as indicators of quality.[25]

In fact, American paper-mold makers, like Nathan Sellers, who began making the essential implements in 1776 and left behind detailed records, affixed the marks

their patrons desired—not only post horns and other familiar European designs, but even the English "Britannia" figure. One American paper-mill owner ordered a single mold with four Britannia devices, a British papermaker's name, and a date of two years previous. Thomas L. Gravell and George Miller, in their treatise on American watermarks, concede the American could have been ordering a mold for the Englishman but consider it more likely the Yankee commissioned it "in order to produce paper at his mill which he could then sell as imported English paper."[26] The backdating points to the latter, since it indicates the purchaser wished to give the appearance of seasoned shipped stock.

The American journalist Hezekiah Niles (1777-1839) railed against such practices. In one issue of his *Weekly Register* (Boston) he told a story of a man who rejected a ream of paper because it was so cheap it had to be American, whereupon the shrewd bookseller exhibited a very high-priced ream which the gentleman promptly purchased. In fact the two reams had come from the same mill bundle! Niles also ridiculed the United States Congress for using paper bearing the watermark of the English royal crown, and he concluded: "Let Congress use paper that is watermarked with a codfish, a hoe-cake, a yoke of oxen, or a race horse,—anything but the royal crown of England."[27]

George Washington was no offender, however. At least, much of his writing and ledger paper was watermarked with a plow upon which sat the figure of Liberty, this being framed with a double circle bearing the president's name and surmounted by an eagle. Washington showed much interest in papermaking, reportedly, when he visited a paper mill in New York State, even accepting an offer to try his hand at dipping up and couching a sheet of laid paper. This legendary sheet was said to have been kept at the mill as a prized relic for many years. To one historian's dismissal of the unverifiable story on the grounds that such a workman's activity would have been unsuited to the holder of so exalted an office, Dard Hunter suggested that "it would seem, Washington could have made just one sheet of paper without losing his rank as gentleman!" [28]

In addition to Washington's, other respectably American watermarks (during the period 1690-1835) included eagles, ships, Indians, crossed arrows, a horse's head and plow, a cherry leaf, the United States Capitol, deer, a bust of Washington, flowers, clover, the arms of Virginia and other states, plus numerous initials, names, dates, and the like (figs. 9.6 and 9.7).[29] According to Gravell and Miller: "In comparison to foreign watermarks of the fifteenth through the seventeenth century, most early American watermarks were quite simple in design. The most common form had initials or a name on one half of the mold and a symbol or device on the other half." [30] An excellent example is the Craig, Parkers one illustrated in the previous chapter, figure 8.3.

Special Watermarks

Innovations in watermarking have largely occurred in response to the production of fake watermarks by forgers and counterfeiters. There are several techniques for creating spurious marks, such as drawing or rubber-stamping them with liquid preparations (e.g., Canada balsam thinned with an equal amount of turpentine) which render the paper translucent.[31] Another amateurish method (which produced the watermark in fig. 9.8) involves smoothing a wet sheet of paper onto a piece of glass, covering with a dry sheet which bears a pattern of the desired mark, and tracing over the design firmly with a stylus (or a ballpoint or medium-hard pencil).[32]

Of course, one approach to duplicating security watermarks—like those placed in prescription blanks for alcohol during Prohibition (fig. 9.9)—was simply to dupe a legitimate paper company into producing paper bearing the marks. For instance, in 1922, two counterfeiters posed as representatives of the (nonexistent) "League for the Enforcement of National Prohibitions." They commissioned a Chicago paper firm to produce 17 by 22 inch sheets with the "league" name watermarked across the top and the all-over "Prohibition" pattern following. The upper line was afterward simply cut off and the remaining paper used to counterfeit forms, some of which were used before federal agents uncovered the scheme.[33]

More determined were the eighteenth-century efforts of the British counterfeiter Charles "Old Patch" Price, who took his nickname from a black eyepatch he wore for a disguise. Although the death penalty had been instituted in 1773 for even copying the "Bank of

Figure 9.8 (*above*). FAKE WATERMARKS range from this rather primitive effort to those produced by standard papermaking techniques.

Figure 9.9 (*right*). SECURITY WATERMARKS, like this all-over "prohibition" pattern, are meant to deter forgers and counterfeiters and to facilitate detection whenever fakery does occur.

England" watermark, Price actually made his own paper by hand in a small mill he had set up, and engraved and printed his own bank notes beginning about 1780. His counterfeits were extremely skillful and effective, even though the swindler was eventually apprehended. He even cheated the executioner, committing suicide by hanging in his prison cell.[34]

As a consequence of efforts such as Price's, methods were sought for creating watermarks that were more difficult to reproduce. The problem was attacked by Sir William Congreve who, in 1818, developed two means of manufacturing colored watermarks. His first involved sandwiching a watermarked sheet of colored paper between two thin sheets of white paper during the "couching" stage of hand papermaking; his second method involved forming the layers in succession on the mold and then couching the three-ply sheet. Congreve also devised a dark "watermark" by couching a sheet of paper over one having the design printed with printer's ink. The Bank of England did not adopt Congreve's proposal, and colored watermarks remained a novelty.[35] Notwithstanding Congreve's invention, until about the middle of the nineteenth century the actual shaping of watermark designs remained relatively unchanged—even the more elaborate ones being comprised of simple outline forms twisted from wire.

The development of the wove mold nearly a century earlier, however, made possible another means of producing the raised watermark design. Invented about 1849 by William Henry Smith of England, it was a method by which the mark was impressed into the wove-wire mesh—in much the same manner as one embosses paper with a notarial seal. Solid areas and subtle gradations in the relief could now be rendered, the end product being what is known as a "light-and-shade" watermark.

Briefly described, the process involves first using small gouging tools to model the desired picture in a layer of wax. This is done with a light underneath, allowing the desired lights and darks to be observed as the thinner and thicker forms are delicately sculpted. Upon completion, the wax relief is coated with powdered graphite and from it is made an electrotype (a metal casting formed by the electrotyping process). Two such dies can then be used to emboss the wire between them.

The resulting watermarks—for examples, simple silhouettelike pictorials or subtly modeled portraits (figs. 9.10 and 9.11)—can be made either by hand molds or cylinder machine (to produce brilliant marks), or by the dandy roll on the common paper machine (which tends to produce inferior, rather dull light-and-shade watermarks).[36] For some identification cards or similar security purposes, a combination

Figure 9.10. DISTINCTIVE WATERMARKS like this silhouette-effect (instead of the usual translucency) are made by embossing the design into wove wire (in the light-and-shade technique) rather than by bending outline shapes from brass wire.

Figure 9.11. LIGHT-AND-SHADE WATERMARKS can yield effects such as shown in figure 9.10, or they can produce the subtle tonalities of a portrait, as in this Cambodian bank note.

Figure 9.12. LAID OR WOVE? The paper of this 1821 receipt has the chain lines of laid paper, but without the wire, or laid, lines. Except for the chain lines, it would be classified as watermarked wove paper. Can you explain the aberration before reading below?

This was most likely a recovered mold, possibly having had damaged wire lines that were removed and replaced by a wove covering.

of single-wire and light-and-shade techniques has been employed.

Occasionally, unfamiliar markings may be found in paper but they can usually be comprehended. An example would be the "ruffled" or blurred laid and chain lines sometimes observed in handmade paper. Such blurring was caused by the coucher's allowing the mold to slip just as he transferred the delicate, newly formed sheet to the felt.[37] Another example—presented as a puzzle for the reader to solve—is illustrated in figure 9.12. Most such enigmas can ultimately be resolved by referring to the published literature and/or through one's own understanding of the basic processes involved in papermaking.

SELECT BIBLIOGRAPHY

Briquet, Charles-Moise. *Les filigrantes. Dictionnaire historique des marques du papier des leur apparition vers 1282 jusqu'en 1600.* 1907. Amsterdam: Paper Pub. Soc., 1968.

Churchill, W.A. *Watermarks in Paper in Holland, England, France, etc. in the XVII and XVIII Centuries. . . .* Amsterdam: M. Hertzberger, 1935.

Gravell, Thomas L., and George Miller. *A Catalog of American Watermarks, 1690-1835.* New York: Garland, 1979.

Nickell, Joe. "Vintage Watermarks: Clues to the Origins of Paper on the Kentucky Frontier." *Journal of Kentucky Studies* 4 (September 1987): 105-15.

10

Stationery & Seals

Writing Paper

Since paper was available in Europe as early as 1102—and thus long before the first printing there (by woodblock from 1423 and by movable type from about 1450)—writing paper long preceded the printing variety.[1] Unlike the thin, tissuelike mulberry-bark paper of the Orient, but like the parchment which it came to replace, European paper was heavy enough so that both sides could be used for writing or printing.[2]

To be used for writing, however, paper required a harder surface to minimize its absorbency; otherwise the ink would spread among the fibers like ink does on blotting paper. An early oriental method was to coat the surface with gypsum, and later (as early as A.D 768) starch was used.[3]

In the Middle Ages it was found that one type of "pounce"—powdered gum sandarac (a resin)—which had been used to degrease and give a final smoothing to parchment, could be used to prevent ink from sinking into paper. Thus the pounce container, the antecedent of the sander, was one of the accoutrements of writing—even as late as 1794, as shown in the following verse from a writing book:

> A pen knife, Razor-metal, Quills, good store;
> Gum sandrick powder, to pounce paper o'r;
> Ink, shining Black, paper more white than snow
> Round and flat Rulers on yourself bestow.[4]

Still, the pounce pot had become more and more unnecessary as paper sized in the paper mills could be obtained with greater ease.

The European paper was "tub-sized"; that is, it was dipped into a hot solution of natural gelatin made from boiled animal scraps (as described in chap. 8), or from leather or parchment cuttings. After sizing, the paper was pressed, dried, pressed once more, and finally smoothed (by hand or machine). The process was employed in Europe from 1337 onward, although the earliest European papermaking treatise to describe it was

published in France in 1693.[5] Another method of sizing, by adding rosin to the paper pulp in the beater, was invented in Germany by M.F. Illig about 1800 but was not used elsewhere until about 1835.[6]

Sizes of paper varied considerably over place and time.[7] Some of the early standard sizes of paper that came to be designated by certain watermarks (such as the fool's cap), were given in the previous chapter. By 1781 the following English *writing* papers were common:[8]

Royal	24 by 19¼ inches
Medium	22½ by 17½ inches
Demy	19 by 15¼ inches
Foolscap	16 by 13 inches

These could be used for legal documents, bound "blank books" (e.g., ledgers), and the like. Smaller sheets could be cut from these as needed. Later, machine-cut commercial papers were sold, as indicated by the following "usual" sizes of writing paper in the United States at the end of the nineteenth and beginning of the twentieth centuries:

Commercial note	5 by 8 inches
Letter	8 by 10 inches
Flat cap	14 by 17 inches
Crown cap	15 by 19 inches
Demy	16 by 21 inches

And there were fourteen larger sizes, in various increments to 31 by 53 inches—the dimensions of a sheet known as antiquarian.[9]

Among the many types of special writing papers is "gilt-edged paper," mentioned by Charles Dickens in 1837 (although deriving from a much earlier fashion of decorating the edges of book pages).[10] So-called Lincoln blue paper—which actually ranged from blue through blue-gray to gray—takes its name from Abraham Lincoln, who used it for a large number of his legal pleadings; it was very common from about 1840 to

Figure 10.1. PRE-ENVELOPE LETTERS were simply folded into a packet sealed with wax or a paste wafer. Prior to the use of postage stamps, the postal charges were written or handstamped on the packet; it was marked "Paid" if prepaid (otherwise the recipient paid for it); and a postmark was affixed to show place and date of mailing. The blank, opened sheet was possibly used to mail a mourning card, because it was sealed with black wax.

1860.[11] "Parchment paper" (or vegetable parchment) was invented about 1857 (first manufactured in the United States in 1885); this paper was made by a process called "parchmentizing," which involved the application of sulfuric acid to unsized paper to destroy its fibrous character.[12] It is often used in food packaging as well as for certificates or the like. "Bond paper" (a term in use by at least 1877) describes a superior writing paper originally used for bonds and similar documents.[13]

European paper was sold by the quire and by the ream. An English or Dutch quire consisted of 24 sheets, whereas a quire containing 25 sheets was usual in France and Italy. A ream was 20 quires, or 480 sheets in England and Holland, 500 in Italy and France. Typically, each quire was folded in half (across the longer side) for packaging.[14]

Letters and Seals

Because quires were sold folded in half, which converted each sheet into a four-page folder, or "folio," the

Figure 10.2. SEALING-WAX MELTERS represented the safest and surest method of melting wax for letters. The antique brass melter (*left*) probably stood on a stove for use. It is shown with a stick of vermilion wax and a block of Civil War–era matches. At right is a brass wax standish consisting of alcohol lamp, ivory-handled ladle, seal (never engraved), and individual colored buttons of wax premeasured for use.

format of letters was affected. They came to be written, not on the open sheet, but on the first page of the folio. If the letter were longer, it was continued on the inside (second and third) pages, and even part of the last page could be utilized. The central portion of the back page was reserved for the address, since, in the period before envelopes, the letter was simply folded, tucked, and sealed into a packet for mailing (fig. 10.1). Even if only the first page of the folio was used, the second leaf (pages three and four) was rarely torn off. One reason was that, because of the customary manner of folding, the two layers allowed a flap to be tucked between them, thus holding the packet in a closed position and freeing the hands so sealing wax or a wafer could be affixed.

Sealing wax was typically molded into sticks (not unlike sticks of Chinese ink) for sale. It consisted of a mixture of beeswax, Venice turpentine (i.e., larch gum), and pigment, usually vermilion, which is bright red to red-orange. Later preparations eliminated the wax entirely, a typical formula calling for shellac (seven parts by weight), Venice turpentine (four parts), and vermilion (three to four parts). Cheaper products might contain substitute mineral pigments and ordinary rosin, with admixtures of such materials as chalk.[15]

Other colors of sealing wax were occasionally employed. For example green wax on documents denoted the official Exchequer Court in medieval England.[16] Black sealing wax was long used to seal mourning letters.[17] "Bronze wax" (no doubt containing bronze powder as the pigment) was mentioned by Dickens in an 1837 novel.[18] Recipes for white, yellow, and green sealing wax are given in an 1894 compendium, and a

Figure 10.3. SEALS (OR "SEALERS") like these usually had signet ends of metal, although some were of semiprecious stones like carnelian. The handles of those at the left are wood; of those at the right, six are sterling silver and three at the extreme right are ivory. See figure 10.4 for an enlargement of the seal in the center foreground.

Figure 10.4. SEAL(ER) AND SEAL (enlarged from fig. 10.3). A textured sealer is shown with a wax seal such as it would have produced; it is on a letter packet postmarked (next to the seal) January 13, 1835.

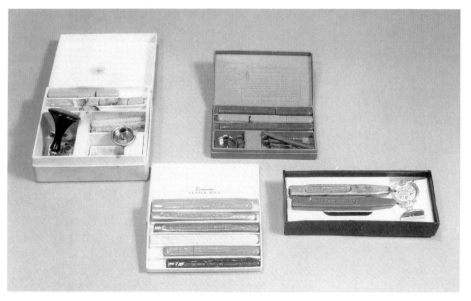

Figure 10.5. LETTER-WAX KITS included (*top*) those complete with miniature candle holders, candles, and seals; those (*right*), such as this relatively recent English kit, with a seal and sealing wax formed as candles that contained paraffin instead of flammable resin; or (*center*) simply a selection of wax sticks. All but the English kit were made by the American firm Dennison Manufacturing Company.

dark brown wax was used about this time by at least one express company.[19]

There were two basic methods of applying the wax. The preferable one involved using a special melter. One designed for the purpose might be a spoonlike device made to rest on a stove, or it might consist of a stand with a means of supporting the ladle over a "spirit" (alcohol) lamp (fig. 10.2).[20] The melted wax was then poured in place and, if desired, an engraved seal (figs. 10.3 and 10.4) was pressed into it. This was done without delay, since the wax set quickly.

The second method of melting the wax—holding the end of a stick in a flame to melt it, and then quickly transferring the blob to the paper—held some risk: the stick could catch fire and behave like a miniature pitch torch (consider the ingredients!), sputtering and dripping flaming drops of wax onto paper, desk, or person. One occasionally sees a blackened seal on a letter or finds a stick of wax with a charred end in an old writing kit. Another problem was that it was difficult to get a sufficient dollop applied in one operation; multiple applications would seal the letter as well as one, but the first deposits would set and keep the seal from making a good, complete impression. Nevertheless, small candlesticks or even taper stands were features of many old inkstands, and small candles were included in nineteenth- and early-twentieth-century letter-wax kits (fig. 10.5).[21]

The term "seal" (old French, *scel* or *seel;* Latin, *sigillum,* diminutive of *signum,* "figure" or "mark") applies to both the impression and the device used to make it. The origins of both lie in the engraved gems and cylinder seals of antiquity, although their use largely died out in the Occident with the fall of the Roman Empire. The use of seals was then revived in the eighth century by the Carolingians, and, in Britain, Edward the Confessor (who reigned from 1042 to 1066) employed the first English royal seal.[22]

In addition to their use for sealing correspondence and thus thwarting prying eyes (not totally effective in any case; see fig. 10.6), seals were used to add the impress of authenticity to documents. They were either applied to the face of the document or attached pendulum-like on a strip of parchment or silk cord—so-called suspended seals. Thus a seal might be employed in lieu of a royal signature, or private seals (at one time most propertied persons had one) might be used as an adjunct to a signature.[23] In addition to the common ones shown in figure 10.3, some had figural handles—for example, a horse's head or a bird—and, of course, there were watch-fob seals and signet rings. Seals were also occasionally improvised from such common items as a thimble, the top of a door key, or the like.[24] Blank seals are frequently found and should not be confused

Figure 10.6. PRYING EYES—as shown in this engraving, "The Postmistress," from about 1840—could perhaps glimpse a word or two from a sealed (pre-envelope) letter if the packet were squeezed open.

with pipe tampers, which are similar.[25] Blank seals were included in writing kits or sold separately, intended to be engraved. Later, seals having stock initials were often sold. With their cast appearance, they are easily distinguished from engraved seals, which have sharply V-cut carvings. Also, sometimes those of the stock variety have the initial stamped in the top of the handle. Among collectible seals, or "sealers," are those which were used by such institutions as Wells Fargo Express and railroads to secure envelopes containing cash receipts.[26]

A substitute for sealing wax, especially for closing letters, was the wafer, a thin disk of paste. Wafers were likewise usually colored with vermilion, although exceptions include a light aqua wafer and black wafers for mourning use that were sold at least as early as 1750.[27]

Wafers were made in a wafer iron, described as "a pincer-shaped instrument, the legs of which terminate in flat blades about 12 inches long by 9 in breadth. . . . The blades are heated in a coke fire, the paste is then put between them, and by pressure formed into a thin sheet of paste, from which discs of the desired size are cut with a punch." [28] The paste itself usually consisted of "flour, mixed with water, gum, and some non-poisonous coloring matter. Fancy wafers are made of gelatine and isinglass in a variety of forms." [29] Wafers were sold in boxes with "a specimen wafer stuck outside." [30] They were kept in special compartments in inkstands, as mentioned in chapter 6 (fig. 10.7).

Wafers can be distinguished from wax on old letters because the wafer was moistened and applied *under* the upper flap of the closed letter packet. Sometimes the paper over the wafer would be scored with a knife or impressed with a textured seal, like that in figure 10.4, to help the paper adhere securely. The placement of the wafer thus stands in contrast to that of the wax seal, which was on the *outside* of both upper *and* lower flaps (and some persons placed a bit underneath for better adhesion). The term "wax wafer" is a hybrid form, occasionally used, but unclear and fundamentally inaccurate.[31]

Wafers were also used for seal impressions on deeds and other documents, the moistened disk being covered with a piece of paper before the seal was applied. This was an adaptation of the custom of using brushed-on paste or glue instead of a wafer, dating back several centuries. Sometimes the piece of paper was creatively snipped to a decorative shape; more often it was a

Figure 10.7. A WAFER DRAWER is a feature of this pewter inkstand of the quill-pen era. Wafer *boxes* were also components of many inkstands or were sold separately. After the introduction of self-sealing envelopes they were used for a different purpose, becoming the forerunners of stamp boxes. This inkstand measures 2⅜ by 3½ inches by 2⁵⁄₁₆ inches high.

Figure 10.8 (*left*). EMBOSSING SEAL. Lever-operated seals embossed paper between two dies. Such seals existed in numerous forms and incorporated a variety of features. This lion's-head model is of cast iron and stands 10¾ inches high. It is marked on the front, "Pat'd Oct. 9, '88."

Figure 10.9 (*below*). WAFER-AND-PAPER SEAL. For many centuries paper squares or ornate shapes were attached to documents with paste or, later, paste wafers and then impressed with a seal. This example has been photographed by backlighting the document to show the vermilion wafer.

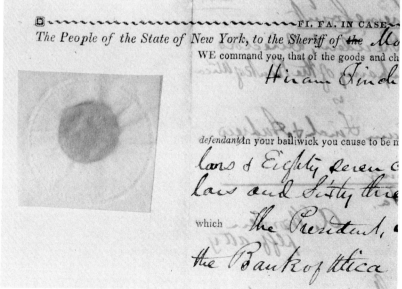

Figure 10.10. ENGRAVED LETTER SHEETS represented an important development in stationery of the mid-nineteenth century. Scenes, like that of this 1846 example, were common.

Figure 10.11. BILLHEADS were another development in printed stationery. These examples are dated (*from top*) 1857, 1860, 1873, after 1881 (unused), and 1894.

simple square.[32] For a time after lever-operated embossing seals (fig. 10.8) replaced hand seals, the same method was continued (fig. 10.9). Eventually, though, the wafer-and-paper overlays were replaced by gummed-paper seals, common in the latter nineteenth century. These continue in use and are typically of glossy red stock or gold foil, die-cut into circles having serrated edges. Often, of course, the paper seal is dispensed with, and the document is simply embossed directly.

Like sealing wax, wafers were employed in sealing the early envelopes but were soon rendered obsolete by self-sealing envelopes. With their advent, letters were affected in various ways. Not only did they no longer bear wax or wafer, but they began to be folded in new ways.

A major development in letter stationery was the production, during the middle of the nineteenth century, of *printed* sheets featuring engraved pictorials at the top. An example would be the scene of a village by the side of a stream plied by boats, with the wording "Stringer's Hotel" above and "Windermere Waterhead" beneath. Another example is shown in figure 10.10. Embossed ornamentation was sometimes com-

bined with the engravings, and printed billheads also began to be common (fig. 10.11).[33]

Another form of printed stationery was that intended for mourning. With matching envelope, the "letter edged in black," as it was known—reflected in a popular song of that title of the 1890s—signified death:

As I heard the Postman whistling yester morning
    Coming down the pathway with his pack,
Oh he little knew the sorrow that he brought me,
    When he handed me a letter edged in black.

Then with trembling hands I took the letter from him.
    I broke the seal and this is what it said.
Come home my boy, your poor old Father wants you,
    Come home my boy, your Mother dear is dead.[34]

Such stationery (fig. 10.12) was an adjunct of mourning, particularly for women, since "death was a religious issue, and by the 1870s, religion itself had become the domain and responsibility of women." [35] "Mourning Goods," referred to in advertisements, would include—in addition to the stationery—"black sealing wax, black leather blotters, and jet paper-knives." [36]

Figure 10.12. MOURNING STATIONERY consisted primarily of black-bordered letter sheets and matching envelopes, sold in boxes like those at the top. Black sealing wax was used in pre-envelope days (*foreground*). A mourning card of 1906 is shown at far left. Of the four letters pictured address-side up, the one on the left is dated 1906 and expresses "appreciation for the love and sympathy shown in your beautiful tribute to the memory of our dear one." Next to it is one of 1911 that tells how "People I work for gave me a real nice black voile dress pattern, a large black velvet bag & $1 in money." The two others are French, and are of more recent vintage: that at lower right is dated 1949, and above it is one postmarked 1953.

The printed black outlines of the stationery—which included calling cards—harken back to black-bordered funeral cards of the seventeenth century.[37] The borders were wide during the first year of mourning, but narrower ones were used for the second year. Mourning stationery was especially common during the latter three or four decades of the nineteenth century. Use declined during the early twentieth century, although Eleanor Roosevelt used mourning stationery, and the custom continued even later in Europe.[38]

Envelopes and Postage

Like their modern counterparts, ancient envelopes were intended to protect the documents they contained and to ensure confidentiality. Most materials used for the document itself—papyrus or parchment, for example—were also physically suitable for its wrapper, and would have been close at hand. The Babylonians even encased their cumbersome clay tablets in thin sheets of clay that were crimped shut and then baked.[39]

As we have seen, the custom eventually developed of simply folding and sealing a letter in such a way that no outer wrapper was necessary. This was especially practical when paper was relatively expensive, although cost was not the deciding factor for diplomatic and royal communication. Hence, Gilbert Burnet wrote in his *History of His Own Time* (referring to about 1714): "A letter from the King of Spain was given . . . by the

Spanish Ambassador, and she tore the envelope, and let it fall."[40] And Jonathan Swift, in his *To Grub Street Poets* (1726), remarked: "Lend these to Paper-sparing Pope. . . . No Letter with an Envelope Could give him more Delight." [41]

It may have been the French who gave renewal to the idea of using envelopes for ordinary correspondence. At least the term *enveloppe* is French, and France established the first purely national postal service in 1464. In 1653 one Renouard de Velayer operated a private Petit Post in Paris where he reportedly sold special envelopes for the purpose.[42] Other sources state that Velayer instead used bands of paper or wafers (sold for two sous, or about a penny) "to indicate that the postage was prepaid."[43] In any event the business scheme failed, reportedly because an enemy of the enterprising Frenchman "began posting live mice in his boxes."[44]

Be that as it may, the use of envelopes was discouraged in England before 1840 by the fact that postal costs were assessed by the sheet. Any form of wrapper, therefore, "would have resulted in double postage being charged."[45] Government-issued letter sheets with postal embossments originated in Sydney, New South Wales, in 1838. The idea was borrowed from earlier proposals made in England by Sir Rowland Hill, then a schoolmaster at Kidderminster. "Rowland Hill advocated a flat rate of one penny for a one ounce letter, regardless of the distance it travelled. By greatly simplifying the postal charges he paved the way for the pre-payment of postage by means of special envelopes

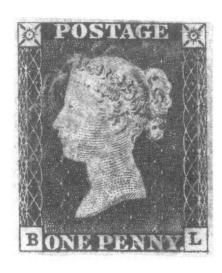

Figure 10.13. FIRST POSTAGE STAMPS. The world's first adhesive postage stamp was the penny black of Great Britain (*left*) issued in 1840. Such stamps were made for local use in the United States from 1842, but the first official issue was the five-cent red-brown Benjamin Franklin stamp of 1847 (*right*). Both stamps were imperforate and had to be cut from sheets with scissors.

or wrappers and by means of adhesive labels which could be stuck on the letter and handed in at any post office." [46]

And so, on May 1, 1840, Britain issued the world's first postage stamp, valid for public use on May 6. Now known to collectors as the penny black (fig. 10.13), it bore a simple profile of Queen Victoria. The stamps had to be cut apart with scissors, but after experiments by an Irishman, Henry Archer, perforations were first used on a British stamp (the one-penny red-brown) in 1850.[47]

Issued with the penny black (and a twopenny blue) were a pictorial letter sheet and an envelope, decorated with allegorical subjects and imprinted "POSTAGE TWO PENCE." It was designed by the English artist William Mulready (1786-1863) but was withdrawn after public reaction was expressed in the form of ridicule and caricature.[48] Nevertheless, envelopes now began to be generally used for mailings.

In America, postal rates prior to July 1, 1845, had been based (as in England) on the number of sheets involved, and so the general use of envelopes was discouraged. But beginning on that date an Act of Congress authorized some local postmasters to issue their own stamps to show prepayment of postage. Called "postmasters' provisionals," they are now highly desirable and usually quite rare and valuable. Two years later, on July 1, 1847, the United States government issued its first stamps, a five-cent red-brown issue featuring Benjamin Franklin (fig. 10.13) and a ten-cent black stamp depicting George Washington.[49]

Prior to the use of stamps, a cover was typically marked with the amount of postage (and stamped "PAID" if it was prepaid). With stamps, however, came cancellations—that is, a means of defacing the stamp to prevent its reuse. With the original 1840 issue Britain used a Maltese cross handstamp cancellation. In

Figure 10.14. POSTMARKS AND CANCELLATIONS. *Postmarks*—introduced in 1661 by the British postmaster general, Colonel Henry Bishop, and thus known as "Bishop's marks"—were intended to reveal delays in postal delivery by containing the date of mailing. *Cancellations* were marks placed on postage stamps to prevent their being used again.

From top: a postmarked "stampless cover" of 1817; two pen cancels, *left*, 1886, *right*, 1858; a postcard—America's first, originally issued in 1873—with a cork cancel of 1875; an 1891 target cancel; another common cancel of 1899; and a flag cancellation, 1900.

Figure 10.15. PRESTAMP LETTERS simply had the amount of postage handwritten or handstamped on them. Most were sealed letter sheets, but some were enclosed in envelopes during the period between their introduction and the issuance of the first adhesive postage stamps.

Figure 10.16. This HAND-DRAWN ENVELOPE of 1859 features a unique pen-and-ink miniature (only about 2⅝ by 4⅝ inches) of a Victorian lady at the fireside. The paper she holds is the address panel, and the portrait on the wall is a Queen Victoria stamp. The envelope's epistle is missing, but it may well have been a love letter. Its wax seal bears the name "Margaret," and it was sent from Dublin to a Mr. Foley in England.

America, from 1847 to 1855, postmasters were instructed to cancel postage stamps with pen and ink—hence the term *pen cancellations* (or *manuscript* cancellations). Later, until 1880, United States postmasters were permitted to use any device they pleased, such as homemade designs cut from cork or wood and known as *cork cancels*. *Target cancellations* were scarce prior to the 1850s but became plentiful in the subsequent decade. *Flag cancellations* were produced by canceling machines, which also printed the postmark and were first used in 1894 (fig. 10.14).[50]

Postmarks, as distinguished from cancellations, are postal markings intended to reveal delays in delivery by containing the date of mailing. In the form of inked handstamps, they were introduced in England in 1661 by the postmaster general, Colonel Henry Bishop, and were thus known as "Bishop's marks." Although postmarks were required by the Massachusetts Colony in 1692, they were handwritten, the stamped "Bishop's mark" type being first used in America in the eighteenth century (New York, 1758; Philadelphia, 1767; Boston, 1769; Albany and Charleston, 1774).[51] The early marks were circular, indicated only month and day, and were made from a variety of materials: engraved boxwood, cast brass, printer's type locked in a holder, molded gutta-percha, and the like.

While an American envelope is reported bearing a date as early as December 28, 1832, envelopes were not common in the United States until the following decade. In New York a printer named Pierson reportedly manufactured the first American envelopes about 1843.[52] At least some of the early productions were of a cheap brown paper, including a specimen in my collection dated 1848 and bearing the circular embossment

on the flap of "J.F. DeSilver, Cincinnati, Ohio." Interestingly, an invoice issued to the superintendent of Indian Affairs in the distant Iowa Territory in 1844 was for "1 Ream Envelope Paper."[53]

With the advent of the new stamped envelopes there continued to exist for a time the old stampless, envelopeless, folded-letter packets with the amount of postage written or handstamped thereon (fig. 10.15). In fact, during the transition period of the 1840s and early 1850s, interesting admixtures of the two are found—envelopes with the old markings, folded letter sheets bearing stamps—as well as the occasional handmade envelope or the unique hand-drawn envelope shown in figure 10.16.

Also during the early period of the envelope many methods of securing the flap were tried: sealing wax and wafer, of course (figs. 10.17-10.19), imitation wax seals (fig. 10.20), "motto seals" (fig. 10.21), brass closures (fig. 10.22), and adhesive envelopes (fig. 10.23). The latter eventually prevailed (although the clasp envelope, fig. 10.24, was a later development). Thus an etiquette book of 1877 advised: "Red sealing-wax is

10.17 (*near right*).   WAX SEALS, originally used to seal letters prior to the introduction of envelopes, were later applied to those wrappers as well.

10.18 (*far right*).   An ENLARGEMENT OF THE SEAL in the previous figure shows the name "Margaret." It is found on the unique envelope illustrated in figure 10.16.

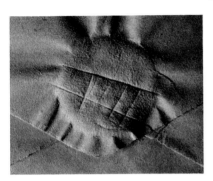

10.19 (*far left*).   A PASTE WAFER (in contrast to a wax seal) was applied *under* the flap, which was then often impressed with a textured seal (like that in fig. 10.4) or scored with a knife (as in this example) to cause better bonding.

10.20 (*near left*).   This IMITATION WAX SEAL was made of glossy red paper embossed to simulate a seal like that illustrated in figure 10.4. The flap has a hole punched in it which allows the paper sticker to adhere to the body of the envelope.

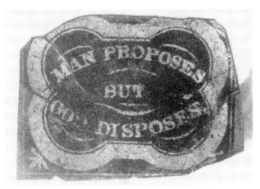

10.21.   "MOTTO SEALS" were small stickers printed with aphorisms like this, or with other wording. Another in my collection, on an 1848 envelope, is a rebus, featuring a picture of an eye, an ✗ surrounded by dots, and the word "return"; translation: "I expects return."

The 1851 envelope on which the above motto seal appears was handmade, being snipped from a piece of paper and fastened with glue. It is also stampless, being merely marked "10" for the amount of postage.

10.22.   BRASS CLOSURES for envelopes included this type, embossed "PAT. MAY 7, 1867." Patented as a "Slide for Fastening Envelopes," United States patent no. 64,608, it was described as follows: "The band passes through the slots of the plate which is attached to the envelope by clinches formed in making the slot." The fastener on this particular envelope was used about 1880.

10.23.   ADHESIVE ENVELOPES, like this "Lipman's Adhesive Despatch Envelope" of the late 1840s or early 1850s eventually became the dominant form.

10.24.   The CLASP ENVELOPE, patented December 9, 1879, as printed on the flap, continues in use but mainly for larger, kraft-paper envelopes.

Figure 10.25. PATRIOTIC COVERS printed with decorative cachets, many hand colored, were common throughout the Civil War. Those intended for the Union citizenry, like the ones shown, were more common than those made for the Confederate populace and expressed pro-loyalist or antisecessionist sentiments.

Used ones are more valuable and, in fact, purists limit the term "covers" to those that "have served postal duty."

Figure 10.26. COMMEMORATIVE COVERS include those heralding a stamp's first day of issue (*top three*) and one commemorating the 100th anniversary of George Washington's birth. The latter has a rubber-stamped cachet; the others—except for the uncacheted 1935 cover—have color-printed cachets.

Collecting first-day covers is a specialized philatelic pursuit.

Figure 10.27. CIVIL WAR POSTAGE. When the southern states seceded from the Union, the United States completely redesigned all its stamps. (The pen-canceled and the target-canceled stamps at lower left were among the reissues.) This was to prevent their use by the Confederacy, which issued its own stamps on a variety of types of paper (*lower right*). Also, when coins were scarce, the United States issued "Postage Currency" (*top*), which was "Receivable for Postage Stamps at any Post Office."

Figure 10.28. An OLD POST OFFICE. Like many other small postal stations, this one in Allen, Nebraska, in 1913 was part of a general store.

only used in business or official letters. The self-sealing envelopes preclude the necessity of using either wax or wafers." [54]

Various modifications of the basic envelope were patented, as was an "Envelope and Letter-Sheet Combined" of 1872. [55] Envelope machines were also patented, the first American one bearing the date of 1849. [56]

Among other developments are the "window" envelope, first manufactured in the United States in 1902, and the "stamped" envelope, preprinted and usually embossed, which began being sold in January of 1841 in England. The first United States ones were issued in 1853. [57]

Following the ill-fated Mulready envelope of 1840 came other pictorial covers, notably a set of ten published by Messrs. Fores of London. They date from the same year and illustrate such activities as courting, making music, dancing, racing, hunting, and shooting; military and civic scenes; and Christmas, the latter being the world's first pictorial Christmas envelope. [58] During the American Civil War, both those loyal to the Confederacy and those loyal to the Union (especially the latter) used "patriotic covers"—envelopes printed with cachets, slogans, and the like—such as the ones shown in figure 10.25. [59] Artistic cachets later came to be used on "first-day covers" as well. The designation applies to envelopes postmarked with the date of a particular stamp's first day of issue; for example, May 6, 1840, for the penny black (fig. 10.26). They are eagerly sought by many philatelists (as stamp collectors call themselves: from Greek *philos*, "fond of," and

ateles "prepaid"). [60]

Historically interesting covers are those that were carried by the legendary Pony Express along its system of relay stations linking St. Joseph, Missouri, and Sacramento, California. In addition to rainproof leather mail pouches, strapped at both the front and back of the saddle, express riders were outfitted with two revolvers and a knife for protection against Indian attacks and holdups. The service began April 3, 1860, and lasted some eighteen months, or until the first coast-to-coast telegraph line was completed. Its closing was announced on October 26, 1861. [61] Some of the famed company's postmarks contain an illustration of a horse plus the words "Pony Express," while others are less immediately recognizable, bearing only the carrier's name, "The Central Overland California and Pikes Peak Express Company." [62]

Additional postal ephemera that may be desirable to specialist collectors include such items as Civil War postal currency (fig. 10.27), photographs (fig. 10.28), stamp boxes and other accessories (figs. 10.29 and 10.30) —even old postal scales (fig. 10.31). [63]

Cards

Visiting cards, greeting cards, and postcards are additional types of stationery—at least in the sense that they often bear handwritten messages, and they have traditionally been sold at printers' and stationers' shops. [64]

Figure 10.29. STAMP BOXES were an outgrowth of the introduction of postage stamps. They invariably have a sloped compartment (*right center*) or a concave one, to facilitate removing the stamps. Some nineteenth-century lap desks have such compartments and thus date from after 1840, when England issued the first stamps.

Left to right, top to bottom: a hand-carved wooden leaf-and-nut inkstand with matching well and stamp receptacle, about 5 by 9½ inches by 2 inches high; a three-compartment wooden box made in Italy, with color decals of facsimile stamps on its lid; another three-compartment box of black japanned papier-mâché, about 1870-80; a brass box with "Shooting an Oil Well, Tulsa, Okla" and an illustration of same on its lid; a brass Victorian box, about 4½ inches long; a metal box with a dragon embossed on its lid; and an ornate pewter box, its lid engraved "STAMPS."

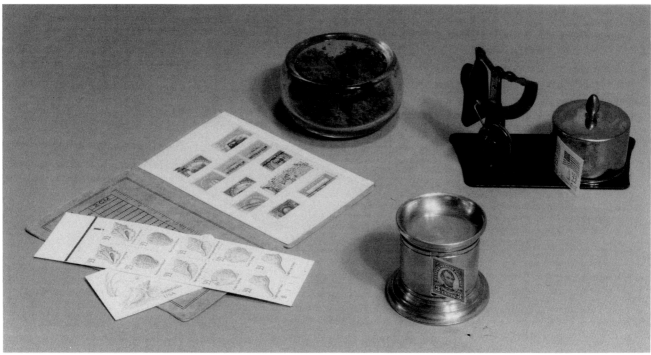

Figure 10.30. STAMP ACCESSORIES include (in addition to stamp boxes, shown in the previous figure) such items as a philatelist's stamp wallet and two books of stamps (*left*); a circa 1920s "sponge cup" for moistening stamps, labels, or envelopes (*center rear*); and two brass coil-stamp dispensers, one a contemporary model with accompanying postage scale (*right*).

A stamp moistener, featuring a moistening pad fastened in an opening in the removable lid in a glass dish, was patented September 21, 1897, and sold by the Moistening Device Company, Pottstown, Pennsylvania. Among later moisteners is a colorful pottery one of a hound's head, whose open mouth contains a red sponge. One of the most common types, usually made of white porcelain, is the so-called "sanitary" moistener that features a revolving moistening roller set in a base containing water; for moistening, the stamp, label, or envelope flap was drawn across the roller. The Sengbusch Self-Closing Inkstand Company made many of these.

The term "card"—that is, a piece of stiff paper or thin pasteboard or cardstock, usually rectangular—is known from as early as 1610.[65] The product itself was manufactured and sold in Europe even earlier, in 1580, and it was made by the Chinese and Persians centuries before.[66] The first machine for forming cardboard, by pasting together sheets of paper, was patented in 1824.[67]

Visiting cards, or calling cards, are used for personal identification in social contexts. It appears their earliest use in Europe was by university students in sixteenth-century Germany, one specimen having been sent as a curiosity to Italy on January 15, 1572. But it was in seventeenth-century France, at the court of Louis XIV (who reigned from 1643 to 1715), that the custom became well established, and simple strips of paper gave way to more elaborately finished cards. The reign of Louis XV (1715-74) saw the development of engraved cards with fanciful landscapes and an autograph signature below. The use of visiting cards soon spread to England and by the late eighteenth century "became a universal fashion in Europe." [68]

The cards were also fashionable in America throughout the Victorian era, and several types came to be recognized: "autograph," or visiting cards, which bore only the individual's name and were typically rendered in script, although usually printed rather than handwritten; address cards, which included the place of residence and were "useful to present when it may be desired to open future correspondence" ; wedding cards, which accompanied wedding-invitation and reception cards and bore the names of the bride and bridegroom; mourning cards; business cards, which were to "contain upon their face the name, business, address and references, if references are used" ; *cartes de visite* (a term originally referring to any calling card but soon limited to photographic calling cards); and presentation cards, used for notes.[69]

Etiquette books attempted to legislate good taste in card selection, as in these 1877 guidelines: "There is no invariable fashion as to their size and shape. At one time they may be long, narrow, small and glazed; at another large, square and unglazed. But one thing good breeding insists upon, and that is that they must always be plain. There must be no stamped ornamentation, no device or flourish of writing, and no printed or engraved border. . . . Cards should be engraved in plain Italian script, not printed, and by all means never written. . . . No person of taste will display his or her photograph upon a *carte de visite*." [70]

Despite such interdictions, as cards became more and more popular, so did the taboo *cartes de visite*, the prohibited pen-flourished cards, and all the forbidden ones that were printed in Gothic type and boldly chro-

Figure 10.31. POSTAL SCALES began to be common after prepaid penny postage was introduced in England, and a patented "Salter's letter balance" or "letter weigher" was a feature of some elaborate inkstands by the late 1870s. The black-painted metal scale at left was made by "Superior," has spring action, and dates from about the 1920s. At right is an earlier, turn-of-the-century scale, its pendulum marked "The Cross Pen Co., Boston."

molithographed, fancy-bordered, and embossed. Among the popular, elaborate types were the "hidden name" card, which featured a pictorial cut-out placed over the name but hinged at one end so it could be lifted back, and the "envelope card," an oversize card to which was affixed a miniature envelope that in turn contained a tiny card or paper for notes.[71]

How the card was to be employed was also regulated:

> A person may make a card serve the purpose of a call, and it may either be sent in an envelope, by messenger or left in person. If left in person, one corner should be turned down. To indicate that a call is made on all or several members of the family, the card for the lady of the house is folded in the middle. If guests are visiting at the house, a card is left for each guest. To return a call made in person with a card inclosed in an envelope, is an intimation that visiting between the parties is ended.[72]

And so on. The fashion of turning down the corner held differing meanings depending on time period and locale.[73]

When cards were received, they were often kept in an open dish on a drawing-room table. Those of socially important persons might be placed on top where they were sure to be noticed by impressionable visitors. One's own cards were carried in a card case made of leather (fig. 10.32) or other material, such as ivory, silver, mother-of-pearl, or tortoiseshell.[74]

Figure 10.32. CALLING CARDS are known from the sixteenth century but became most common in the Victorian period.

Center, printed cards; *left,* "sample books"; *right,* a leather card case; *front,* an engraved copper printing plate of a calling card (wrapped in paper and tied with string); and *rear,* an etiquette book with a cover illustration of a card with a turned-down corner.

Related to the visiting card was another type—the "presentation card" mentioned earlier—which could be used as "a very neat and convenient substitute for a note, to accompany a book or any other gift; or for a Christmas or New Year's greeting." For example, "Mrs. Bouligny sends her Christmas greetings to Mr. Leslie, and begs his acceptance of the accompanying trifle, as a token of her regard. Christmas, 1875."[75] Sometimes the note was penned on the back of a visiting card, as in this example:

> Thine own wish, wish I thee.
> This Joyous Yule-Tide.
> 1890.[76]

Such examples show the close relationship between visiting and greeting cards—particularly valentines, although the earliest were handwritten love missives prompted by Saint Valentine's Day. An example is one that the diarist Samuel Pepys recorded had been given his wife in 1667, consisting of "her name writ upon blue paper in gold letters."[77] As to the commercial variety, "Valentines had achieved popularity in the last few decades of the [eighteenth] century, especially in Eng-

land and America, as a natural development of the little pictorial visiting cards which had become fashionable. The high cost of postage limited their sale at first, but by about 1815 most towns had introduced a local penny post and the sending of elegantly engraved pictorial valentines with 'paper lace' floral borders turned 14th February into the postman's busiest day of the year."[78]

Once printed by copperplate engraving, valentines began to be lithographed after 1830.[79] From about 1810 to 1860 lacy valentines were especially common, and afterward many valentines were decorated with pressed flowers, feathers, shells, artificial jewels, and the like, although "the craze was in decline by the 1880's."[80] Nevertheless, novel, yet cheaper, cards flooded the market in the mid-1890s, many made in Germany. Among them were cards which opened into three-dimensional shapes, comprised of brightly colored tissue paper in a honeycomb effect.[81] Such a feature can still be seen in many of today's valentines.

The golden age of valentines (ca. 1840-79) had passed, however, and "despite the Edwardian substitute of Valentine postcards, and a mild revival in the 1920's, St. Valentine's Day today is an unexciting affair

Figure 10.33. VALENTINES have been popular for more than three centuries. *Left*, an elaborate chromolithographed folded card of the Gay Nineties with lace-paper appliqué, complete with its embossed-paper envelope; *bottom center*, a folded card of about 1920; *bottom right*, a folded card of 1947; *top center*, two valentine postcards of 1909 and 1916; and *upper right*, two die-cut cards of 1937 and 1931.

when compared with its former status" (fig. 10.33). [82]

Like valentines, popular Victorian Christmas cards derived from the fashion of using visiting cards. The first Christmas card intended for general distribution was comparable to today's card in size; designed and etched by John Calcott Horsley and published by Sir Henry Cole in 1843, it measured 5⅛ inches tall by 3¼ inches wide.[83] It did not set the early standard, however, and there were few Christmas cards until 1860, when the British publisher Charles Goodall and Son began to market small, brightly colored cards intended for Christmas visits. Then "from Christmas visiting cards it was a short and logical step to a card sent ahead of time to carry the season's greetings."[84]

Later in the nineteenth century, Christmas cards grew in size, although the small visiting-card type continued in use until about 1910.[85] They were typically printed in rich colors by chromolithography and often decorated with silk fringes, satin, or mother-of-pearl as well. Frequent designs included animals and fish, children and young women, flowers and summer scenes until about 1900, when Christmas postcards from Germany became popular and tended to feature subjects like Santa Claus (a thinner, more quaintly attired figure than the rotund, red-suited one of today), snowscapes, fireside scenes, and the Nativity. (Until that time most religions had disapproved of the cards.) Also prior to the turn of the century, cards usually went unsigned, instead being accompanied by the visiting card of the sender.[86]

As with valentines and Christmas cards, other greeting cards essentially derived from the visiting type. They included cards celebrating Easter, wishing a happy New Year, or extending other greetings.[87] Some

Figure 10.34. GREETING CARDS, apart from the valentine, date from after 1843, when the first commercial Christmas card was published in England.

Left column, from top: Thanksgiving postcard, 1912; birthday card in original cellophane wrapper, 1946; birth announcement card with envelope, 1921; Christmas card, 1928. *Right column, from top:* a calling-card-size (1⅛ by 3⅜ inches) New Year's card, copyrighted 1876; "My Greeting" Christmas card, signed "Aunt Kate 1893"; a fringed, chromolithographed "compliments of the Season" card, by Raphael Tuck and Sons, 1890s; and two Christmas cards, 1907 and 1910.

Figure 10.35. POST CARDS were first issued in Austria in 1869, followed by France and England in 1870; the first United States card, 1873, is shown at the upper left. Picture postcards followed and were avidly collected during their heyday, from about 1880 to 1914.

Left column, from top: the first postcard issued by the United States, with cork cancel, 1873; a chromolithographed "A Merry Christmas" postal, 1913 (*left*); a chromolithographed card with added "glitter" decorations and writing, 1908 (*right*); a card with a cut silhouette pasted on, unused but probably early 1900s (*left*); a 1913 "realphoto" card (*right*). *Right column, from top:* two leather postcards, 1908 and 1906; souvenir postcard of Great Salt Lake, Utah, with a tiny bag of salt affixed, 1947; a 1944 picture postcard "furnished for the convenience of men in the armed services by the Travel and Information Department of the Oregon State Highway Commission"; an envelope for English "Pictorial Post Cards," early 1900s.

cards were all-purpose ones, typically featuring floral designs and blank message panels, including one with a handwritten wish, "May you have many happy birthdays," dated 1881. Stylistically similar cards—ones descended from the previously mentioned presentation cards—include such interesting forms as an All Fools' card, actually an invitation to a party of April 1, 1898; temperance cards, such as one of 1878 urging, "Add to Knowledge, Temperance"; and memorial cards, having black borders and thus related to mourning cards,

which were sent out about a week after a funeral to friends of the deceased.[88]

Later trends in most greeting cards paralleled those of the valentine and Christmas cards already described. Mother's Day and sympathy cards became popular only after the Second World War, however, and cards addressed to particular relatives (grandmother, brother, aunt, etc.) are of still more recent vintage.[89]

In addition to cards made by Charles Goodall and Son, mentioned earlier, were those of his English rivals—Marcus Ward and Company, which featured Kate Greenaway's popular round-eyed Victorian children; De La Rue and Company; and Raphael Tuck and Company, later Raphael Tuck and Sons—and, in America, L. Prang and Company, whose founder, Louis Prang, made America's first Christmas card in 1874. The American Greeting Card Company was established in 1908, and Hallmark Cards (which later became a household name with its slogan, "When you care enough to send the very best") in 1910. According to Sharron Uhler, curator of the Hallmark Historical Collection, the founder of Hallmark Cards, Joyce Hall, began in 1910 by selling picture postcards printed by others from a shoebox stored under his bed and later, about 1915, turned to the manufacture of his own greeting cards.[90] An assortment of greeting cards is illustrated in figure 10.34.

Another type of card, the postcard, was an inevitable outgrowth of the increasing tendency for cards to bear handwritten notes.[91] A Philadelphia businessman printed the first postcard in 1861. Austria produced the first government-sanctioned postcard, October 1, 1869, but other countries soon followed: France and England in 1870, the United States in 1873. The first commercial "picture postcards"—a term that distinguishes those having any sort of artistic or photographic illustration from the usual government-issued variety—may have appeared in France in 1870, during the Franco-Prussian war. Except for a facsimile printed in 1910, however, none of these has been discovered.[92]

Because of their cheapness and convenience—aided by the permissiveness of etiquette books, which allowed "many of the formalities of letters" to be dispensed with—postcards were immediately popular.[93] In England, on the first day of sale, crowds at the general post office had to be regulated by police.[94]

Although postal regulations in the United States and Britain had tended to discourage privately issued cards, by the turn of the century the situation had begun to change: In America the postage on private cards was lowered from two cents to the same one-cent cost of government postals, and in England larger, privately issued cards for use with postage stamps were allowed. In both countries—in Great Britain from 1899 and the United States from 1907—one side was permitted to bear both address and message space, freeing one full side for an illustration.[95]

A postcard-collecting craze resulted, with chromolithographed and embossed postals flooding the market from Germany and Austria, and cards of high quality also being produced in the United States.[96]

They were collected in fancy albums and used to cover lampshades, screens, and wastebaskets. Many cards

Figure 10.36. HANDMADE POSTAL. This greeting postcard was drawn in pencil and completed in watercolors (3⅜ by 5⁷⁄₁₆ inches). It is undated but imitative of cards in the decade after 1908, when Thanksgiving cards were especially common (see fig. 10.34).

were produced in series and sets and the picture postcard also became the medium on which manufacturers and retailers could advertise their wares for very little investment. There were funny cards: some, depicting Blacks, mothers-in-law, women, and henpecked husbands, do not seem as funny today as they may have seemed in the last century. There were cards made for every special occasion, every holiday, and to appeal to people of every age and personality. Not a city or town existed that didn't have its Main Street recorded for posterity on picture postcards sold at the local drugstore.[97]

The photographic cards were of two basic types: some were photographs reproduced by printing from plates; the others were not reproductions but actual photographs and thus were in limited, even one-of-a-kind, editions.[98] As well, "postcards were embossed, die-cut, and sometimes had added material such as feathers, fabric, or real hair. For the children, there were paper doll cards, puzzle cards, and 'installment' cards, mailed on four successive days until all four received made up a single picture and poem. The variety of collectible picture postcards is enormous and represents a rather complete picture of the Edwardian era" (figs. 10.35 and 10.36).[99]

By 1914 the craze ended, partly because of World War I and partly because of "the arrival on the market of newfangled greeting cards." In that year the National Association of Greeting Card Manufacturers was formed, and the National Association of Post Card Manufacturers announced it would hold no convention.[100] Then, in the 1960s, the old cards were rediscovered by a new wave of collectors and were searched for in albums, in bundles in trunks, in flea markets, and elsewhere. Most desirable are those in the heyday of the art—that is, before World War I—and

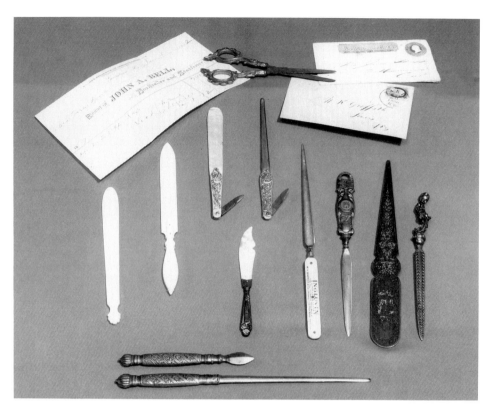

Figure 10.37. PAPER KNIVES typically had blades of ivory or pearl (*group of four at left*) and were used to slit folded paper in lieu of cutting with scissors. Letter openers (*right*) are pointed paper knives designed for slitting the flaps of envelopes—the one at the bottom is with a matching ink-eraser knife. At the top left is a receipt from a bookseller and stationer for "1 Paper Knife," dated 1892. It sold for $1.50.

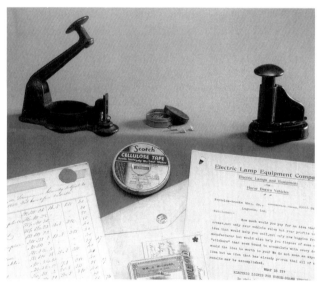

Figure 10.38. PAPER FASTENERS range from the centuries-old ribbon-and-wax fastener (*left*) to such recent means as Scotch tape (*center*), introduced in 1930. Above and below are various brass fasteners, many of which were patented in the latter third of the nineteenth century. Also shown is an early stapler (*upper left*) and a device that makes a fastener out of the paper itself.

The cast-iron stapler is embossed on the bottom: "PAT. SEPT. 25, 1877, REISSUED JULY 12, 1881, PATENTED IN EUROPE—1877, APL. 14, '80, FEB. 20, '82." The other device was invented by George P. Bump and predates the 1912 document on which it was used, shown immediately below it. A later model was issued United States patent no. 1,104,622, July 21, 1914. Bump's company was Bump's Perfected Paper Fastener Company, La Crosse, Wisconsin. As explained in a Carrithers office-equipment catalog of about 1925, after they were inserted "a slight pressure slits papers, makes a tongue and automatically tucks this tongue through the slit, all in one operation." The catalog also illustrates a rival "Dexter Paper Fastener," and in my collection is a "Paper Welder," which fastens by embossing.

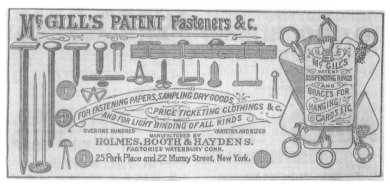

Figure 10.39. This ADVERTISEMENT FOR FASTENERS shows many of the brass devices used for fastening paper that were patented prior to its appearance in the September 1888 issue of *Lippincott's Monthly Magazine*, p. 21.

collectors usually specialize in some topic, limit themselves to "tourist" cards (subspecializing, usually, in a particular locale), or otherwise focus their collecting efforts.[101]

Paper Accessories

Among the many items used in connection with writing paper is the paper knife, whose origins are, perhaps, as old as paper itself. When a large sheet of handmade paper required cutting to provide smaller sheets, it was folded, the fold was flattened, a paper knife was inserted, and the fold was slit open.[102] The knife was also used—in fact still is used in libraries—to "open" the inadvertently uncut pages of old books.[103]

Since only the edge of the knife was used, a point was unnecessary, and paper knives typically had rounded blades (i.e., shaped rather like tongue depressors).[104] The blades of the Victorian knives were usually of ivory or mother-of-pearl, preferred because of their smoothness, and the handles were of silver or other material.

A type of paper knife, having a characteristically more slender, pointed blade, is the letter opener. Actually the term is somewhat misleading, since the implement was designed for opening envelopes (and thus postdates their introduction); it was not used to slit open the earlier folded-and-sealed letters. To do so would have damaged the letter itself; instead, the wax

was broken or the paper was simply torn in a half-circle around it.[105] Both paper knives and letter openers are shown in figure 10.37. Careful slitting remains the best way of opening an envelope, since ripping at the flap or tearing off one end damages the envelope and could injure the letter itself.

Other related items include those involved in securing papers. The wax-and-ribbon fastener (fig. 10.38) appeared by the thirteenth century.[106] In addition to sealing wax and wafers, nineteenth-century fasteners included various patented devices (figs. 10.38 and 10.39), "bank pins" (straight pins), and wire staples. Introduced about 1875, the latter were applied by "clumsy cast-iron machines, which had to be loaded with individual staples. Later, staplers were built to accommodate a strip of 25 staples at a time, but to work such a device the user had to whack the contraption with a mallet. Finally, in the early 1900's, lever-action staplers solved the delivery problem—and the staple boom was on" (fig. 10.38).[107] The paper clip was a British invention of about 1900.[108] Of course some form of brushed-on paste, gum, or glue (the latter term should be reserved for that made from animal parts) has been employed since ancient times. For example, starch paste was used to fasten sheets of papyrus end-to-end to form scrolls of up to forty meters long.[109] Nineteenth- and twentieth-century ink manufacturers sold a variety of such materials (often in the same containers used for their writing fluids). Carter's, for

Figure 10.40. PASTE AND MUCILAGE. Both were sold in "cones"—the same used for ink—as well as jars having reservoirs for water and brush (*upper left*). Also shown are, *right front*, a mucilage bottle made of green glass with a rubber-applicator top; *lower left*, a "Kwik Stick" bottle, with a metal flange marked "Spread with this," of about the 1920s; and, *center*, a chromolithographed advertising card for Chases Liquid Glue, probably about 1890.

Our Popular Stationery Outfit.

It consists of 1 quire of fine quality Writing Paper and Envelopes to match, 2 sticks of Sealing-wax, 1 seal (any initial you desire), 1 hammered-brass Candlestick, miniature size, 2 small Wax Candles, 1 rubber Initial Stamp for stamping the Stationery (any initial you desire), 1 box Gold Bronze with Sizing for stamping initial in gold bronze, 1 Pad, and 1 Brush.

Given for one new name. Price, $1. Postage and packing, 20 cts., when sent as a premium or purchased.

Figure 10.41 (*far left*). STATIONERY PACKAGE of the Warren Mills, probably dating from just after the end of the Civil War, contains octavo-size folio sheets of ruled notepaper. It remains sealed in its paper wrapper, just as it came from the manufacturer.

Figure 10.42 (*near left*). STATIONERY OUTFIT. Writing paper, envelopes, wax seal, and other materials were included in this boxed set featured as a premium item in the October 28, 1886, issue of *The Youth's Companion.*

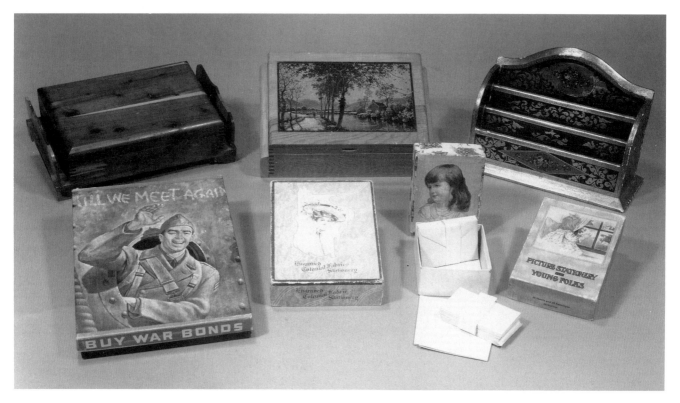

Figure 10.43. STATIONERY CONTAINERS include, *front,* cardboard boxes that held the sheets and envelopes when they were sold; *rear, left and center,* wooden containers that, after emptying, could be used as jewelry boxes. On the right is a stationery rack for use on a desk. The cardboard boxes were used for (*from left*) World War II "General" brand "Fine Papeteries"; "Engraved Colonial Fabric Stationery"; and two brands of children's stationery, the smaller box measuring 3½ by 4¼ by 1⅝ inches. The wooden chests (*from left*) include a cedar one with letter-holder ends and a hardwood box with a halftoned color picture pasted on the cover. The stationery rack is hand painted and gilded.

example, in 1919 advertised "Cico Paste, Photolibrary Paste, Cement, Glue Pencils, Great Stickist Mucilage" (fig. 10.40).[110] On September 8, 1930, the Minnesota Mining and Manufacturing Company introduced an adhesive, transparent cellophane tape (fig. 10.38) that displaced an earlier, gummed-tissue tape.[111]

Writing paper, often with accessory items, was packaged, sold, and stored in various forms (figs. 10.41-

10.43). After being written, letters might be placed in letter holders, delivered in letter bags and mail sacks, then stored by the recipient as keepsakes in letter boxes (figs. 10.44-10.46). Receptacles for other types of documents included bill holders, document containers, and card racks (figs. 10.47-10.49). Victorian ladies' magazines featured directions for sewing and embroidering such assorted cases as a "postage card case," a case for

Figure 10.44. LETTER HOLDERS included those for incoming mail (mailboxes) as well as outgoing mail (letter racks and holders), all sometimes doing double duty. Shown are a cast-iron mailbox with a hasp for a padlock; a notched wooden letter rack, about 18¾ inches high; and two metal holders, one with a plate embossed "Letters." Except for such identifiers, the latter type can be confused with napkin holders, although some, especially the handmade ones sold by arts and crafts sellers, are intended for either use. More often than not, if a manufactured one has uprights of *unequal* height—such as the two illustrated—they are letter holders. And of course there were holders of quite different designs. Although the holders are shown with a postmarked letter and telegram, they would have been used primarily to collect letters *for* mailing.

Figure 10.45. "THE LETTER BAG" is the title of this 1870 steel engraving. The courier has delivered the gentleman's correspondence and seems to await learning whether there may be a reply, while her ladyship anxiously views the key's approach to the padlock.

Figure 10.46. LETTER BOXES are not always easy to distinguish from other such containers, although size is an indicator. The carrier-pigeon illustration on the lid of this dovetailed, late-Victorian box, however, leaves little doubt as to its function. The box measures 3⅝ by 7¹³⁄₁₆ inches by 3⁷⁄₁₆ inches high. The hasp is missing.

Figure 10.47. BILL HOLDERS include the common bill spindles (*rear center and right*), sometimes advertised as "Standing and Hanging Files." Also shown are two large clips and two "arch files." The rearmost clip was made by Esterbrook, the steel-pen manufacturer, and features a patented ball-bearing action. The other clip is a spring-action one; its insert was missing and has been replaced by a calendar such as it might have contained. At left front is a "Shannon Arch File" that was commonly fastened to a clipboard in place of the clip and was used in conjunction with a "file perforator," that is, a two-hole punch. The one at the rear is the same except it is embossed with the name "Yawman and Erbe Mfg. Co., Rochester, N.Y." The file received United States patent no. 774,410 on November 8, 1904.

Figure 10.48. DOCUMENT CONTAINERS include (*from left*) dispatch cases, a metal letter file, a Civil War–era tin document tube, two deed boxes, and (*right front*) a lawyer's homemade combined document and writing box. The leather bag at the front is probably of late-nineteenth-century vintage. Behind it is a circa World War I military dispatch case with "U.S." embossed on the flap. The letter file is olive-drab painted metal, but similar ones shown in the circa-1925 office-supply catalog of Carrithers and Company, Chicago, were of wood, or binder board, or of both, or were made of "the best material . . . covered with a black leatherette-back printed in gold." The document tube measures about two inches in diameter by nineteen inches long. The deed boxes are of black-painted metal, the bottom one having a hasp for a padlock, the upper having a built-in lock. The box at right front belonged to a Frankfort, Kentucky, lawyer of Swiss ancestry, Jacob S. Luscher, early in this century. Homemade from an "Empire Bolts" box, it is covered with paper and has decorative, hand-cut paper trim and a leather hasp. Inside, in one corner, is an inkstained oilcloth retainer for a bottle of writing fluid, and in the lid are pen loops and two pouches of the same material: one, marked *P*, has pen nibs; the other, marked *S*, was apparently for stamps.

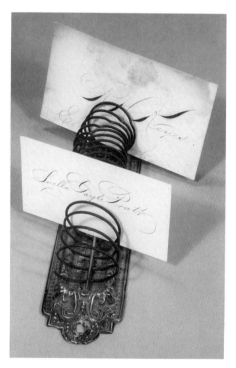

Figure 10.49. "CARD RACK" was the name of this item when it was patented in 1866, but similar coils were later sold as pen racks or letter holders. The cards shown are handwritten. The "Card Rack" was patented October 2, 1866, by James Adair of Pittsburgh, as United States patent no. 58,363; reissued August 4, 1868, as design no. 3,061. Adair's design may not have been the first of its kind. In any case, similar wire coils—mounted on either a pressed-glass or enameled-iron base—were listed in the circa-1925 office-supply catalog of Carrithers and Company, Chicago, as, respectively, "Dixie Glass Pen Rack" and "Diamond Pen Rack"; see also figure 2.19. A contemporary model, by Diversified Designs, Inc., of Cleveland, Ohio, is an "Organizer" for "File Folders, Letters, Messages, Envelopes"; it is a large, blue-painted coil with the heavy wire forming its own supports.

Figure 10.50. PAPERWEIGHTS served a decorative, as well as functional, purpose for a century and a half. *Clockwise from left front:* an advertising paperweight; a paperweight inkwell, containing colorful glass flowerlike designs; a "glass knob weight," advertised in the circa-1925 office-supply catalog of Carrithers and Company, Chicago; an onyx weight with a brass Scottie; and a millefiori paperweight of about 1940, imitative of its then century-old antecedents and measuring about 2⁹⁄₁₆ inches in diameter by 1¼ inches high.

holding "accounts and various memoranda," another for "visiting cards, letters, etc.," a multipocketed "dispatch-case," and a "case for [writing] tablets."[112] Tablets represented one method of holding sheets of note or letter paper; another was the loose-leaf notebook, such as the ring binder, one form of which was invented in 1908.[113]

Related to these paper-holding devices is the simple paperweight. Although they may have existed in earlier times, paperweights of the now-familiar type first appeared in France and Venice as a product of glass-blowers in the 1840s. They are still in use, although more for their decorative than their functional value,

since central air-conditioning has largely replaced fans and open windows.

Among the early whimsies were a type known as millefiori ("thousand flowers"). They contained colorful "canes" of glass and cross sections thereof, arranged in decorative patterns, the earliest known ones dating from 1845. Other glass paperweights have encapsulated fruit or flowers, birds, or other figures or objects; some contain winter scenes that "snow" after being inverted, those with marble or china bases being preferred over those with wood or plastic ones; other varieties include those with decorative bubbles, swirls, or the like (fig. 10.50). And there are paperweights of endless variety that are not made of glass at all, instead being of stone or metal, even a stag's hoof.[114] There were also paperweight inkwells (fig. 10.51) as well as paperweight wafer stands.[115]

Although they might have widely divergent origins, such accessory items, like the fundamental ones of pen and ink and paper, were brought together at two locations: the stationer's counter and the writer's desk. At the latter transpired the activity for which all were intended.

SELECT BIBLIOGRAPHY

Blair, Arthur. *The World of Stamps and Stamp Collecting*. London: Hamlyn, 1972.

Bowyer, Mathew T. "Postmarks." *Antiques Journal*, April 1974, 45.

The Encyclopedia of Collectibles. Alexandria, Va.: Time-Life Books, 1978-79. Includes entries on greeting cards, postcards, valentines.

"Envelope." In *Stories behind Everyday Things*, ed. Jane Polley. Pleasantville, N.Y.: Reader's Digest, 1980. Brief history of letter wrappers.

Frost, S.A. *Frost's Original Letter-Writer*. New York: Dick and Fitzgerald, 1867. Typical Victorian guide to correspondence—with sample letters, guidelines on etiquette, etc.

Oakley, Robert L. "Collecting Wax Sealers." *Antiques Journal*, February 1973, 10-12.

PART 4

Writing

Yet the mere inspection of a small number of these relics of antiquity, may convince anyone of the reality and distinctness of those progressive changes in the modes of writing upon which such discriminations are founded. The architecture of different periods is not more characteristic of the ages to which it belongs, than is the style of writing in manuscripts; nor is there less certainty in determining questions of antiquity in the one case, than in the other.

—Isaac Taylor
*History of the Transmission
of Ancient Books*
1827

11
The History of Written Forms

Ancient Beginnings

The origins of writing lie in the rock drawings of the later Paleolithic period (20,000-10,000 B.C.). Those petroglyphs (carvings) and petrograms (paintings), which are believed to have served mystical as well as decorative functions, eventually evolved into forms of written expression. In such pictographic or ideographic writing (i.e., picture- or idea-writing), simple pictures represented words—whether concrete objects (e.g., a circle could stand for "sun") or more abstract concepts (the sun could signify "day" or "time"). The pictures could be strung together to create narratives.[1]

The earliest extant examples of writing are from a pictographic system used by the Sumerians in southern Mesopotamia, between the Tigris and Euphrates rivers, about 3500 B.C. It was followed (ca. 3200 B.C.) by a modified version called cuneiform (from the Latin, meaning "wedge shaped"; fig. 11.1). This writing system was later (ca. 2500 B.C.) adopted by the Semitic Akkadians, that is, the Assyrians and Babylonians and it continued in use until about the third century B.C. (figs. 11.2 and 11.3).[2]

Cuneiform characters were impressed into the moist clay of tablets (or sometimes cones or prisms) with a

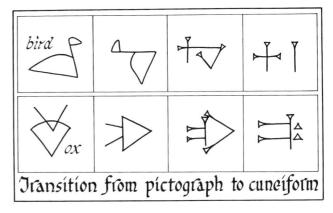

Figure 11.1. CUNEIFORM, or "wedge-shaped," writing evolved from a pictographic system used by the Sumerians. It was later adopted by the Assyrians and Babylonians.

reed stylus. The soft clay, which allowed mistakes to be rubbed out with a thumb, was subsequently baked into the hard, durable form that has helped ensure the survival of many tablets.[3] According to William Rodger,

> Cuneiform was used for every writing task, including legal proceedings and documents. When archaeological sites are explored in modern Iraq, or other regions whose ancestors wrote in cuneiform, many

Figure 11.2 (*far left*). This BABYLONIAN CLAY TABLET in cuneiform writing is a receipt for beer, from about 2112-2004 B.C. It is about 1⅜ inches wide by 1⁷⁄₁₆ inches high by ⁷⁄₁₆ inch thick.

Figure 11.3(*left*). This CYLINDER SEAL is from the reverse side of the Babylonian clay tablet in figure 11.2. Such seals were impressed from stone cylinders having intaglio (recessed) carvings which were rolled across the soft clay.

Figure 11.4. HIEROGLYPHIC WRITING began with simple pictographs but evolved into a phonetic form of writing. The above hieroglyphics accompany an illustration of King Shishak with captives on a sculpted wall at Karnac, tenth century B.C. From L.W. Yaggy and T.L. Haines, *Museum of Antiquity: A Description of Ancient Life* (Nashville: South Western Publishing, 1880), 935.

Figure 11.5. HIERATIC SCRIPT. *Hieratic,* or "priestly," writing is descended from the ancient hieroglyphics but is less recognizably pictorial. This papyrus fragment features a colored illustration of a portal with portions of four lines of Egyptian script.

Figure 11.6. The EVOLUTION OF EGYPTIAN SCRIPT represented a gradual simplification of form. Three characters of a hieroglyphic "book hand," or writing used for manuscripts (*left column*), are shown with their later equivalents in hieratic and demotic script.

Figure 11.7. This HEBRAIC SCROLL illustrates the form of the book prior to the development of the codex, or bound volume. Actually this scroll, dating from the second millennium B.C., records the Pentateuch, or the first five books of the Bible. From L.W. Yaggy and T.L. Haines, *Museum of Antiquity: A Description of Ancient Life* (Nashville: South Western Publishing, 1880), 921.

Figure 11.8. CHINESE WRITING MATERIALS, shown here in contemporary form, have remained relatively unchanged since ancient times. In addition to the various brushes are, *center,* a brush rack, a bamboo pen at its base, and a roll-up brush holder; *right,* an ink stick and a grinding stone; and *upper left,* a hanging scroll.

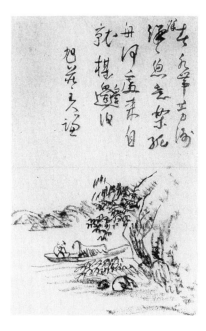

Figure 11.9. CHINESE BRUSH CALLIGRAPHY is the traditional means of rendering the nonalphabetic Chinese writing, as in the example above this sketch from a late-nineteenth-century artist's sketchbook.

small and large clay tablets bearing these bizarre inscriptions are discovered. Until rather recent times the deciphering of cuneiform posed a sticky problem but today, thanks to the efforts of such scholars as Sir Henry Rawlinson, it can be interpreted without difficulty. Many tablets prove to be land grants, transfers of property, and various sorts of licenses, which conform surprisingly closely to more modern laws. The normal shape is not rectangular, as might be expected, but like a dinner roll, and quite thick. A single document might weigh as much as several pounds, so if early legal scribes complained of being buried under tons of work they were not far from correct.[4]

Both cuneiform and the other major script (or handwritten form) of the ancient Near East, the Egyptian hieroglyphics system, evolved from ideographic into phonetic writing (in which symbols came to represent sounds) and then syllabic writing (wherein syllables were combined to make new words).[5] The earliest-known hieroglyphics (from *hieros*, "holy," and *glyphein*, "to carve") date from about 3000 B.C. (fig. 11.4). Some 600 years later a cursive form developed, known as *hieratic* (priestly) and during 2000-1790 B.C. the vertical line was replaced by the horizontal one, written from right to left (fig. 11.5). In the seventh century B.C. there appeared a third form, *demotic* (of the people) which was a further, rather scribbled derivative of the hieratic. It was used by the populace until about A.D. 470 (fig. 11.6).[6]

Following syllabic writing came the creation of the alphabetical system, wherein characters represented individual sounds rather than syllables. The origins are murky, but the Phoenicians, who lived along the western coast of the Mediterranean, appear to have been the inheritors of earlier, Semitic alphabetic writing, which they developed into a vowel-less system about 1000 B.C. From the ancestral Semitic alphabet developed Hebrew, Arabic, Persian, and other scripts (fig. 11.7). China, however, failed to develop an alphabet, its brush-written writing instead combining ideograms and phonograms (figs. 11.8 and 11.9).[7]

European Developments

From Phoenician traders the Greeks came in contact with the alphabet. Since its twenty-two consonants were more than were needed for Greek, the extra signs were converted into vowels. The first letter of the Phoenician alphabet, ⫷ , whose name, *aleph*, meant "ox" (of which the character was a simple picture, with its triangular head and horns adapted from an earlier Egyptian hieroglyphic), became the Greek *alpha*, or *A*. The second letter, *beth*, became Greek *beta*, or *B*, and from the two comes our word "alphabet." Of the ear-

Figure 11.10. The GREEK ALPHABET, which was used for this ancient (ca. 1000 B.C.) altar inscription, was the basis for our own, Roman, alphabet. From L.W. Yaggy and T.L. Haines, *Museum of Antiquity: A Description of Ancient Life* (Nashville: South Western Publishing, 1880), 563.

liest Greek inscriptions (fig. 11.10), like some early Latin ones, some read up and down, some from right to left, some left to right, and some alternating. The latter writing was termed *boustrophedon*, meaning "ox-turning": that is, when an ox plows a furrow it turns at the end of it and proceeds in the opposite direction.[8]

About 700 B.C., the Romans adopted the Greek alphabet while it was still in development.

> From the standard Greek alphabet the Romans took A, B, E, Z, H, I, K, M, N, O, T, X and Y with hardly any change at all. The letter B, for instance was merely a rounded form of the Greek character. Remodeling and finishing other Greek letters, the Romans produced C (and G), L, S, P, R, D and V. F and Q were taken from two old characters abandoned by the Greeks themselves. And that makes twenty-three.
>
> . . . At first the Romans dropped Z entirely, then found they could not get along without it. When they allowed Z to return to the alphabet, it had lost its place in the regular order [it was sixth in the Greek alphabet] and had to get to the end of the line. We have kept Z there ever since.
>
> The three missing letters, J, U and W, were not used by the Romans at all. U and W developed from V about a thousand years ago, and J developed from the letter I about five hundred years ago.[9]

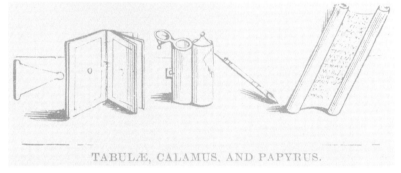

Figure 11.12. This ROMAN BRONZE COIN, issued during the reign of Galerius, (A.D. 305-11), illustrates a further example of all-capital Roman writing. Note the similarity to today's common printing type.

Figure 11.11. The ROMAN ALPHABET contained only capital letters like the ones making up this Latin inscription. Minuscules (small letters) developed later. From L.W. Yaggy and T.L. Haines, *Museum of Antiquity: A Description of Ancient Life* (Nashville: South Western Publishing, 1880), 247.

Figure 11.13. ROMAN WRITING MATERIALS included (*from left*) a double-leaf wax tablet, for writing on with a stylus; a double inkstand, probably for red and black ink; a reed pen; and a papyrus roll. From L.W. Yaggy and T.L. Haines, *Museum of Antiquity: A Description of Ancient Life* (Nashville: South Western Publishing, 1880), 283.

Like their predecessors, the Romans carved inscriptions in stone, embossed them on coins, and also wrote on papyrus with reed pen and ink (figs. 11.11-11.13). They employed formal "square capitals," as well as a later, more freely written form, "rustica." Except for initials, headings, and the like, it replaced square capitals in book manuscripts in the fifth century A.D. The Romans also had an even freer, cursive or near-cursive script—similar to one of the Greeks—used for correspondence, accounts, and various informal writings.[10]

Another Roman book hand (as scripts used for manuscript volumes are termed) was the "uncial" (the name deriving from the fact that the characters were commonly an *uncia*—a Roman inch—high; they were actually developed by the Greeks as early as the third century B.C.). Uncials were a rounded form that began to emerge in Latin manuscripts of the second century A.D., became dominant for book use in the fourth, and remained so until the ninth century.[11] In the meantime—about the seventh century—word separation and punctuation began to appear; before then words were run together SOTHATTHEYLOOKEDLIKETHIS-ANDWEREDIFFICULTTOREAD.[12]

From the uncial script, which was comprised of *majuscules*—capital letters—that required only two guidelines for lettering, there developed half-uncials, which show a tendency toward *minuscules*—"small" letters—and required four guidelines because of the presence of ascender and descender strokes. Half-uncials existed briefly in the third century but were revived in the sixth. They became the national hand of Ireland, and Irish half-uncials attained their most perfected expression in *The Book of Kells*, the intricately beautiful gospel book found in the church at Kells, County Kilkenny, Ireland, and dating from about 700 (fig. 11.14).[13]

The full ascendancy of minuscules awaited the resumption of western European cultural progress; this was after three centuries of instability following the fall of the Roman Empire. Then in 789 the emperor Charlemagne (Charles the Great, 742-814), in an attempt to restore some order as well as revive culture in the Frankish or "Holy Roman" Empire, issued a famous decree. It ordered that all writings—literary works, legal and ecclesiastical documents, and so on—were to be rewritten in a standard hand. Now known as

Figure 11.14. EVOLUTION OF ROMAN SCRIPTS. Classic Roman "square capitals" were lettered with a chisel-edge pen, as was the less-formal *rustica* style, although the pen was held at a different angle. The latter was displaced for routine manuscript use by the rounded "uncials." From them developed "half-uncials" which anticipated true minuscules, or small letters.

Figure 11.15. GOTHIC SCRIPTS. "Gothic" was a term of derision applied to an extreme type of script that evolved from the Caroline minuscule. Also called "blackletter" because of its appearance, it became a distinct style in the twelfth century and came to exist in three major forms as shown.

the Carolingian or Caroline minuscule (after Charlemagne), the script used for this massive undertaking represented the final development of the small letter. The script was created, not single-handedly, as legend holds, by Alcuin of York, but by what Alcuin himself termed a "crowd of scribes." Moreover, it was not an entirely new creation but a development from a variety of national styles that had evolved from the previous Roman hands—notably a pre-Caroline cursive minuscule produced by Frankish scribes. In fact, the Caroline alphabet itself continued to evolve into a progressively more graceful and more finished form—reaching its ultimate flowering in the eleventh and twelfth centuries (fig. 11.14).[14]

With widespread dissemination of the Caroline script, rendered in different locales by scribes with varying degrees of training, it was inevitable that divergent forms would arise. Among these so-called national

Figure 11.16 (*below*). SCRIPT TO TYPE. When printing from movable type appeared in Europe in the fifteenth century, manuscript hands became models for typefaces. Note the similarity of the hand-lettered rotunda script, on the late-medieval parchment antiphonary page at left, to that of the sheet of paper at far right, printed in Venice in 1503. The calligraphy on the seventeenth-century sheet of antique laid paper in the center is similar to today's common roman type. The latter sheet measures 9³⁄₁₆ by 15⁷⁄₁₆ inches.

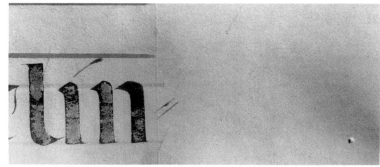

Figure 11.17 (*left*). MARKING PARCHMENT preparatory to lettering, as in this late-medieval example, involved ruling margins and guidelines, scribing them with a stylus. Note the impressed lines. Note also the lightly scribbled numeral "2," which may have related to the laying out of the page.

Figure 11.18 (*above*). A PRICK MARK in the parchment (*lower right*) coincides with the base of the line of lettering, which it was apparently used to indicate during the laying out of the page.

Figure 11.19 (*below*). An ILLUMINATED MANUSCRIPT like this one, which is probably late-fifteenth-century Italian, has initial letters or other embellishments rendered in colors, gilding, or the like. The letter at left is done in red and purple. At the upper right are "rubrications," that is, words done in red.

hands, or styles, that evolved from the Caroline was "Gothic," or "blackletter," script.

"Gothic" was a term of derision applied by later Renaissance humanists who thought the style reminiscent of the Goths, the fifth-century barbarians who invaded Rome. It tended to narrowness (some say as a means of conserving parchment) and hence angularity, features that, when rendered by the chisel-edged quill, resulted in exaggerated contrast between heavy vertical strokes and hairline horizontal ones. Because they tended to be written closely together, and Gothic letters like *i*, *m*, *n*, and *u* could cause confusion, there came to be placed over the *i* a distinguishing stroke that later developed into a dot.

Gothic script became a distinct style during the twelfth century in northern Europe, where it predominated during the next three centuries, and spread elsewhere in Europe as well. As a book hand, it existed in three essential forms: an angular variety know as *textura;* a rounded version, developed by the Italians, called *rotunda* (or "round-" or "half-Gothic"); and various near-cursive forms known under the heading *bastarda* (fig. 11.15). The Gothic became especially popular in Germany, where it was adopted as a typeface by the early printers and where it continued in use to modern times (fig. 11.16).[15]

The Medieval Scribe

By the time the parchment codex (or bound book) had displaced the papyrus roll, before the fourth century, Christian books (as a result of the Christianizing of the Roman Empire) had superseded non-Christian ones. Increasingly, scholarship became the province of the church, and it maintained a monopoly from the sixth to the twelfth century. Characteristically, monasteries maintained libraries and operated scriptoria. A scriptorium was a room set apart for the scribes, or it consisted of carrels, individual cells where monks transcribed, "illuminated," and bound the manuscript volumes.[16]

In the scriptorium the typical copyist worked on a writing board placed across the extended arms of his chair, his parchment sheet secured by a thong. At hand were his various implements: a container of pumice, an inkhorn, a supply of quills, a narrow parchment ruler, an awl, a sharp knife, and a boar's tooth.[17]

The scribe began by preparing his parchment sheets, which were double, or folio, ones—that is, having two leaves, or four pages, when folded. Each sheet of the massive Carolingian Bibles represented one sheep; the completed volume would thus have derived from a flock of some two or three hundred animals.[18]

With his knife the scribe scraped off any encrustations and rubbed the surface with pumice so that it would retain ink better. He measured off the various margins and guidelines, placing prick marks or scribbling notations where necessary, then scratched the lines with a stylus (figs. 11.17 and 11.18). Carefully cutting his quill to a chisel edge, he dipped it into the inkhorn and began writing the main text. He worked from a copy placed before him, unlike the Roman practice of having the text read aloud while several scribes wrote simultaneously. He left spaces for the rubrication and illumination. In a large scriptorium these would be filled in by others, there being specialist craftsmen for the various stages of bookmaking.[19]

Scribes corrected minor mistakes by scraping with a knife and polishing the area with a boar's tooth or similar implement before relettering. They sometimes remedied larger errors with resignation and even humor: for example, an omitted line or verse might be added at the top or bottom of the page, a rope carefully drawn around the text or attached to it, and the figure of a penitent scribe placed in the margin to tug the text into place.[20]

The rubricator next completed his work. The rubrics—small initial letters or headings—were done in red (hence the term, derived from the Latin word *ruber*). It is from the fact that saints' days in medieval calendars were always rubricated that we obtain the expression "red letter day." Sometimes the rubricator used a combination of colors, such as red and yellow or red and blue.[21]

Afterward, the "illuminations" were rendered. The term once strictly denoted embellishments of gold or silver and referred to their reflective quality, "thus giving the impression that the page has been literally illuminated."[22] At least one source, however, maintains the "origin" of the term lay in the fact that the illustrations were intended to "shed light upon the text."[23] In any case, illumination now broadly refers to "the embellishment of a letter or writing with colours, etc."[24]

Medieval decorative treatment of initial letters, used to begin manuscript sections, ranged from the relatively simple (fig. 11.19) to highly elaborate ones with miniature paintings or with complex arabesques and geometric designs, like those in *The Book of Kells*.[25] Letter and surrounding background were both usually decorated, and the treatment may be described as—in addition to gilded and rubricated—"textured," "foliated" (ornamented with leafy designs and tendrils), "inhabited" (having birds, animals, etc.), and "historiated" (illustrated with figures in historical or legendary situations).[26]

The illuminator, responding to instructions that had

been lightly scribbled in the area the initial or illustration was to fill, sketched the design with a lead marker, made a careful drawing with diluted ink, applied any gilding (by painting in the size and laying on and burnishing the gold), and finally filled in the colors and added outlines and highlights.[27]

After the pages were completed and checked for errors by a corrector, they were folded, gathered, sewn, and bound with wooden boards that were covered with leather and perhaps encrusted with gold, ivory, or jewels.[28] The book was then ready for bishop or king.

With the rise of universities in the twelfth century, the church's monopoly on book production began to decline. There grew a class of secular artisans—parchmenters, scribes, illuminators, bookbinders, and other craftsmen—employed in lay workshops which began to produce manuscripts commissioned for private use. Now, not just ecclesiastics and princes could have books, but so could mere nobles and wealthy merchants. In addition to Bibles, psalters, and gospel lectionaries, there began to be histories, herbals, bestiaries, and other volumes. A type known as the book of hours (a private devotional book, formerly an adjunct to the psalter) arose in the thirteenth century, as did pocket-sized Bibles. And vernacular books (books written in the vernacular or native, as opposed to classical, languages—Chaucer's *Canterbury Tales,* for example, in English, and Dante's *Divine Comedy,* in Italian) appeared in the fourteenth century, by which time books were being marketed widely through booksellers.[29]

Figure 11.20. CURSIVE WRITING, or that in which the letters have connecting strokes, tends to develop as script is produced with more and more speed. The secretary hand descended from a cursive form of bastarda and combined with italic to produce English round hand. It, in turn, was the precursor of Spencerian and later hands.

The Renaissance

About the first quarter of the fifteenth century there appeared in Florence a script developed by the Italian "humanists," so named because of their philosophical focus on human concerns. As part of an evolving "renaissance," or rebirth, of learning, they turned to the culture of antiquity for models of excellence. Thus, for the "new" script, the humanistic scribes adopted Roman capitals and a neat, round version of Caroline minuscules which they believed Roman because many

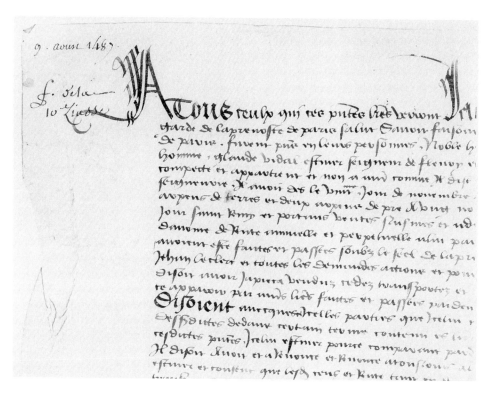

Figure 11.21. FRENCH BASTARDA SCRIPT, in a cursive form, was used for this parchment legal document written in Old French and dated 1487. From the script developed the English secretary hand.

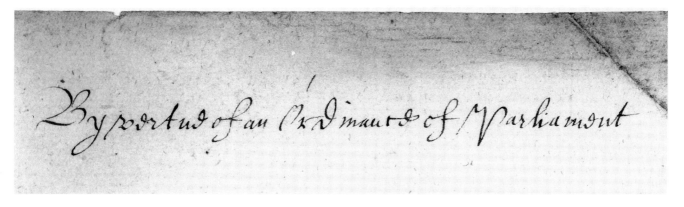

Figure 11.22. SECRETARY HAND is the name given to this style of English handwriting that descended from bastarda and in turn was a precursor (with italic) of round hand. This example reads, "By vertue of an Ordinance of Parliament." Note the Gothic influence on the capitals, and the distinctive forms of *c* and *e*. The cardinal's hat watermark in figure 9.5 is from this sheet of antique laid paper.

of the Roman classics had been copied in it during the earlier Carolingian Renaissance.[30] They termed this hand *lettera antica*, "antique letters," but it has become known as humanistic antiqua or Renaissance minuscule.[31] A cursive form developed, became increasingly slanted due to the rapidity with which it could be written, and otherwise evolved into the late-fifteenth-century manuscript hand *cursiva humanistica* (fig. 11.20).[32] Because it was widely disseminated by the scribes of the Papal Chancery, it became generally known as *cancellaresca*.[33] It became popular throughout Europe in the following century as a typeface the French dubbed "Italic."[34]

In England, the humanistic antiqua style was introduced in the early sixteenth century, and by mid-century it had become an alternative to the English script then current: the "secretary" hand.[35] This was a cursive handwriting the roots of which can be traced to the half-century period of 1260-1310. At that time there was an increasing demand for writing by the English populace.

> Great monasteries began late in Henry III.'s reign to keep elaborate court-rolls and account-rolls of their manors. Changes in land tenure under Edward I. led to a vast output of deeds dealing with little bits of land. A little later allusions to the "paper of the market" show a new and cheap writing material fostering the growth of ephemeral business records. And lastly, legal documents were coming to be written in French and English, and by persons unskilled in the elaborate system of abbreviations which learned Latinists had devised to shorten their labour. In these conditions, the requirements for a popular hand were speed and simplicity rather than beauty, and even at the cost of a high degree of legibility.[36]

From this artless "popular hand," which was a de-

rivative of a cursive form of Gothic bastarda obtained from the French (fig. 11.21), there evolved the native English hand that became known in the sixteenth century as secretary (figs. 11.20 and 11.22).[37]

The secretary hand and its more legible rival, the Italian hand, were used literally side by side during the English Renaissance. For example, a letter of 1570 from Elizabeth I is written in secretary, the more everyday hand, but the queen has penned the closing and her signature in italic, or what Shakespeare's Malvolio termed "the sweet Roman hand."[38] Early seventeenth-century examples of English writing were also frequently part italic, part secretary. The result was that, by the end of the century a new, albeit hybrid, form—English round hand—had developed.[39]

Round hand was helped into being by the influence of popular penmanship copybooks printed by copper-plate engraving. The engraver's tool was ill-suited to reproducing the products of the writing masters' chisel-edge pens, but instead produced a different type of thick and thin strokes that encouraged their imitation. Thus, as Joyce Whalley states, citing various seventeenth-century examples, "there was an inclination for the pen to follow the graver, rather than the graver to follow the pen."[40]

Consequently, the pen began to be cut to a pointed rather than chisel shape. And just as the engraving burin produced a hairline when moved lightly on the metal plate but a heavier stroke when pressed so as to cut more deeply, the pointed pen now yielded a similar effect: upstrokes, in which the sharp point lightly touched the parchment or paper, were thin, whereas downstrokes, in which pressure caused the two points of the split pen to separate, were contrastingly swollen or "shaded." The pointed pen now moved more swiftly than the square-cut one and facilitated fluid penmanship (fig. 11.20).[41]

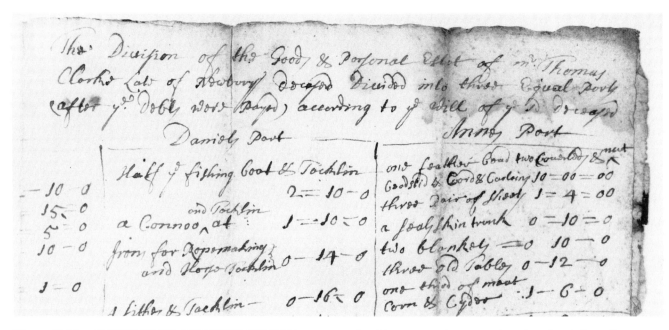

Figure 11.23. "MAYFLOWER CENTURY" SCRIPT is one name for this seventeenth-century American hand. In reality, however, it is merely a transitional form between secretary (it still preserves the quaint *e* shown in the previous figure) and round hand.

This example is from an estate-settlement document of about 1680: "The Division of the Goods & Personal Estat of M^r. Thomas Clarke Late of Newbury Decased Divided into three Equal Parts (after ye Debts were Payed) according to ye will of ye sd Deceased." Listed under "Daniel's Part" is "Half ye fishing boat & tacklin" (i.e., tackle), and so on; among the items listed under "Anne's Part" are "one feather bead," "a seals skin trunk," and "one third of meat Corn & Cyder"; the "widows part" is not shown here.

American Systems

In early America, handwriting trends followed those of the mother country. From the landing of the Pilgrims at Plymouth Rock in 1620 until the end of the century, the dominant hand was one that has been called "the 'Mayflower Century' Style of American Writing," showing secretary and italic features but blending to round hand by century's end (fig. 11.23).[42]

It was followed by the American round-hand system (about 1700-1840), which retained the features of its English forebear: a "copperplate" appearance resembling engravers' script, with hairline upstrokes and "shaded" downstrokes (figs. 11.24 and 11.25). The letter forms were rounded and often contained flourishes (refer to fig. 1.3).[43] Also, the writing commonly featured such forms as superscript abbreviation (e.g., the use of raised letters in such contracted forms as "W^m" for "William" and "Rob!" for "Robert") as well as the archaic long *s*, most often used as the first letter of an *ss* combination, which thus would somewhat resemble *fs* or even *p* (see fig. 14.3 for examples).

The modified round hand (ca. 1840-65), as its name indicates, was basically a round-hand system but incorporated stylish modifications as found in early editions of the copybooks of Platt Rogers Spencer and of the Payson, Dunton, and Scribner system. It includes what

can be termed "unsystematic 'Spencerian'"; in other words, it was a transitional form between old round hand and soon-to-be-codified "Spencerian."[44]

The popular "Spencerian" system (1865-90) represented the fruits of the two ostensibly competing systems: that of Payson, Dunton, and Scribner, who had issued the first modern copybooks in 1851, and Spencer, who had published a series of copy slips three years earlier.[45] The two influenced each other until together they created a new style. It featured more angular connecting strokes, had very little shading on the small letters and more space between them, plus a distinctive set of capitals and a slant set at fifty-two degrees from the horizontal. The result was a fashionably new, American hand that could be rendered with more speed than the old round hand, and for a time "Spencerian" became synonymous with penmanship (fig. 11.26).[46]

"Modern vertical" (1890-1900) was a reversion to a slower, more legible hand, almost printed and lacking both slant and contrast in shading. According to one authority: "It had a printed type form with angular and arcade features and elongated approach and terminal strokes. It was heavy with constant pen pressure."[47] It was entirely too slow, and it passed from the American school system after only ten years (fig. 11.27).[48]

A number of "basic popular systems" (1890-1945)

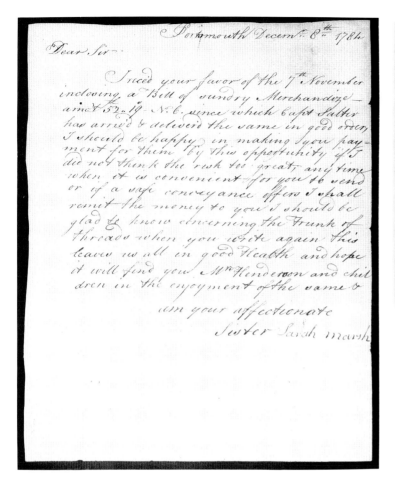

Figure 11.24. ROUND-HAND SCRIPT, as in this American letter, dated 1784, has an appearance like copperplate engraving, with hairline upstrokes resulting from a pointed pen and "shaded" downstrokes caused by the points of the split pen tip separating under pressure.

Figure 11.25. ENGRAVERS' SCRIPT shows a striking resemblance to English round hand—both styles influencing each other in the seventeenth century, when penmanship books were printed from engraved plates. In this 1914 White House invitation and admission card, the married couple's name has been skillfully penned by an engrosser (or master penman) in imitation of the writing *printed* from an engraved plate.

also characterized the period subsequent to the Spencerian. Sharing a free movement of the arm, the systems were termed "American arm movement writing." They included the American Book Company, Palmer, and Zaner-Bloser methods. They lacked the heavy pressure shading of Spencerian, were easy and fast to use, and were popularized by the commercial schools (fig. 11.28).[49]

Finally, various mixed forms represent the period from 1945 to the present, and these were influenced by the ballpoint pen:

> Writers were now able to scribble out a check holding it in their hand, or take notes in the field. Desks were not needed. But a physical change also occurred as writers began to write with their fingers and not their wrist or arm. Letters became smaller, cramped, and often found to have groups of two or three letters and then a break in the middle of the word, or letters tapered smaller as the fingers reached without moving the wrist resting on the paper. The old pen and ink system taught

arm movement with line after line of practice circles or zig-zag lines [of] neat and even pressure strokes. This was no longer thought important.[50]

In addition to these mainstream American hands, there was also an "angular hand" that was "taught to and written by many women during all of the last century."[51] Back hand, or writing done with a backward rather than a forward slant, is essentially a variant rather than a distinct hand, one common, in fact, to many left-handed writers. Nevertheless, it was taught by at least one American writing master, Nathaniel Duren Gould (1781-1864), as "an easy and fashionable hand for letter writing."[52] Of course, it is also an easy—if not necessarily successful—means of disguising handwriting, as for anonymous character-assassination missives known as poison-pen letters.[53]

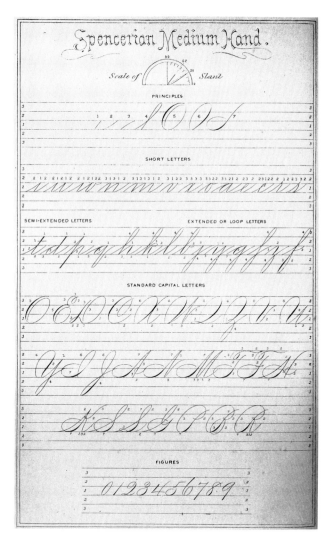

Figure 11.26. SPENCERIAN SCRIPT was named for its major developer, Platt Rogers Spencer. It derived from round hand but had only selective, as opposed to systematic, shading and other features that made it a distinctively American hand. From *Spencerian Key to Practical Penmanship, 1877,* by H.C. Spencer.

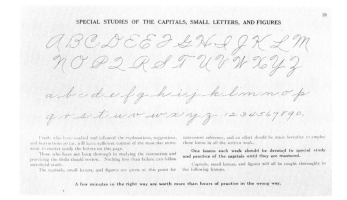

Figure 11.27. VERTICAL WRITING was taught in American schools from 1890 to 1900. This page from a copybook of that period shows a printed example, followed by three attempts of a budding penman to reproduce it. The fact that the style was too slow led to its abandonment at century's end.

SPECIAL STUDIES OF THE CAPITALS, SMALL LETTERS, AND FIGURES

Figure 11.28. The PALMER METHOD was one of the most widely taught systems of "American arm movement writing." Practice drills involved making endless ovals and spirals, in addition to practicing the actual letters, as a means of obtaining freedom in movement.

Figure 11.29. "PENNSYLVANIA DUTCH" FRAKTUR. German immigrants to America made folk-art productions out of their baptismal and similar documents, which are known as frakturs, after the script employed. Many were elaborately embellished with birds, hearts, and other motifs; others (like the 1850 one from which this is a detail) were only filled in on printed forms and hand colored. (The full document is shown later, in fig. 13.13.)

One foreign hand that was much employed in America, particularly in the late eighteenth and early nineteenth centuries was *fraktur*, a derivative of the old Gothic bastarda hand of the Middle Ages (fig. 11.15). It was brought to America by German immigrants who settled in Pennsylvania (as well as parts of Maryland, Virginia, and Ohio) and who became known (erroneously) as "Pennsylvania Dutch" (a corruption of *Deutch*, meaning "German"). The hand (in a hodgepodge of variants) was employed for their elaborately embellished manuscript certificates for birth, baptism, and the like. These folk-art productions ranged from the amateurish to the skillful, depending on the ability of the penman, who was usually a schoolmaster or minister. In addition to the entirely hand-rendered certificates—painted with colorful birds, flowers, hearts, and other motifs—later ones were filled in on partially printed sheets decorated with hand-colored wood engravings (see detail in fig. 11.29). Now themselves known as frakturs, these documents have become highly desirable and valuable (comparable to samplers), and thus it is not surprising that skillful forgeries on genuine old paper have become the bane of collectors.[54]

Printing and Related Developments

A number of alternatives to ordinary writing deserve mention, the most significant being printing, which played a major role in the Renaissance and profoundly influenced the written word.

Long after wood-block prints and printed books originated in the Orient (an eighth-century scroll was found in southern Korea) such printing began to appear in Europe.[55] Wood-block prints were introduced there by 1423 (the earliest known date), and block-printed books soon followed.[56]

By 1436, the German goldsmith Johann Gutenberg (ca. 1397-1468) was selling partnerships in some unspecified invention, now assumed to have been printing from movable type. It is thought that he was producing at least experimental work between 1440 and 1450, but the first example of known date is a papal bull of 1454 printed in Mainz. Approximately a year later the famous Latin Bible now known as the Gutenberg or "42-line" Bible appeared—the first significant book printed from interchangeable metal type, and a masterpiece by any standard. The debts Gutenberg incurred in the process left him in financial ruin, however, and he lost his printing equipment as well as the Bibles; he lived his final years on a pension, forgotten and nearly blind.[57]

It is noteworthy that Gutenberg's approach was to imitate manuscript books. Not only was his type derived from the fifteenth-century German Gothic script then current (believed to have been designed with the assistance of a scribe, Peter Schoeffer), but many copies were printed on vellum instead of paper, and copies were hand rubricated and illuminated.[58] Reportedly, this was "to give the effect of a hand-copied manuscript, as desired by the printers, who did not wish their invention discovered."[59]

Be that as it may, printing's association with calligraphy continued during its spread throughout Europe. The following dates represent the first printing from presses in each country:

Italy	1465	Spain	1474
Switzerland	1468	England	1476
France	1470	Denmark	1482
Holland	1473	Sweden	1483
Belgium	1473	Portugal	1487
Austria-Hungary	1473		

Presses were established in all major cities in Europe by century's end. Books printed during that period are called incunabula—"in the cradle"—and are valuable collectors' items.[60]

Italian developments provide an example of this relationship between script and print that is important in today's printed word. There had existed a disparity in the two elements of the humanistic hand: the Roman capitals had serifs (short terminal cross strokes; fig. 11.14), whereas the minuscules were a serifless, or sans-serif, variety. As a consequence, the humanistic scribes attempted to harmonize them by adding serifs to the latter. Thus, when printing arrived in Italy, that script served as the model for the native type style, now called "roman" and used on this very page.[61]

A relationship between manuscript writing and early printing also characterized the origins of printing in England. William Caxton (ca. 1422–91), who first set up a press at Bruges in Burgandy, now Belgium, in 1474, did so in association with a calligrapher and illuminator named Colard Mansion, who had worked in the library of the duke of Burgandy. There, in that year, Caxton published the first book in English. In 1476 he returned to England and established a press at Westminster. His first book there of known date (1477) was *The Dictes or Sayengis of the Philosophers*, which was soon followed by others, including Chaucer's *Canterbury Tales* and Malory's *Morte d'Arthur*. Caxton's and other early English volumes were invariably printed in bastarda or some other form of Gothic, now often but misleadingly called "Old English."[62]

Although printing soon had a negative impact on professional scribes—one lamented in paying his taxes in 1480 that the invention had cost him so much copywork he could scarcely buy clothing—the overall

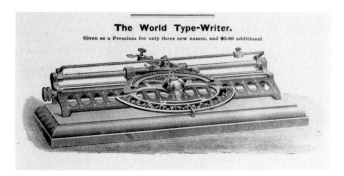

Figure 11.30. EARLY TYPEWRITERS. Following Remington's marketing in 1873 of Christopher Latham Shole's typewriter, many competing models were patented. Among them were ones that operated on the type-wheel, rather than type-bar, principle, like this model advertised in the October 28, 1886, issue of *The Youth's Companion.*

Figure 11.31. The OLIVER TYPEWRITER (shown here with its accessory kit) was first patented in 1894. It was one of the most successful of the early "visible" typewriters; the earliest machines did not permit viewing of the line being typed. The Oliver's arched, nesting type bars struck downward from either side, in contrast to the front-stroke models that later became standard.

effect was different.[63] By giving impetus to the new revival of learning (Gutenberg's invention roughly coincides with the beginning of the Renaissance), printing greatly aided the spread of literacy. Not only did an increasing number of people desire to learn to write, but there were increasing markets for those who could pen a good script, as well as for those professionals who could teach them.[64]

Printing in the New World began in Mexico City in the 1530s, and the first actual press in North America was established in 1638 at Cambridge, Massachusetts, by Stephen Daye. No copies survive of Daye's first productions, an almanac and the *Freeman's Oath,* although forgeries of the latter created a sensation when they were "discovered" in 1985.[65] As colonies spread in the United States, and later, as settlements increased westward, so did printing.[66]

When, in 1886, the German-American Othmar Mergenthaler invented the Linotype machine—a complex device that set and cast type a line at a time, and so industrialized printing—he employed a keyboard, a concept that already had an interesting history.[67] As part of his work on the telegraph (conceived in 1832 and used for the first time on May 24, 1844, between Baltimore and Washington), Samuel F.B. Morse had developed a keyboard as part of "what was virtually a teletype system."[68] Produced (before 1845) in conjunction with Alfred Vail, Morse's keyboard anticipated those later used by the typewriter and the Linotype. In 1846 a patent was issued to Royal Earle House whose message-recording machine replaced the dots and dashes of Morse's telegraphic code with roman type.[69]

The concept of the typewriter is even earlier, dating from 1714, when Queen Anne issued a patent to the English engineer Henry Mill for "an artificial machine or method for the impressing or transcribing of letters singly or progressively one after another, as in writing,

Figure 11.32. THE TYPIST, as shown in this 1913 photograph with her Oliver typewriter, came invariably from the ranks of women. While some would see the machine as a means of her enslavement, in 1923 the authors of *The Story of the Typewriter* asserted: "The typist blazed the path by which other women entered every department of business."

whereby all writings whatsoever may be engrossed in paper or parchment so neat and exact as not to be distinguished from print."[70] There is no proof, however, that such a machine was ever used or that any model ever existed.

In 1784 a machine was reportedly invented "for embossing printed characters for the blind."[71] Again, nothing further is known of this pre-typewriting device except that it foreshadowed the modern Braille system, the raised-dot code invented by a fifteen-year-old blind French boy named Louis Braille in 1824, which made possible today's Braille typewriters.[72]

The first United States patent on a typewriting machine was issued in 1829 to William A. Burt of Detroit, who called his invention "the Typographer."[73] It used a type-wheel rather than individual bars. It was followed in 1833 by a French "Ktypographic" machine, which had a circular array of type bars that struck downward on a common center.[74] The two principles embodied in these machines form the basis for later typewriters.

A progression of ingenious American devices followed, including one machine with a piano-like keyboard and other elaborate affairs with names like "typograph," "Pterotype" (winged type), "Patent Printer," and "Mechanical Chirographer."[75] Still, most were too slow to be effective.[76]

The first successful commercial "Type-Writer," as he named his machine, was the invention of Christopher Latham Sholes (1819-90). Sholes was a Milwaukee journalist and printer who built some twenty-five to thirty models in the period of 1867-1873, following his invention of a machine for numbering the pages of blank books. A final model was sold in 1873 to E. Remington and Sons (the great firearms company during the Civil War), which marketed it the following year. The machine was developed by an employee of Remington's sewing-machine department, and the first "Model 1 Remington" actually resembled a sewing machine: it was mounted on a stand and had a foot-treadle to operate the carriage return.[77]

Soon, Mark Twain had typed a letter to his brother on a Remington, confessing he was "greatly taken with it." Twain subsequently became the first author to submit a typewritten manuscript, *Life on the Mississippi*, to a publisher.[78]

Remington's first catalog promoted Shole's invention as "a beautiful piece of furniture" and even suggested that "persons traveling by sea can write with it when pen writing is impossible." Its success, of course, came not at sea but in the world of commerce, where it won slow but sure acceptance.[79]

Other typing machines began to be marketed in the late 1880s and 1890s as their popularity grew. A few,

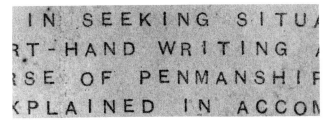

Figure 11.33. EARLY TYPEWRITING was done entirely in capitals, and sometimes in a sans-serif type, as in this 1889 letter from a commercial college advertising instruction in shorthand, typing, and penmanship.

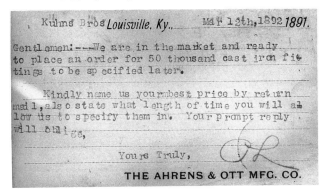

Figure 11.34. FAULTY ALIGNMENT, as in the machine that typed this 1892 postcard, is a problem that can occur over time. Such divergences are among the features that give a machine its individuality and help to distinguish it from others of the same make and model.

such as the Hammond (patented in 1880), had type-wheels (fig. 11.30), but most were type-bar models like the Remington. The latter presented a problem in that the construction required the operator to lift the carriage in order to view the writing line. This was rectified by a series of machines advertised as "visible" typewriters, notably the Columbia Bar-Lock (1888), the Williams (1890), and the Oliver Typewriter (1894; figs. 11.31 and 11.32). Later, "visible" machines operating on the now-familiar front-stroke principle displaced most others—the first significant one being the 1897 Underwood. The L.C. Smith, the Royal, and the front-stroke Remington were among the successful followers.[80]

Many of the first machines typed only in capital letters (fig. 11.33), but in 1878 Remington added the shift-key mechanism, which had two type characters (uppercase and lowercase, to use the printer's terms) mounted on each bar.[81] Alignment was among the early typewriter problems (fig. 11.34) and so was "a certain prejudice against the typewritten letter," but in the 1890s the machine's office potential was fully realized and success was assured (fig. 11.35).[82] The electric typewriter followed, after 1920, and the computerized "word processor" (still featuring Shole's basic key-

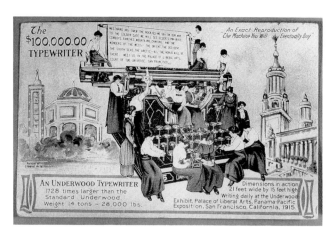

Figure 11.35. The TYPEWRITER ADVERTISEMENT on this old postcard dates from long after the machine was entrenched in the business world. Featured is a giant typewriter "1728 times larger than the Standard Underwood" that was a novelty at a 1915 exposition. Note that only women are shown in attendance.

board arrangement) began to be common in the 1970s.[83]

A "shorthand typewriter" known as Stenotype was invented in 1906 and continues in use—primarily for legislative, conference, and court reporting—as does a similar machine called the "Stenograph." Both employ keyboards and print roman letters in various positions and combinations along a continuous paper tape. This strip automatically folds into the back of the machine.[84]

Handwritten shorthand is not only older than machine shorthand but can be traced back to ancient times. Its earliest form may have been a Greek system used by historians such as Xenophon to record the words of Socrates and other notables. Shorthand was used by the Romans, after 63 B.C., in the form of a system employing some five thousand signs to represent words. It was called *notae Tironianae* (notes of Tiro) after its developer, Marcus Tullius Tiro. He was a learned slave who was freed by Cicero (106-43 B.C.) and became his secretary, preserving the statesman's orations for posterity. Tironian stenography became common throughout the Roman Empire. Written with *styli* on wax tablets that could easily be rubbed smooth for reuse, it continued in use for several centuries.[85]

In later times, stenography (literally, "narrow writing," hence "shorthand") was employed in one or another of its transitory forms to preserve Saint Augustine's sermons, record Shakespeare's plays, and take down President Wilson's speeches. It was also used by Samuel Pepys, who wrote his famous diary in Shelton's Shorthand (and may have been the first to use the term "longhand" to distinguish one form from the other), and by Charles Dickens, who employed the Gurney System in his early years as a Parliamentary reporter.[86]

Modern shorthand stemmed from the development of phonographic systems (the first one was published in 1750), wherein characters were used to represent the *sounds*, rather than the spellings, of words. Sir Isaac Pitman (1813-97) was knighted by Queen Victoria for the system he developed in 1837, and which was brought to America in 1852 by his brother. For his Stenographic Sound-Hand, later called "Phonography" and finally "Pitman's Shorthand," Pitman classified sounds scientifically and arranged his system accordingly. It was characterized by light and shaded consonant strokes, by disjoined dots and dashes to indicate vowels, and divergence of strokes at various angles.[87]

In contrast is the system of Light-Line Phonography, later called "Gregg Shorthand." Devised by John Robert Gregg (1867-1948), it was published in England in 1888 and brought to America in 1893 by Gregg himself. It was more smoothly curvilinear, was based on the slant of longhand, featured vowels formed without pen lifts, and was generally more akin to cursive writing than Pitman's system. Possibly for that reason it came to be the dominant style in shorthand schools around the world.[88]

During the third quarter of the twentieth century, both handwritten shorthand and machine shorthand increasingly gave way to the use of tape recorders, particularly with the development of pocket models. According to one writer, "On the horizon is the futuristic voice-operated typewriter, which, when perfected, will be able to type verbal dictation either directly from a person or from a prerecorded tape."[89]

SELECT BIBLIOGRAPHY

Backhouse, Janet. *The Illuminated Manuscript.* Oxford: Phaidon, 1979.

Degering, Herman. *Lettering: Modes of Writing in Western Europe from Antiquity to the End of the 18th Century.* New York: Pentalic Corp., 1965.

Gaskell, Philip. *A New Introduction to Bibliography.* New York: Oxford Univ. Press, 1972. Treats early handpress printing, bookbinding, etc.

Jackson, Donald. *The Story of Writing.* New York: Taplinger, 1981. A nicely illustrated history of writing from its earliest forms to the present.

Morgan, Marvin, "Handwriting Systems and Penmanship." *Identification News,* July 1985.

Nesbitt, Alexander. *The History and Techniques of Lettering.* 1950. New York: Dover, 1957.

Ogg, Oscar. *The 26 Letters.* New York: Crowell, 1948. A history of the origin and development of the alphabet.

Rendell, Diana J. "The Development of Writing." In *Autographs and Manuscripts: A Collector's Manual,* ed. Edmund Berkeley, Jr., 3-27. New York: Scribner's, 1978.

The Story of the Typewriter, 1873-1923. Herkimer, N.Y.: Herkimer County Historical Society, 1923.

12
The ABC's of Penmanship

Early Writing Masters

The appearance of popular writing books in the sixteenth century resulted from the confluence of two major trends. First, the spread of learning fostered by the Renaissance meant a general increase in reading and writing, and, second, the rising prominence of commerce provided opportunities for those who could successfully wield a pen.

Such writing manuals (called "copybooks" when they have specimens of writing to imitate) first appeared in Italy—the earliest being Sigismondo Fanti's *Theoretica et practica*, published in Venice in 1514, followed by *La operina* by Ludovico degli Arrighi in 1522. Arrighi's text was the first general-instruction manual in *cancellaresca*, or chancery script. Later manuals were issued by Dutch and French writing masters—an example being Pierre Hamon's *Alphabet de l'invention des lettres en diverses escritures*, of 1561.[1]

The copybooks of English masters began to be common in the seventeenth century, facilitated by copperplate engraving.[2] They included Edward Cocker's *The Pen's Transcendencie* (1667), John Seddon's *The Pen-man's Paradis* (1695), and John Ayers's *A Tutor to Penmanship* (1698), among many others. These master scriveners influenced a still larger number of professional penmen, and during the early decades of the eighteenth century English copybooks began to dominate the field.[3]

Among the latter manuals must be mentioned the classic text *The Universal Penman*, by George Bickham, which was actually issued to subscribers in fifty-two installments from 1733 to 1741. Bickham was both a master calligrapher and an engraver, a combination which ensured a proper rendering of the book's 212 plates (fig. 12.1). These were engraved by Bickham from writing specimens produced by him and his fellow writing masters, the following being a partial roster: John Bickham (probably a relative), Willington Clark, William Leekey, Samuel Vaux, Gabriel Brooks, John

Figure 12.1. "THE UNIVERSAL PENMAN," from which this plate (no. 89) was reproduced, was an important eighteenth-century English copybook. As such, it provided alphabets, specimens of script, and examples of pen-flourishing art (note the fish at bottom) for copying. It was issued by the calligrapher-engraver George Bickham in installments from 1733 to 1741.

Figure 12.2. The NEW ENGLAND PRIMER was the first widely used book in colonial American schools. This page is reproduced from an edition printed after 1727.

Figure 12.3. "TOM THUMB ALPHABET" is the name of the little alphabet book containing this entry. While "A was an ARCHER, And shot at a Frog" can be traced back to *A Little Book for Little Children*, published in England in 1702, another entry shows its Americanized form: "K was a King, once of England." Measuring about 6¾ inches square, the hand-colored booklet was published by Sheldon and Company, New York, after 1864.

Day, John Shortland, Richard Morris, Emanuel Austin, and Moses Gratwick.

Some of Bickham's contributors were further identified, such as Nathaniel Dove ("Master of the Academy in Hoxton") and William Kippax ("in Great Russel Street, Bloomsbury"). John Holden signed a plate and added: "To the worthy M.ʳ Joseph Champion, of London, this Plate is humbly Inscrib'd." Champion himself wrote: "Invented, & Written by Joseph Champion, Master of the Boarding School in King's-Head-Court, S.ᵗ Paul's Church-Yard."[4] Champion artistically lettered many of the plates, including those of the scripts shown in appendix 1.

The earliest American writing masters came from England in the seventeenth century and taught secretary, court, italic, and other hands.[5] Like their counterparts in the motherland, many produced copybooks. Among the earliest was the mid-seventeenth-century *Plain and Easy Directions to Faire Writing*, by the Reverend Lewis Hughes. This manual (only a single leaf of which is known) was published in London but "set forth for the benefit of the new planted Vinyards of the Lord Jesus in Virginea, Sommer Islands and New England." It featured *printed* letters which the student was to trace over.[6]

The first American manual to reproduce handwriting was a compendium on various subjects published by Benjamin Franklin and D. Hall. Titled *The American Instructor or Young Man's Best Companion*, it was published in Philadelphia in 1784. The first true copybook originating in America was *The Writing Scholar's Assistant*, published at Worcester, Massachusetts, in 1785 by Isaiah Thomas. It was followed by many others.[7]

Still, it was not the publishing of copybooks that provided American writing masters their livelihood. Rather, it was in the schools that most found gainful employment, putting young "scholars" through their penmanship exercises.

American Schools

Schools of one kind or another were common in New England. Although by 1647 each Massachusetts township was required to operate a school, free public schools were a relative rarity. Typically, colonial children to the age of nine were tutored in a "dame school" conducted by a widow or housewife. She received a small sum for teaching the ABC's, reading, and spelling. These were invariably small schools of a dozen children or fewer, commonly held in a meetinghouse.[8]

The earliest "books" used in such schools consisted of a paddlelike oak board on which was pasted a printed leaf—containing the alphabet, Lord's Prayer, and so on—covered with a thin protective sheet of translucent horn. Such simple items were called "hornbooks" although many were more elaborate productions that eliminated the paper and so with it the horn (and are sometimes called "battledores"):

Hornbooks were often bound in brass, leather, ivory, or silver. Some are made completely of ivory or silver with the letters hand-painted on the ivory or engraved on the silver. Still other hornbooks are framed in silver filigree. Hornbooks of carved English oak have not only hand-carved letters but also typical geometric carving similar to that on Elizabethan furniture. A German hornbook has letters printed in gold. Hornbooks were also stamped on tin, worked in needlework, and stamped with wooden molds from which gingerbread hornbooks were made to be sold at English fairs. A hornbook has been found with the wires and beads of an abacus fastened to its back; another hornbook has the head of a wooden doll at the top of the frame, and an American hornbook with a printed lesson and illustration from a Philadelphia primer of 1821 is framed in wood with a short turned-wood handle. A unique jumping-jack hornbook was made in Germany in the nineteenth century.[9]

Today because hornbooks are scarce and "immensely valuable" they rarely come on the market, and when they do they are usually bought by financially well-endowed institutions.[10]

Hornbooks were succeeded by the cardboard battledore—actually a varnished card or folder printed with alphabet, numerals, and Lord's Prayer, for example, and decorated with illustrations of nursery rhymes or the like. Battledores were forerunners of *The New England Primer,* the first book that saw general use in colonial schools. Printed between 1686 and 1690, the first copies were subsequently reprinted in varying editions over a period of a century and a half, the earliest surviving one having been published in Boston in 1727 (fig. 12.2).[11] *The New England Primer* was followed by other primers (figs. 12.3 and 12.4), spellers (notably Noah Webster's *American Spelling Book,* first issued in 1783 and popularly known as the blue-backed speller), and readers (including the famous McGuffey Readers; they were printed between 1836 and 1895 and later reprinted by Henry Ford and by the American Book Company).[12]

Young ladies attending the dame schools learned needlework, and their repertoire of stitches was presented in the form of a sampler. Stitched on a background of homespun linen, the sampler featured designs, ranging from the simple to the challenging, together with an alphabet, the stitching of which served as a further learning exercise.

Samplers were sewn by poor girls as well as rich, and were of two basic types. The first was a "plain," or "marking," sampler (fig. 12.5), so named because it was a means by which the girl learned how to cross-stitch initials on the family textiles (a practice later transferred to indelible ink). Sometimes the pupil "worked" a second, "fancy" sampler, which typically featured one or more alphabets, together with some pictorial element such as floral designs or a building. Most valuable in today's American market are native, rather than European, "fancy" samplers, signed and dated, the earlier the better.[13]

Figure 12.4. TEACHING ABC's has traditionally been done through a variety of aids, including primers and ABC books, alphabet blocks and cards, and other means. To teach a schoolchild to *pen* the alphabet, the writing master "set the copy" (e.g., placed a row of specimen letters across the top of the copysheets) as shown at the upper right; the example was then imitated by the student, row on row.

The two small primers date from 1848 (*left*) and 1843 (*right*); the *New Primer* was published in New York by Johnstone and Van Norden, 1823; the large primer is missing its front cover but probably dates from the mid-nineteenth century. The cards and ABC book were printed by chromolithography, probably before the turn of the century. The copysheets are signed "Mary A. Kuhl" and dated 1846.

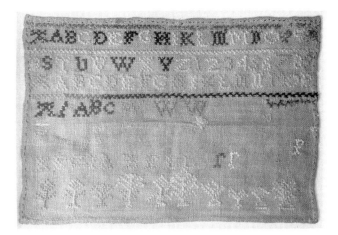

Figure 12.5. "MARKING" SAMPLER. A beginning sampler—such as this early nineteenth-century one, signed "Kezia Bell"—helped prepare a young girl to mark the family textiles. Later she might also "work" a "fancy" sampler.

Such a "fancy" or "fine" sampler would have been produced at a school for young ladies. Few girls, however—even among those whose parents could afford it—continued their education past dame school.[14] Other things were expected—helping at home or even being indentured—prior to a girl's intended marriage.

In contrast, boys often went on to the more highly regarded "wrighting schoole" which—as was said of one in 1667—would "teach children to writte and to keep accounts." That was a private school, but a public one was operating in Boston in 1684. Referred to as the Writing School in Queen Street, it only admitted boys seven years of age or older, and then only if they were already able to read. Two other writing schools flourished in Boston, the North Writing School (established in 1700) and the South Writing School (1719), both continuing (after a brief interruption with the outbreak of war in 1775) until 1789.[15]

Figure 12.6. "A COLONIAL SCHOOL-ROOM" (as envisioned by an artist for an 1884 primary history) was conducted under firm discipline. The master of the "writing school" provided the quill pens, as shown by the supply kept on the schoolmaster's desk.

Figure 12.7. This PRACTICE ALPHABET, penned in an old record book about 1840, was amateurishly done, probably by a young "scholar." Ostensibly a round-hand script, it has "shaded" strokes that are especially unsystematic.

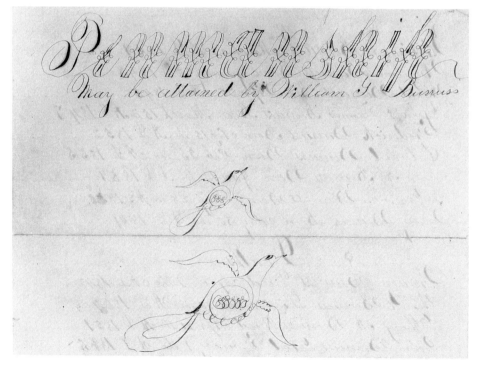

Figure 12.8. This PENMANSHIP EXERCISE, including a beginner's attempt at pen flourishing, may have derived from a self-instruction manual. The tremulous lines result from being slowly drawn. Penned on the back of a handwritten family record, it dates from the early 1870s.

The writing-school master provided, or at least cut, the pupils' quill pens and saw that they were held correctly and that the student sat properly at the desk with his ruled paper or writing book before him (fig. 12.6).

> Then came the demonstration of the strokes of the letters in due order, of the letters themselves, and eventually of the letters joined into words and the words arranged in improving sentences that are still remembered in the pejorative term "copybook maxims." The master wrote the model for the lesson at the top of a fresh page in the learner's writing book—this was called setting the copy. It was then the pupil's business to reproduce the copy as nearly as he could, studying each thick and thin, every curve and join, line after line to the bottom of the page under correction of the master.[16]

Typical of later writing schools was one advertised in a New York periodical in 1796. The advertisement specifies penmanship among the subjects taught at "A Day and Evening School," although it does not state the master's qualifications. In the same publication, however, a lengthy advertisement for "The New York Commercial, Classical and Mathematical School" touted the accomplishments of William Milns, author of the *Penman's Repository*, whose "Running-hand copies" would be available to students. As the advertisement noted, "an elegant and ready command of the pen" was "absolutely necessary to every one who aspires eminently to succeed in a Commercial and growing country."[17] To such end the writing master was willing to contribute.

Writing-System Instruction

In 1791 John Jenkins of Boston published his *Art of Writing*, which remedied the lack of an effective *system* of teaching beginning writing. Jenkins's solution to the problem was to discover, from a "critical investigation," that "nearly the whole alphabet was composed of six principal strokes or lines." Thus Jenkins replaced the old writing masters' method (having students copy model letters) with a systemized approach that required learning basic strokes, then combining them to form letters.

Jenkins asserted that his system was "so contrived, that young gentlemen and ladies, who have not been under advantages to learn to write, may immediately become, not only their own instructors, but instructors of others." As one authority remarks concerning this almost missionary approach: "This was utter heresy, and Jenkins had only himself to thank for opening the

gates to a crowd of self-annointed professors of penmanship."[18]

These self-taught scriveners multiplied in the nineteenth century, many serving as schoolmasters at greater or lesser institutions. Others became "roaming instructors who traveled throughout the countryside holding penmanship classes in private homes or in the village school or setting up shop on a street corner to write flourished calling cards."[19] Some of the amateurish products produced by students of this period are shown in figures 12.7 and 12.8.

Like their English counterparts, American writing masters seem to have been perpetually engaged in squabbling over the methodology of writing instruction.[20] Some idea of the atmosphere can be gleaned from Benjamin Franklin Foster's little manual *Writing and Writing Masters: the Principles of the Former Developed, and the Fallacies of the Latter Exposed* (1854). Snorts Foster: "In no department of the diversified business of education have there been so many puerile attempts at improvement as in that of teaching children to write. It is impossible to say, with any degree of certainty, what number of 'new and easy systems' have been issued from the press during the last fifty years, but the list would astonish any one who had not investigated the subject. It is a fact, however, that the art of writing is less understood and worse taught at the present day than it was a century ago, notwithstanding the number and skill of its elucidators."[21] Foster also stated:

> The most elaborate, and by far the most useful work which has appeared on the subject of penmanship, in any age or country, was published in 1804, at Salem, Massachusetts. The author, Henry Dean, taught writing with the most distinguished success for many years at Salem, and subsequently established himself as a writing-master in New York. . . .
>
> Dean, in common with Butterworth, Guoinlock, Langford, Tompkins, Bland, Carstairs, Paton, Hemm, and all other teachers of celebrity, insists upon the practice of large text hand, as a preliminary step in the process of teaching writing. "Men long accustomed to old habits," says Dean, "quit them with reluctance; and with the prejudiced it will be a sufficient objection that this is a new system. But hoary-headed error is not on that account venerable, nor has long-continued absurdity any prescriptive claim to respect."[22]

Of a rival of Dean, Foster asserted: "The only novel system worthy of notice, is that published by Joseph Carstairs, of London, in 1814. The inventor of this marvellous system claims great credit for originality; but these claims, as I shall show, rest on a very sandy foundation."[23] After a lengthy analysis of Carstair's system, Foster concludes: "Here then is the distinction

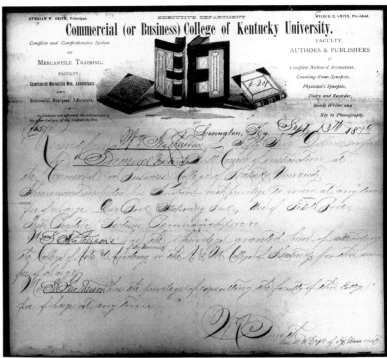

Figure 12.9. PLATT ROGERS SPENCER (1800-64) was an educator and calligrapher known for developing and teaching "Spencerian" penmanship, of which his flourished signature is a specimen. It dominated in the latter half of the nineteenth century. This engraved portrait appeared as a frontispiece in *Spencerian Key to Practical Penmanship,* by his son H.C. Spencer (New York: Ivison, Blakeman, Taylor, 1877).

Figure 12.10. SPENCERIAN SCRIPT was appropriately used for this business-college receipt of 1879, which lists "Tuition . . . Stationery, Ink, Use of Text Books, Tests, Practice, Lectures, Penmanship, &c, &c." The signature "W.R. Smith" is also in Spencerian; compare with Spencer's in figure 12.9.

between the *old* and the *new* systems: Dean starts from the fingers and hand, and gradually unites the free motion of the arm: Carstairs starts from the *shoulder,* and descends to the hand and fingers;—in other words, puts the 'cart before the horse!' The systems published by Dolbear, Root, Badlam, Dunton, French, etc., are simply modifications of Carstairs' plan, with the important difference, however, that these wiseacres reject the initiatory process of large-hand *in toto!* " [24]

The upshot of all the competing systems (as discussed in the previous chapter) was a relatively new, essentially American script. It was known as "Spencerian" after its major developer, Platt Rogers Spencer (fig. 12.9).

Spencer (1800-64) was the descendant of the English native John Sponsor, who settled in Massachusetts in 1636. According to a brief biography, "Young Spencer was always passionately fond of penmanship, writing in his early years upon anything procurable—sand, snow, ice, brick, bark, the fly-leaves of his mother's Bible, etc., and by permission of a kind old cobbler, upon the leather in his shop." [25] Spencer taught his first writing

class at age fifteen. Aspirations for college and the ministry were thwarted by alcoholism, but he was reportedly cured by a devoted wife after they "secluded themselves in the forests of Geneva, O." He held minor country offices, compiled a local history, became an abolitionist, and devoted himself to "universal freedom and education"—in particular to the teaching of penmanship (by class instruction, and with various publications of 1848-63) and the founding of business colleges (work carried on by his sons who also published texts on penmanship). [26] Spencer made "Spencerian" synonymous with "penmanship" and strongly influenced the systems that followed (figs. 12.10 and 12.11).

Among the advocates of self-instruction was Thomas E. Hill (fig. 12.12), whose "Self-Instructor in Penmanship" comprised the first part of his compendium *Hill's Manual of Social and Business Forms: A Guide to Correct Writing* (issued in various editions beginning in 1873). Hill had this to say about the then-current status of penmanship:

Two styles of penmanship have been in use, and each in turn has been popular with Americans in the past fifty years; one known as the round hand, the other as the angular writing. The objection attaching to each is, that the round hand, while having the merit of legi-

Figure 12.11. COPYBOOKS provided specimens for the novice penman to imitate. Most later ones had a line of copy printed across the top of each page, the remainder being lined for use by the copyist.

First column, from top: 1880 "Indiana Commercial Writing Book"; a "Columbia Practical System Vertical Writing" book of about the 1890s; and a "Spencerian Penmanship Vertical Edition" manual of 1895.

Second column, from top: two Palmer Method teacher's manuals, 1931 (*left*) and 1925, and a "Palmer Method of Business Writing" copybook of 1917; a "Zaner Method" manual 144, copyright 1915, and a "Zaner & Bloser Method Writing" manual 96, copyrighted in 1909; and a "Muscular Writing" booklet of 1920 by W.S. Benson and Company, which sold for nine cents.

Third column, from top: "Champion Method" business writing manual, 1921; an open copybook, showing a completed page; and a "cursive" writing book of 1951.

Figure 12.12. THOMAS E. HILL, educator and penman, was the author of an 1873 business compendium featuring a segment, "Self-Instructor in Penmanship." Hill produced the excellent example of pen flourishing shown later in figure 12.34. Note Hill's Spencerian signature.

Figure 12.13. POSITIONS IN WRITING—both incorrect (*upper right*) and correct—were illustrated in *Parson's Hand-Book of Forms: A Compendium of Business and Social Rules* (1882; Edgefield, Tenn.: J.E. White, 1906), 19.

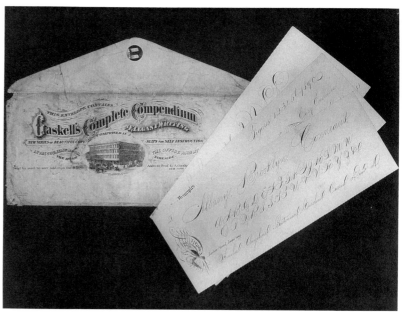

Figure 12.15. GASKELL'S COPY SLIPS were part of his "Complete Compendium" intended for self-instruction in penmanship. It included the assortment of slips, an instruction manual, an "ornamental sheet," and a case—all "sent by mail to any address for $1.00."

Figure 12.14. G.A. GASKELL did much to promote self-instruction in penmanship with his mail-order text and copy slips. Gaskell, a noted practitioner of pen-flourishing art, signed his name, as did many of his fellow penmen, with Spencerian flourishes.

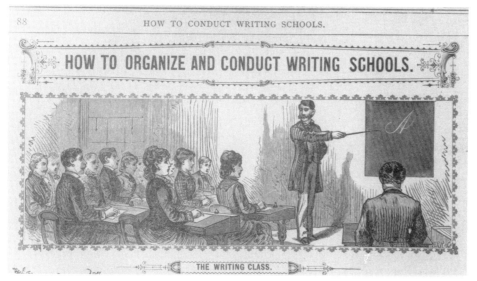

Figure 12.17. A PALMER METHOD button, like another Palmer one picturing a quill and scroll, was given to one who "mastered" the requisite drills in the Palmer Method manual. The button measures about ⅞ inch in diameter.

Figure 12.16. CONDUCTING WRITING SCHOOLS. In his zeal to promote penmanship, G.A. Gaskell not only provided self-instruction in the art but taught how to set up and teach penmanship classes, from securing a suitable schoolroom with blackboard, to putting up posters "in the smaller villages," collecting tuition, and teaching a twelve-lesson course. In his 1884 *Gaskell's Compendium of Forms*, from which this illustration is taken, he admiringly describes one of the greatest of such instructors: "Spencer, the originator of the Spencerian System, was, without doubt, the most successful itinerant of his time. . . . His arrival in a village was heralded as the event of the year."

bility, requires too much time in its execution; and the angular, though rapidly written, is wanting in legibility. The best teachers of penmanship, of late, have obviated the objections attaching to these different styles, by combining the virtues of both in one, producing a semi-angular penmanship, possessing the legibility of the round hand along with the rapid execution of the angular.

To the Duntons, of Boston, and the late P.R. Spencer, as the founders of the semi-angular penmanship, are the people indebted for the beautiful system of writing now in general use in the schools throughout the country.[27]

Such self-instructors employed illustrations to show what the early writing masters would have demonstrated in the classrooms—for example, how to hold the pen and the correct and incorrect positions of the body (fig. 12.13).[28] As well, they provided analyses of the individual letters, and set forth alphabets and other specimens for copying.

One of the greatest purveyors of such instructional material was G.A. Gaskell (fig. 12.14). In the 1870s and 1880s he was issuing Gaskell's "Compendium of Penmanship," which consisted of instructional book, copy slips, "ornamental sheet," and case (fig. 12.15). Gaskell also published a periodical, *The Penman's Gazette and Business Educator.* His 920-page *Gaskell's Compendium of Forms* was sold by subscription and went through numerous editions. It not only featured penmanship (in addition to bookkeeping, letter writing, business forms, and countless other subjects), but also taught "How to Organize and Conduct Writing Schools" (fig. 12.16).[29] This shows him to be a true disciple of Jenkins.

The successors to the Spencerian system were the popular systems devised by A.N. Palmer, Zaner-Bloser, and others. Austin Norman Palmer (1859-1927) was a noted American penman and educator who developed the system of handwriting bearing his name (discussed in the previous chapter), introducing it in 1888. The Palmer Method "employed muscles of the forearm in producing a simple rotary style" and was widely taught in schools in the United States in the early 1900s.[30] His A.N. Palmer Company published copybooks for grade-school students and Palmer Method teachers' manuals, as well as other publications, including *The Palmer Method of Business Writing* (fig. 12.11) and the periodical *American Penman,* of which Palmer was editor. The company also issued "Palmer Method" buttons (fig. 12.17) and certificates of proficiency, with the name filled in, of course, in Palmer-style handwriting and bearing the facsimile signature of A.N. Palmer.[31]

The Zaner Method of Penmanship is still taught by the Zaner-Bloser Company of Columbus, Ohio— "Handwriting Publishers Since 1895." That date

marked a new era in the partnership of Charles Paxton Zaner (d. 1918) and Elmer Ward Bloser (1865-1929). They had met as students at a penmanship school, where they later served together as instructors. Before becoming partners in 1891, Bloser taught at two other schools (including the Spencerian Business College in Cleveland at the request of Platt R. Spencer, Jr.), and Zaner had founded the Zanerian Art College in 1888. That school soon became the Zanerian College of Penmanship, operated by the Zaner-Bloser Company, which over subsequent years published writing manuals, manufactured and sold its patented "finger-fitting" penholders, and trained young men and women in "arm movement writing," engrossing, and illuminating. Prior to his death in a "train mishap" in 1918, Zaner had become a renowned penman and practitioner of pen-flourishing art. Bloser continued the company's work, including publishing the *Business Educator,* until his own death, when he was succeeded by his sons.[32]

Two forms of handwriting are typically taught in schools. *Manuscript* writing is actually hand printing (using capital and small letters), taught in the first two grades; *cursive* (or connected) writing (such as the Zaner or any of about twenty other systems) is usually taught from the third grade. The emphasis is on writing that is both easily read and easily written.[33]

Artistic Penmanship

Systems like the Palmer and Zaner methods, and the Spencerian before, were the products of trends toward a more easily rendered hand (while retaining legibility). As one man expressed his desire for such a script in 1828, "I should be glad if some engraver would publish a set of small or running hand copies—a free, slanting, easy running hand, with very little difference between up or down strokes, fit for letter writing; I am confident, if made known there would be a great sale for them."[34] The wish for the script to exhibit little contrast between strokes was based on the fact that producing the consistent up-thin, down-thick strokes of round hand was a slow process, one more suited to artistry than to the practical requirements of the business world.

Indeed, it was for purely aesthetic reasons that some of round hand's distinctive features—flourishes on the capitals, and selective "shading"—were retained for Spencerian script before ultimately being eliminated from the modern systems. And so today, wherever artistic concerns are preeminent, as in engraved invitations and many other commercial and graphic-arts applications, flourishes and shadings may well be resurrected.

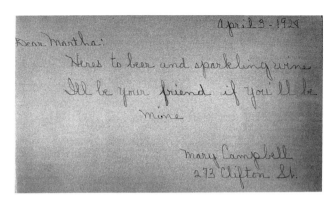

Figure 12.18. RULER WRITING is occasionally seen, as in this 1928 schoolgirl's autograph album. Observe the unnatural, straight-edge perfection of the bottoms of the letters, caused by the pen being drawn against the ruler, which was held in place for each line. The tails of the letters were added subsequently.

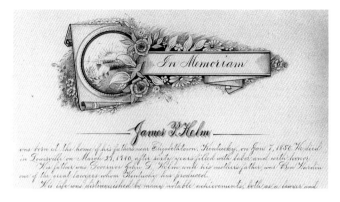

Figure 12.19. PROFESSIONAL ENGROSSING. This memorial declaration (commissioned in 1910 by a bar association for a lawyer's widow) features a combination of skillful calligraphy with artistic drawing (see the following figure).

Figure 12.20. ENGROSSER'S "SIGNATURE." The master penman who calligraphed the memorial declaration shown in the previous figure signed with this artistic trademark. He was listed in a Louisville, Kentucky, city directory at the time, under "Card Writers" as "M.R. Teesdale"; his was the only such listing.

Still, in an era when such ornate features are no longer taught, the old writing—even decidedly amateurish efforts like those shown earlier (figs. 12.7 and 12.8)—may seem elegant to those unfamiliar with such script. At the same time, contemporary penmanship may seem undesirably "plain," even when rendered with skill. Thus the impulse to create something with aesthetic appeal (while avoiding shadings and flourishes) could be expressed in unusual forms. An example would be the stylized writing illustrated in figure 12.18: a combined backhand and ruler-written script, it was produced by a 1920s schoolgirl for a friend's autograph album.

Even in the heyday of the great writing masters, the degree of embellishment was often one of preference. For example, about 1616 the English master Martin Billingsley described as "unnaturall" any "strange, borrowed or inforc'd tricks and knots in or about writing other then [sic] with the celerity of the hand" (i.e., with speed).[35] Yet Edward Cocker (1631-76), whose work tended toward the opposite extreme, was unrepentant:

> Some sordid sotts
> Cry downe rare knotts,
> But art shall shine
> And envie pine
> And still my pen shall flourish.[36]

The gulf between the two extremes regarding embellishment can be attributed partly to individual taste and partly, perhaps, to the intended purpose—the handwriting of a letter, say, versus the engrossing, or calligraphy, of a diploma or certificate that is meant for display (figs. 12.19 and 12.20).

One wishing to imitate the work of the earlier penmen must become aware of how the type of pen had a direct bearing on the writing it produced. An example (as discussed in chap. 1), would be the use of the "broad" (or chisel-edged) pen for certain styles of lettering. Nineteenth-century attempts to reproduce the thick and thin strokes of medieval writing (Gothic, for example, which has a long tradition of use for diplomas and the like) were unsuccessful because penmen were trying to imitate the strokes with pointed pens. It was not until this century, when the great calligrapher Edward Johnston determined how the medieval quill had actually been cut, that the way was paved for the current revival of interest in calligraphy.[37]

Most modern, popular books on the subject are confined to the use of the broad pen.[38] They illustrate how to hold it at an almost constant angle of forty-five degrees so that, for instance, the left stroke of the *A* will be thin, the right one thick (fig. 11.14).[39] Unlike the thick and thin strokes of round hand, which require an alternating light and heavy pressure on a pointed pen, those of such styles as italic (*cancellaresca*) or "Old English" (Gothic) largely result from the shape of the broad pen itself.[40] Such styles are thus relatively easy to learn.

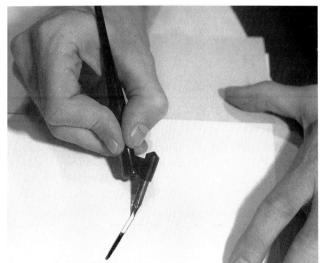

Figures 12.21-12.24. USING THE OBLIQUE PENHOLDER is the secret to producing round-hand script.

12.21 (*top left*). Hold the "oblique" penholder with the right hand as shown (resting the hand on a blotter or card to protect the sheet of paper from perspiration or soiling) and hold the paper with the left hand. Since the holder cannot be dipped into a narrow-mouthed india ink bottle, one can use an old Skrip ink bottle which has been cleaned and filled with suitable ink to take advantage of the "top well" feature.

12.22 (*top right*). Very lightly push the pen upward to produce a hairline stroke, yet not so lightly as to allow the pen to skip. If the pen snags, try dulling the point slightly or replace the pen with an older, more worn one; or use a harder finish paper or adopt a lighter touch.

12.23 (*bottom left*). On downstrokes, exert pressure on the pen to cause the nibs to separate and thus produce a "shaded" stroke. Practice hairlines and shades, then—with a round-hand alphabet as a model—practice making letters and then words.

12.24 (*bottom right*). "Ink failure" (note the two "nib tracks") allows the split in the pen to be clearly seen. The serious student should consult a specialized text on the subject.

$$ABCDEFGHIJKL$$
$$MNOPQRSTUV$$
$$WXYZ \quad Roundhand$$
$$abcdefghijklmnopqrst$$
$$uvwxyz \quad 1234567890$$

Figure 12.25. This ROUND-HAND ALPHABET was lettered by the author just as shown in figures 12.21-12.24. See also the similar alphabets in Appendix 1.

Figure 12.26 (*right*). PEN/SCRIPT VARIETY. The choice of pen must depend on the type of script desired. The three basic categories of pen have here been used to create lettering expressive of various times and moods, all taken from my commercial work.

The chisel-edge or "broad" pen was used for the entire lines of "Courier," "Spring," "Celtic," "Colloquium," and "Honors"; it was also used for "March 22-24" in the bottom line. The pointed nib was, of course, used for the round-hand script of "Victorian."

The stylographic pen was used for all outlining, and a round ("Speedball" brand "B"-nib) pen was used for "Star" and "Computers." The heavy strokes of "Computers" and the shadows of "Grand Opening" were outlined and filled in with the stylographic pen.

Figure 12.27. COMMERICAL LETTERING often combines special-effect styles with pictorial elements to create logos, headings for posters or advertisements, and similar uses. In these commercial examples I attempted to harmonize content and treatment.

While the lettering above was all rendered by hand, for lettering that is to be reproduced by printing, transfer sheets of rub-on letters, available from art stores, are often used. They come in a variety of styles, from printers' typefaces to special-effect and calligraphic lettering. The stipple shading of the comedy/tragedy masks and the wavy-line background of "Subs & Salads" were also done by hand, using a stylographic pen; however, the mechanically halftoned areas of "film" and "Pavement" were done with commercially printed transfer overlays, also available from art stores. Some such means of rendering gray areas for a black-and-white printing plate is necessary.

Figure 12.28. LETTERING AND DESIGN. An appropriate arrangement of lettering and other elements—called "layout" by graphic artists—is a challenge that must be met in order to produce posters, advertisements, or the like that are eye-catching, readable, and aesthetically pleasing. A good design with mediocre lettering will triumph over excellent lettering placed in a poor layout. I did the examples shown here as posters or flyers, except for the "Student's Guide," which was a booklet cover.

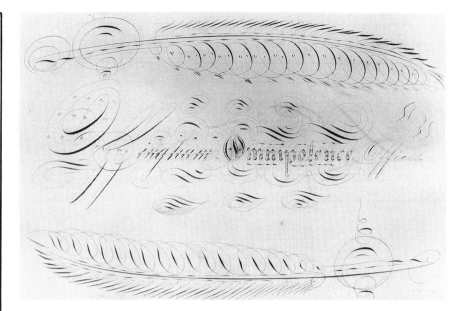

Figures 12.29-12.32. MASTER PENMAN'S PROMOTIONALS. New England writing master Horace Jones advertised penmanship classes in 1852.

12.29 (*top left*). Jones's flyer was posted in the Manchester, N.H., vicinity to advertise his writing lessons. So that prospective students could judge the quality of his own penmanship, like the examples in figures 12.30-12.32, he promised, "Specimens may be seen at the Post Office."

12.30 (*top right*). A pen-flourished quill—like the two that frame this round-hand and Gothic lettering—was a popular subject for calligraphic art, since the quill was emblematic of penmanship.

12.31 (*center right*). Flowers and birds, including the swan, were other popular subjects for pen flourishing by masters like Horace Jones. Flourished initials, like the *N*'s of "Names" and "Namesake," as well as penned configurations (sometimes called "dingbats") were also common.

12.32 (*bottom right*). A detail of Jones's work reveals the graceful lines that characterize skilled pictorial calligraphy, although his examples do not match those of the greatest masters.

Position of the Hand in Flourishing.

Figure 12.33. INSTRUCTIONS FOR FLOURISHING, such as this illustration of how to hold the pen, were common in late-nineteenth-century compendiums (like Thomas E. Hill's 1875 *Manual of Social & Business Forms*) as part of their treatment of penmanship. Stated Hill, in the caption to this engraving: "In executing broad sweeps with the pen, and assuming a position that will give greatest command of the hand in flourishing, the position of the pen in the hand should be reversed [from that used in writing]; the end of the penholder pointing *from* the left shoulder, the pen pointing towards the body, the holder being held between the thumb and two first fingers, as shown above."

Another example of the pen's effect on writing concerns the rendering of round hand (and, to a lesser degree, the later Spencerian script). Originally, the natural curvature of the left-wing quill, placed in the right hand, compensated for the forward slant of the script. But the holders used for the later metal pens lacked this feature, being straight, and so the hand had to be shifted to an awkward angle.[41] As a consequence Sampson Mordan and William Brockedon obtained a patent about 1831 for an "oblique" steel pen (i.e., one angled to the right). One satisfied user stated at the time: "Messrs. Mordan and Co.'s pen supplies a perfect remedy for this defect, for the oblique direction of the slit being that in which the writing usually slopes or leans, at an angle of about thirty-five degrees, both nibs are brought equally down upon the paper, the writer is not confined to any particular position, but may use the pen freely and without the restraint of attitude directed by teachers of writing."[42]

A better solution was to create an oblique *holder* so that any commonly available pen could be used. Such an implement was referred to in an 1893 story about the World's Columbian Exposition: "But on their way out, they stopped long enough for Harry to have his name written by a woman card-writer, who used a pen set

Figure 12.34. BEAUTIFUL FLOURISHING, as in this specimen by Thomas E. Hill, depends on the elements of curvature, arrangement, and contrast. Note that two *heavy* lines never cross.

'Skew-shaw' [at an angle] on its handle. She added his residence—the State only—and the date. It cost him five cents."[43] The oblique holder—specifically recommended for round-hand script in an instructional text—is shown being used to pen the script in figures 12.21-12.24; a round-hand alphabet produced by this technique is shown in figure 12.25.[44]

In addition to the "broad" and pointed pens, which produce different types of contrasting strokes, pens like the ballpoint and stylographic pen yield lines of relatively uniform thickness. Consequently the stylographic pen is much used by graphic artists in outlining, ruling borders, drawing and filling in certain letter forms, doing illustrations, and so on. For heavier uniform-width strokes, borders, and so on, the Hunt Pen Company's "Speedball" B-series nib or similar pen is commonly used.[45]

Figures 12.26 through 12.28 illustrate the use of assorted letter forms. All were produced by the pens described above, ranging from the ancient to the modern, and were hand lettered by the author for various

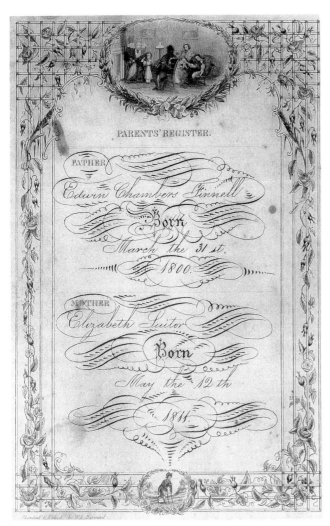

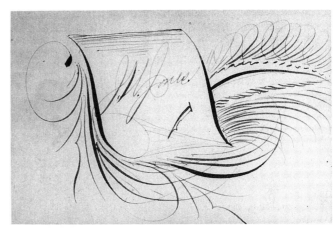

Figure 12.35. This FLOURISHED BIBLE RECORD represents an attempt to adorn the treasured names and dates in an appropriate fashion. Close inspection of this mid-nineteenth-century example shows tremulous hairlines that betray their slowly drawn nature.

Figure 12.36. A CALLIGRAPHIC CALLING CARD of the Spencerian period features a pen-flourished design of a scroll pierced by a quill. The card measures only 1¹¹⁄₁₆ by 3¼ inches.

Figure 12.37. GOOD AMATEUR FLOURISHING is exhibited in this signed and dated calligraphic bird, but observe the crossing of heavy strokes. It was penned in an 1880s autograph album.

clients. They include logos, other special-effect lettering, poster designs, and the like.

Representing great penmanship skill are calligraphic drawings produced by pen flourishing—also known as "the art of ornate pictorial calligraphy," "ornamental pen drawing," and "Spencerian Work."[46]

The latter term is actually a misnomer, since flourishing art long antedates Spencer. In fact it developed alongside round hand and was common by the seventeenth century, as shown by the work of Cocker and others.[47] It continued in the eighteenth century in texts like Bickham's *The Universal Penman*, which reproduced not only ornately flourished borders and dingbats, but also graceful swans, fish, cupids, and other intricate pictorial configurations.

The nineteenth century saw an increase in pen flourishing, partly attributable to a proliferation of writing teachers (figs. 12.29-12.32) and "lesser itinerant penmen," as well as to copybooks like *The Penman's Paradise* of 1848.[48] This book's scant fourteen pages nevertheless provided examples of flourished initials, flowers, birds, and fish.[49] Other texts followed, such as Gaskell's and Hill's, featuring instructional illustrations (fig. 12.33) and flourished art for copying (like that by Hill himself, given in fig. 12.34).[50]

Novice penmen tried their hands at the difficult art with mixed results. An example shown earlier (fig. 12.8) features tremulously penned birds that could best be described as resembling dead ducks. Respectable amateur examples include the Bible record shown in figure 12.35 and the calling card in figure 12.36. A more ambitious effort, the bird shown in figure 12.37, lacks the perfection of professional examples but still elicits praise.

Flourishing art continued into the twentieth century but was becoming anacronistic. As handwriting eliminated the flourishes and shaded strokes that also comprised pictorial calligraphy, the latter was left looking increasingly dated. And when the ballpoint displaced the traditional pen, an era in the history of penmanship had finally come to a close.

SELECT BIBLIOGRAPHY

Bickham, George. *The Universal Penman*. 1741. New York: Dover, 1954. Classic eighteenth-century penmanship book with engraved plates of alphabets, pen-flourished pictures, and so on.

Lupfer, E.A. *Fascinating Pen Flourishing*. Columbus, Ohio: Zaner-Bloser, 1951. Republished as *Ornate Pictorial Calligraphy*. New York: Dover, 1982.

Nash, Ray. *American Writing Masters and Copybooks: History and Bibliography through Colonial Times*. Boston: Colonial Society of Massachusetts, 1959.

———. *American Penmanship, 1800-1850*. Worchester, Mass.: American Antiquarian Society, 1969.

Whalley, Joyce Irene. *The Student's Guide to Western Calligraphy: An Illustrated Survey*. Boulder, Colo.: Shambhala, 1984.

13

Written Documents

Documents and Desks

In a legal sense, a document—from the Latin *documentum*, originally "a lesson" or "example"—is anything which can provide evidence or proof and is also written or can otherwise be "read"—a soldier-artist's sketches of a battle, for example. The term usually refers, however, to printed or handwritten texts which can provide information bearing on some subject.[1]

The related term "record" (Latin, *recordari*, "to recall to mind"), is often applied to that which preserves something permanently in memory. Examples would be such "documents" as the carved inscriptions on Roman monuments, although *archival* records are usually meant. Thus an old diary, lodged in a university library collection might be characterized as representing, say, a "record" of an early New England village. In a more specific sense, records are legal or administrative documents preserved as permanent accounts of the transactions they describe. Examples include a business's carbon copies of its typewritten letters, and official duplicates of deeds hand copied by a county court clerk into weighty "blank books."[2]

At the desk (or some improvised equivalent) have been written these documents of our past. It was there that pen and ink and paper were brought together in the act of writing—composing a letter, posting entries in a ledger, or drafting a will. In fact, writing desks (the term is not a redundancy: there were *sewing* desks, for example) evolved as a means of combining a support for writing and a container for stationery.

Whereas the desk of the Middle Ages was essentially a workbench-easel used by professional scribes for producing their illuminated pages, as writing became more common, the household desk evolved with the Bible box or writing box.[3] Its early form did not assert its intended purpose, since it was only a flat-topped container for writing materials (fig. 13.1). Some of these boxes, however, contained small pigeonholes, and with the addition of a slanted lid came the recognition, in

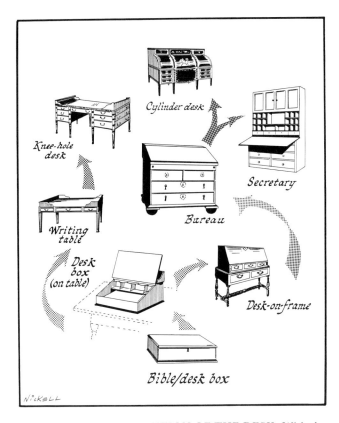

Figure 13.1. The EVOLUTION OF THE DESK. With the addition of a sloping lid, the writing box (*bottom*) combined the essential features of a desk: a surface for writing and a container for writing materials. From this desk box other forms developed.

their external design, of their true purpose. These desk boxes were common throughout the seventeenth century.[4]

Later in the century the box was given its own support, and with such desks-on-frame the desk became a separate piece of furniture. It was eventually made as a single unit, like the one used by Nathaniel Hawthorne, shown in figure 13.2.[5] Such a desk sometimes had a shelf beneath or, more commonly, a

147

Figure 13.2. HAWTHORNE'S DESK. Often called a "schoolmaster's desk," this type, which evolved from the desk-on-frame, was also used by storekeepers and others. This one was used by the great novelist while he held a position in the customhouse at Salem, Massachusetts, from 1846 to 1849. (Illustration from Albert Bushnell Hart, *How Our Grandfathers Lived*, New York: Macmillan, 1938, p. 261.)

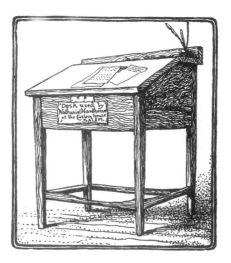

OVER **4000** IN USE.
THE **NEEDHAM**

Type-Writing Cabinet and Office Desk Combined.

The advantages of our Desks are that they can be adjusted to every known type-writing machine. We supply them to fit the **REMINGTON, CALIGRAPH AND HAMMOND.** By patented mechanical construction they can be changed from Typewriter Desk to Office Desk instantly. ARE ORNAMENTAL. Are dust-proof when closed. Are solid and substantial, and without exception the best type-writing desks made. Over **4000** now in use. Used in the offices of The Century, Harper & Brothers, Youth's Companion, and other first-class offices. 6 styles of desks. Address for Catalogue

CLOSED AS DESK.

The **NEEDHAM CO.** 292 Broadway, N.Y.

Figure 13.3. ROLLTOP DESKS derived from the French cylinder desk and became popular in the late nineteenth century in America. This undated advertisement in my collection is probably from the 1890s.

drawer.[6] There documents could be stored: tied in a packet or kept in a box.

As early as 1660 was invented the *escritoire*, or *bureau*, (from the French term for the woolen cloth, *bure*, with which it was covered), although it did not become common until about 1700. The bureau—simply a desk atop a chest of drawers—continues to be a standard form. It was a forerunner of the secretary—a desk surmounted by a bookcase or similar unit—and later types. With their pigeonholes and assortment of drawers, these desks usually served as their owners' offices at a time when there was relatively little paperwork. Some desks, such as those of the late-eighteenth-century Chippendale style, even had a secret compartment, used for storing important documents.

Another type of desk that derived from the *escritoire* was the cylinder desk (*secrétaire a cylindre*), a French invention of about 1750 (fig. 13.1). It was, in turn, the forerunner of the American rolltop desk, which became popular in the late nineteenth century. Some rolltop desks were massive, with expanses of pigeonholes and other compartments, used for filing an increasing amount of paperwork (fig. 13.3).[7]

Along a second, major evolutionary line, the ordinary table obviously gave rise to the specialized writing table, which was in turn the forerunner of the kneehole-type desk. The one shown (fig. 13.1) was used by George Washington from 1789 to 1790.[8] In a version with *columns* of drawers (the lower ones usually designed to hold file folders and so replace pigeonholes) and its rear opening covered by a "modesty panel," it became the standard office desk. It was known as a "pedestal" desk because of the columns.[9] In use, it was

typically graced with a "desk set" of matching pieces, like the brass group shown in figure 13.4.

Such, at least, is a basic outline of the desk's evolution. Its progenitor—the desk box itself—never really disappeared, but instead became the portable, or lap, desk that was common in the eighteenth and nineteenth centuries. Typically, these desks were boxlike models so designed that when opened they provided a sloping writing surface. They usually featured compartments for pens, traveling inkwell and matching sander, stationery, and (after 1840) stamps. Among the popular Victorian varieties were those of "Turnbridge ware" (i.e., wood decorated with intricate veneer mosaics, an art form that originated in 1720) (figs. 13.5-13.7).[10]

The Bible box, or desk box, was also the basis for a variety of later writing boxes, including those pictured in figure 13.8, as well as writing kits (fig. 13.9). Of course some pocket-size kits, like that shown in figure 13.10, took other forms.

Among the desks which may not appear to fall readily into either of the two main divisions are the common school variety shown in figures 13.11 and 13.12.[11] In their basic form, a combining of table and chair features with stowage space for writing materials, they harken back to early types; note the pen ledge, special hole for inkwell, and the shelf for books, copy sheets, and other papers and materials.

Indeed, the fact that desk boxes were known in ancient China and Egypt demonstrates that the history of the desk and that of the written document are interwoven.[12] As the one became more common and ceased

Figure 13.4. A DESK SET, like this one of brass, often graced the top of a desk from the end of the nineteenth century to the middle of the twentieth.

Clockwise from center: inkstand, stamp box, calendar, letter holder, and blotter. The items are displayed on a desk pad of blotting paper.

Figure 13.5. This LADY AT A LAP DESK, perusing a letter, represents what would have been a familiar Victorian scene. Lap desks were a folding version of the slant-top desk box.

Figure 13.6. LAP DESKS typically folded for travel or storage and had compartments for paper, pens, and inkwell. Early ones also featured matching sanders, and models after 1840 often had stamp compartments. Shown with the oak box at left are a wood-veneer box (*right front*) and a painted wooden box with a chromolithographed paper appliqué.

Figure 13.7. The "McCLELLAN GIFT WRITING DESK," which sold for only twenty-five cents, was linked to the popularity of the famous Union general and Democratic rival of President Lincoln. Described as a "portable writing-desk" it could have been similar to ones in either the previous or the following photograph.

The McClellan Gift Writing-Desk.

Something New for Agents.

Something New for Agents.

A portable writing-desk, containing three kinds of the following articles: Writing paper, envelopes, pen, pencil, pen-holder, blotting-paper, and a bottle of ink. EACH DESK CONTAINS A GIFT OF JEWELRY, ECLIPSING ALL AND EVERY GIFT JEWELRY ARTICLES OFFERED TO THE PUBLIC.

The retail price for the McClellan Gift Writing-Desk IS ONLY **25** CENTS! Agents wanted all over the country. For particulars address, with stamp, W. H. CATELY, 102 Nassau Street, New York City.

Figure 13.8. WRITING BOXES. These leather-covered writing cases were popular in the last quarter of the nineteenth century and featured traveling inkwells, pen compartments, pockets for papers, and stationery compartments with combination blotter/lids. The one at left slides open; others lift up. The box at right front measures 8 by 12 by 1½ inches (closed).

Figure 13.9. WRITING KITS can include boxed sets of matching writing implements (*left*), a metal writing box (*center rear*), and portfolios (*right*). The boxed sets include penholder, seal, letter opener, and eraser knife; the late-nineteenth-century "French ivory," or celluloid, set at the left also features a mechanical pencil. The writing box has two glass inkwells and various compartments including a match safe and a tip-up holder for a candle. At right rear is an embossed-leather portfolio of about the 1850s with a locking flap; the imitation-leather "writing portfolio" is marked "Souvenir of San Francisco, Calif., 1939."

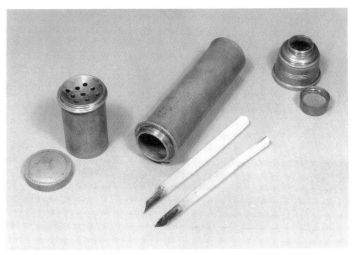

Figure 13.10. This COMPACT WRITING KIT (*left*) contained a sander, a pen case (quills not original), and an inkwell—all of brass. Closed (*above*), it was suitable for carrying in a pocket or saddlebag. The kit measures 1⅛ inches in bottom diameter by 5¹¹⁄₁₆ inches long.

to be the exclusive province of the professional scribe, so did the other. Later, when typewriters took over much of the burden of writing, desks (usually pedestal desks) incorporated "pull-out" or "drophead" design "typewriter racks."[13] By the 1980s, two of every three households in the United States had at least one desk, the latest styles being specially designed for computers.[14]

Some Important Records

Because the content of a record or document (say an original Civil War–era deed) is invariably multidimensional, it can hold quite different values for different persons. A collector may desire it for one reason (as for the signature of a rebel officer), while a historian may prize it for another (possibly as an indicator of the war's influence on southern property values). Or it might provide evidence of one sort for an attorney (for example, as a link in a "title search") but evidence of another import to a genealogist (maybe a clue to the location of the old family burying ground).

Thus a document regarded as worthless by one may be considered priceless by another—especially, as a collector or dealer soon learns, if nostalgia or sentimental value is involved. For example, an old letter, for which one might generously offer a dollar, might not be for sale at any price if it were written by the owner's grandfather. Such familial ties have helped ensure the preservation of family records, many of which have worth independent of personal attachment and beyond the measure of money.

Of the significance to genealogical research, Gilbert H. Doane states, in his *Searching for Your Ancestors:*

Sometimes old letters, diaries, and other family papers exist. One or two old letters, in faded handwriting,

Figure 13.11. The SCHOOL DESK of wood and cast-iron construction, like this "New Peabody" model, was the mainstay of the classroom. The back of each seat held a desk for the next student. Note the inkwell in the hole, the penholder in the groove, and the wooden pencil box.

Figure 13.12. PUPILS AT DESKS similar to that in the previous figure were models of late-Victorian deportment.

Figure 13.13. FAMILY RECORDS took many forms: Bible records, certificates (including the "Pennsylvania Dutch" fraktur at left rear), and other papers. The tin document case contained family and professional documents of a Virginia physician who headed west to Missouri about 1844.

Rear: the fraktur (see detail in fig. 11.29) is dated 1850; the marriage certificate, 1912.

Left front: family records have been entered into an 1888-89 pocket memo book and, uniquely, the back pages of a salesman's "subscription book"—a slim version of an actual book with blank pages intended for names and addresses of those wishing to purchase it.

Right center: "The Illustrated Historical Family Record Album" was never used. The leatherbound Bible, published in 1850, contains records of births, marriages, and deaths; a citizenship paper and a "reward of merit" had been inserted among its pages.

Right front: the tin document case contains physician's documents of about the 1830s and 1840s, four "Family Record" sheets from Bibles, a diploma, a letter of introduction, and other documents.

Figure 13.14. "FAMILY RECORD" is the heading of this chromolithographed register that has been filled in with pen and ink (ca. 1916) and framed. The photographs under glass show children in their coffins—poignant mementos mori then and now.

Figure 13.15. This MARRIAGE CERTIFICATE of 1866 featured pasted-on photographs of the couple. It was chromolithographed in Boston by L. Prang and Company. (Later, in 1873, Louis Prang created the first American Christmas card.)

Figure 13.16. "REWARDS OF MERIT" were teachers' gifts to deserving little "scholars." Most were printed—either by engraving, wood engraving (typically hand colored), or chromolithography. A handwritten reward of about the 1860s is shown at the upper right. One on a lace-paper folder, dated 1856, is at the upper left. It reads "Reward of Merit to Miss Sallie G. Scruggs for correct deportment and conformity to the rules of the Bourbon Female Institute during the session ending June 19th 1856." It measures 4½ by 7 inches.

badly worn along the creases, may contain clues to places of residence or details of family history which would otherwise be completely lost in the obscurity of the past. Sometimes a dull old diary will contain, interspersed among accounts of the weather, notes of baptisms, weddings, and funerals. Old family account books are another source of information, perhaps meager, but sometimes very illuminating. Even the framed sampler, worked by Great-Great-Aunt Hannah at the age of eleven, may prove to be of value. Don't overlook such items, for everything is grist to the genealogist's mill.[15]

Among the most important family documents for the genealogical searcher is the Bible record, as Doane demonstrates by devoting much of a chapter to it. He says in part:

Occasionally a son was sufficiently interested in his family, when he was married and was about to start his own family life, to copy from the original Bible, kept by his father, the data which it contained. But this rarely happened, for, I regret to say, our ancestors were not always of a genealogical turn of mind, and generally did not think of doing such a thing. Young people are always more interested in the future, as they should be, than in the past, however much they can learn from it. Generally speaking, late in the eighteenth century and early in the nineteenth, a young couple, newly married and just starting out in life, either received a brand-new Bible as a gift from parents or well-wishers, or bought one with their first spare cash. It was a period during which "respectable people" still belonged to a church

and read the Bible regularly. Sometimes they would enter their family names, but more frequently they were content to enter only the dates of their own births, that of their marriage, and then, from time to time as the children came along, the records of their progeny. Fortunately, in many nineteenth-century Bibles parents entered the name of the place as well as the date of birth. This was a century of great movement, as families by the thousands were migrating westward, staying but a few years in one place and then moving on as they heard of richer lands.[16]

Not all family registers are in Bibles: see figures 13.13 and 13.14. Moreover, there are marriage certificates (figs. 13.13 and 13.15), baby books, frakturs, and many other valuable records.

Old wills are other important genealogical documents. Although few are passed down in families, copies are recorded in will books maintained in city and county depositories. Since children are typically named in them (but rarely are parents) they are an excellent source for proof of descent. Also, wills occasionally give evidence of a family rift, as by stating that someone is "cut off with a shilling" (or, later, a dollar). Gilbert Doane cautions, however, that such wording "has more than one implication in family history" (for example, that heir may have received an earlier settlement).[17]

Old parchment or paper documents may also be found that begin, "This Indenture. . . ." The term refers to a mutual agreement between two parties whereby each has a duplicate copy. Originally, these were cut

Figure 13.17. AUTOGRAPH ALBUMS derive from the German *alba amicorum* of the sixteenth and seventeenth centuries and became especially popular during the era of Victorian sentimentality. Apart from their occasionally interesting content—perhaps a pen-flourished bird like that shown in figure 12.37—their frequently dated entries make them good reference sources for specimens of ink and handwriting.

with an irregular, or *indented* line from the same sheet, or from two sheets overlapped before cutting, so that the two copies could subsequently be placed together—like two pieces of a puzzle—to demonstrate their interconnected relationship.[18] (Note the top of the eighteenth-century parchment document shown earlier in fig. 1.2.)

Among the miscellaneous diplomas, certificates, and other documents of achievement that may be found mounted in an album, displayed in a frame, kept in a box or chest, or even, like one example shown in figure 13.16, inserted in the pages of a Bible, are "rewards of merit." Presented to deserving students as incentives, some eighteenth-century rewards took the form of silver tokens, but paper rewards became common by century's end. They were handwritten and decorated with pen flourishing, cut-paper ornamentations, or hand-colored bird or flower designs.

Nineteenth-century rewards were rarely handmade but instead were printed in quantities, arranged several to a sheet, which the schoolmaster cut apart as needed. Many were illustrated with wood engravings that were then hand colored. After 1850, chromolithographed cards became common, printed on glossy cardstock and often embossed (fig. 13.16).[19]

Old autograph albums are also frequently found among the family "archives" and so turn up at estate sales. Their use traces back to the German *stammbuch*, or *album amicorum*, of the sixteenth and seventeenth centuries. Originally, this type of album contained

Figure 13.18. This AUTOGRAPH-ALBUM PAGE features hand-drawn "calling cards." The one in the center is that of a Confederate infantryman.

coats of arms, but they were later displaced by sketches, verses, and other entries. By the eighteenth century the custom of keeping an album had spread to England and elsewhere in Europe. Late in that century and early in the next, silhouettes and locks of hair became common additions. Many of the early books were handmade, with covers of cardboard or even wallpaper.[20]

As early as the 1820s, in New York, autograph albums began to be published with engraved scenes.

Victorian sentimentality contributed to the popularity of albums, and in the last half of the century they proliferated, often having chromolithographed pictures, printed quotations, pages of alternating pastel colors, and leather covers with embossed, chromolithographed, and gilded decorations. Plush covers also became fashionable. Late in the century this autograph album became the hobby of very young schoolgirls, and it declined both in physical quality and content: covers were made of imitation leather, and artistic sketches and original poems tended to disappear (figs. 13.17 and 13.18).[21]

The collecting of third-party autographs—those not addressed to oneself—probably followed from the popularity of the sixteenth-century *alba amicorum* described earlier. Although William Wordsworth, Edgar Allan Poe, Francis Scott Key, and other poets are known to have penned a verse or two in an autograph album, and they and other notables may have occasionally signed elsewhere on request (fig. 13.19), the autographs of famous persons generally had to be obtained indirectly.[22] Unfortunately, during the nineteenth century they were often snipped from letters and documents which were then discarded—such autographs being known as "cut signatures."[23]

Actually the term "autograph" (from the Greek words *auto* and *graphos*, i.e., "self-writing") refers not only to a signature but to any writing, even if unsigned, that is in the hand of its author. An entire text penned by the author is called a holograph (fig. 13.20).[24] Technically, a "signature" may consist of an entire name plus title or be only an initial if that were a customary way of signing. Many writers have had variant signatures, like Queen Victoria, who sometimes signed with her first name, sometimes "V.R.I." or "V.," and sometimes simply, "The Queen." Fifteenth- and sixteenth-century monarchs frequently used a "sign manual" (a penned device comprising initials of their names and often their titles, interconnected by loops). A "paraph" was a distinctive flourish or swirl added to a signature (fig. 13.21); common in the eighteenth century, it was sometimes used instead of the signature, thus concealing one's identity except to the initiate.[25]

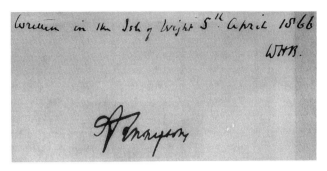

Figure 13.19. AUTOGRAPH OF ALFRED, LORD TENNYSON was signed in 1866, when the British poet laureate was living on the Isle of Wight.

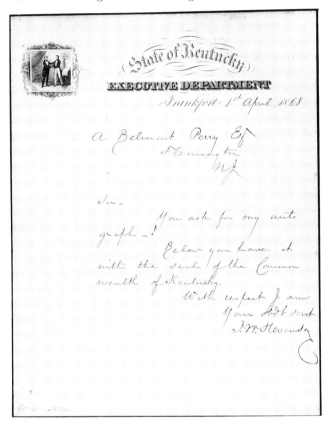

Figure 13.20. A HOLOGRAPH LETTER is one entirely in the writing of the author, like this example from a Kentucky governor. Dated 1868, it was in response to a request: "You ask for my autograph—Below you have it."

Figure 13.21. AUTOGRAPH OF THE AMERICAN PATRIOT William Williams, who was a signer of the Declaration of Independence. He penned this signature (with paraph) in 1764. This was in his capacity as town clerk of Lebanon, Connecticut, a post he held from 1756 to 1801.

Figure 13.22. REVOLUTIONARY-ERA WRITING MATERIALS included such items as a pewter "countinghouse" inkstand with quills, quill knife, seal and wax, sander, and early spectacles resting on a 1790s "Waste Book," as some of its later pages are headed—that is, a daybook of accounts. The papers are shown in the following photograph.

Another device used instead of the signature was a mark—commonly a cross or circle—added by the signer after a scribe had written out the name. Called a "signum," it was used more than a milennium ago by Charlemagne and was common during the eleventh, twelfth, and thirteenth centuries. Whatever was the case with its early usage, it came to be employed (along with the scribal words "his mark") by those unable to write.[26]

Those who engage in autograph collecting—or philography (from the Greek, meaning "love of writing")—employ standard designations for different types of autographs. A signed holographic missive is an "autograph letter signed" (A.L.S., plural A.Ls.S.), whereas a text signed by the author but written by another is a "letter signed" (L.S.) Other terms (more or less self-explanatory, with *S* added if signed) include: autograph document (A.D.); autograph manuscript (A.Ms., plural A.Mss.); autograph note (A.N.); and autograph quotation (A.Q.). If signed, a typed letter, document, or manuscript is autographic (and designated, respectively, T.L.S., T.D.S., and T.Ms.S.).[27]

Collectors naturally have diverse interests. Either the novice or veteran collector may be a generalist or specialist (and there are good books available for each).[28] The latter might concentrate on the autographs of British poets, for example, or the signers of the Declaration of Independence (fig. 13.21).

Apart from autographs, philographers also collect and study documents for their historical and cultural value. Interesting collections can be assembled around various themes such as any of the American wars,

Figure 13.23. COLONIAL AND REVOLUTIONARY DOCUMENTS provide tangible links with an important period of American history.

Top: a partially printed and filled-in colonial arrest warrant—4 by 13¾16 inches—issued in the name of George III and dated in "the Ninth Year of Our Reign"—that is, 1769.

Left center: a record of the "sales of 5 half Barrels of gun Powder," 1770.

Lower left: the pay authorization for a Revolutionary War officer, 1778.

Right center: a bill of the 1770s issued to Dr. Timothy Darling, a Revolutionary War surgeon; on the verso is a notation of 1785 by his executor.

Bottom right: a promissory note issued by the Connecticut Treasury, 1781, and subsequently voided by use of a "cut cancel."

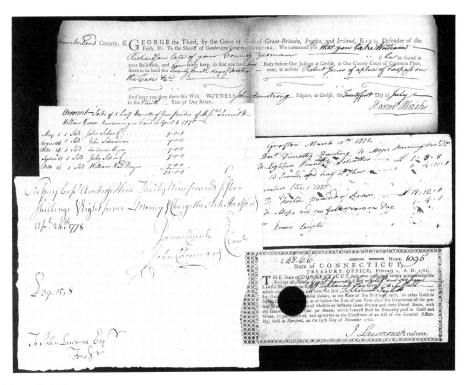

Figure 13.24 (*below*). COLONIAL CURRENCY. This two-shilling note was issued by the Pennsylvania General Assembly in 1773. Such colonial notes—which were actually signed in ink on their face—can have autographs of notables like Benjamin Franklin. On the verso of this bill is printed: "To counterfeit is death."

possibly including writing materials or military artifacts of the period (figs. 13.22-13.33). Other themes might be slavery, steamboats, westward expansion, telegraphy, quackery, or temperance and prohibition (figs. 13.34-13.39). Billheads can be found that relate to many trades and subjects (fig. 10.11).

The philographer's interest may be piqued by almost anything that is written, including humble memoranda, account books, letters, and assorted papers and related items (figs. 13.40-13.46).[29] Frequently, these exhibit distinctive features that serve as signposts of their historical and cultural context and that can have bearing on document analysis, as for authentication and dating, treated in part 5.

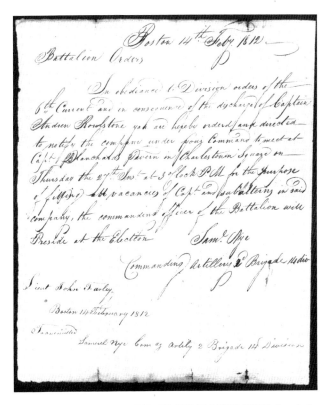

Figure 13.25. This WAR OF 1812 DOCUMENT, headed "Battalion Orders," directed a company of soldiers "to meet at Capt. Blanchards Tavern in Charlestown Square." This was in order to fill—by election—the vacant positions of captain and subalterns.

Figure 13.26. CIVIL WAR WRITING ACCOUTREMENTS might include the following (*counterclockwise from candle and tintype*): pottery "cone" ink bottle, Silliman pocket inkwell, tin document case, leather-covered diary, lap desk with patriotic covers and a letter on a sheet of stationery printed with a portrait of General McClellan, and pen and two-piece penholder in a case. The large document (about 10 by 15¼ inches) records the 1862 issue of clothing, waterproof blankets, and other equipment to a member of the Pennsylvania Volunteers.

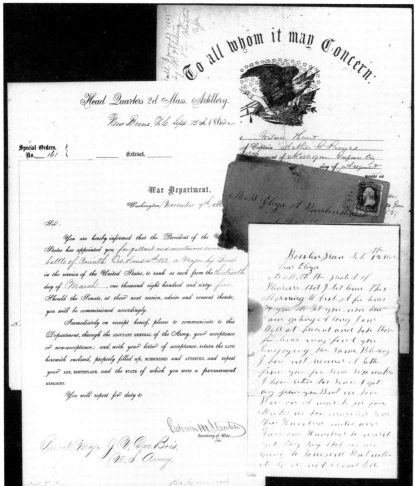

Figure 13.27. These UNION DOCUMENTS include papers both military (such as "special orders") and private (e.g., soldiers' letters). Significant content would add to the commercial value of these or any documents, in addition to making them intrinsically more valuable.

Upper left: special order of 1864, detailing a private as "Hospital Cook," and so on.

Lower left: notification of a presidential promotion to major "for gallant and meritorious service," dated 1865; this document has the rubber-stamped signature of Secretary of War Edwin M. Stanton.

Upper right: discharge of a corporal from the Michigan Infantry, dated 1865.

Lower right: an envelope with its contents, a soldier's letter edged in red and blue to his sweetheart, dated 1862; the writer states he has "Bin on March for four weeks," had his "likeness taken," expects to embark on a six-day march to Louisville, hopes to see her, and vows he will "remain your Love untill death."

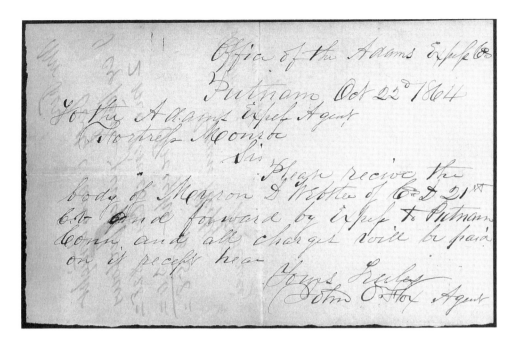

Figure 13.28. This RECEIPT FOR A SOLDIER'S CORPSE is a grim reminder of the carnage of the Civil War. Issued by the Adams Express Company in 1864, it was for shipment of a Union soldier's body to Fortress Monroe, Virginia.

Figure 13.29. CONFEDERATE DOCUMENTS are generally somewhat more valuable than their Union counterparts. Shown here are a soldier's letter, a military telegram, and Louisiana and official Confederacy bank notes.

Top: this soldier's letter of 1862 details a dispute over payment of a debt, which the addressee has requested in gold rather than Confederate currency and which thus serves as a commentary on the decline of the latter.

Right: the telegram, dated 1861 from Jackson, Tennessee, concerns trains carrying carloads of lumber; it measures 5⁷⁄₁₆ by 8¾ inches.

Left: unlike Union currency, southern bank notes were signed in ink on their face, thus aiding in distinguishing the genuine bills from their countless reproductions.

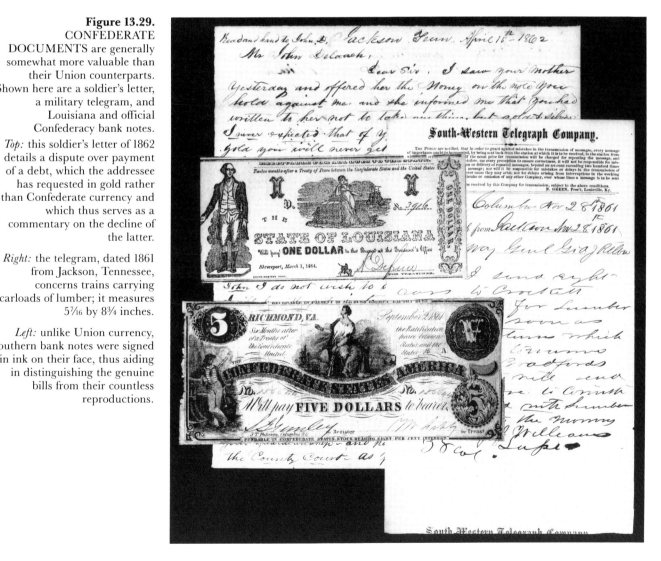

Figure 13.30. WORLD WAR I WRITING MATERIALS typically included the fountain pen. One company made a small model with a ring rather than a clip, advertised for soldiers. Shown are a pen and filler bottle, a letter and picture postcard, a leather dispatch case, and (*upper right*) a writing kit in a canvas case that contains stationery, a blotter, and a mechanical pencil.

Figure 13.31. DOCUMENTS OF THE GREAT WAR include such items as a 1917 British "letter card" (*upper left*), marked "Opened by censor"; a "field service post card" of 1918 (*left center*); two picture post cards (*bottom*) and two letters (*upper right*); the envelopes with the letters are franked "Soldiers Mail" and "Officers Mail."

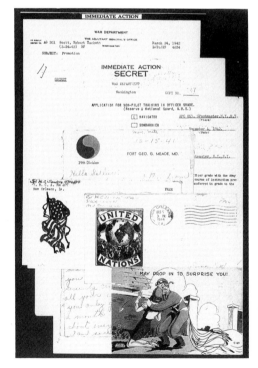

Figure 13.32. WORLD WAR II PAPERS include (*from top*) documents marked "immediate action" and "secret," an airplane navigator's application, a soldier's letter, two cacheted franked envelopes, and a similarly marked cartoon postcard. The "secret" document of 1942 concerns "Return of Cadres from the Newfoundland Base Command."

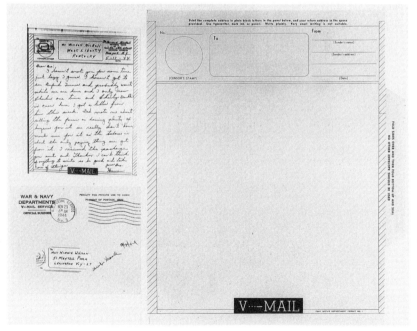

Figure 13.33. WORLD WAR II "V-MAIL" consisted of letters written on official letter sheets (*right*), then reduced to microfilm for shipment overseas, and finally converted to small photostats (*upper left*) of about 4¼ by 5⅛ inches; these were placed in window envelopes for mailing (*lower left*). V-mail holiday greetings were also provided for the soldier to fill in and send.

The Oath of Registration.

THE STATE OF ALABAMA: ..Madison..COUNTY.

I, ...Thos J. McNeill...., do solemnly swear, that I will henceforth faithfully support, protect, and defend the Constitution of the United States, and the Union of States thereunder; and that I will, in like manner, abide by and support all Laws and Proclamations which have been made during the existing rebellion with reference to the Emancipation of Slaves,—So help me God.

T. J. McNeill

SWORN TO and subscribed before me, this ....5.... day of .... ~~1865~~ 1872

Mr. Michael Polmer

1859, To the Sheriff of Frederick County, Dr.

To / State Levy $ 80	Slave $	Pers'l Property $ 4	$ 84
/ County Levy $ 140	/ Parish Levy $ 1 00		2 40
Land Tax $			

Received Payment, $3.24

D. S.

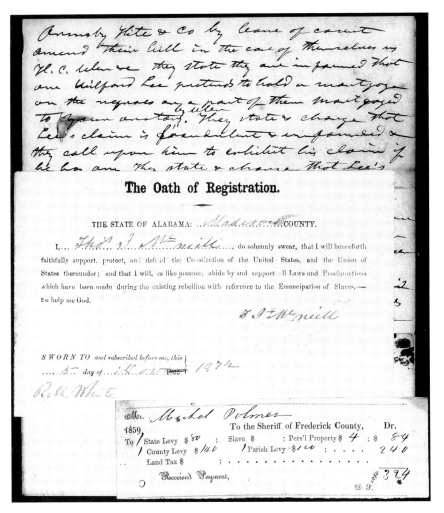

Figure 13.34. DOCUMENTS RELATING TO SLAVERY are reminders of a shameful era of America's past and of consequential secession and war. Shown are a legal document, loyalty oath, and tax receipt—all mentioning slaves.

From top: a handwritten document of 1845 referring to "a mortgage on the negroes"; a rather late—1872—loyalty oath, signed by a former rebel who promises to obey "all Laws and Proclamations made during the existing rebellion with reference to the Emancipation of Slaves"; and an 1859 tax receipt with a space for recording slaves as a revenue source.

New-Orleans, May 21 1866

Steamer T. D. Horner, Brother

Bought of DAVISON & HUGHES,

Wholesale Grocers and Dealers in Boat Stores,

41 Front Street and 42 Fulton Street.

FIFTH STREET COAL YARD.

Steamboats supplied with Coal at the Dock, foot of Fifth street.

New Albany, Ind., April 21st, 1866

Bought of J. H. FAWCETT,

STEAMSHIP SUPPLIES, ENGINEERS STORES & TOOLS.

MACHINERY OF ALL DESCRIPTIONS. AGRICULTURAL IMPLEMENTS &c.

To Steamer UNITED STATES, Dr.

Marks. To Freight on

Received Payment.

Clerk.

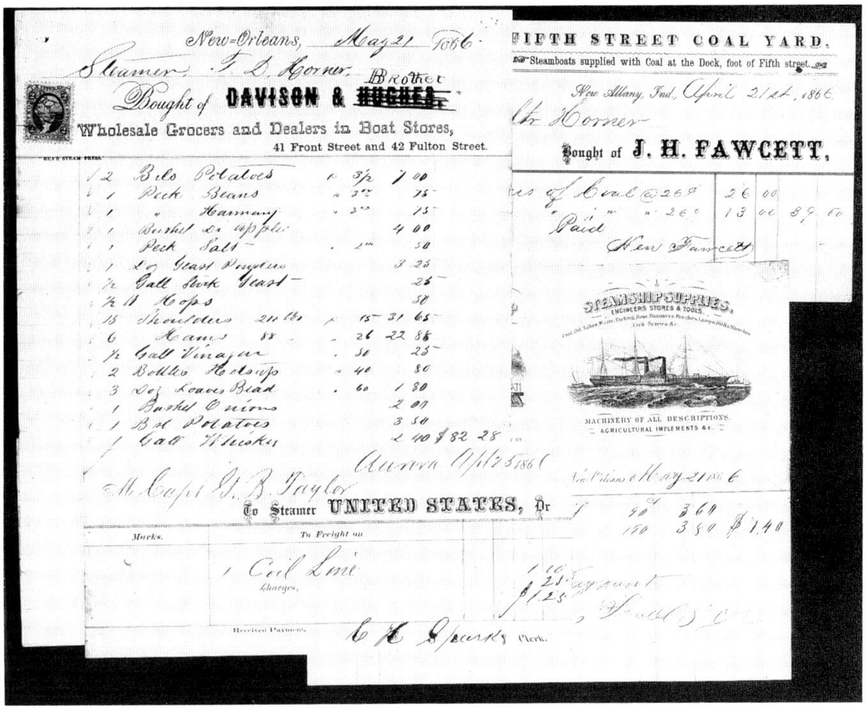

Figure 13.35. STEAMBOAT MEMORABILIA could include such papers as these 1860s invoices. Researching the steamers referred to—here the *United States* (*lower left*), and the *T. D. Horner* (*other bills*)—could add an interesting dimension to collecting.

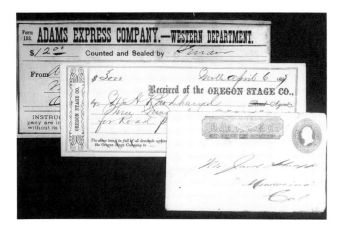

Figure 13.36. PAPERS OF THE OLD WEST could relate to the gold rush of 1849, or to famous lawmen or notorious outlaws, or some other aspect—as, in this instance, to stagecoach and railway-express companies.

The Adams Express Company was once the largest such carrier in America, and was thus the frequent target of train robbers; notable among them were the Reno gang, until the legendary Pinkertons caught them a few at a time and they were lynched by vigilantes.

Top, the company's envelope, marked "Western Department" and used to send cash, and a letter in 1890. *Center,* an 1867 stage-line receipt in the amount of $3,000 "for road purposes". *Bottom,* an envelope carried "Over our California and Coast routes" by the famous Wells, Fargo and Company, containing a vintner's receipt of 1874, sent from San Francisco to Mendocino.

Figure 13.37. TELEGRAMS (from the Greek *tele,* "far," and *gramma,* "a writing") began to compete with letters after 1844, when Samuel F.B. Morse installed the first experimental telegraphic line between Washington, D.C., and Baltimore. In addition to a telegraph key and the booklet "How to Write Telegrams Properly" are shown a telegram sent by the South-Western Telegraph Company in 1861 (*upper left*), and Western Union telegrams of about the turn of the century, with envelope (*lower left*), and of 1949 (*center right*). The text of the latter was received on a strip of paper by a *teleprinter,* then cut into individual lines and pasted on the form. Also shown (*lower right*) is a "telegram" postcard.

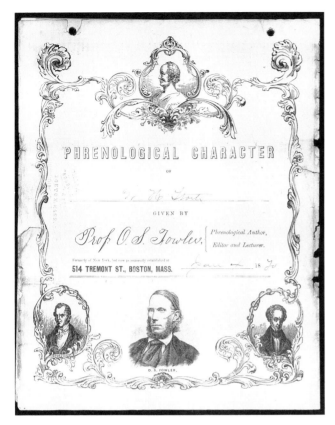

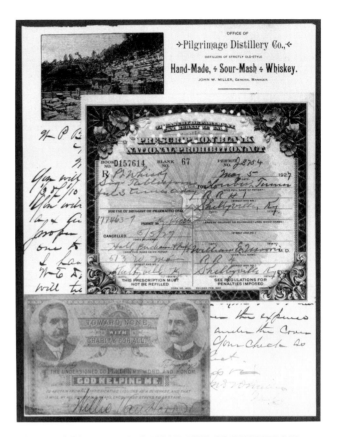

Figure 13.38. This PHRENOLOGICAL REPORT of 1870, prepared by "Professor" O.S. Fowler of Boston, is among the documents pertaining to quackery that amuse the collector as well as provide insight into an earlier time. Attached to this cover sheet by brass grommets are five handwritten pages that comprise the "character" analysis. The cover sheet and last page are embossed, "CHAS. A. GRAHAM, PHONOGRAPHIC REPORTER, BOSTON, MASS."; in other words, the analysis was taken down in shorthand.

Figure 13.39. TEMPERANCE AND PROHIBITION DOCUMENTS represent another class of collectibles, an outgrowth of the extremes of intemperance and intolerance. A late-nineteenth-century temperance pledge (*bottom*) and a 1927 whiskey prescription entered under the National Prohibition Act (*center*) are shown with an 1898 distiller's letterhead bearing the curious name "Pilgrimage Distillery Co." The pledge card—marked by a waterstain across its middle—measures about 3⅜ by 5⅜ inches.

Figure 13.40. MEMORANDA. Even informal notes can be significant relics of the past together with their associational items.

From left: a leather-covered notebook of about the 1830s and 1840s, containing recipes for ink, gunpowder, and so on; a "mammy" memorandum-pad holder with a pencil serving as the broom handle; a recent brass-"hand" memo clip; a "Magic Memo" slate that erases when the covering film is lifted; two pocket memorandum/account books, about 1890. *Foreground:* an "ivory book," the fan-like pages of which allow pencil notations and erasure; it is similar to two such reminders known to have been kept by Thomas Jefferson, who used them for quick notations which he later transferred into larger memorandum books.

Figure 13.41. "BLANK BOOKS" were volumes of blank (or ruled) pages intended for accounts or the like. This open book of the 1790s contains lists of goods brought from Europe, with a record of ships' voyages, and so on. Note the left-hand page, headed "Voyage from Ostend" and having the subheading "Dutch Goods" near the bottom of the page. Also shown are an 1840s account book (*far left*) and an 1850s Texas general-store ledger.

Figure 13.42. DOCKETED LETTER. In earlier times many folded papers—like this "stampless cover" of 1817—were filed, standing on end, with a docket (label or brief abstract) written across the top for reference purposes.

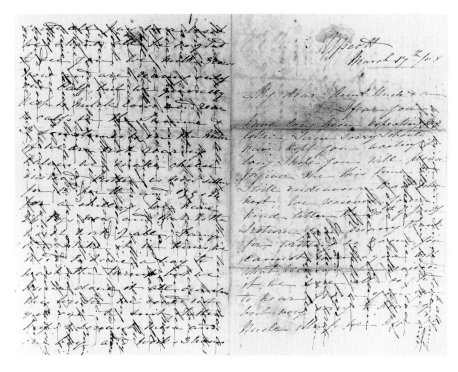

Figure 13.43. CROSS WRITING, produced by turning the page and writing across the lines at right angles, was a common mid-nineteenth-century practice. Used at a time when paper was still relatively expensive, it was also prompted by English and American postal rates. This specimen is dated 1858; another in my collection is a year earlier. Mary Todd Lincoln wrote at least one cross-written mourning letter in 1869.

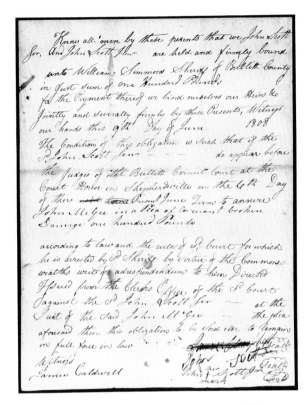

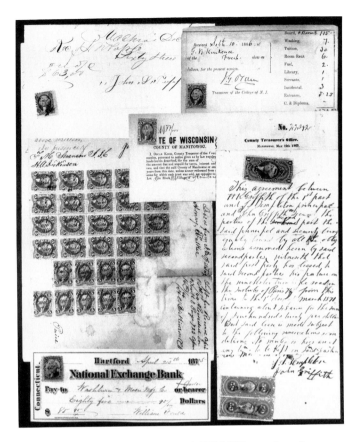

Figure 13.44. This CLERICAL DOCUMENT was prewritten—probably by a deputy clerk on a rainy day—and filled in later. By using stock language and leaving blank spaces (portions of which remain, together with some crowding, as evidence of the practice), one could prepare a number of such legal forms in advance, thus having them available when needed. This example is from Bullitt County, Kentucky, and dated 1808. Note that the last signer has made "his mark."

Figure 13.45. DOCUMENTARY STAMPS were issued as a means of collecting federal government revenues, the first American ones dating from 1862. They were no longer required after December 31, 1967.

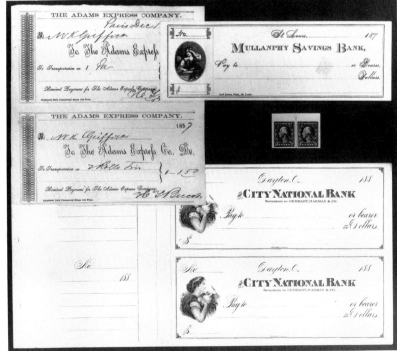

Figure 13.46. IMPERFORATE PAPERS. Although perforations for stamps were introduced in Britain in 1854, the separation of receipts, checks, and similar papers, including some stamps, continued to be done by hand with scissors or knife until a later time.

Duplicating

As long as man has written letters and other documents, he has sought to maintain records of them by reproducing them in some form. As one authority points out: "The humble beginnings of this great urge are to be found in apparatus which was in common use in Nineveh [in ancient Assyria] as far back as 1,000 years B.C. This was a simple hand duplicator, consisting of an engraved cylinder mounted in a frame, and when rolled over a slab of soft clay it created a copy which was then dried in the sun. From such apparatus the present widespread use of reproduction methods has evolved."[30]

Throughout the Roman era and the medieval period, document reproduction was done by scribes who laboriously hand copied texts. In fact, the practice continued well into this century, when, for example, many county clerks were still recording wills, deeds, and other such documents into blank books.

In the meantime, though, certain labor-saving tricks and gadgets were devised. For example, surveyors from as early as the eighteenth century (Daniel Boone among them) and into the twentieth, used a simple but effective method to facilitate copying the plat drawing on survey documents. While the text still had to be written out by hand, the drawing needed to be carefully plotted only once (using a protractor and scale) and then—with the use of pin pricks at each "corner"—the configuration was transferred to an additional two or three sheets placed beneath. All that remained was to connect the prick marks with inked lines (fig. 13.47).[31]

Such time-saving tricks were insignificant, however, in comparison to a method of copying documents that predominated during the same period. That was the method of making "letterpress" copies, patented in 1780 by James Watt (inventor of the modern condensing steam engine). This involved writing with a specially thickened "copying" ink, placing upon it a dampened sheet of tissue paper, and pressing the sheets together in a "letter-copying press." In this way, a copy of the writing was transferred to the tissue (figs. 13.48-13.50).[32]

The ink used in this process was made glutinous by the addition of sugar or gum or glycerine. According to an 1882 source, copying inks "must be rather thick, not dry too quickly, and soften when moistened again, without becoming too fluid," in which case they would run.[33]

The use of thin paper (sometimes called "flimsy") allowed the lifted-off writing to be read from the opposite side (thus eliminating the need for a mirror).[34] Also, "copying-books" permitted several letters to be distributed among their pages and pressed at one time.

Figure 13.47. COPYING PLAT DRAWING. Surveyors like Daniel Boone frequently made duplicates of survey documents by using pin pricks to transfer the configuration to additional pages. This detail is from a document drawn up by one of Boone's fellow surveyors in 1817.

Still, an unhappy user of 1879 stated: "Press Copying-books have an unlucky knack of coming to pieces."[35]

Copying presses were of two types: the screw press, like one used by George Washington, who also had his own specially watermarked tissue paper, and the roller press, like the model shown in figure 13.49.[36] Another method of making copies was a device (similar to the pantograph) that used two interconnected pens; as one was being used, the other traced a copy on an adjacent sheet of paper. Thomas Jefferson was smitten by the ingenious device, as revealed by a letter he wrote to a friend in 1805:

Our countrymen are so much occupied in the busy scenes of life, that they have little time to write or invent. A good invention here, therefore, is such a rarity as it is lawful to offer to the acceptance of a friend. A Mr. Hawkins of Frankford, near Philadelphia, has invented a machine which he calls a polygraph, and which carries two, three, or four pens. That of two pens, with which I am now writing, is best; and is so perfect that I have laid aside the copying-press, for a twelvemonth past, and write always with the polygraph. I have directed one to be made, of which I ask your acceptance. By what conveyance I shall send it while Havre is blockaded, I do not yet know. I think

Figures 13.48.-13.50. LETTERPRESS COPYING could be achieved with documents first written with a special, viscous ink; when a copy was desired, a damp sheet of tissue paper was placed against it, and the sheets were pressed, thus transferring a copy of the writing to the tissue. The thin paper allowed the resulting reversed writing to be read from the opposite side. Invented by James Watt in 1780, the process was—for its day—the equivalent of photocopying.

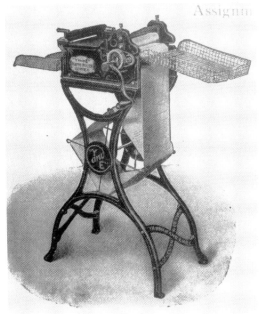

Roller Copier

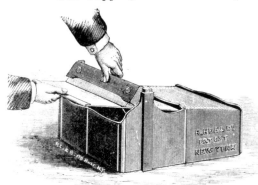

PATENT DAMPENING TABLETS,

For Copying Letters and Legal Documents.

This indispensable addition to the ordinary Copying Press comprises a substantial iron case or water box, with a pair of rubber wipers, so arranged that the simple act of taking a Tablet out of the water, and passing it between the wipers, removes the surplus water from both sides, and prepares the Tablet for immediate use.

At one pressure of the press any number of manuscripts may be copied, including many duplicates of each page when desired; an invaluable aid to the merchant and the legal profession, where many letters and documents are to be copied in duplicates, with exactness and great dispatch.

The subscribers manufacture and keep for sale, at wholesale and retail, a large assortment of LETTER-COPYING PRESSES, combining tasteful designs with the best workmanship.

R. HOE & CO.,

29 & 31 Gold St.. New York.

13.48. By dampening an entire copying tablet, as described in this advertisement (from the Mar. 25, 1871, issue of *Harper's Weekly*), multiple pages could be copied at one pressing.

13.49. Copying presses were of two types: screw presses, like the one preferred by George Washington, and roller copiers, like the one in this 1916 illustration (from Rupert P. SoRelle, *Office Training for Stenographers*, New York: Gregg Pub. Co., 1916, p. 89).

13.50. An original letter promoting Bowman's Copying Books, shown with its letterpress copy on tissue paper (overlapped for comparison).

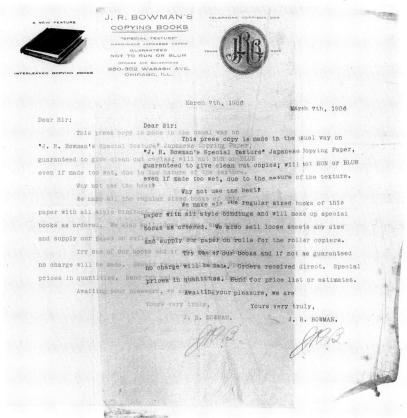

you will be pleased with it, and will use it habitually as I do; because it requires only that degree of mechanical attention which I know you to possess.[37]

Despite Jefferson's enthusiasm, however, Hawkins's invention was completely overshadowed by the copying press, which lasted well into the twentieth century. Copying pencils and copying ribbons for typewriters expanded the possibilities of the technique.[38]

The use of carbon paper represented an alternate method of copying letters that became common with the introduction of the typewriter. There followed the development, in the 1950s, of NCR paper—the acronym representing both No Carbon Required and National Cash Register, after the company that developed it. The copying properties of NCR paper are based on the interraction of the two chemical substances with which the two surfaces of the paper have been treated.[39]

All such methods were limited to one or, at best, a few copies; whenever a considerable number was required, some other manifolding (multicopying) process was necessary. The simplest of these was the hectograph, which was made possible by the development of aniline dyes (the first in 1858). In one form, the master copy was written with aniline ink or pencil (usually purple); the writing was then transferred to a thin slab of gelatin treated with glycerine; this was then dampened and a blank sheet placed upon it, rubbed, and peeled off. Numerous copies (about 300) could be lifted off, one at a time, in this fashion.[40]

A "spirit" (solvent) process form of hectographic duplicating is more efficient and has continued in common use. In this process the writing or typing is done on a sheet of paper having a special dye-coated sheet placed behind it. This produces a reversed, master image on the back of the sheet, which is then fastened to a rotating drum. Copy sheets, moistened lightly by solvent, thus have a minute amount of the color transferred to them.[41]

A large class of copying machines involves the use of some form of stencil. Among the most successful of such devices—which have included the "cyclostyle" and the "trypograph"—has been the "mimeograph."[42] Often referred to simply as the "mimeo," it was patented in 1876 (and improved in 1880) by Thomas A. Edison as a "method of preparing autographic stencils for printing." The stencil is made by typing (without ribbon) or

writing with a stylus on wax-coated fiber sheets, thus leaving porous lines through which ink can pass. Modern electrical models—in which the stencil is placed over an inked pad mounted on a revolving drum—are capable of yielding as many as 5,000 copies.[43]

Modern duplicating methods include photocopying processes—notably xerography, invented by Chester Carlson. He produced the first copy in 1938, but the process was not publicly demonstrated until 1948. Unlike other methods, which require sensitized paper, xerography instead produces an image by means of a special photoconductive plate. The image is made up of pigment particles held on the plate by electric charges; the particles are then transferred to paper and fixed by heat.[44] As a result of one trademark for the process, photocopies—even when produced by the other methods—are often called "Xerox copies."

With large models that can copy in color, enlarge and reduce, and even collate and staple pages, photocopiers now dominate the duplication field. Together with word processors, which can also turn out limitless copies, they are revolutionizing the production—and reproduction—of documents.

SELECT BIBLIOGRAPHY

Altick, Richard D. *The Scholar Adventurers*. New York: Macmillan, 1951. Describes scholars' quest for literary documents—diaries, letters, etc.

Aronson, Joseph. *The Encyclopedia of Furniture*. New York: Crown, 1938. s.v. "Desk."

Benjamin, Mary A. *Autographs: A Key to Collecting*. Rev. ed. 1963. Reprint. New York: Dover, 1986.

Berkeley, Edmund, Jr., ed. *Autographs and Manuscripts: A Collector's Manual*. New York: Scribner's, 1978.

Cunha, George Martin, and Dorothy Grant Cunha. *Conservation of Library Materials*. 2d ed. 2 vols. Metuchen, N.J.: Scarecrow Press, 1971. Standard work on conservation recommended for the serious collector.

Hamilton, Charles. *Big Name Hunting: A Beginner's Guide to Autograph Collecting*. New York: Simon and Schuster, 1973.

———. *Collecting Autographs and Manuscripts*. Norman: Univ. of Oklahoma Press, 1961.

Hector, L.C. *The Handwriting of English Documents*. London: Arnold, 1958.

Whalley, Joyce Irene. *English Handwriting, 1540-1853*. London: Her Majesty's Stationery Office, 1969.

PART 5

Examining Documents

It is therefore necessary to examine all the writings relating to a case. . . . We may often, too, find a thread broken, or wax disturbed, or signatures without attestation; all of which points, unless we settle them at home, will embarrass us unexpectedly in the forum.

—Quintilian
Institutio Oratoria
ca. A.D.88

14

Decipherment

The effectiveness of written language naturally depends on its ability to be read—an ability that can be limited by several factors: *reader unfamiliarity*, as with foreign languages or archaic scripts, the province of the paleographer; *writing deformity*, such as that distorted by palsy, or scribbled in haste; *physical deterioration*, for example, charred texts or faded writing; and intentional *writer obfuscation*, as in secret writings, such as cryptograms.[1] Each of these limitations on readability has potential remedies.

Reader Unfamiliarity

A classic example of triumph over an unintelligible language was the decipherment of the ancient Egyptian writings. The key was the celebrated Rosetta Stone, a stele (upright tablet) of black basalt, acquired by the British upon the surrender of Alexandria in 1801. It bore an inscription of 196 B.C., promoting the policies of the boy-king Ptolemy V, which was repeated three times: first in hieroglyphics, then demotic script, and finally Greek. Since the latter was known, it allowed Egyptologists, notably Jean François Champollion (1790-1832), to uncover the rebuslike mysteries of hieroglyphics. Champollion's work eventually permitted routine translation of the ancient texts.[2]

With cuneiform, proper names and titles found at the beginning of many inscriptions provided the first real clues for decipherment. In turn, they allowed several sound values to be established and bit by bit, as a result of the work of paleographers like Sir Henry Rawlinson (1810-95), the various cuneiform languages were eventually interpreted.[3]

Today, most instances of indecipherable texts caused by one's unfamiliarity with the written forms are due not to "lost" languages, but rather to merely foreign ones or else to antiquated scripts. The former problem usually has a simple solution: finding someone who is literate in the requisite language. Professional translators exist (as do stenographers if the writing is in shorthand) and may be identified through the yellow pages or other sources. The local librarian may be able to assist. Language teachers at high schools and colleges are often only too glad to help, particularly if the material is relatively short, or they may be enticed with a fee. With lengthy texts, unless a word-by-word transcription is absolutely necessary, the translator may be able to provide an abstract (summary) that will solve the problem at a reasonable price—particularly if he or she is alerted to potential points of significance in advance.

Antiquated scripts—such as the secretary hand used for much Elizabethan English and colonial American writing—presents a problem for the budding scholar and the amateur genealogist. For such scripts, however, there are available many charts (like those of figs. 14.1 and 14.2 as well as those in app. 1) that help identify the unfamiliar forms with their array of variants. There are also specialized texts that should be consulted by the serious investigator.[4]

Compared to secretary, round hand presents relatively little difficulty. The uninitiated can be bewildered by the long *s*, however, reading it as *f* or, in combination with the regular *s*, as *p*. Beginning searchers working on their family trees among the musty records of county courthouses are often seen confusedly copying down "Rop?" and "Map?" until, if they are lucky, some deputy clerk or experienced visitor explains the matter and helps provide the correct "Ross" and "Mass[achusetts]." In one published index the surname "Hosfort" was incorrectly given as "Hoffort," a misinterpretation obviously caused by the long *s* (fig. 14.3).[5]

Round hand's lookalike letters—notably, common forms of capital *L* and *S*—are another source of confusion and result in many mistaken interpretations ("Lawyer" for "Sawyer," for instance). Other frequently mistaken sets of letters are *T* and *J* and (in the secretary hand) *K*, *P*, and *R*. The problem is even more

Figure 14.1. SECRETARY HAND: MAJUSCULES. The capital, or uppercase, secretary letters exhibit quaint, difficult-to-read features attributable to their derivation from Gothic (bastarda) script. This chart displays some of the more common variants. Note that *I* and *J* were interchangeable, as were *U* and *V*.

Figure 14.2. SECRETARY HAND: MINUSCULES. The small, or lowercase, secretary letters can also present difficulties in reading, notably the *c*, which often resembles an *r*, and the *e*, which the novice can mistake for *o*. Other problem letters include the *r* and the long *s*.

acute with the cursive lowercase letters, especially those comprised of minims (short downstrokes): *i, m, n, u,* and *w*.

Abbreviations and other contracted forms represent yet another difficulty.[6] Sometimes they are signaled by a period (or colon) and/or superscript letters; an apostrophe is rarely seen, but a mark placed above the missing letters is common (fig. 14.4).[7] This is a very old practice: In the 1487 French parchment shown in figure 11.21, for example, "chūn" is given for *chacun*, "each." In many old manuscripts the straight line came to represent *m* or *n*, especially with double letters; thus $\overline{m}$ and $\overline{n}$ were often used for *mm* and *nn* until the late eighteenth century.[8]

Quite often, however, shortened forms of words are employed without any accompanying indicator and, if they are roughly scribbled as well, can present difficulty. Typically though, they are common forms recognizable as such, and in any case are usually understandable from the context. If not, there are special guides that can be consulted.[9]

Similar problems stem from unfamiliar terms. The abbreviation "Hdmet," for example, may not be much

more puzzling than the actual word *hereditament*, nor "L.S." more unfamiliar than the term *"Locus Sigilli"* (fig. 14.5). *The Oxford English Dictionary* or a legal lexicon will usually help clarify the usage, and special glossaries have been compiled for the purpose.[10]

Orthography (spelling) represents a related problem. The notion that there is a single way to spell a word is a relatively modern one. For example, in the fourteenth line of hieroglyphics on the Rosetta Stone, the word for *writing* appears in four different forms: the second and third are represented pictorially (respectively, by a picture of a man writing, and by a pen with an inkwell), while the first and last are different spellings of the word. In Shakespeare's time, the famous bard's name saw some fifteen variant spellings (e.g., "Shackspere").[11] Much "creative" spelling is rooted in phonetics, and thus Americans like Daniel Boone, for example, betray their archaic-English ancestry with spellings like "rad" for "red" and "clark" for "clerk."[12]

To achieve proficiency in reading old manuscripts, E.E. Thoyts states,

I would advise the careful study of an old deed, one of

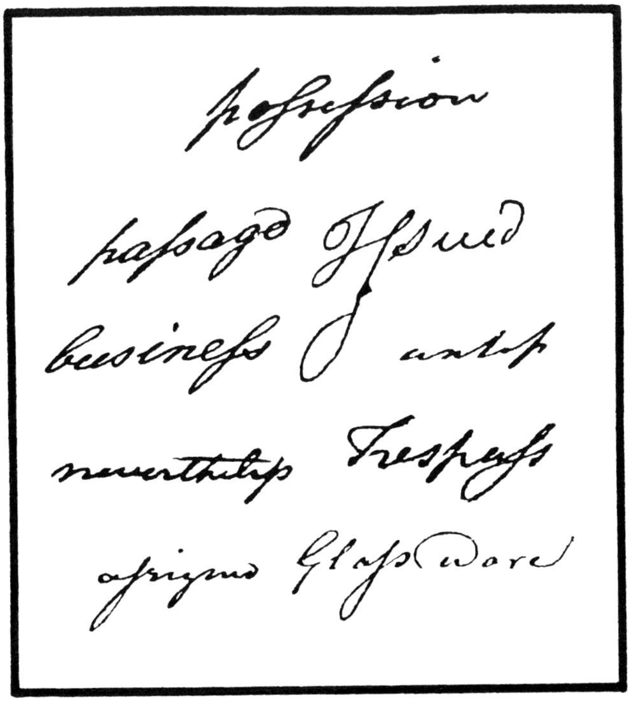

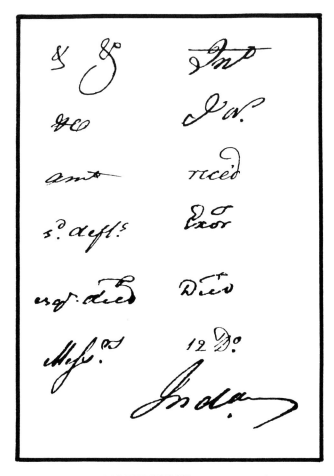

Figure 14.3. The LONG *S* in the secretary hand and (as illustrated here) in round hand is a problem for novices who frequently mistake it for *f. From top:* "possession," "passage," "Issued," "business," "unless," "nevertheless," "Trespass," "assigns," and "Glassware." Note that sometimes the combined long and regular *s* resemble a *p.*

Figure 14.4. ABBREVIATIONS represent another decipherment problem. *First column:* "&" (two versions), "&c." (i.e., et cetera), "amount," "said defendants," "esquire deceased," and "Messieurs"; *second column:* "John," "James," "received," "Executor," "Deceased," "12 Ditto," and "Indiana." Note the use of bars or other marks over words to indicate omitted letters, and the use of superscript.

those written late in the seventeenth or early in the eighteenth century, because these deeds give the phraseology or form of sentences, and are often written in English in a fairly clear hand, freer from contractions than earlier manuscripts, and the beginner has so many new things to discover and learn that it is well to commence by not attempting too much at the first start. An acquaintance with the style of words used in legal language is a good groundwork to commence with. Spread out the parchment before you; never mind the fact that only a word or two, or even only a chance letter here and there catches your eye. Then set to work to compare the letters of the words you do know with the letters in other words which at the commencement looked so strange to you.

It was in this way that Egyptian hieroglyphics were first successfully studied.

She also says:

> Beware of too imaginative guesses. Although this fault is easily remedied, still, it is better to spell a word out letter by letter, however unintelligible and depressing the result at first may be. It is so easy to take a name or word for granted, and an idea once seized upon is not quickly eradicated, and may bring about absurd re-

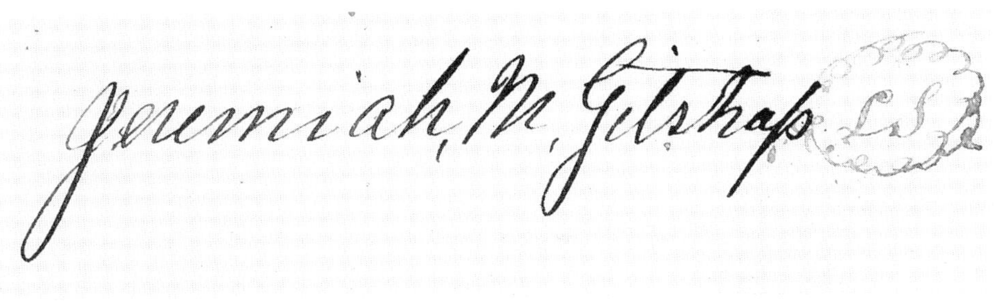

Figure 14.5. The ABBREVIATION "L.S.," which often accompanies signatures on old documents, stood for *Locus Sigilli*, Latin for "place of the seal."

sults and deductions. Do not ponder too long over a word which puzzles you, but go on, leaving gaps in your copy with a stroke underneath corresponding with or leaving sufficient space for the missing word. These spaces can then be filled in afterwards, when the general sense of the document has been mastered, and the aspect of the particular style of writing has become familiar. Then it will be found that words hitherto seemingly unintelligible resolve themselves into readable form, and although apparently impossible to decipher at the first reading, later on they present no difficulty. A little practice and patience soon overcome the difficulties of the first start, and after that the progress is rapid.[14]

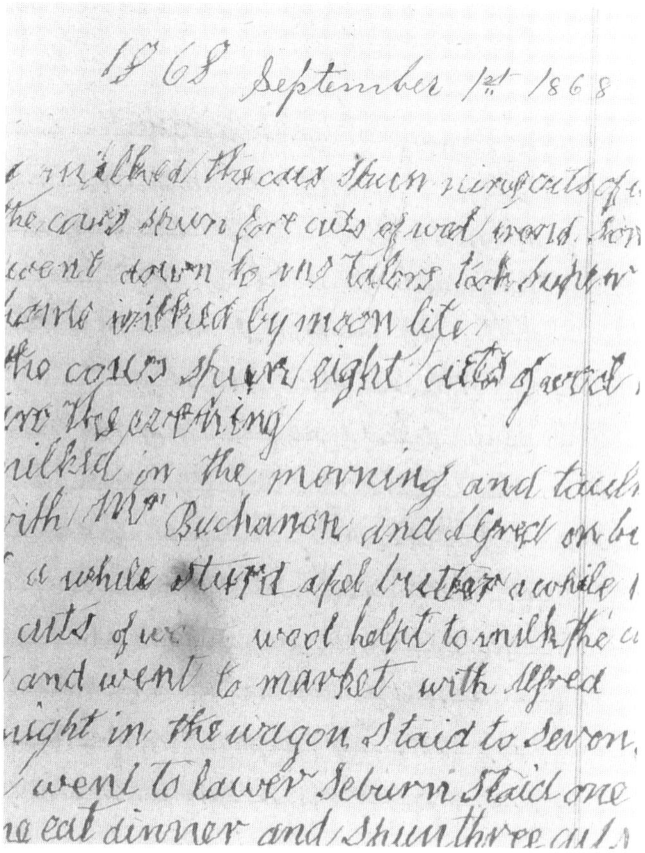

Writing Deformity

Of course, even when the system of writing is familiar to the reader, a particular individual's handwriting may yet present difficulties. The script may be altered by some physical debility of the writer (shaky writing can result from old age, for example), or its legibility may suffer from hasty scribbling (fig. 14.6). Again, some writers have their own peculiar way of making certain letters that can cause confusion.

An example will illustrate how eccentricities on the part of a writer (in this instance coupled with the reader's unfamiliarity with the writing system as well) can cause a misinterpretation to occur. A phrase in an old document (relating to the fabled "lost silver mines" of eastern Kentucky) had been transcribed and published as "the Cardinal points of the Camp aforesaid." Now, this makes no sense whatever, and, in fact, the correct phrase is a standard one: "the cardinal points of the compass" (i.e., north, south, east, and west). But (as the original showed) the clerk had made his *o*'s like *a*'s and had left gaps in words, so that—with the use of a long *s*—the word had appeared as "Camp afs." Had the transcriber written it as such (placing his interpretation of "afs" in brackets), as he should have, the cause of the error would have been more immediately apparent. Of course it would never have occurred— despite the original writer's deceptive penmanship— had the transcriber been familiar with the long *s* and the stock phraseology of old legal documents.[15]

In attempting to interpret a difficult handwriting, as in all cases of decipherment, one begins with known elements—such letters and whole words, here and there, as may readily be apparent—and uses those as keys to unlock further meaning. For example, a beginning letter that looks like an *R* but is followed by an unmistakable sequence *n-o-w* must actually be a *K*; and so what might have been interpreted elsewhere in the text as the surname "Ritner" may instead be "Kitner"—a fact that might be confirmed when actual in-

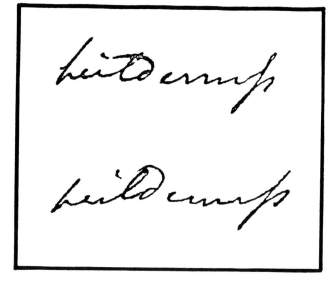

Figure 14.6. TREMULOUS WRITING, the frequent result of age or illness, can represent still another legibility problem, as in this journal entry of 1868.

Figure 14.7. A COMPOSITE TECHNIQUE can sometimes demonstrate a correct interpretation of a difficult-to-decipher word or phrase. Here, the puzzling word at the top is duplicated by the one following, which is a paste-up of known letters and letter combinations taken from elsewhere in the same document. The word is "wilderness."

Figures 14.8-14.9. ENHANCEMENT OF FADED WRITING.

14.8. Ultraviolet light has many applications in the examination of documents, including enhancing faded ink.

14.9. Photograph made with ultraviolet illumination enhances writing on this 1876 German-American baptismal certificate.

stances of the writer's *R* turn up further on in the writing for comparison.

One thus begins to assemble a specimen alphabet for a given handwriting that can be applied to particularly difficult words. The assemblage may be purely mental, or it could take the form of a chart, comprised of letters and words clipped from photocopies. For demonstrating an interpretation to others, when the same word (or phrase) cannot be found elsewhere in the text for one-on-one comparison, a *composite* word (or phrase) may be pasted up from a photocopy (fig. 14.7).

Perseverence in studying a text usually pays dividends. After perusing a given handwriting for a time, one becomes (so to speak) acclimatized to it. Then that which was difficult may be read with relative ease, and the "impossible" may become only the difficult.

Physical Deterioration

Texts that would otherwise be easy to read are frequently diminished in legibility by a variety of causes—fading ink for one example. Since the most common old ink was the iron-gallotannate variety (as discussed in chap. 5)—wherein the vegetable compounds can decompose and the iron oxidize—there have long been remedies for its regeneration.

An 1850s text, for instance, states that when such an ink "becomes yellow, pale or indistinct" due to age, "if the written surface be then carefully washed or even moistened with the infusion of nut-galls, it will be rendered blacker, and if before indistinct will become legible. This may sometimes be better accomplished by

first applying a weak solution of oxalic acid or very dilute muriatic (hydro-chloric) acid, and then delicately laying on the infusion of galls."[16] The acid renders the oxidized iron slightly soluble again so it can combine with the gallotannates of the nutgall solution. Instead of the latter, a solution of tannic acid can be employed.

A panoply of other chemical treatments is available, but this approach should be avoided if at all possible. Quite often ultraviolet light will dramatically enhance the old iron-gall or weak carbon-ink writing by causing the paper to fluoresce slightly, thus making the ink appear black by contrast (figs. 14.8-14.9).[17] With iron-gall or even other varieties of ink, photographing with special filters can often provide beneficial results.[18]

Infrared photography is a standard technique for restoring writing that has become obliterated, although sometimes, of course, no technique will succeed. It was employed with great success with portions of the Dead Sea scrolls that had become darkened with age. And it is routinely used in forensic laboratories to restore writing on charred documents and writing that has been erased or deliberately obliterated with ink.[19]

The technique may succeed when an ink that is transparent to infrared has been applied to one that is opaque to it.[20] Such was the case with Charles Dickens's correspondence, many of his letters having had passages inked out by protective family members. Infrared photography enabled scholars to read the obliterated portions, which contained references to "Nelly" and thus confirmed what had long been rumored: Dickens had indeed kept a young mistress named Ellen Ternan.[21]

Figure 14.10.
SUBSTITUTION CIPHERS, like this example from an 1870s autograph book, were popular with schoolchildren. Deciphered as "Asa Wallace. Mor[g]antown. W. Va.," it matches a name and address found elsewhere in the album and apparently rendered with the same pen and ink. The pencil-written cipher above—of the so-called "pigpen" type—has not been deciphered.

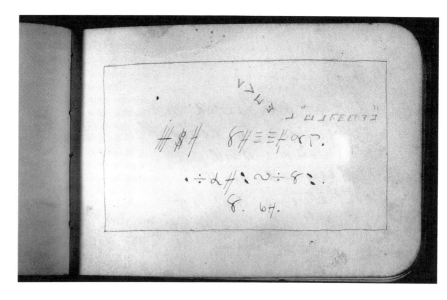

Figure 14.11. This CIPHER KEY from another autograph album shows that numbers were substituted for certain letters while remaining letters went unchanged. Can you read the entry following the key?

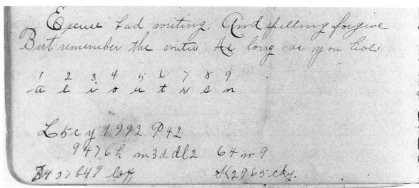

Today, argon laser light is increasingly being applied in cases heretofore reserved to ultraviolet and infrared examination—often with greatly improved results.[22] As well, specially filtered high-intensity light is now being offered as a less expensive substitute for the laser.[23]

Quite a different technique is applied to the indentations that remain from erased pencil writing or that have been left on a sheet of paper which was beneath the original when it was written. They can often be enhanced by oblique lighting (also known as "low angle grazing light"). This causes the otherwise indistinct text to appear in shadow, thus contrasting with the background. As with most such laboratory techniques, the results may be photographed for a permanent record.[24]

Secret Writing

Among the most difficult texts to comprehend are those deliberately obfuscated in some fashion that limits readership to select initiates. Such "secret" writings include cryptograms (codes and ciphers), as well as texts hidden from view by various means (e.g., by use of invisible ink).

Codes are cryptographic systems wherein arbitrary symbols (or words, etc.) stand for certain whole concepts (such as words, phrases, or the like). For example:

11111 = Do not transmit by letter
11112 = Transmit by wire in code
11113 = Transmit at your discretion

Such code groups with their "plaintext" equivalents are usually given in a code book (a sort of cryptographic dictionary). By theft, bribery, the salvage of sunken ships, and the like, foreign governments attempt to secure code books, without which codes are most difficult to crack.[25]

A simple code was apparently used by Charles Dickens as a means of signaling his mistress by telegram whether or not to join him when he was on tour in America. Discovered among the blank pages at the back of an old pocket diary of 1867, it reads:

Tel: all well means *you come*
Tel: Safe and well, means *you don't come*
To [William Henry] Wills. Who sends the Te. on to
Villa Trollope
fuori la porta S'Niccolo Florence [where Dickens's mistress was visiting].[26]

More suceptible of being solved are ciphers—that is, cryptograms in which the *letters* of the plaintext are transformed so as to conceal its meaning (the result being the "ciphertext"). In *transposition ciphers* the actual letters of the plaintext are retained but are transposed (scrambled) in some systematic fashion. *Substitution ciphers* have some symbol (possibly a number or another letter) that replaces each letter—either singly (e.g., 1 for *A*, 2 for *B*, and so on) or in pairs (*XM* for *TH*, for instance), or in some other manner (figs. 14.10 and 14.11).

Solving a cipher begins with the determination of whether it is a transposition or a substitution cipher. If the message is comprised of letters of the alphabet and contains about fifty words or more, a frequency count can be undertaken to see which letters appear most often. If those are the same (or nearly so) as those expected in an ordinary text—namely, *E* first, followed by, respectively, *T, A, O, N, R, I, S,* and *H*—then a transposition cipher is indicated.[27] Knowledge of the various transposition systems will assist in the deciperment, which is usually more difficult than solving a substitution cipher.[28]

If, on the other hand, the frequency count yields, in order, a sequence such as *Q, L, W, B, K, G, P, Z,* and *N* (or if the characters of the message are represented by symbols), then a substitution cipher is indicated. Suppose, in a given message, that *Q* and *L* thus appear to represent *E* and *T*—an interpretation seemingly confirmed as correct by the message's containing several instances of the three-letter combination *LNQ*, probably "the." One can adopt those letters, including *h*, as provisionally "known." Now other letters can probably be inferred and blank spaces filled in: *LNWL* is "th—t" (i.e., "that"), and a new piece of information (*W = A*) is gained. Proceeding in this manner, one is usually able to solve a simple substitution cipher without much difficulty. Excellent treatises on the subject—many with useful lists such as "pattern words" and various charts—are available to assist the cryptanalyst in his or her work.[29] Instructive short stories that feature deciperments of simple substitution ciphers include Sir Arthur Conan Doyle's Sherlock Holmes story, "The Adventure of the Dancing Men," and Edgar Allen Poe's "The Gold Bug."[30]

Secret writings other than cryptograms include those written in sympathetic ink (discussed in chap. 5). These can often be revealed by ultraviolet light.[31] Various other methods of producing secret texts, including

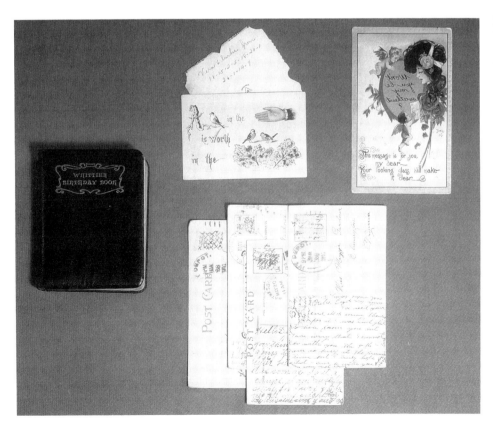

Figure 14.12. SECRET WRITING could take many forms: shorthand, used in the diary at left; ciphers, written on the reverse of a valentine and a rebus card; mirror writing, shown here in printed form but also penned on the back of the card; and concealed messages, hidden under postage stamps on these 1911-13 postcards that the sender mailed to his sweetheart at a girl's school.

mirror writing and concealing messages under postage stamps, are shown in figure 14.12. With methods like the latter, decipherment is not the problem; rather it is discovering the existence of the secret writing in the first place.

Whatever the decipherment problem, knowledge coupled with experience, aided by creative thinking and tempered by good judgment, will—time and energy permitting—usually result in a degree of success.

SELECT BIBLIOGRAPHY

Beardsley, Niel F. "The Photography of Altered and Faded Manuscripts." *Library Journal* 61 (1936): 96-99.

Ceram, C.W., ed. *Hands on the Past: Pioneer Archaeologists Tell Their Own Story.* New York: Knopf, 1966. Includes case studies of deciphering ancient texts and treats advances in computer decipherment.

Gardner, Martin. *Codes, Ciphers, and Secret Writing.* New York: Pocket Books, 1972.

Kirkham, E. Kay. *The Handwriting of American Records for a Period of 300 Years.* Logan, Utah: Everton, 1973. Guide to reading old round-hand writing.

Pratt, Fletcher. *Secret and Urgent: The Story of Codes and Ciphers.* Garden City, N.Y.: Blue Ribbon Books, 1942.

Tannenbaum, Samuel A. *The Handwriting of the Renaissance.* New York: Columbia Univ. Press, 1930. Standard treatise on the English secretary hand.

Thoyt, E.E. *How to Decipher and Study Old Documents*, 2d ed. 1903. Reprint. Detroit: Gale Research, 1974.

15

Age Determination

In addition to decipherment, a common problem for the document detective is the need to determine the age of a writing. Although, fortunately, most letters, legal papers, and other written materials do bear dates, many do not, or the dates are uncertain due to indecipherable writing or subsequent damage. Moreover, in the case of questioned documents (discussed in the following chapter), the penned date may be bogus, and uncovering that fact may resolve the question of authenticity.

Yet no matter how important may be the need, "it is not a simple matter to determine the age of a document," according to a forensic text, which adds, "Obviously the fixing of an exact date is an impossibility in the absence of eyewitnesses to the making of the document."[1] Nevertheless, a number of indicators can assist in establishing a probable age: the writing materials and type of writing employed, as well as such factors as evidence from the content itself. According to Osborn's *Quesioned Documents:*

> Under certain circumstances almost any element or phase of a document may have a bearing on the question of age and when critically examined may furnish evidence either for or against the contention that a document or part of a document is of a certain specified date.
>
> The actual age of a document is ascertained by a study of all the means by which it was produced and the actual conditions under which it was kept. All the external evidence bearing on the question should be thoroughly investigated. The phraseology throughout and the subject-matter of the document should be examined with reference to all the known conditions and facts that may be connected in any way with the case.[2]

Writing Materials as Age Indicators

Among the diverse elements that can help reveal a document's age are those of pen and ink and paper, discussed earlier in parts 1 through 3 and summarized in specific chronological charts in appendix 2.

Pen identification, for example, is an obvious adjunct to dating, since writing implements have evolved over time: the ancient "broad" (chisel-edged) pen (reed or quill) yielding to the pointed quill, thence to the steel pen, the fountain pen, including the distinctively stylographic variety, and, in more recent times, the ballpoint, porous-tip, and roller-ball pens (fig. 15.1). For all of these there are time periods—of varying degrees of specificity—with which they are associated (see app. 3).

Likewise, writing fluids have value in determining the age of a writing—from the carbon and iron-gallotannate inks of ancient times, to the iron-gall varieties containing indigo or logwood, to such later types as aniline and nigrosine inks. Simple tests for identifying the common inks of old documents—involving removal of an insignificant sample and testing with chemical reagents (figs. 15.2 and 15.3)—are detailed in appendix 3. More sophisticated tests of ink—such as neutron activation analysis and thin-layer chromatography—are available and can often provide decisive results. For example, detailed tests of the ink used in some forgeries of works by William Carlos Williams proved it had not been manufactured until a year after the poet's death.[3]

Paper offers especially valuable dating potential. Whether it is handmade—and if so, whether antique laid, laid, or wove pattern—or was produced by paper machine is of obvious significance. A watermark can provide very useful evidence (fig. 15.4); an obvious example is that of a "1799" watermark in one sheet of some minister's sermons I was attempting to date. Chemical tests to determine, for example, the presence of wood pulp (see app. 3) can also help to establish a minimum age for a document. Even how a paper has been used can have dating value, as was the case with the supposed "original" of Abraham Lincoln's letter to the widow Bixby; the document expert Charles Hamil-

Figure 15.1. PEN IDENTIFICATION CHART. From the ancient quill to the modern ballpoint, pens leave evidence of their form in the lines they trace.

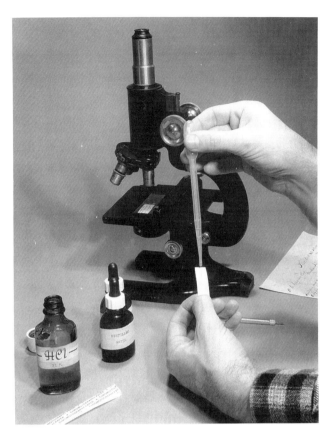

Figures 15.2-15.3. INK IDENTIFICATION TESTS

15.2 (*above*). A small sample of ink is transferred onto moistened chromatography paper by gentle rubbing with a suitable instrument.

15.3 (*right*). Various reagents are applied to the sample; color changes indicate the identity of such inks as iron-gall, logwood, nigrosine, and carbon.

ton observed that it was not folded correctly for envelopes of Lincoln's time.[4]

In the case of very old paper, or such other materials as Egyptian papyri or medieval parchments, radiocarbon dating can establish a time frame accurate to within an estimated 150 years. A small piece of the document about the size of a fingernail must be sacrificed, however, and the expense of the technique limits its use to only the most significant cases.[5]

Some of the other elements that can have evidential value in attempting to establish a date are paper fasteners, postmarks and postage stamps, seals, perforations and hole-punchings, and the presence of writing sand in the ink or indications of the use of a blotter (fig. 15.5).[6]

Dating Handwriting and Printing

Just as writing materials have changed over time, so have the styles of script, whether they be the evolving forms of Egyptian writing (hieroglyphic, hieratic, and demotic scripts), or the transition styles from Greek and Roman lettering to the Carolingian and Gothic hands of, respectively, the early and late Middle Ages, or the changing trends in English and American penmanship from secretary to round hand to later scripts (fig. 15.6). Of course, it should be kept in mind that any

script can be imitated by a skilled forger, and that outmoded forms (such as the long *s*) may persist in the handwriting of elderly persons even after new trends have become generally established. Despite such caveats, however, the stylistic evidence from the script—taken together with all additional factors—can help establish an approximate time frame for a document (see app. 2 for chronological charts that will provide assistance).

Like handwriting, printing can also offer dating evidence, since particular typefaces make their first appearance at known dates, as do processes employed in producing printed illustrations.[7] While an extended discussion is beyond the scope of the present study, the serious student is encouraged to consult reference works and to seek the help of antiquarians in learning to distinguish, for example, wood engravings from steel engravings, and chromolithographs from halftone prints (figs. 15.7- 15.10).[8] Some useful dates relating to printing are given in the chronological charts in appendix 2.

Clues from Internal Evidence

Internal evidence—that is, evidence from the content of a document—can often provide valuable dating information as well. An example is the case of the infamous "Beale Papers" of Virgina legend. According to these papers, one Thomas Jefferson Beale and a company of adventurous comrades in 1818 discovered a fabulous gold and silver lode in the American West, transported their treasure to Virginia, and concealed it in a rock-lined vault whose location is supposedly recorded in an unsolved cipher. The story surfaced in an 1885 pamphlet that told how a man named Robert Morriss had met Beale while Morriss was, in his own words, "keeping the Washington Hotel." Through research, however, I demonstrated that the Morriss account was probably written by a hoaxer. For instance, Morriss had not acquired the Washington *Inn* (its real name while Morriss owned it) until three years *after* Beale had allegedly wintered with him there. Among other indicators—sufficient to discredit the documents—was the word *stampeding*, a form of the Spanish noun *estampida*, apparently not used before about 1883 yet present in a "Beale" letter of 1822. A linguistic analysis subsequently showed that the author of the 1885 pamphlet had the same distinctive writing style as the author of the Beale Papers.[9]

Even as simple a "document" as an old tree in Louisville, Kentucky—inscribed "D. Boone. Kill a Bar. 1803."—was revealed as spurious on the basis of the date alone: In that year Daniel Boone was serving as a magistrate in Missouri, having already lived there a few years and not returning to Kentucky until about 1810.[10]

Figure 15.4. EARLY WATERMARKS can provide valuable dating evidence. Shown are some of the common types, each having many variants.

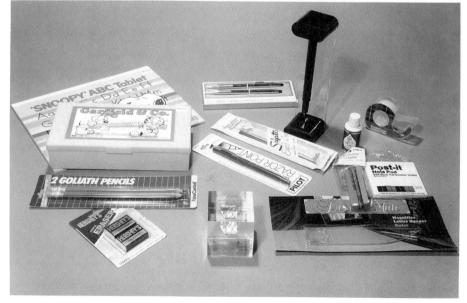

Figure 15.5. THE OLD AND THE NEW. Although all of the writing materials grouped here date from the latter twentieth century, many are basically carryovers from the Victorian era, for example (apart from their plastic construction), the pencil box and letter opener. Some, like the "roller" pen and the pen-and-ink correction fluid (or "white out"), leave an unmistakable mark of time upon a document.

Clockwise from holder with suspended magnetic pen: a bottle of Liquid Paper Pen & Ink Correction Fluid; Scotch Magic Transparent Tape in dispenser; a pad of Post-it notepaper ("Self-Stick Removable Notes"); a disposable stapler (*to left of pad*); a combination magnifier, letter opener, and ruler; a Lucite paperweight encapsulating a real doubloon from a shipwreck; erasers packaged like tiny Hershey's chocolate bars; FaberCastell Goliath pencils; a Garfield plastic pencil box; a Snoopy ABC Tablet; a Cross boxed pen and pencil set ("Fine writing instruments since 1846"); a Scripto "roller" pen; and a Pilot porous-point pen.

Figure 15.6. SCRIPT STYLES, as discussed in chapter 11, represent another factor with potential for dating a writing.

The document sleuth should be alert to any factual error in a writing that may indicate it was produced at a later date. Such internal evidence can assume crucial importance in situations in which the usual evidence from the writing materials is absent. That was the case not only with the aforementioned "Boone" tree but with the Beale papers as well, since the "originals" had supposedly perished in a fire.

Among the reference tools that may assist the investigator in attempting to establish a correct date is a perpetual calendar. For example, suppose the date of a letter is unclear—due, say, to a torn-off last digit, as in "Saturday, February 24, 183(?)." According to the perpetual calendar, Saturday fell on the twenty-fourth of February only once in the decade of the thirties, namely in 1838.

Combined Factors

Assessing multiple factors can help establish a time frame for an undated document or one whose date is questioned, as explained in a forensic text: "For example, if the model of the typewriter used to produce the document was not made before 1911, a minimum age can be set. Similarly, if the watermark of the papers was not used by the manufacturer after 1920, another probable maximum can be fixed. The use of a ball point pen would likewise limit the age." [11]

Figure 15.7.
WOOD ENGRAVINGS were popular from the late eighteenth to the late nineteenth century. They are impressions from woodblocks with lines cut in recess with a steel graver.

Figure 15.8 (*below*). STEEL ENGRAVINGS—prints from engraved steel plates—have been used since at least 1819. Note the dashed- line technique in the facial area and the various hatchings and cross-hatchings; compare with the illustration on any American currency, all of which is printed from engraved plates.

Figure 15.9.
CHROMOLITHOGRAPHS—
lithographs printed from multiple
color plates—originated in the late
1830s and continued into the 1920s
(especially for color postcards).
Magnification reveals both solid-
color and stippled areas.

A case in point is a scrap of antique paper I wished to date. It bore a cardinal's hat watermark (fig. 9.5) similar to examples dating from about 1649-52.[12] The secretary-hand script (fig. 11.22) was consistent with this time period, and a quirk of phraseology seemed to settle the matter: instead of referring to an *act* of parliament, it used the word "ordinance"; according to the *Oxford English Dictionary,* "The Acts of the Long Parliament after 1641 were at first called *Ordinances.*"[13] Thus, evidence from the paper and the handwriting, together with internal evidence, dovetailed to provide an estimated date of circa 1650.

Another example comes from a Tennyson autograph that had been framed (with an engraved portrait of the poet) so that it appeared to be a "cut signature." When removed, however, it was revealed as a larger piece of paper bearing an inscription. (It is shown in fig. 13.19.) Helping to authenticate the autograph was internal evidence from the inscription, together with a study of the writing materials and comparison of the signature with known specimens. Signs of age, although not of

themselves proof of authenticity, were also part of the total equation. These signs included oxidization of the ink and yellowing of the paper (cellulose degradation), both at one end and in an area around the signature corresponding to a cut-out rectangle in the mat.

The advisability of considering multiple factors was demonstrated by the case of Mark Hofmann, the purveyor of fake Mormon papers and other bogus historic documents, who eventually resorted to two bombing murders in an attempt to cover his crimes. Hofmann was a knowledgable document dealer who used old paper, made his own ink, and employed artificial aging techniques to create sophisticated forgeries that fooled many experts. (I was twice consulted in the case of Hofmann's notorious "white salamander letter," once by an assistant district attorney regarding Hofmann's chemical "aging" of iron-gallotannate ink, and again by a handwriting expert concerning the type of pen believed to have been employed.)

One of Hofmann's imaginative creations was a copy of the "Oath of a Free Man"—known as the first exam-

Figure 15.10.
HALFTONE
REPRODUCTIONS
exhibit a characteristic
"screen" pattern of dots
under magnification.

ple of printing in America, although no actual specimen of it had ever been found. The forger had pasted up authentic old type characters in order to have a printing plate made, and he apparently used an artificial aging technique that fooled one laboratory into concluding the ink's bonding to the paper demonstrated an age of some three hundred years.[14] Typographical anomalies and other factors, however, allowed investigators to expose the forgery.[15]

Almost anything can provide a clue, as Osborn makes clear: "It frequently happens that names of persons, firms, or corporations, names or numbers of streets, or references to events or transactions in a questioned document have a conclusive chronological significance and prove it was made after a certain definite date. Even a post office cancelling stamp may have a most important date significance or a postage stamp design may have a definite date value. Names of officers on a letterhead or a telephone number may have positive date value."[16] By being alert to all such possibilities, the examiner can often succeed in restoring to a document a lost date, or in exposing as more recent a writing that pretends to a certain antiquity.

SELECT BIBLIOGRAPHY

Damon, P.E., et al. "Radiocarbon Dating of the Shroud of Turin, *Nature*, 337 (1989): 611-15. Demonstrates the possibility of dating small samples—in this instance, cloth—by carbon-14 testing.

Grant, Julius. *Books and Documents: Dating, Permanence, and Preservation*. New York: Chem. Pub., 1937. Useful, if not error-free, text with data on dating manuscripts.

Nickell, Joe. "Discovered: The Secret of Beale's Treasure." *Virginia Magazine of History and Biography* 90 (1982): 310-24. A case study in dating the text of a questioned manuscript that had supposedly been destroyed accidentally.

Osborn, Albert S. *Questioned Documents*. 1910. 2d ed. Montclair, N.J.: Patterson Smith, 1978. Classic forensic text with much data relevant to determining the age of a writing.

16

Questioned Documents

A third major class of document problem is the frequent need to determine the authenticity of a writing. According to Osborn: "A document is usually questioned because its origin, its contents, or the circumstances and story regarding its production, arouse serious suspicion as to its genuineness, or it may be adversely scrutinized simply because it displeases someone by its unexpected provisions." Whatever the reason for its being suspected, once a document has in fact been questioned, then, insists Osborn, "everything about it should be promptly and thoroughly examined."[1]

Of course, an important aspect of many disputed-document investigations is the determination of age, which (as discussed in the previous chapter) may not only be a goal in itself but can also have profound relevance as to authenticity. Thus the document detective may seek to learn whether an undated writing can be attributed to a particular time period (and if so, the implications thereof to the inquiry at hand), or whether a dated writing was actually produced when alleged.

Other common problems are those in which one seeks to determine the identity of an unknown writer of a document; the source and/or age of typewriting; whether a signature or other writing was made by a particular individual, or was instead made by a secretary or other person or is actually a forgery; and whether the document has been altered, as by erasures, additions, deletions, and so on, and, if so, why.[2]

The earliest recorded instances of handwriting examinations are from third-century Rome. Roman jurists set forth protocols for the detection and proof of forgeries, and during the sixth century the emperor Justinian established additional guidelines. Persons who were especially skilled in writing could give testimony as to the authenticity of a disputed text, largely based on "resemblance or similitude of hands." The Roman approach prevailed in western Europe for the next millennium.[3]

The same held true in England for ecclesiastical courts, but in other English judicial proceedings common law had rendered it all but impossible for handwriting to be authenticated except by testimony of eyewitnesses to the original writing. By the seventeenth century—at least in France, where handwriting experts were called "master writers"—a more "scientific" (i.e., systematic and detailed) approach to handwriting comparison began to prevail. The Frenchmen F. Demelle in 1609 and J. Raveneau in 1666 advocated analysis of such elements as the manner in which the pen was held and moved (determined, respectively, by the trace of the nib and by line quality), speed of writing (judged by the density of the strokes), and letter formation.[4]

In colonial America, protocols for judging genuineness of writings naturally followed English common-law practices, but after the Revolution most state jurisdictions began to allow the testimony of experts, who were permitted to give an opinion in such matters. Little is known about this period of comparatively little activity, but handwriting identification became increasingly common in courts of the eastern United States in the latter part of the nineteenth century.

The first significant modern text that attempted a detailed, scientific approach to questioned documents—including chemical tests for detecting alterations—was *Disputed Handwriting*, written by W.E. Hagan in 1894. Albert S. Osborn (1858-1946) dominated the period at the turn of the century, publishing a pioneering article on typewriting identification in 1901 and his monumental *Questioned Documents* in 1910.[5]

Forgery

Although there are many types of challenges for the manuscript sleuth, the uncovering of forgery is among the most persistent and pressing. Indeed, it is to the forger that the specialized field of document examination owes its very existence: "Since the earliest instances of the use of a written form as a means of communication, there have undoubtedly been instances of alteration of documents with the intent of changing their meaning or values, or of a fraudulent *de novo* fabrication of documents. Forgery has surely been practiced in every country and civilization with a literate populace; collaterally, for as long as the alteration of documents has existed, some means has been required to establish their validity or to establish that a forgery has in fact taken place." [6]

In earlier centuries, widespread illiteracy meant that forgery was largely confined to the upper classes and often entailed imitation, not of a signature but of its practical equivalent: a seal. Whereas faking a king's seal could be punished as treason, forgery of a lesser signet was only punishable commensurate with the injury caused.

Forgeries flourished in European churches in the fifteenth century: "Clerics comprised the majority of those who could read and write, and a number of them forged and sold papal bulls and dispensations for high prices. On occasion they also supplied themselves with documents that could improve their own power or position; university professors not infrequently engaged in the same practice." [7]

Forgery became an increasingly common crime with the advance of literacy, and it became a statutory offense in England in 1562. At that time, the forger could be fined, pilloried, mutilated by having his ears cut off or his nostrils slit, or punished by perpetual imprisonment and/or confiscation of land. [8] Eventually, daring forgers began to achieve a measure of notoriety. George Psalmanazar (ca. 1679-1763) posed as a Japanese and fooled scholars with fictitious writings on Formosa. [9]

The teenage poet Thomas Chatterton (1752-70) produced a remarkable series of poems—penned in pseudo "earlie Englisshe" on parchment and allegedly written by a fifteenth-century monk named Rowley. Chatterton had intended to reveal his deception once his verses had been acclaimed by his literary contemporaries, but when the works were examined and denounced as fakes, the seventeen-year-old prodigy committed suicide. His tragic death was much lamented by the later romantics, including Samuel Taylor Coleridge and John Keats. [10]

William Henry Ireland (1777-1835), the son of a London engraver and author, forged letters of Elizabethan notables and an impressive array of Shakespearean documents. These included annotated volumes from his library, contracts with actors, notes and receipts, drawings, an expression of love to Anne Hathaway, manuscript fragments of *King Lear* and *Hamlet*, and, finally, an entire manuscript drama, *Vortigern and Rowena*. But after the play was laughed off the stage of Drury Lane Theater, Ireland's productions

Figures 16.1-16.3 (*top to bottom*).   CRUDE FORGERY.

16.1. A mourning card, purportedly signed by "Mrs. A. Lincoln," bears little resemblance to the smoothly penned script of the widowed first lady.

16.2. Sketchily produced, heavily retouched characters are further proof of forgery.

16.3. Additional confirmation of forgery is found on closer inspection, which reveals traces of the pencil first used to draw the signature. Traces are visible at the lower-right leg of the *A* along its left side and at the bottom of the period.

were increasingly suspected and he eventually published a confession, an *Authentic Account of the Shakespearian MSS* (1796). [11]

Among other notorious forgers were the nineteenth-century American penmen Robert Spring (1813-76)

Figures 16.4-16.5. "POSTHUMOUS" SIGNATURE of Robert E. Lee.

16.4 (*left*). A bogus signature of the Confederate general has been added, in brown ink, to a genuine *carte de visite* of Lee's time.

16.5 (*above*). Inspection reveals the signs of a slowly drawn forgery: irregular pen pressure and tremulous line quality.

and Joseph Cosey (b. 1887), who forged papers of Washington, Franklin, and other American heroes. Cosey even produced an entire draft of the Declaration of Independence in Jefferson's handwriting.[12] Notable forgers in this century have been Clifford Irving, who wrote an "autobiography" of Howard Hughes; Konrad Kujau, who produced the multivolume "Hitler diaries"; and Mark Hofmann, who forged Mormon and other papers, then turned to bombing-murders in an attempt to prevent exposure.[13]

Detecting forgeries can be a challenging endeavor, since not all fakes are as easy to spot as the crude effort shown in figures 16.1-16.3. For example, the infamous "white salamander letter," purporting to relate early Mormon history but actually a forgery by Mark Hofmann, went undetected by the laboratory of the Federal Bureau of Investigation. I later spotted it as a fake from a photograph, due to the manner in which it was folded and other indications, while the handwriting expert Charles Hamilton and forensic examiners were already preparing a case against Hofmann.[14]

Although the following list of common signs that can point to forgery does not constitute a complete treatise on the subject, it should prove helpful for the autograph collector, archivist, and others with an interest in manuscript material. One should bear in mind, however, that some indicators are just that, not in themselves proof of inauthenticity but rather requiring evaluation in connection with additional evidence, while others (for example, a watermark that did not originate until

after the date penned on the document) would immediately betray forgery.[15]

1. Incorrect writing materials, including pen, ink, paper, and other elements. For example, Charles Hamilton tells how one forger's victim, who had purchased a manuscript poem allegedly written by Lord Byron, should have "read the watermark—1834, ten years after Byron's death."[16] See appendixes 2 and 3 for data on writing materials that can help unmask the inauthentic.

2. Incorrect writing characteristics for time period indicated. The style and form of a writing (see part 4) should be consistent with the time and place it was supposedly produced. As Osborn states: "to be entirely safe and successful the forger in America in many instances must have some historical knowledge of American handwriting; fortunately he seldom uses it."[17] For instance, Hamilton says of one early Cosey forgery, "the Palmer-method script does not suggest the eloquent flourishes of the Revolutionary era."[18] On similar grounds, I exposed a fake Daniel Boone letter.

3. Off-scale writing. The forger often unconsciously shrinks the writing of his subject; according to Hamilton this is "probably because of a psychological desire to conceal his fraud by making it less easy to read." Robert Spring's "G⁰ Washington," for example, was typically only one-half to two-thirds that of the first president's own signature.[19] Or a forger may inadvertently enlarge a diminutive handwriting by copying from a facsimile that is not to scale, as from a book. It should be cautioned, however, that "writing situations will change the size of writing"; for instance, a small signature box on a printed form might result in a signature's being smaller than normal for an individual.[20]

4. Uncommon forms. Beware of any form—particularly of a signature—that is different from a given writer's usual one. For example, in a forged letter of Charles Dickens, a forger "neglected to note Dickens' normal complimentary close."[21] As another example, amateur forgers have often used the wrong form of signature for Abraham Lincoln. Lincoln customarily used "Abraham Lincoln" for official papers but not (with three or four exceptions) for letters; for those he used "A. Lincoln" (or rarely, in letters to intimates, "A.L." or "Lincoln"); he never used "Abe."[22]

5. Evidence of tracing or prior drawing. Traced signatures represent a very common type of forgery. They typically have "all the characteristics of unnatural handwriting, with its appearance of having been drawn and with the lack of spontaneity and natural variations."[23] The forger may first have traced the lines with a sharp instrument, thus leaving telltale indentations distinguishable under the microscope from the pen's, or with a pencil, thus leaving pencil marks (as in the detail of the forgery shown in fig. 16.3) or erasures.[24]

6. Irregularity in strokes and retouching. Normal handwriting is freely executed and thus usually characterized by light upstrokes and "feathered" beginning and ending strokes, indicating speed. In contrast, forged writing often has an unnatural attention to detail, is belabored, hesitant, and often shows evidence of pen lifts and retouching strokes that are absent from genuine handwriting.[25] An extreme example is shown in fig. 16.2.

7. Tremulous writing. This is another unnatural trait that indicates a slowly drawn movement, unlike the smooth strokes of confident, natural writing. It is a common indication of forgery but must be distinguished from the tremulous writing of age, illness, or "illiterate writing."[26] For instance, to determine whether the "R. E. Lee" autograph of figs. 16.4 and 16.5 was genuine, several authentic Lee signatures penned prior to his death were inspected: none was shaky.

8. Writing applied to old paper. Old paper often loses its sizing, with the result that new writing leaves a suspicious, fuzzy appearance, like that of writing done over an erasure (fig. 7.13).[27] If the old paper had been folded before the new writing was added, this may also be detected by the spreading of ink along the fold, since folding can make the paper more porous.[28] In one case it was demonstrated that a fold across a sheet occurred *after* the signature was written but *before* the body of the

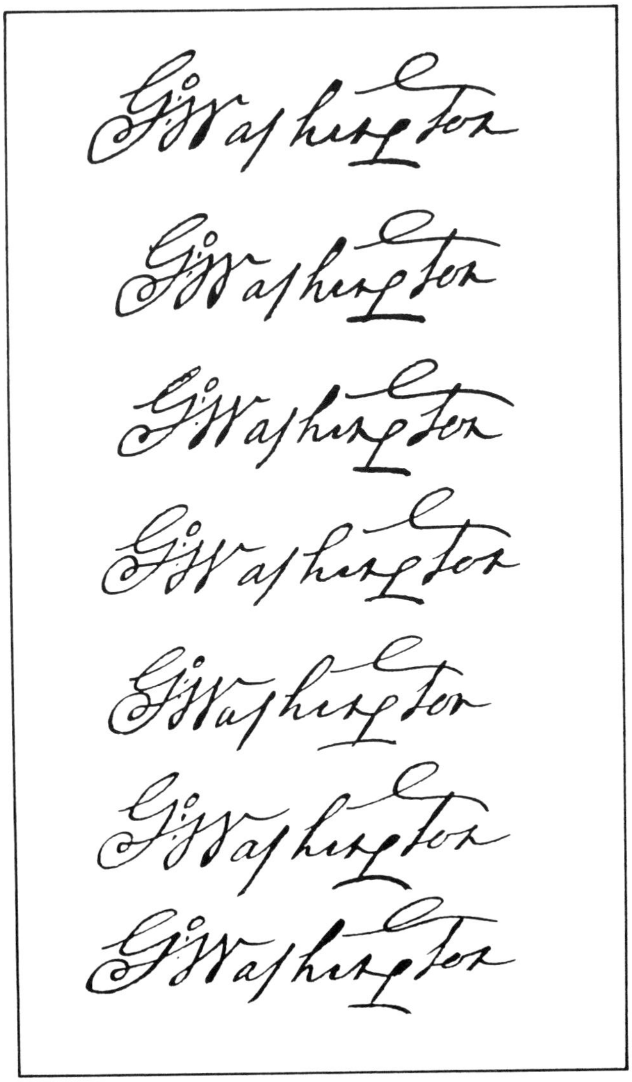

Figure 16.6. FORGER'S PRACTICE SHEET is one of many required in preparation for a freehand forgery. With sufficient practice, a skilled penman can produce a signature which closely resembles that of his target and which lacks the tremors and amateurish efforts. These beginning examples were done, appropriately, with a quill.

document; this demonstrated the signature was written first and, in fact, the document consisted of a forged text over a genuine signature.[29]

9. Evidence of artificial aging. In order to impart to a document an appearance of age, the forger often resorts to heating the document, either by holding it over a stove or baking it in an oven; exposing it to sunlight (or carbon-arc lamps or ultraviolet lights); treating it with chemicals; staining it with tea, coffee, or dirt; or crumpling or otherwise abusing it.[30] States Kenneth Rendell, "These forgers seem to be unaware that most autograph material is in good condition, and that persons normally wrote letters and documents on paper that was in good condition, without holes or other defects."[31] Careful inspection—possibly laboratory examination—may reveal signs of artificial aging. Examination with ultraviolet light showed that Mark Hofmann chemically treated some of his documents in order artificially to age—that is, oxidize—his iron-gall ink.[32]

10. Other factors. A careful study of a disputed text might reveal an incorrect format, content with factual errors, or any of a number of other anomalies that could indicate forgery. Again, it is important to study everything related to a questioned document.

Finally, something should be said about provenance (the history or chain of ownership of a document, published book, manuscript, or the like). It is always desirable to learn the true provenance of a work, and the loss of provenance (as by the removal of a page from a scrapbook, sentiment album, or other volume that might have a traceable provenance) is most regrettable. Still, as Roy L. Davids says regarding questions of authenticity: "Provenance can be important, but it can never be unimpeachable—externals must always be inferior to a thorough examination of the manuscript itself."[33] Worse, provenances can themselves be faked. As Charles Hamilton cautions:

> *Do not be misled by dealer markings on a document, or by penciled notations or by repairs or by evidence of prior mountings or framing.* Skilled forgers often rig such details, thus beguiling their victims into the belief that the document has long been accepted as genuine and has already passed under critical eyes. Printed descriptions of the suspect document from old sales catalogues are of very little value, since many oldtime autograph dealers and auction houses sold autographs "as is," and the philographic market is peppered with fakes that have passed through the hands of various dealers during the last century.[34]

Obviously, provenance will hold more interest concerning a sensational work, and the refusal of the possessor of an item to state where and how he obtained it—the cases of the "Vinland map" and "Hitler diaries" come to mind—must be interpreted accordingly. Certainly, contradictory stories with regard to provenance (again the "Hitler diaries" case is an instance) or evidence of faked provenance should prompt the most thorough investigation and examination of the work in question.

It should be stressed that a skilled forger—using correct materials and relying on freehand skill, supported by considerable practice (fig. 16.6)—can achieve a high degree of perfection. Fortunately, however, as one forensic text reports, "perfect forgeries are so rare that it is doubtful if many document examiners have ever seen one."[35]

Handwriting Identification

As Charles E. O'Hara states in his *Fundamentals of Criminal Investigation*, "The majority of questioned document cases are concerned with proving authorship."[36] The manuscript detective may seek to know, for example, whether an unsigned document was written by a particular individual (an anonymous letter by a suspect, for instance) or whether a letter or document was actually written by the individual whose signature is affixed to it.

In such cases the correct procedure involves obtaining known *standards* (authentic specimens of a subject's handwriting), which are then compared with the questioned writing. As O'Hara explains:

> The principles underlying the comparison of handwriting are similar to those on which the science of fingerprint identifications is based. No two products of man or nature are identical, and differences are perceptible if a sufficiently close study is made. Through years of practice each individual acquires permanent habits of handwriting. The group of characteristics which form his script constitutes an identifiable picture. In comparing two specimens of handwriting the expert searches for characteristics which are common to both the questioned and standard writing. If the characteristics are sufficient in kind and number and there are no significant unexplainable differences, he may conclude that the writings were made by the same person.[37]

Before such a comparison is made, however, the examiner carefully examines the questioned writing. Gideon Epstein, a noted document expert, has stated: "In the comparison and identification of handwriting, the first thing that must be done is that the disputed writing or the disputed signatures . . . must be examined to determine that the signatures are naturally executed, freely executed, executed with what we consider careless abandon or unconscious effort, and that the habits that are there are in fact unconscious, habitual movements. . . . And that they were not drawn or traced or in some manner forged."[38] Second, the expert examines the known or standard writings to determine what the genuine handwriting habits of the individual are. Third, and finally, the examiner compares the disputed writing with the standards.[39]

Characteristics which form a basis for the comparison include *quality of line* (affected by pen position, pressure, rhythm, speed, tremor, skill, and other factors), *form* (including proportions, slant, beginning and ending strokes, flourishes, and the like), and *spelling and punctuation* (a consequence of education).[40]

Oftentimes, in presenting evidence of authorship to a jury, the examiner prepares a chart consisting of

Figures 16.7-16.14. "GENUINE FAKES" comprise autographic material that is not forged, yet is not quite authentic.

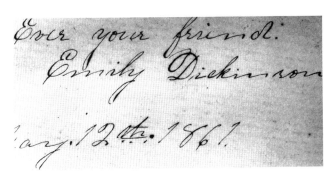

16.7. This "Emily Dickinson" signature is from a genuine nineteenth-century autograph album; however, it was penned, not by the famous poet, but by another young lady of the same name.

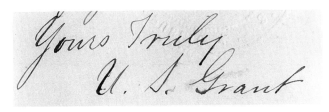

16.9. The signature "U.S. Grant" was sold to the author as a "forgery" because the writing did not resemble that of the Union general. Actually a forgery would probably bear a close resemblance, and, as it happens, the letter was a copy written out by a notary public. His attestation and seal are found on the verso.

16.10. "Martin Van Buren" is actually a proxy signature—one signed for him by his secretary. The document, of course, is entirely legal.

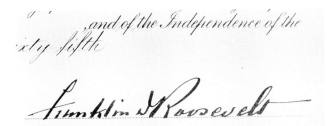

16.13. "Franklin D. Roosevelt" is a *printed* signature on a postmaster's commission—that is, it was on the plate that printed the blank form. The commission—which bears the authentic signature of the postmaster general—was that of my late father, J. Wendell Nickell, who received it in 1940 and who served as postmaster at West Liberty, Ky., for the subsequent thirty-four years.

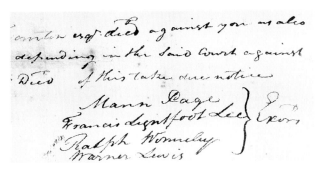

16.8. This "Francis Lightfoot Lee" signature is actually no such thing. Rather, this entire document—"signatures" and all—is a copy in a clerk's hand. Note the similarity of the "Francis" in the text above the signatures to that of the "signature" of the famous signer of the Declaration. Such copies were routine in the days before photocopiers.

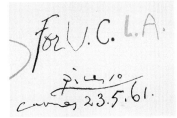

16.11. "Picasso" is from an original lithograph; the name was "signed on the plate."

16.12. "Edwin M. Stanton" is a rubber-stamped signature on a Civil War document.

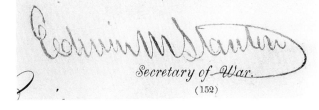

16.14. "G? Washington" is an engraver's copy of the first president's autograph, here reproduced from an old book.

Figure 16.15. This COLLECTION OF FAKES includes reproduction documents and Confederate currency (on imitation parchment!), a brass inkstand (*center*) and (*from left*) a pewter inkstand, a small Carter's "cathedral" ink bottle, and an imitation-ivory (plastic) letter opener.

photographically enlarged letters, words, or other distinctive characteristics from the two writings. Those from the questioned document are arranged in one column and those from the standards in another, so that a side-by-side comparison can be made.[41] This allows "instantaneous perception" of the similarities.[42] Occasionally, a composite technique (like that shown in fig. 14.7) is employed.[43]

It should be noted that modern forensic document analysis eschews measuring exact heights or spacings, although *ratios* are considered, or any kind of exact meaurements in writing, because of the variations that normally occur.[44] This is in contrast to the practice of some graphologists—those who attempt to determine personality from handwriting.[45]

Another cautionary note concerns "class" characteristics in writing. These are features common to a given handwriting system and thus shared by numerous writers; it is therefore paramount that these not be mistaken for *individual* characteristics.[46]

"Genuine Fakes"

An important category of autograph consists of those which are neither fish nor fowl, as it were—neither quite "genuine" nor yet forgeries. We might term them "genuine fakes." They are frequently encountered and are the bane of the autograph collector. Still, the document sleuth will find them interesting, instructive, and sometimes amusing.

One type is represented by the Emily Dickinson signature shown in figure 16.7. An absolutely authentic signature, just as it appears in an old autograph album in my collection, it is nevertheless worthless. That is because it was not written by *the* Emily Dickinson, the American poet, but by another of the same name. Their signatures bear no resemblance. In his article "Confused Identities," Joseph E. Fields discusses such cases of "identical names"—the two James Madisons for instance—and explains how to avoid mistaking the one for the other.[47]

A second category of signature that is at once genuine and not is represented by three subtypes (as illustrated in figs. 16.8-16.10). That of Francis Lightfoot Lee (1734-97), signer of the Declaration of Independence, is from a *clerk's copy*—that is, the entire document, including Lightfoot's "signature," is in the hand of a clerk—the document probably having been made as a file copy (fig. 16.8). That of U.S. Grant (1822-85), the famed Civil War general and eighteenth president of the United States, is from a letter which I purchased as a "forgery"; instead it is a *notarized copy*, being clearly identified as such on the verso (fig. 16.9). And that of Martin Van Buren (1782-1862), the eighth president of the United States, is what is termed a *proxy signature*;

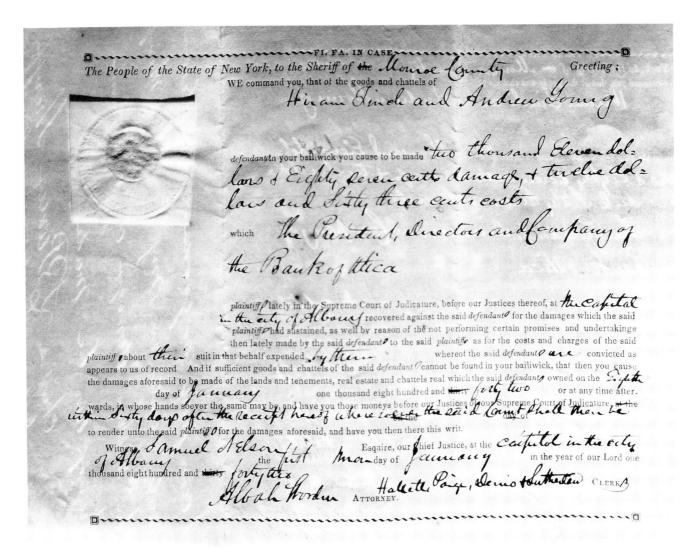

Figure 16.16. "GHOST WRITING"—the mirror-image script shown here in white—has been revealed by argon-laser light. Such writing can be produced by the corrosiveness of ink causing offsetting onto paper in contact with it (as by a document being folded on itself). Sometimes the writing is visible to the unaided eye in the form of faint brown traces, the result of cellulose degradation. Photo by John F. Fischer.

that is, it was legally signed for Van Buren, like so many other land grants, by his secretary, whose name appears below, immediately following the word "By" (fig. 16.10).

A third category of "genuine fakes" is the reproduction signature. That of Pablo Picasso (1881-1973), the great artist, is actually not a mere reproduction but is from an *original lithograph* "signed on the plate" and produced in a limited edition (fig. 16.11). That of Edwin M. Stanton (1814-69), Lincoln's secretary of war, is a *rubber-stamped signature* (fig. 16.12). That of Franklin D. Roosevelt (1882-1945), three times president of the United States (fig. 16.13), is a *printed signature*—printed with the rest of the document (with blanks that were filled in later), in this instance a postmaster's commission. And that of George Washington (1732-99) is an

engraved signature, copied by an engraver and printed in an old book (fig. 16.14). Numerous facsimile documents, documents reproduced in imitation of the original, are frequently encountered by the manuscript sleuth (fig. 16.15). These include Lincoln's letter to Mrs. Bixby, the script of which is actually a forgery; a draft of the Gettysburg Address—often, ridiculously, printed on imitation parchment, whereas Lincoln naturally used paper; and others, including General Order No. 9, relating to the surrender of the Confederacy, signed by Robert E. Lee.[49]

Still another category is the *robot signature*, which falls somewhere between the proxy and the reproduction signature. It is one produced by such devices as the Autopen or Signa-Signer, both of which utilize a mechanical pattern to counterfeit precisely their owner's signature using his or her own ballpoint or other pen. They are used by movie stars, presidents (first by John F. Kennedy), and others who have an extensive correspondence. Any robot signature produced from the same pattern will be identical to another (that is, the two will exactly superimpose) although the master pattern can be changed often, to the consternation of autograph collectors.[50]

Laboratory Analysis

Although financial considerations may limit sophisticated laboratory analyses to criminal matters or to sensational cases like that of the "Hitler diaries," the range of scientific possibilities is quite broad.

Laser examination, for example, has considerable potential and may succeed in revealing some hidden traces that remain invisible to ultraviolet and infrared examination.[51] One such application is shown by a photograph of a document in my collection made by the forensic analyst John F. Fischer (fig. 16.16). Laser light revealed "ghost writing" on the document—that is, invisible offsetting of handwriting caused by the corrosive properties of the ink and common to many old documents.

Laser technology is also used to discriminate between similar inks when other methods may prove unsuccessful.[52] Thin-layer chromatography, commonly employed in forensic laboratories to analyze inks and paper samples, played a major role in uncovering the "Hitler diaries" hoax.[53] Simpler—but nevertheless forensically routine—"spot" tests of inks and paper are given in appendix 3.

Recovery of faded, obliterated, and charred writing and that done in invisible ink was discussed in chapter 14. Other techniques or analyses are available for identification of typewriters, checkwriters, and handstamps; detection of forged stamp impressions and cancellations; detection of various alterations, such as erasures; development of fingerprints from documents; identification of various markings (e.g., staple holes), stains (including blood), and foreign matter. Additional capabilities range from the routine to the exotic.[54]

Such techniques can play a crucial role in document examination but, of course, there is no substitute for a keen mind nourished on factual knowledge and experience, bolstered by a willingness to persevere, and governed by a desire for the truth. That should be the document detective's ultimate goal.

SELECT BIBLIOGRAPHY

Hamilton, Charles. *Great Forgers and Famous Fakes: The Manuscript Forgers of America and How They Duped the Experts.* New York: Crown, 1980.

Harrison, W.R. *Suspect Documents: Their Scientific Examination.* London: Grafton, 1937.

Mitchell, C. Ainsworth. *Documents and Their Scientific Investigation.* London: C. Griffin, 1935.

Morton, A.Q. *Literary Detection: How to Prove Authorship and Fraud in Literature and Documents.* New York: Scribner's, 1978.

Osborn, Albert S. *Questioned Documents.* 1910. 2d ed. Montclair: Patterson Smith, 1978.

Rendell, Kenneth W. "The Detection of Forgeries." In *Autographs and Manuscripts: A Collector's Manual*, ed. Edmund Berkeley, Jr., 73-91. New York: Scribner's, 1978.

They Write Their Own Sentences: the FBI Handwriting Analysis Manual. Boulder, Colo: Paladin, 1987. Introduction to the work of the Document Section of the FBI Laboratory.

APPENDIX 1

Eighteenth-Century Scripts

German Text.

Round Text.

Square Text.

Round Hand.

Engrossing.

Secretary.

Joseph Champion Scr.

Old English Print.

Italick Print.

Roman Print.

Italian Hand.

Court Hand.

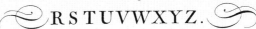

The Chancery.

Champion Scrip.

Reproduced from George Bickham's *The Universal Penman* (1741; repr., New York: Dover, 1954), 210-11.

APPENDIX 2
Chronology of Writing & Writing Materials

Pens

624 A.D.   Earliest certain reference to quill pen.

10th cent.   Legendary invention of a pen that carried its own supply of ink.

1565   German-Swiss naturalist Konrad von Gesner, described what may have been the first wooden pencil (a piece of graphite in a wooden holder).

1662   Pencils made in Nuremberg, Germany, having leads molded from graphite dust mixed with adhesives.

1663   Samuel Pepys recorded that he had a reservoir pen.

1700   Early reference to steel pens (made in France).

1723   Detailed description of a French fountain pen published in English.

Ca. 1748   Steel pen produced in France but unpopular due to stiffness and price.

1761   Kaspar Faber founded great pencil-making dynasty at Stein, Germany.

1770   British chemist Joseph Priestly announced that a certain vegetable gum—renamed "rubber"—could be used to rub out pencil marks.

1780   Steel pens made in England by Samuel Harrison.

Ca. 1785   Pencils became common but not for writing letters or documents.

Late 18th cent.   Nicoles Jacques Conté (1755-1805) developed the modern process of mixing graphite with clay to make pencil leads, which were then fired in a kiln.

1803   Metal pens marketed with some success in London.

1808   Bryan Donkin obtained the first patent for metal pens (England).

1809   Joseph Bramah patented a machine for cutting a quill into separate nibs to be used with a holder.

             U.S. patent for "metallic writing pen" issued to Peregrine Williamson.

             First two English patents issued for reservoir pens.

1810   Rhodium-tipped gold pens in use.

1818   Charles Watt patented a method of giving a metallic cast to quills by dipping them in nitromuriate of gold.

1819   English Penograph reservoir pen was patented; the flow of ink to the metal or quill nib had to be periodically replenished by means of a small lever.

1820   Modern type of metal pen nib invented.

1822   Machine-made steel pens introduced in England by John Mitchell.

             Invention of "patent ever-pointed" (i.e., mechanical or propelling) pencil.

1824	Englishman James Perry began making pens on a large scale.
1830	Perry patented a more flexible metal pen, with additional slits and a hole above the central slit.
	First American patent for a fountain pen awarded to D. Hyde of Reading, Pa.
Ca. 1845	The steel pen had by this time become fully accepted.
1849	Early patent for a stylographic pen, termed an "ink pencil."
Ca. 1850	Glass pens known by this time.
1857	"Copying" pencils were first made.
1858	First steel-pen company established in United States by Richard Esterbrook, Jr., who began by selling English pens.
	Patent by Hyman L. Lipman of pencil with eraser—prototype of later "penny pencil."
1861	First large-scale pencil manufactory established in United States (in New York) by John Eberhard Faber.
	Esterbrook began manufacturing his own Esterbrook nibs.
1866	"Indelible" pencils (containing methyl-violet, graphite, and binder) patented; wetting converted writing to inklike form.
Ca. 1870s	Pens marketed that held a stick of concentrated ink which was dipped in water for writing.
Early 1870s	Advertisements for fountain pens became common, for example, Prince's Improved Fountain Pen and the Darling Self-Supplying Penholder.
1870s	Stylographic pen became popular (see 1849).
	Stub pen "rare" at this time.
1884	First truly successful fountain pen marketed by Lewis E. Waterman, who created effective "feed."

1888	John J. Loud obtained U.S. patent for a reservoir pen with a rotatable ball, intended for marking cartons and the like. George S. Parker established his own fountain-pen company.
1890	Cartridge fountain pens, originally utilizing glass vials, patented (see 1955).
1895	Rotatable-ball marking pen (see 1888) marketed.
	Paper-wrapped pencils, invented by Blaisdell, patented.
1907	Lever-filler mechanism for fountain pens invented by W.A. Sheaffer.
By 1927	Stub pens represented about one-third of total pen consumption.
1935	Modern ballpoint briefly marketed in Prague.
1938	Ballpoint independently invented by two Hungarian brothers.
Early 1940s	Refillable "brush pen" marketed (forerunner of later felt markers).
1944	Ballpoint pen adopted by the United States Army.
1945	Ballpoint began to be marketed on a large scale in New York City.
1951	Felt-tip markers introduced (see 1964).
1954	Parker introduced its first ballpoint, the Jotter, with several new features.
1955	Parker introduced the Liquid Lead Pencil, a ballpoint with an erasable graphite ink.
	Sheaffer popularized cartridge fountain pens (see 1890).
1964	Fiber-tip pen (fine-pointed and intended for writing) marketed in Japan and the United States.
1979	Eraser Mate pen marketed by Paper Mate.

Ink

Ca. 3d millennium B.C.	Egyptians were using a carbon ink, made from lampblack and gum or glue.
2d cent. A.D.	Iron-gallotannate inks *may* have been used this early on Greek parchments.
7th cent.	Mention of an iron-gall ink in writings of Bishop Isidore of Seville.
11th cent.	Detailed directions for manufacture of an iron-tannate ink given by monk Theophilus in his treatise *On Divers Arts*.
	Gradual transition from carbon ink to iron-gall ink began. In the Middle Ages, carbon ink was sometimes added to iron-gall ink.
By 1382	The term "inkhorn" (various spellings) used in English.
1465	Earliest known mention of blotting paper in English; however, use of sand predominated for blotting until ca. 1800.
By 1474	References made to existence of a *standish*—that is, a stand for inkwell and other items.
1552	Possibly earliest mention of sandboxes, in Richard Huloet's *Abecedarium* (considered the first English dictionary).
1598	Specific mention of "inke-maker" as a tradesman.
By 1690	Ink powder sold in England.
1763	Extract of logwood added to iron-gall ink. Logwood inks probably introduced (see 1848).
1770	Indigo first used as principal coloring agent of ink.
1772	Probably the earliest advertisement for glass ink bottles, by Manheim (Pennsylvania) Glass Factory: newspaper advertisement listing "Inkes of all sorts."
1776	Reportedly, the first use of sympathetic inks for diplomatic/espionage purposes.
1780	Letterpress copying process—and hence "copying" ink—invented by James Watt.
Ca. 1800	Blotting paper came into general use (see 1856).
1813	First American patent issued for an inkwell.
Ca. 1816	Colored inks using pigments first manufactured in England.
1816	First American ink manufactory, Maynard and Noyes Company, Boston, established.
1820s-1880s	"Umbrella" (paneled cone) ink bottles popular.
1825	Thaddeus Davids Ink Company—a major American ink manufacturer—established.
1834-36	Henry Stephens set up an ink factory in London and introduced indigo-containing iron-gall ink—that is, a "blue-black" ink.
By 1838	Stephens was advertising "a Carbonaceous Black Writing Fluid" which was "proof against every known chemical agent." He also advertised blue and red inks.
1840	Early figural "ink": log-cabin-shaped bottle made for "Log Cabin and Hard Cider" presidential campaign of William Henry Harrison and John Tyler.
1848	Potassium chromate type of logwood ink probably first used commercially.
Mid-19th cent.	Inkstands with quill holes began to be replaced by those having pen racks.
	S. Silliman and Company of Chester, Connecticut, made a large variety of inkstands, most with glass wells surrounded by an air chamber to prevent ink freezing.
1856	First coal-tar aniline dyestuff (Perkin's mauve) discovered; such synthetic dyes later used in colored inks.

Blotting paper began to be made on a large scale by the paper machine. By this time sanders—for dusting on writing sand to blot ink—were effectively supplanted.

1858	Carter Ink Company established.
Before ca. 1860	Ink bottles had scar on bottom from "pontil" rod.
1861	Synthetic indigo introduced for inks.
By 1867	Gray ink eraser (of "sand rubber") was being sold by A.W. Faber.
1867	Nigrosine ink first produced commercially.
1889	Early spring-and-float, self-closing inkwell patented by the Davis Company.
1903	Popular "self-closing" inkwell patented by Sengbusch Company.
1914-16	Patented ceramic figural inks—"Mr. and Mrs. Carter Inx"—sold by Carter.
Ca. 1920	Carter's RYTO blue-black ink sold in cobalt-blue "cathedral" bottles.
1922	Formulation of Skrip ink (sold, since 1933, in a bottle with a top-well feature).
1924	Screw-on caps for ink bottles, although used earlier, became common with standardization of bottle threads.
Through 1950s	Blotters dwindled in use because of the advent of the ballpoint pen.
1957	Benchmark for close of dip-pen era: United States Post Office Department notified branches (June 13) that pens and inkwells were being replaced by ballpoints.

Paper

Early 1st cent. A.D.	Paper first made by Ts'ai Lun in China.
751	Chinese skilled in papermaking captured by Arabs in battle at Samarkand; thus papermaking soon spread through Arab dominions.
By 768	Starch used to size oriental paper.
1042-1066	During his reign, Edward the Confessor employed first English royal seal.
By 1102	Paper available in Europe.
1109	Earliest extant European paper manuscript (Sicily; written in Arabic and Greek).
1150	Paper mill established in Spain.
1276	First mention of paper mills in Europe (Italy).
1282	First European watermarks used (Italy): a form of Greek pommée cross.
Ca. 1285	Watermarks began to contain initials of papermakers.
By 1307	Names of papermakers began to appear in watermarks.
1309	Paper first used in England, soon becoming common there.
By 1337	"Tub-sizing" of paper (dipping in hot solution of natural gelatin) employed.
1348	Paper mill established in France.
1390	Paper mill built in Germany.
Ca. 1450	Paper began to be used on an increasingly large scale with the beginning of book printing.
1464	First purely national postal service established in France.
1495	First English paper mill built in Hertfordshire by John Tate.
By 1500	Some mills began to use watermark designs to indicate paper quality.
16th cent.	"Countermarks"—secondary watermarks—added to the other half of the paper mold.

16th cent., cont.	Apparently the earliest use of visiting cards in Europe (Germany; see 1643-1715).	1792	First bleaching of paper (England).
Ca. 1540	A "glazing hammer"—a mechanical means of polishing paper—came into use in Germany and spread throughout Europe early in the next century.	1793	First paper mill in early American frontier completed at Georgetown, Kentucky, by Craig and Parkers.
1580	Cardstock manufactured and sold in Europe.	1796	First embossing of paper (England).
By 1610	The term "card"—that is, stiff paper or thin pasteboard or cardstock—known.	1798	Papermachine invented by Nicholas-Louis Robert (France); patented the following year.

Apparently the earliest use of visiting cards in Europe (Germany; see 1643-1715).

Ca. 1540 — A "glazing hammer"—a mechanical means of polishing paper—came into use in Germany and spread throughout Europe early in the next century.

1580 — Cardstock manufactured and sold in Europe.

By 1610 — The term "card"—that is, stiff paper or thin pasteboard or cardstock—known.

1643-1715 — The custom of using calling cards (see 16th cent.) became well established during the reign of Louis XIV of France.

1661 — Postmarks (inked handstamps) introduced in England by a Colonel Bishop and known as Bishop's marks.

1680 — The Hollander, a machine for macerating materials into paper pulp, invented in Holland.

1687 — First coloring of paper (Europe).

1690 — First American paper mill founded near Germantown, Pennsylvania, by William Rittenhouse; produced the first American watermark, the single word "Company."

1692 — Postmarks (handwritten) required by the Colony of Massachusetts Bay.

Ca. 1720 — Wooden "glazing rolls" displaced the use of the glazing hammer.

Ca. 1755 — "Wove" mold originated in England, apparently at the behest of John Baskerville.

1757 — First use of wove paper in European book printing (England).

1758 — First stamped postmarks in America used in New York (see 1661, 1692).

1765 — First experimental paper made from straw (see 1829).

Ca. 1770 — First machine ruling of lines on paper (England).

1792 — First bleaching of paper (England).

1793 — First paper mill in early American frontier completed at Georgetown, Kentucky, by Craig and Parkers.

1796 — First embossing of paper (England).

1798 — Papermachine invented by Nicholas-Louis Robert (France); patented the following year.

Ca. 1800 — Beginning of rosin-sizing of paper (Germany). Not used elsewhere until about 1835.

1800 — First "practical" paper made from wood. Ground-wood paper was not produced on a significant commercial scale, however, until 1846; the first ground-wood pulp was produced commercially in the United States in 1867.

1807 — First "loading" of paper with filler material (Europe).

1809 — First hot-pressing of paper (United States).

1809 — First "cylinder" paper machine in operation (at Hertfordshire, England, mill of John Dickinson).

Ca. 1810 — Fourdrinier paper machine—basis of modern papermaking—perfected in England; fully operational at beginning of 1812.

1816 — America's first "endless-paper-making" machine developed by Thomas Gilpin in Delaware and in operation the following year.

1820 — Heated "drying cylinders" for paper machines patented in England.

1825 — Earliest patent for a dandy roll (for marking machine-made paper with pseudolaid pattern and/or watermark) issued in England.

1827 — First American Fourdrinier machine, imported from England, in operation on October 14.

1829	Straw paper produced commercially at Chambersburg, Pennsylvania (see 1765).
	First American-made Fourdrinier machine (see 1827) began making usable paper.
Mid-1830s	Machine-made paper had become relatively common; the United States was the world's dominant paper producer.
Ca. 1840	Envelopes began to be common in England.
Ca. 1840-60	So-called Lincoln blue paper was common.
Ca. 1840-79	The golden age of valentines.
1840	Britain issued the world's first postage stamp on May 6.
1840s	Engraved letter sheets—stationery with engraved pictorials at top—became common in England.
	Decorative glass paperweights appeared in France and Venice as a product of glassblowers.
1842	Postage stamps made for local use in the United States (see 1847).
Ca. 1843	First manufacture reported of American envelopes (in New York by a printer named Pierson).
	First Christmas card intended for general distribution (England).
1847	First ground-wood paper produced commercially (in Saxony).
	First official U.S. postage stamps issued.
Ca. 1849	"Light-and-shade" watermark process invented by William Henry Smith of England.
1849	First American envelope machine patented.
By 1850	Virtually all U.S. paper—with 443 mills in operation—was machine-made.
1851	The first "useful" paper made from chemically processed wood fibers (soda process).
1854	Photographic calling cards—*cartes de visite*—first mentioned.
Ca. 1857	"Parchment paper" (or vegetable parchment) invented (see 1885).
1857-60	First use of esparto grass in paper in England (first used in the United States in 1869).
1860	Famed Pony Express service began April 3; its closing was announced Oct. 26, 1861.
1861-65	"Patriotic covers" (envelopes with pro-Union or Confederate cachets) issued during the Civil War.
	The Confederacy experienced chronic paper shortages during the Civil War.
1867	First successful commercial production of ground-wood paper in North America.
1869	World's first government-sanctioned postcard issued (Austria).
1870	First French and English postcards issued.
1873	First U.S. postcard issued.
1874	First American Christmas card, printed by Louis Prang.
Ca. 1875	Wire staples introduced, applied by "clumsy cast-iron machines."
By 1877	The term "bond paper" in use.
1879	Clasp envelope patented.
Ca. 1880	Sulphite-process wood paper first made on a commercial scale in England (in America in 1882).
1885	"Parchment paper" (see ca. 1857) first manufactured in the United States.
Ca. 1900	Paper clip invented in England.
1902	"Window" envelope first manufactured in the United States.

1908	The American Greeting Card Company established.
1910	Hallmark Cards established by Joyce Hall, who began to manufacture his own greeting cards about 1915.
1930	Cellophane tape introduced.

Writing

3500 B.C.	Pictographic writing system used by Sumerians.
Ca. 3200 B.C.	Sumerian system became modified into "cuneiform" (wedge-shaped) writing.
Ca. 3000 B.C.	Earliest known Egyptian hieroglyphics.
Ca. 2500 B.C.	Cuneiform writing system adopted by Assyrians and Babylonions.
Ca. 2400 B.C.	Development of cursive form of Egyptian hieroglyphics known as hieratic (priestly) script.
2000-1790 B.C.	Vertical line in Egyptian writing was replaced by horizontal one, written from right to left.
Ca. 1000 B.C.	Vowel-less alphabetical system developed by Phoenicians.
7th cent. B.C.	Egyptian demotic script—derived from hieratic—appeared.
Ca. 700 B.C.	Romans adopted Greek alphabet (adopted in turn from Phoenicians).
2d cent. A.D.	"Uncials" (a rounded form of Roman letters) emerged (see 4th-9th cents.).
Ca. 3d cent.	Earliest known examples of Egyptian Coptic writing (formed from Greek uncial and demotic letters).
3d cent.	Half-uncials existed briefly (see 6th cent.).
By 4th cent.	Parchment codex (or bound book) had displaced papyrus scroll.
4th-9th cents.	Uncials became dominant for book use.
5th cent.	"Rustica" replaced Roman square capitals in book manuscripts, except for initials, headings, and so on.
6th cent.	Half-unicals, which foreshadowed minuscules, revived, becoming national hand of Ireland; attained most perfected expression in *Book of Kells*.
6th-12th cents.	Church maintained monopoly on scholarship; monasteries operated scriptoria, where "illuminated" manuscripts were produced.
Ca. 7th cent.	Punctuation and separation of words began to appear.
742-814	Small letters, or minuscules, became fully developed during the reign of Charlemagne as part of script known as "Carolingian minuscule."
11th-13th cents.	Gothic or text script developed; replaced Carolingian minuscule as principal script in books.
By 14th cent.	Technique of copper engraving known, but early examples in Germany and Italy date from the following century.
14th-15th cents.	Gothic script continued in vogue in northwestern Europe.
By 1423	Woodblock printing introduced in Europe.
Ca. 1450	First printing (in Europe) from movable type.
1476	First printing in England from an English press.
Late 15th cent.	Evolution of English secretary hand (descended from a cursive form of Gothic bastarda).
16th cent.	German *stammbuch*, or *album amicorum*, flourished; prototype of later autograph albums.
Early 16th cent.	Humanistic antiqua style script introduced into Britain from Italy.
1514	First writing manual appeared (Italy): Sigismondo Fanti's *Theoretica et practica*.

1530s	First printing in the New World began in Mexico City.
Mid-16th cent.	Humanistic antiqua, or italic hand, replaced Gothic as the dominant script throughout Europe; became a substantial alternative to the English secretary hand.
17th cent.	Evolution of scripts continued throughout the century to the ultimate development of the English round hand.
	Copybooks of English writing masters began to be common.
	Desk boxes were common throughout the century; they gave rise to the household desk (a box with its own support, known as a desk-on-frame) in the latter part of the century.
Early 17th cent.	Writing characterized by mixture of styles, combining features of both secretary and italic.
1638	First press in North America established at Cambridge, Massachusetts, by Stephen Daye.
Mid-17th cent.	Early American writing manual (published in London but specifically intended for the colonies) featured *printed* letters which the student was to trace over.
	The letter *J* began to be used at this time but did not see general use until late in the eighteenth century.
1686-1690	First copies of *New England Primer* printed, the first book that saw general use in colonial schools.
1700-1840	The American round-hand system continued to exhibit the features of the old English round hand.
1714	Patent issued in England for a typewriter (which, however, may never have been made or used).
1784	First American manual to reproduce handwriting was published by Benjamin Franklin and D. Hall.
By 1790	Use of wood engraving for book illustra-

	tion popularized by Thomas Bewick.
1791	John Jenkins of Boston created a *system* of teaching beginning writing that required learning basic strokes, rather than merely copying model letters.
1792	Alleged use of steel engravings in France for artistic purposes (see 1819).
1796	Invention of lithography by Aloysius Senefelder in Munich.
1804	First use of the term "lithography."
1819	First successful commercial exploitation of steel engraving (see 1792).
1829	First U.S. patent on a typewriting machine—"the Typographer"—issued; machine used a type-wheel rather than individual bars.
1837	Development of chromolithography by Gottfried Engelmann, who obtained a French patent.
Ca. 1839	Chromolithographs began to appear in English books.
1840-65	Writing was typically a modified round hand; it characterized the transition from round hand to Spencerian.
1865-90	Spencerian system (after Platt Rogers Spencer) predominated; a distinctively new, American hand.
1874	First successful commercial "type-writer"—invented by Christopher Latham Sholes—marketed by E. Remington and Sons.
1882	Halftone printing process patented.
1886	Linotype machine invented by the German-American Othmar Mergenthaler.
1888	Palmer Method of handwriting introduced.
1890-1900	Modern vertical writing taught; reversion to a slow but legible writing, lasting only ten years.

1890-1945	"Basic popular systems" of "muscular arm movement writing" predominated.
1895	Zaner-Bloser system of handwriting introduced.
1906	Edward Johnston's *Writing and Illuminating and Lettering* (London) revived interest in calligraphy; Johnston determined correct "broad pen" form of the medieval quill.
1945-present	Writing characterized by mixed forms, influenced by the ballpoint pen; writing largely done with fingers rather than wrist or arm.

Examining Documents

1st cent. A.D.	The Roman scholar Quintilian expressed the need "to examine all the writings relating to a case" lest there be found "a thread broken, or wax disturbed, or signatures without attestation."
3d cent.	Earliest known handwriting examinations (Rome); jurists set forth protocols for proving forgery.
6th cent.	The Roman emperor Justinian established protocols for legal use of handwriting comparison.
6th-16th cent.	The Roman approach (that is, persons skilled in writing could give opinions on authenticity based on "similitude of hands") prevailed in western Europe, except England, where eyewitness testimony was required.
15th cent.	Forgeries flourished in European churches, where clerics forged and sold papal dispensations.
By 16th cent.	Autograph collecting common throughout Europe.
1562	Forgery became statutory offense in England; punishment could range from a fine to the forger's having his ears cut off.

17th cent.	The Frenchmen F. Demelle and J. Raveneau wrote treatises describing the "scientific" approach to handwriting comparisons (involving analysis of pen position, speed of writing, letter formation, etc.).
1774-78	Paleographer Karsten Niebuhr distinguished three types of cuneiform and learned one was alphabetic.
1796	William Henry Ireland published confession of his forgeries, an *Authentic Account of the Shakespearian MSS.*
1799	Discovery of the Rosetta Stone.
1801	Rosetta Stone obtained by British; subsequently, it allowed Egyptologists to decipher hieroglyphics.
1822	Champollion discovered key to Egyptian writing.
1887	Discovery of the Tel-el-Amarna tablets in upper Egypt; provided valuable paleographical information on ancient cuneiform script.
Late 19th cent.	Handwriting identification became increasingly common in eastern U.S. courts.
1894	Publication of the first significant modern text on questioned documents: W.E. Hagan's *Disputed Handwriting*, which described physical and chemical tests for detecting alterations, and so on.
	French anthropologist-criminologist Alphonse Bertillon made erroneous determination of handwriting evidence in the Dreyfus case, resulting in Dreyfus's wrongful imprisonment for treason; the case stimulated the need for reform and scientific advancement in the field of document examination.
1901	A.S. Osborn published a pioneering article on typewriting identification in the November issue of the *Albany Law Journal*; at this time Osborn was the major expert in the field of questioned-document examination.

1906   Edward Johnston's *Writing and Illuminating and Lettering* not only revived interest in calligraphy, but also in materials used by the ancients, especially the correct "broad pen" form of the medieval quill—knowledge important to the paleographer.

1910   Publication of the first edition of A.S. Osborn's monumental *Questioned Documents*.

Before 1920s   All questioned-document examinations in the United States done by private consultants.

1929   Creation of the first forsensic science laboratory—the Scientific Crime Detection Laboratory, in Chicago—under private endowment; within a year or two affiliated with Northwestern University School of Law.

Ca. 1931   First American woman to become a professional document examiner: Katherine Applegate Kesler, at the Scientific Crime Detection Laboratory.

1932   Laboratory added to the FBI; began with one microscope and a single examiner.

1942   Creation of the American Society of Questioned Document Examiners.

1950   Founding of the American Academy of Forensic Sciences, with questioned document examination included as a discipline.

1956   Ordway Hilton's *Scientific Examination of Questioned Documents* published; an attempt to update the subject.

1977   American Board of Forensic Document Examiners, Inc., organized.

APPENDIX 3

Laboratory Identification of Pens, Inks, & Papers

Pen Identification

The identification of the class of pen with which a writing was done should be undertaken in good light with a strong lens, preferably a stereomicroscope. If possible, a blotted portion should be chosen (or at least a place where the ink is somewhat thin); treatment of old writing with oxalic acid reagent has also been recommended.[1] Illustrations of the major types of pens and the writing they produce are given in part 1; see figure 15.1 for a ready-reference chart.

A quill usually produces a line of uniform intensity across its width, and due to its flexibility there is often considerable contrast in thickness between upstrokes and downstrokes. Writing done with a metal pen, however, is characterized by its heavy strokes (the downstrokes) having darker, sharper outlines; as the points of the split nib separate under pressure they scratch into the paper, abrading it and rendering it more porous and also creating furrows that can retain additional ink. The outlines are called "pen tracks" or "nib tracks." It should be noted, however, that a fire-hardened quill may also leave nib tracks and that, in any case, nib tracks should not be confused with the dark margins common to nigrosine ink.

Osborn observes that "Quill pens were also very frail and it was frequently necessary to repair them, and this often made a decided change in the appearance of parts of the same extended document."[2] Writing done with the stub pen has a distinctive appearance (fig. 15.1); however, some other steel-pen writing occasionally resembles it. To distinguish the latter, one should examine the tops of rounded letters—like the *e*—where the pen moves *to the left*: in ordinary steel-pen script these strokes will be thin (i.e., lack shading), whereas with stub-pen writing they will be thick ("shaded") due to the characteristic width of the pen.[3]

Obviously, a fountain pen will leave its own evidence of a continuous ink flow, whereas a dipped pen yields sequences of writing with graduated intensity as it progressively runs out of ink and must be dipped again. It should be recalled, however, that the "ink spoon" device shown in figure 3.3 can considerably extend the amount of writing that can be done with a single charging of an ordinary dip pen.

The so-called stylographic pen also yields a continuous ink flow; it produces a line of near-uniform width—on both upstrokes and downstrokes (fig. 15.1)—because of its distinctive construction. The ballpoint pen also produces a line of even width, but the viscous ink and rotatable ball application give the line a distinctive appearance easily recognized under magnification. A more recent variety of ball pen—termed "roller ball" or "floating ball"—utilizes a free-flowing ink. Such pens thus produce "a mark that falls somewhere between the ball-point and the fountain pen."[4]

Porous-tip pens—most of which have pointed tips of felt, nylon, or other porous material—produce lines of relatively uniform width that lack either nib tracks or evidence of roller application. They leave ending strokes that often have a "dry" appearance.

Ink Identification

Appearance sometimes provides an indication of the type of ink. For example, Osborn points out that nigrosine ink lines "have peculiar, dark, microscopic extreme edges, like a very narrow black border and this ink also sometimes shows a peculiar metallic luster and also a distinct secondary color when observed at a certain angle of light."[5] More commonly, iron-gall ink is evidenced by its corrosiveness, and it is not uncommon to see words actually "burned" through the paper.

Sophisticated tests to identify inks include thin-layer chromatography, infrared luminescence photography, spectrographic analysis, and many others.[6] Simpler standard analyses are spot tests employing various reagents. Osborn, Mitchell, and others describe several of these reagents which make it possible to distinguish

Figure A.1. MICROCHEMICAL TESTS to identify ink require only tiny samples to be removed from a pen stroke; a bulb pipette is then used to apply reagents, and the reaction, if any, is observed under the microscope.

many inks.[7] The Cunhas, following a number of forensic sources, present a chart showing twelve reagents and their reactions with seven types of writing ink.[8]

They apply a drop of 5 percent acetic acid directly onto the tail of a letter, let it stand briefly, then lift it off with a blotter on which are then added the other reagents. Osborn recommended making tests directly on the pen strokes, followed by careful washing and blotting.[9] An alternate method is described by Kenneth Rendell who advises that a "pinhead-size spot of ink" be removed with a scalpel and the test be observed under the microscope (fig. A.1).[10] If conducted properly, these procedures cause little damage, although Osborn does caution against clumsiness.[11] Objections may be raised, however, in the case of a rare document. Another problem is that no one reagent identifies all inks, and some reagents may yield similar reactions with more than one type; thus, multiple tests are required.

In an attempt to minimize these problems, John F. Fischer and I have developed a simple methodology especially intended for identification of black (or brown-appearing) inks on historical documents. Our protocol begins with the transfer of an insignificant amount of ink onto a piece of chromatography paper (or filter paper or other similar paper that has been tested with reagents for neutral reactions). First the paper is lightly moistened with distilled water, placed over a heavy pen stroke, and carefully rubbed with a small burnishing tool with moderate pressure (figs. 15.2 and 15.3).

Onto this transferred ink specimen is added a drop of a 20 percent solution of hydrochloric acid, and the reaction is carefully noted: an iron-gall ink is bleached, leaving a yellow residue; a blue reaction is characteristic of an iron-gall variety to which has been added a blue colorant; red indicates a logwood variety (either logwood ink or an iron-gall ink with logwood); and carbon ink (e.g., india ink and printing inks) and nigrosine ink yield no reaction to the reagent.

After the reaction is noted, a drop of a second reagent—a saturated solution of potassium ferrocyanide—is added. The result is interpreted in light of the preceding one. If the hydrochloric acid produced a reaction consistent with an ordinary iron-gall variety, and if the second test yields a prussian-blue color, iron-gall ink is thus demonstrated. If the first reagent produced a red color and there is no reaction with the second, logwood ink is identified; if, however, the red changes to prussian blue in the second test, the ink is shown to have been an iron-gall one to which logwood had been added.

Should the ink still undergo no reaction, either a variety of carbon ink or nigrosine is indicated, and the differentiation is made by the addition of a third reagent, a solution of sodium hydroxide, which causes nigrosine to run dark violet. Carbon inks are not affected by this or any reagent and are thus identified by negative evidence.

Paper Identification

As discussed in chapter 9, two types of paper are distinguished according to the pattern of the mold screens involved: the early European paper, characterized by close parallel lines (laid lines) crossed by heavier, wider-spaced lines (chain lines), is known as *laid* paper; that with an overall fine-mesh pattern, often scarcely discernible, is called *wove* paper. Commonly, an emblematic device (bent to shape from wire) was sewn to the screen, and it also left an imprint, or *watermark*. Small, round, accidental "watermarks"— caused by water dripping from the vatman's hands— are often found in old handmade paper (fig. 8.5).

Early machine-made paper—necessarily an unwatermarked, wove variety because it was produced on a continuous woven-wire belt—also sometimes exhibits an accidental watermark; it shows as a line of stitches and results from the seam in the belt (fig. 8.13).

Machine-made wove paper—like that of daily newspapers—tears easily in a straight line in one direction but with difficulty and irregularly in another. This effect of a "grain" imparted to the paper is due to the direction it ran when being formed on the paper machine. But tearing a sheet in two is a poor test for a document! Instead, double the paper first in one direction, then another, each time pressing gently on the bend. (CAUTION: Do not crease the paper!) If there seems about the same amount of springiness in either direction, handmade paper is indicated; if the paper "gives" more easily when pressed along one bend, then along that bend is the apparent direction of the grain. This is, however, a subtle test, and practice on sheets of newsprint (afterward tearing the sheet to check how successful has been the determination) is recommended.

The invention of the dandy roll (a cylinder with an embossing surface in the laid pattern, possibly bearing a watermark design also) made possible the manufacture of a pseudo–laid paper. As the wove paper was formed on the paper machine, the dandy roll impressed its design into the wet fibrous mass. The resulting lines lack the sharp clarity of those in true, handmade laid paper, however.[12] Also, according to Berkeley, "one can, with a magnifying glass and a strong light source, determine that the marks are pressed into the upper side while the wove wire marks are still visible on the lower side."[13]

The introduction of ground-wood pulp for papermaking, and later of chemically processed pulp, were among further developments. Knowledge of such aspects of paper manufacture is vital to detecting many forgeries. Obviously a letter written on machine-made paper but bearing a date prior to the invention of the paper machine is prima-facie spurious. Or, as happened in a Louisiana case, a will written on paper that was not marketed until some four years after the testator's death—as proved by the watermark—would be an obvious fake.[14]

Among the useful laboratory tests of paper are those for lignin—the presence of which is an "infallible indication that a paper is machine-made."[15] Reagent tests (used in conjunction with the microscope) involve using a scalpel to remove a minute sliver of paper from an edge, moistening and teasing the fibers on a microscope slide, then blotting; the addition of Herzberg's Stain as a reagent will yield the following color reactions:

wine red: cotton and linen
blue, gray, or blue-violet: purified cellulose (chemical wood, bleached straw)
yellow-green (changing slowly to blue green): lignified cellulose (ground wood, straw, manilla)[16]

Relative percentages of mixed fibers can be estimated. Julius Grant discusses at some length the dating evidence to be derived from the fiber content, as well as from such nonfibrous constituents as rosin sizing.[17]

Other laboratory techniques applied to paper include the use of ultraviolet fluorescence to distinguish certain constituents and to detect artificial watermarks.[18] For a further forensic discussion of paper, see Osborn, and Lyter and Brunelle.[19]

NOTES

1: The Quill

1. Oscar Ogg, *The 26 Letters* (New York: Crowell, 1948); Donald Jackson, *The Story of Writing* (New York: Taplinger, 1981), 14-45; Joyce Irene Whalley, *Writing Implements and Accessories: From the Roman Stylus to the Typewriter* (Detroit: Gale Research, 1975), 11-15. **2.** William Bishop, "Pens, Pencils, Brushes and Knives," in *The Calligrapher's Handbook*, 2d ed., ed. C.M. Lamb (New York: Pentalic, 1968), 43. **3.** Bishop, "Pens," 33. **4.** *Encyclopaedia Britannica* (hereafter *Ency. Brit.*), 1910-11, 21:83; s.v. "pen." **5.** Bishop, "Pens," 34. Advertisement in the *Kentucky Gazette*, May 8, 1818. **6.** Quoted in Whalley, *Writing Implements*, 30. **7.** Bishop, "Pens," 33. **8.** Nathaniel Dearborn, *American Text Book for Letters*, 1846, cited in Lilian Baker Carlisle, "How to Make a Quill Pen," *Antiques Journal*, Sept. 1973, 38. **9.** Berenice Ball, "Writing Tools and Treasures," part 2, *National Antiques Review*, Sept. 1973, 17; Philip Mason, "The Lost Art of Quill Pen Making," *Early American Life*, Apr. 1975, 40. **10.** Carlisle, "How to Make a Quill Pen," 37; Charles Dickens, *Bleak House* (1853; repr., New York: Norton, 1977), 403. The cardboard box is illustrated in Alec Davis, *Package and Print: The Development of Container and Label Design* (New York: Potter, 1968), plate 86. **11.** Ball, "Writing Tools," 17. **12.** Ibid. **13.** Jackson, *Story of Writing*, 84. **14.** Quoted in Whalley, *Writing Implements*, 24-25. **15.** Jackson, *Story of Writing*, 118. **16.** Bishop, "Pens," 29-30. **17.** Jim Tucker, "George Washington's Knife," *National Knife Magazine*, Aug. 1983, 23-26, 39. **18.** Bernard Levine, *Levine's Guide to Knives and Their Values* (Northbrook, Ill.: DBI Books, 1985), 176; Bishop, "Pens," 28-31. **19.** Bishop, "Pens," 31. **20.** Dearborn, *American Text Book*, cited in Carlisle, "How to Make a Quill Pen," 36. **21.** Bishop, "Pens," 30. **22.** *Encyclopedia Americana*, 1980, s.v. "quill pen." **23.** Quoted in Ray Nash, *American Penmanship, 1800-1850* (Worcester, Mass.: American Antiquarian Society, 1969), 57. **24.** The stand-up model is mentioned in Whalley, *Writing Implements*, 39, and one can be seen in the Victoria and Albert Museum, London. **25.** Quoted in ibid., 24-25. **26.** Ball, "Writing Tools," 17. **27.** James P. Maginnis, *Reservoir, Stylographic, and Fountain Pens*, Cantor Lectures, Society for the Encouragement of Arts, Manufactures and Commerce (London: William Trounce, 1905), 9; Whalley, *Writing Implements*, 19. **28.** E. Kay Kirkham, *The Handwriting of American Records for a Period of 300 Years* (Logan, Utah: Everton, 1973), 5.

2: Durable Pens

1. *Ency. Brit.*, 1910-11, 21:83-84, s.v. "pen." **2.** Bishop, "Pens," 83. **3.** Jackson, *Story of Writing*, 130. **4.** Whalley, *Writing Implements*, 41. **5.** Quoted in Jackson, *Story of Writing*, 130. A brief reference to steel pens, dated 1733, is given in Maginnis, *Reservoir Pens*, 10. **6.** Quoted in Maginnis, *Reservoir Pens*, 10. **7.** Edmund Berkeley, Jr., ed., *Autographs and Manuscripts: A Collector's Manual* (New York: Scribner's, 1978), 30. **8.** Julius Grant, *Books and Documents: Dating, Permanence, and Preservation* (New York: Chem. Pub., 1937), 43. **9.** Rudolph J. Bodmer, ed., *The Book of Wonders* (New York: Presbrey Syndicate, 1915), 15. Harrison's pen

is illustrated in Maginnis, *Reservoir Pens*, 10. **10.** *Chambers's Encyclopedia*, 1967, 10:552, s.v. "pen." **11.** Maginnis, *Reservoir Pens*, 11; *Ency. Brit.*, 1910-11, 21:83, s.v. "pen." **12.** Bodmer, *Book of Wonders*, 16. **13.** Ibid. **14.** *Ency. Brit.*, 1910-11, 21:83, s.v. "pen." **15.** Quoted in Jackson, 133. Perry's patent number, 5933, is given in Maginnis, *Reservoir Pens*, 11. **16.** Thomas Hood, "Ode to Perry: The Inventor of the Patent Perryan Pen," in *The Complete Poetical Works of Thomas Hood*, ed. Walter Jerrold (London: Henry Frowde, 1906), 304-307. **17.** On the education system, Jackson, *Story of Writing*, 133. On "Perryian Limpid Ink," Walley, *Writing Implements*, 82-83. **18.** Jackson, *Story of Writing*, 134. **19.** *Ency. Brit.* 1910-11, 21:83, s.v. "pen." **20.** Ibid. **21.** See Gillott's advertisement reproduced in Whalley, *Writing Implements*, 44. **22.** Jackson, *Story of Writing*, 134. **23.** Bodmer, *Book of Wonders*, 17. A similar description is in Maginnis, *Reservoir Pens*, 12-13. **24.** Mary L. Richmond, *Shaker Literature: A Bibliography* (Hancock, Mass.: Shaker Community, 1977), 184; Nash, *American Penmanship*, 58. Williamson's patent appears in *List of Patents for Inventions and Designs, Issued by the United States, from 1790 to 1847 . . .* (Washington, D.C.: J. and G.S. Gideon, 1847), 324. **25.** *Ency. Brit.*, 1973, 17:546-48, s.v. "pen." **26.** Quoted in Nash, *American Penmanship*, 58-59. **27.** Kirkham, *Handwriting of Amer. Records*, 5. **28.** Albert S. Osborn, *Questioned Documents*, 2d ed. (Montclair, N.J.: Patterson Smith, 1978), 160. **29.** According to the *Oxford English Dictionary* (hereafter, *OED*), the stub pen, which has a broad point, is so named from the original reference to "a worn quill pen" (which would have a blunt point). **30.** Maginnis, *Reservoir Pens*, 9. **31.** *Ency. Brit.*, 1910-11, 21:83, s.v. "pen." Robert John Thomas, "Doughty's Rhodium Pens"; letter to the editor, *Mechanics' Magazine* 9 (1828): 405. **32.** Frazer and Geyer Co., catalog of Lincoln Fountain Pens, 1900; reproduced in the *Pen Fancier's Magazine*, Mar. 1984, 16-20. **33.** Elizabeth D. Beckman, *Cincinnati Silversmiths, Jewelers, Watch and Clockmakers* (Cincinnati: B.B. and Co., 1975), 68. **34.** *Ency. Brit.*, 1910-11, 21:83, s.v. "pen." **35.** Cliff Lawrence, *Official P.F.C. Pen Guide* (Dunedin, Fla.: Pen Fancier's Club, 1982), 59. **36.** Johnson Smith and Co., novelty catalog (Detroit: Johnson Smith, 1941), 84. **37.** William Baddeley, letter to the editor of *Mechanics' Magazine* 28 (1837-38): 135-36. **38.** Otto Young and Co., annual jewelers' catalog for 1889. **39.** Bill Poese, "Peep Shows," *The Antiques Journal*, Apr. 1974, 17-18, 52. **40.** Betty Rivera and Ted Rivera, *Inkstands and Inkwells: A Collector's Guide* (New York: Crown, 1973), 194. **41.** Jane Weaver, "Strawberry Pen-Wiper," *Peterson's Magazine* 48 (1865): 136. **42.** "Ornamental Pen-Wiper," *Godey's Lady's Book* 89 (1874): 556-57. **43.** Rivera and Rivera, *Inkstands and Inkwells*, 195.

3: Reservoir Pens

1. Osborn, *Questioned Documents*, 154. **2.** Albertine Gaur, *Writing Materials of the East*, quoted in Jackson, *Story of Writing*, 162. **3.** Samuel Pepys recorded in a display of the Penographic fountain pen, Science Museum, London; reproduced in Whalley, *Writing Implements*, 62. M. Bion, *The Con-*

struction and Principal Uses of Mathematical Instruments, trans. from the French by Edmund Stone (London, 1723). **4.** Bion, *Construction of Mathematical Instruments,* quoted in Maginnis, *Reservoir Pens,* 69. **5.** Edward Johnston, *Writing and Illuminating and Lettering* (1906; repr., London: Pitman, 1979), 20.

6. Maginnis, *Reservoir Pens,* 14. **7.** English patents in ibid., 15-19. **8.** "Soluble-Ink Pens," having a fixed nib and "a sliding tube provided with a rod or bar of solidified soluble coloring compound, arranged to be adjusted in the longitudinal bore of the pen-holder, and in relation to the pen-point," were patented in the United States, Jan. 1, 1878 (no. 198,812). Another U.S. patent, for a pen with "a solid writing composition for supplying the nib of the pen with ink," was issued May 21, 1878 (patented in England, Sept. 18, 1874). **9.** Display of Penographic fountain pen, Science Museum, London; reproduced in Whalley, *Writing Implements,* 62. **10.** Ibid.; see British patent no. 4389/1819.

11. Advertisement in *Harper's Weekly,* Jan. 6, 1872. **12.** Ibid. **13.** Ibid., Jan. 4, 1873. **14.** Grant, *Books and Documents,* 44. Cliff Lawrence, *Official P.F.C. Pen Guide* (Dunedin, Fla.: Pen Fancier's Club, 1982), 17. A U.S. patent on a stylographic pen of Jan. 27, 1857 (no. 16,514) refers to "the ink pencil" patented by E. Jordan, Nov. 20, 1849. A plungerless model, patented in 1809, is described in Maginnis, *Reservoir Pens,* 21. It was intended for use in making what would later be called carbon copies; states Maginnis: "Common writing ink flowing from the point of the pen will give the first impression; the other copies are obtained by having previously placed alternate sheets of a transfer paper, described in the specification, and sheets of thin writing-paper, under that upon which the original writing was being executed. The pressure of the pen, acting as a stylus, reproduced the writing." **15.** Glen Bowen, *Collectible Fountain Pens* (Glenview, Ill.: Glen Bowen Communications, 1982), 248-50.

16. *Ency. Brit.,* 1973, 17:547, s.v. "pen." **17.** For a chronological list of Parker's inventions, see Bowen, *Collectible Fountain Pens,* 17-21; Jackson, *Story of Writing,* 165. **18.** Maginnis, *Reservoir Pens,* 38; the pen had a piston operation. **19.** Bowen, *Collectible Fountain Pens,* 11-12, 107. **20.** *Ency. Brit.,* 1967, 10:553, s.v. "pen." Patents of Apr. 29, Sept. 16 and 23, 1890; see the *Pen Fancier's Magazine,* Mar. 1984, 6-7. Bowen, *Collectible Fountain Pens,* 256, 118.

21. The *Pen Fancier's Magazine,* Pen Fancier's Club, 1169 Overcash Drive, Dunedin, Fla. 33528; *Pen World,* P.O. Box 6666, Kingwood, Tex., 77325-6666. The text by Lawrence, *Official P.F.C. Pen Guide,* is available from the Pen Fancier's Club, and that by Bowen, *Collectible Fountain Pens,* may be had by writing him care of *Pen World.* For restoration of fountain pens, see advertisements in *Pen World* and *Pen Fancier's Magazine.* **22.** Lawrence, *Official P.F.C. Pen Guide,* 3; Glen Bowen, "Fountain Pens: Advice from a Collector," *Early American Life,* Dec. 1983, 27-28. **23.** John J. Loud, U.S. patent no. 392, 046 (Oct. 30, 1888). **24.** *Ency. Brit.,* 1973, 17:548, s.v. "pen." **25.** "Fountain-Pen Scramble," *Fortune,* July 1946, 144.

26. Don Wharton, "Mighty Battle of the Pens," *Nation's Business,* Nov. 1946, 53-54, 98, 100. Jane Polley, ed., *Stories behind Everyday Things* (Pleasantville, N.Y.: Reader's Digest, 1980), 244. **27.** On smudging, Charles Panati, *The Browser's Book of Beginnings* (Boston: Houghton Mifflin, 1984), 78-79; modern ballpoint inks have oil-free dyes in fast-dry solvents. Kirkham, *Handwriting of American Records,* 5, referring to ballpoints of 1950-53, whose ink faded when exposed to light. **28.** Bowen, *Collectible Fountain Pens,* 15. **29.** Ibid., 15, 21, 79. **30.** Joseph Nathan Kane, *Famous First Facts* (New York: Wilson, 1981), 454.

31. Jackson, *Story of Writing,* 168. **32.** Ibid. **33.** *Ency. Brit.,* 1973, 17:548. s.v. "pen." **34.** Ibid. **35.** Ibid. **36.** *New Standard Encyclopedia,* 1982, 10:170, s.v. "pen."

4: The Pencil

1. See fig. 3.4; see Laughlin advertisement on front cover of *Pen Fancier's Magazine,* May 1983; advertisement for Hawkes's pen in *Harper's Weekly,* Jan. 4, 1873; Wharton, "Battle of Pens," 100; see discussion of the Liquid Lead Pencil in chap. 3; the 1903 advertisement was reproduced in Bowen, *Collectible Fountain Pens,* 30-31. **2.** Polley, *Everyday Things,* 245; *Ency. Brit.,* 1973, 17:549, s.v. "pencil." **3.** *Ency. Brit.,* 1960, 17:461, s.v. "pencil drawing." **4.** Cennino Cennini, *The Craftsman's Handbook* (Il Libro dell'arte), trans. Daniel V. Thompson (New York: Dover, 1960), 7-8. **5.** *Ency. Brit.,* 1973, 17:549, s.v. "pencil"; Polley, *Everyday Things,* 245.

6. *Ency. Brit.,* 1973, 17:549-50, s.v. "pencil." **7.** Ibid., 550. See also (for mention of square leads) *Ency. Brit.,* 1910-11, 21:86, s.v. "pencil." **8.** *Ency. Brit.,* 1973, 17:549-50, s.v. "pencil." Gesner's 1565 treatise is titled, *De omni rerum fossilium genere;* a drawing of Gesner's pencil is given in Edward De Bono, ed., *Eureka! An Illustrated History of Inventions from the Wheel to the Computer* (London: Thames and Hudson, 1974), 50. **9.** *Ency. Brit.,* 1973, 17:549-50, s.v. "pencil." **10.** Bodmer, *Book of Wonders,* 466. See also *Ency. Brit.,* 1960, 9:18, s.v. "Faber," and 1980, 4:19, s.v. "Faber, (Johann) Lothar von and John Eberhard."

11. Monroe's factory is mentioned in Kane, *Famous First Facts,* 454. **12.** Bob Dvorchak (Associated Press), "Pencil Company Doubts Product Will Be Obsolete," *Lexington* (Ky.) *Herald-Leader,* Jan. 27, 1985. **13.** Ibid., Bodmer, *Book of Wonders,* 467-69; *Ency. Brit.,* 1973, 17:550, s.v. "Manufacture of Lead Pencils;" *Mechanics' Magazine* 31 (1839): 174-75. **14.** Carrithers and Company, Chicago, office-supply catalog (in my collection), ca. 1925, 150-58 (hereafter cited as Carrithers catalog). **15.** Ibid., 157; the indelible pencil was patented July 10, 1866 (U.S. patent no. 56,180); see Kane, *Famous First Facts,* 454.

16. *Ency. Brit.,* 1973, 17:550, s.v. "pencil." Blaisdell's patent was no. 549,952, Nov. 19, 1895; see Kane, *Famous First Facts,* 454. **17.** Polley, *Everyday Things,* 245; *Ency. Brit.,* 1973, 17:550, s.v. "pencil." **18.** U.S. patent no. 19,783, Mar. 30, 1858. **19.** U.S. patent no. 18,265, Sept. 22, 1857. **20.** U.S. patent no. 89,109, Apr. 20, 1869.

21. *OED,* 1961, 7:634, s.v. "pencil-clasp." Point protectors and lengtheners are common items in the Carrithers catalog, 152, 155, 162. **22.** *The Youth's Companion,* Oct. 28, 1886, 415 (illus). **23.** See Rivera and Rivera, *Inkstands and Inkwells,* 193, for a photograph of such a box. **24.** Illustrated in *Hearth and Home* (which gave such boxes as premiums to those who sold four subscriptions), June 1921, 13. **25.** "Invention of the Ever-pointed Pencil," *Mechanics' Magazine* 27 (1837), 32.

26. S. Mordan and Co. advertisement in Pigot and Co.'s *Metropolitan New Alphabetical Directory* for 1827 (reproduced in Whalley, *Writing Implements,* 121). **27.** Catalog of Otto Young and Co. (Chicago, 1889), 474; the terms "magic pencils" and "screw pencils" are employed. **28.** "Lownds's Ever-pointed Pencil and Pen-case," *Mechanics' Magazine* 27 (1837), 351, 360. **29.** *Ency. Brit.,* 1973, 17:550, s.v. "pencil." **30.** Ibid.

31. Jefferson's purchase is shown on a page of his account book, in James Munves, *Thomas Jefferson and the Declaration of Independence* (New York: Scribner's, 1978), 103. **32.** Munves, *Jefferson;* Jefferson's numerous strike-outs and insertions, however, suggest the extant pages are his primary drafts. **33.** The pencil is specifically prohibited, even for notes to the closest friends, in Alexander L. Sheff and Edna Ingalls, *How to Write Letters for All Occasions* (New York: Permabooks, 1948), 173. Earlier, nineteenth-century books simply specified that only black ink was to be used, as in Mrs. E.B. Duffey, *The Ladies' and Gentlemen's Etiquette* (Philadelphia: Porter and Coates, 1877), 120.

5: Writing Fluids

1. A.B. Davis, "The Chemistry of Inks," in *Chemistry in Industry*, ed. H.E. Howe (New York: Chemical Foundation, 1925), 190. **2.** M. Therese Fisher, "Ink" in Lamb, *Calligrapher's Handbook*, 72. **3.** Supplement to *OED*, 1976, 2:308, s.v. "ink." **4.** Ibid. For a description of the process of "rubbing down" Chinese stick ink, see M.C. Oliver, "The Design of Manuscript Books and Inscriptions," in Lamb, *Calligrapher's Handbook*, 150. **5.** Davis, "Chemistry of Inks," 190-91. **6.** *The History of Ink, Including Its Etymology, Chemistry, and Bibliography* (New York: Thaddeus Davids, n.d. [ca. 1856-60]), 14. **7.** Ibid., 9-15. **8.** Alfred Fairbank, *The Story of Handwriting* (New York: Watson-Guptill, 1970), 90. **9.** De Bono, *Eureka!*, 47. **10.** Theophilus, in a twelfth-century text, *On Divers Arts*, trans. John G. Hawthorne and Cyril Stanley Smith (New York: Dover, 1979), 42. **11.** Fisher, "Ink," 73; Fairbank, *Story of Handwriting*, 90; *World Book Encyclopedia*, 1984, 8:3, s.v. "gall." **12.** Daniel V. Thompson, *The Materials and Techniques of Medieval Painting* (New York: Dover, 1956), 81-82. **13.** J. Bronson and R. Bronson, *The Domestic Manufacturer's Assistant and Family Directory in the Arts of Weaving and Dyeing* (1817; republished as *Early American Weaving and Dyeing*, New York: Dover, 1977), 202. **14.** "The best blue galls" mentioned in Elijah Bemiss, *The Dyer's Companion* (1815; repr., New York: Dover, 1973), 290; "Aleppo galls" mentioned in *History of Ink*, 18; *World Book Encyclopedia*, 1984, 8:3, s.v. "gall." **15.** In Fisher, "Ink," 71. **16.** Edward Cocker, *The Pen's Triumph*, 1658, quoted in Whalley, *Writing Implements*, 78. **17.** Thompson, *Materials of Medieval Painting*, 84; Grant, *Books and Documents*, 114-15. **18.** Osborn, *Questioned Documents*, 469. **19.** Examples are J. Bronson and R. Bronson, *Domestic Manufacturer's Assistant*, and Bemiss, *Dyer's Companion*. As another example, a book titled *The New Family Receipt Book* was cited with reference to ink making in *Mechanics' Magazine* 2 (1824): 63. **20.** In fact, "Frontier merchants stocked copperas by the keg, since it was needed in the making of ink and in drying materials for clothing," according to Frances Dugan and Jacqueline Bull, eds., Ebenezer Hiram Stedman, *Bluegrass Craftsman* (Lexington: Univ. Press of Kentucky, 1959), 189 n. 6. **21.** The *Kentucky Gazette* (e.g., issues of May 3 and 24 and June 7, 1788) lists such writing materials as ink powder, writing paper, and penknives. **22.** A recipe, "To make an excellent Black Ink Powder, &c.," is given in Bemiss, *Dyer's Companion*, 289. **23.** See *OED*, 1961, 5:302, s.v. "ink." **24.** In *The Moving Market; or, the Cries of London, for the Amusement of Good Children*, 1815, reproduced in Whalley, *Writing Implements*, 80. **25.** Rivera and Rivera, *Inkstands and Inkwells*, 195. **26.** William E. Covill, Jr., *Ink Bottles and Inkwells* (Taunton, Mass.: William S. Sullwold, 1971), 10. **27.** "A Trip through Inkland," in *The Story Your Ink Bottle Tells* (Boston: Carter Ink Co., 1919; repr. in the *Pen Fancier's Magazine*, Feb. 1984, 26-27). **28.** Timothy Hilton, *Keats and His World* (New York: Viking, 1971), 16; a portrait of Stephens is included. **29.** William Baddeley, letter to editor of *Mechanics' Magazine* 25 (1836): 229-31. The letter, dated June 9, refers to Stephens's "new writing fluid," which has the properties described.

30. Thompson, *Materials of Medieval Painting*, 81-82. **31.** On indigo used by Stephens, Grant, *Books and Documents*, 114-15; Osborn, *Questioned Documents*, 468-69. **32.** Stephens advertisements in *Robson's London Directory for 1838* and an 1843 issue of the *Polytechnic Review*, both reproduced in Whalley, *Writing Implements*, 81, 82. **33.** An advertisement in an 1843 issue of the *Polytechnic Review*, reproduced in Whalley, *Writing Implements*, 82. **34.** Osborn, *Questioned Documents*, 451-52; Grant, *Books and Documents*, 44; C.A. Mitchell, "Section on Writing, Stamping, Typing, and Marking Inks," in Alfred Henry Allen, *Allen's Commercial Organic Analysis*, vol. 5 (1927; rev. ed., Philadelphia: Blakiston, 1948), 207. **35.** Bowen, *Collectible Fountain Pens*, 116-17; Whalley, *Writing Implements*, 84. **36.** Fisher, "Ink," 73. **37.** Ibid. **38.** Thompson, *Materials of Medieval Painting*, 178. **39.** Jackson, *Story of Writing*, 85. **40.** Grant, *Books and Documents*, 116, and Davis "Chemistry of Inks," 192, among many others, use the term "ink" for such preparations, which could well be called "paint," the general distinction relating to their viscosity and whether the colored fluids were used in association with writing; *History of Ink*, 55. **41.** Thompson, *Materials of Medieval Painting*, 60, 97-98, 102-03. **42.** Ibid., 76, 50-60. **43.** Ibid., 89, 145, 160, 175-77. **44.** Ibid., 116, 135, 169. **45.** Charles Hamilton, *Great Forgers and Famous Fakes: The Manuscript Forgers of America and How They Duped the Experts* (New York: Crown, 1980), 265-66. **46.** Carter's gold ink "for fancy writing" and white ink "for fancy and ornamental writing on dark surfaces, marking in photo albums, etc.," was advertised in the Carrithers catalog of about 1925, p. 128. **47.** "To Make an Indelible Ink, for Marking Linen, &c.," *Mechanics' Magazine* 1 (1823): 47. **48.** John Marquart, *Six Hundred Receipts, Worth Their Weight in Gold* (Philadelphia: John E. Potter, 1867; repr., Paducah, Ky.: Troll Publishing, n.d.), 76. **49.** U.S. patent no. 133,197, Nov. 19, 1872. **50.** Ordway Hilton, *Scientific Examination of Questioned Documents* (Chicago: Callaghan, 1956), 283-84. **51.** Ibid., 284; "Ink," in *The New Student's Reference Work*, ed. Chandler B. Beach (Chicago: F.E. Compton, 1910), 926; K.L. Armstrong, *Hill's Educator and Library of Reference* (Chicago: George M. Hill, 1894), 397; recipes for "Red Copying Ink" and "Violet Copying Ink" are also given on the same page, the latter containing glycerine. **52.** Armstrong, *Hill's Educator*, 398. **53.** Mitchell, "Section on Writing Inks," 233-43. **54.** Ibid., 243; *Ency. Brit.*, 1960, 12:361, s.v. "ink." **55.** *History of Ink*, 38-39. **56.** Kane, *Famous First Facts*, 321; *Collier's Ency.*, 1985, 13:27, s.v. "ink." Wellcome's Magic Ink was sold by H.S. Wellcome of Garden City, Minn., probably during the third quarter of the nineteenth century. Its label stated: "Write with quill or golden pen on white paper. No trace is visible until held to the fire, when it becomes very black." For illustration of label, see Davis's *Package and Print*, n.p. **57.** Martin Gardner, *Codes, Ciphers, and Secret Writing* (New York: Pocket Books, 1972), 81-82; *History of Ink*, 39; Hilton, *Scientific Examination*, 132-33. **58.** Armstrong, *Hill's Educator*, 399; on magnetic inks, *Academic American Encyclopedia*, 1982, 11:178, s.v. "ink." **59.** Carrithers catalog, 187, 195, 204, 216. **60.** Covill, *Ink Bottles*, 194, fig. 834; on waterproof drawing inks, *New Standard Encyclopedia*, 1982, 6:110, s.v. "ink." **61.** Covill, *Ink Bottles*, 10, 92 (fig. 385), 183 (fig. 791), 209 (fig. 894); the illustrated bottle of "perfumed" ink is embossed "ALLING'S PERFUMED INK/ROCHESTER, N.Y."; the "frost-proof" ink was manufactured by "The Anti-Fraud Ink Co. Washington, D.C."; and the blue writing fluid was manufactured by "The Snow Ink Co., Nashua, N.H." **62.** On ink tablets, ibid., 98, fig. 418; these particular tablets were sold in a bottle embossed

"DE LUXE INK TABLETS" and "DE LUXE MFG. CO. CHICAGO." The bottle appears to be an early twentieth-century one. On "vanishing ink," *Fun Catalog* (Scotch Plains, N.J.: Abracadabra Magic Shop, 1987-88), 14.

6: Ink Containers

1. Marquart, *Six Hundred Receipts*. His recipes for common black ink call for a gallon of water, although that was reduced by boiling. **2.** See the recipes in chap. 5. **3.** Advertisement quoted in *OED*, 1961, 5:303; Joe Nickell, "Vintage Watermarks: Clues to the Origins of Paper on the Kentucky Frontier," *Journal of Kentucky Studies* 4 (Sept. 1987): 109. **4.** Joe Nickell, "Old West Liberty, Ky., General Store Ledger: Name Index and Commentary," typescript (1983). **5.** Bemiss, *Dyer's Companion*, 289; the *OED* (1961, 5:303) cites a source as stating: "Ink-Powder . . . is nothing else than the substances employed in the composition of common ink, pounded and pulverised." Such a mixture was apparently not instantly ready for use upon adding the water, which Bemiss specified was to contain vinegar or "sour beer," but was to be "kept warm, and frequently shook together." Whalley, *Writing Implements*, 83; Covill, *Ink Bottles*, 411. **6.** *OED*, 1961, 5:303; see also Whalley, *Writing Implements*, 88-89. **7.** George Neumann, *Early American Antique Country Furnishings: Northeastern America, 1650-1800* (New York: McGraw-Hill, 1984), 333. **8.** Reproduced in Jackson, *Story of Writing*, 63. **9.** Whalley, *Writing Implements*, 85, cites illustrations in medieval manuscripts. **10.** Ibid., 85-86. **11.** *OED*, 1961, 5:302-3, 305. **12.** Rivera and Rivera, *Inkstands and Inkwells*, 31; Whalley, *Writing Implements*, 88-93. **13.** *OED*, 1961, 10:821. **14.** Rivera and Rivera, *Inkstands and Inkwells*, 174-75. **15.** *OED*, 1961, 5:305. **16.** Glassware manufacturer's catalog reprinted under the title *Whitall, Tatum & Co. 1880*, and with a historical introduction (Princeton, N.J.: Pyne Press, 1971), 48. **17.** An example is the second definition of "inkstand," given as "an inkwell," in *The American Heritage Desk Dictionary* (New York: Houghton Mifflin, 1981), 505. **18.** *OED*, 1961, 5:302. **19.** Cecil Munsey, *The Illustrated Guide to Collecting Bottles* (New York: Elsevier-Dutton, 1970), 120. **20.** Ibid., 23. **21.** Covill, *Ink Bottles*, 12. **22.** Munsey, *Collecting Bottles*, 120; the 1816 date is also given on a later (1855) Maynard and Noyes's advertisement reproduced in Covill, *Ink Bottles*, 14; the 1825 date is also shown on some later Thaddeus Davids Co. ink-bottle labels (which state, "Manufactory established 1825"), for which see fig. 750 in Covill, *Ink Bottles*, 172. **23.** Covill, *Ink Bottles*, 117, 12. **24.** Grace Kendrick, *The Antique Bottle Collector* (New York: Harcourt, 1971), 25. **25.** Ibid., 23-43; Munsey, *Collecting Bottles*, 30-36, 47-50. **26.** Kendrick, *Antique Bottle Collector*, 65. **27.** Ibid., 43-44. **28.** Ibid., 45-49. Glass-stoppered carmine inks are shown in an 1880 catalog (*Whitall, Tatum & Co. 1880*); see also Covill, *Ink Bottles*, 10. **29.** In addition to Covill's text is Lavinia Nelson and Martha Hurley's *Old Inks* (Salem, Ore.: Old Time Bottle Pub. Co., 1967), which, however, is illustrated only with line drawings. **30.** See *Whithall, Tatum & Co. 1880*, 48; Munsey, *Collecting Bottles*, 120. **31.** Covill, *Ink Bottles*, 153. **32.** Albert Christian Revi, *American Pressed Glass and Figural Bottles* (New York: Nelson, 1964), 395; the log-cabin ink patent was issued Apr. 15, 1884, to Emil Herckner (see Covill, *Ink Bottles*, 154-55). **33.** Revi, *American Pressed Glass*, 391-95; Covill, *Ink Bottles*, 147-68. **34.** "For a bottle to qualify as a figural bottle, by definition the shape of the bottle must be mostly figural in makeup," according

to Munsey, *Collecting Bottles*, 96. **35.** Actually cobalt is added to make the blue color. See Kendrick, 51-57, for more on colored glass.

36. See fig. 819 in Covill, *Ink Bottles*, 190. **37.** The L.H. Thomas Co. sold one such model as a "Practical Inkstand"; see the bottle illustrated at the upper right in fig. 5.12. **38.** Covill, *Ink Bottles*, 364-81, 386-91; Neuman, *Early American*, 333-34. **39.** Several examples of wells sold both separately and incorporated into inkstands are shown in the Carrithers catalog of about 1925, 137-40. **40.** Ibid., 140. **41.** The correspondent signed himself "Bolnhurst" and his letter was headed "Pencils," *Mechanics' Magazine* 8 (1828): 40. **42.** Covill, *Ink Bottles*, 393; a Silliman price list is reproduced on 394. **43.** The patent was to Oliver Barber, Hartford, Connecticut. See *List of Patents for Inventions*, 323. **44.** Revi, *American Pressed Glass*, 336. **45.** Covill, *Ink Bottles*, 337-47. **46.** Both are featured in the Carrithers catalog of about 1925, 138-40. See also Covill, *Ink Bottles*, 345; Rivera and Rivera, *Inkstands and Inkwells*, 56. **47.** Covill, *Ink Bottles*, 342. **48.** Roger Hawthorne, "American Glass Inkwells and Ink Bottles," *Spinning Wheel*, Dec. 1969, 20. **49.** Rivera and Rivera, *Inkstands and Inkwells*, 12. **50.** Ibid., 11-38. **51.** An Italian earthenware inkstand of about 1500 is in the Boston Museum of Fine Arts; illus. in Rivera and Rivera, *Inkstands and Inkwells*, 120. **52.** Crolius's price list reproduced in Harold F. Guilland, *Early American Folk Pottery* (Philadelphia: Chilton, 1971), 41. **53.** Revi, *American Pressed Glass*, 363, classes the ceramic figure set as bottles but they were sold as "inkstands" (Rivera and Rivera, *Inkstands and Inkwells*, 112), apparently without ink, and were obviously intended to be kept, filled, and refilled. **54.** Covill, *Ink Bottles*, 243-45, 325. **55.** Ibid., 245; Munsey, *Collecting Bottles*, 51; Rivera and Rivera, *Inkstands and Inkwells*, 60-70. **56.** Covill, *Ink Bottles*, 265-76; Rivera and Rivera, *Inkstands and Inkwells*, 73. **57.** Rivera and Rivera, *Inkstands and Inkwells*. **58.** "Inkwells: Practical Elegance for Writing Desks," *The Encyclopedia of Collectibles* (Alexandria, Va.: Time-Life Books, 1979), vol. IL, p. 7. **59.** Illustrated in Covill, *Ink Bottles*, 411. **60.** Guilland, *Folk Pottery*, 191. **61.** Covill, *Ink Bottles*, 403.

7: Ink Problems

1. The little drawing appears in *The Poetical Works of Thomas Hood*, vol. 2: "Humorous Poems" (Philadelphia: Porter and Coates, n.d.), 110. **2.** Bemiss, *Dyer's Companion*, 288. **3.** *OED*, 1961, 5:302. **4.** Ibid., 303. **5.** Charles Dickens, *Nicholas Nickleby* (1838), chap. 8; cited in *OED*, 1961, 5:303. **6.** Munsey, *Collecting Bottles*, 120. **7.** "Safety Inkstands" (inkwells) were described as "one of the most widely used" in the Carrithers catalog, 137. On the same page, similarly shaped "Practical Inkstands," intended "for hotel, school, office and home use," were likewise designated "unspillable." **8.** A blotter so used is in my collection. **9.** *OED*, 161, 5:302. **10.** Charles Dickens, *Bleak House* (1853; Norton Critical Edition, New York: Norton, 1977), 43. **11.** Armstrong, *Hill's Educator*, 453; italics in original. Modern ballpoint-ink stains, most often found on fabric, require a different approach. Place the stain side down on absorbent cloth and drop on naptha (lighter fluid) or carbon tetrachloride (cleaning fluid), tamp, move to a clean area on the absorbent cloth, and repeat. Or apply all-purpose, heavy-duty liquid detergent and rinse thoroughly (*Compton's Encyclopedia*, 1978, 7:200-201). **12.** Mary A. Benjamin, *Autographs: A Key to Col-*

lecting, rev. ed. (1963; repr., New York: Dover, 1986), 152.
13. *Ency. Brit.*, 1960, 17:230, s.v. "paper."   **14.** "Pounce Boxes and Sand Shakers," *Antiques*, July 1947, 36. The article gives the date of the *Abecedarium* as 1572, but 1552 is the correct date, as provided in *Ency. Brit.*, 1960, 7:338, s.v. "dictionary."
15. John Amos Comenius, "Ars Scribendi," *Orbis Sensualium Pictus*, ca. 1655; cited in *OED*, 1961, 2:39, s.v. "Callis-sand"; see also "Pounce Boxes and Sand Shakers," 36.
16. Illustrated in Covill, *Ink Bottles*, 410-11.   **17.** Whalley, *Writing Implements* 91-92.   **18.** Ibid., 90-91; Rivera and Rivera, *Inkstands and Inkwells*, 196-98; "Pounce Boxes and Sand Shakers."   **19.** Rivera and Rivera, *Inkstands and Inkwells*, 197.
20. "Pounce Boxes and Sand Shakers"; Rivera and Rivera, *Inkstands and Inkwells*, 196-98; Covill, *Ink Bottles*, 402-10. Many sanders are illustrated in each source.
21. "Pounce Boxes and Sand Shakers." See Rivera and Rivera, *Inkstands and Inkwells*, plate 4 (following p. 88), for an inkstand with sander dated ca. 1890.   **22.** Hunter, *Papermaking*, 476; Grant, *Books and Documents*, 42; W. Horman, *Vulgaria*, 1519, cited in Hunter, 476.   **23.** Huloet's full statement was, "We dry a writing with Blotting-paper, or Calis-sand out of a Sandbox."   **24.** Grant, *Books and Documents*, 43.   **25.** *Records of the Moravians of North Carolina*, 5:2269-2326, cited by Hunter, *Papermaking*, 508.
26. Ibid., entry of June 30, 1791; *New Standard Encyclopedia*, 1982, 10:77, s.v. "paper."   **27.** Charles Dickens, *The Pickwick Papers* (1837; Signet Classic ed., New York: New American Library, 1981), 553; Dickens, *Bleak House*, 120.   **28.** Herman Melville, *Moby Dick*, 1851, cited in "Pounce Boxes and Sand Shakers."   **29.** Kane, *Famous First Facts*, 119 (citing *Paperworld*, Aug. 1881). Kane states (erroneously) that this was the first blotting paper made in America.   **30.** Quoted in "Pounce Boxes and Sand Shakers."
31. According to the dealer K.C. Owings, Jr., Antiques Americana, North Abington, Massachusetts.   **32.** U.S. patent no. 131,056, Sept. 3, 1872.   **33.** The term "desk pads" was used in the Carrithers catalog of about 1925, 104.
34. Whalley, *Writing Implements*, 92, 129-30. Mention of a "blotting-pad" is found as early as 1591, according to *The Shorter Oxford English Dictionary on Historical Principles*, 1973, 1:206, s.v. "blotter."   **35.** Osborn, *Questioned Documents*, 461, 576.
36. Dickens, *Pickwick Papers*, 495.   **37.** The illustrations of the series of steps are reproduced in Jackson, *Story of Writing*, 68.   **38.** Interview with Ella Nickell (secretary-bookkeeper since 1935), June 14, 1988.   **39.** "Steel erasers," in Carrithers catalog, 162; "steel scrapers," in William Rodger, *The Official Guide to Old Books and Autographs*, 2d ed. (Orlando, Fla.: House of Collectibles, 1979), 76; "ink erasers," in Sears, Roebuck and Co. catalog (Fall 1900), 138; "ink knives," in "Inkwells: Practical Elegance for Writing Desks," p. 13.   **40.** Carrithers catalog, 162.
41. *The F.H. Collins Company Price List and Illustrated Catalog of Picture Frames and Artists' Materials* (Fort Worth, Tex.: F.H. Collins Co., 1894), 44.   **42.** Carrithers catalog, 163.
43. Ibid., 162.   **44.** Osborn, *Questioned Documents*, 547.
45. Armstrong, *Hill's Educator*, 386.
46. The Carrithers catalog shows the "Inky Racer" kit in a cardboard box with a cartoon-style drawing of a black runner; later kits were in metal canisters and the illustration was a stick figure; still later, kits were labeled "Carter's Two Solution Ink Eradicator."   **47.** Interview with Ella Nickell, June 14, 1988.   **48.** *Ency. Brit.*, 1980, 10:688, s.v. "laser and maser."
49. Carrithers catalog, 140.   **50.** Quoted in Whalley, *Writing Implements*, 78.
51. *OED*, 1961, 5:303, s.v. "ink-horn."   **52.** *Mechanics'*

Magazine 15 (1831): 270.   **53.** Ibid.   **54.** This use of salt probably explains the reference to it in Ben Jonson's play of 1606, *Volpone* (Prologue, lines 33-34): "All gall and copperas from his ink he draineth, / Only a little salt remaineth"; a footnote to the lines in *The Norton Anthology of English Literature*, 4th ed., (New York: Norton, 1979), 1117, asserts that salt is "not an ingredient of ink." Armstrong, *Hill's Educator*, 416.   **55.** Rivera and Rivera, *Inkstands and Inkwells*, 194.
56. Fairbank, *Story of Handwriting*, 91.   **57.** Bemiss, *Dyer's Companion*, 290.   **58.** Label illustrated in Covill, *Ink Bottles*, 183.   **59.** Silliman price list reproduced in ibid., 394.

8: Papermaking

1. Bodmer, *Book of Wonders*, 13-14.   **2.** Chandler B. Beach, ed., *The New Student's Reference Work* (Chicago: F.E. Compton, 1910), 3:1418.   **3.** Charles R. Anderson, *Lettering*, expanded ed. (New York: Van Nostrand Reinhold, 1982), 22-24; Jackson, *Story of Writing*, 22, 33.   **4.** H.W. Janson, *History of Art* (Englewood Cliffs, N.J.: Prentice-Hall, 1963), 165.   **5.** *Ency. Brit.*, 1960, 17:281, s.v. "parchment."
6. Johnston, *Writing and Illuminating*, 139.   **7.** Rodger, *Official Guide to Old Books*, 132.   **8.** Thompson, *Materials of Medieval Painting*, 24-30; *Ency. Brit.*, 1960, 17:281, s.v. "parchment"; Jackson, *Story of Writing*, 37; Dard Hunter, *Papermaking: The History and Technique of an Ancient Craft*, 2d ed. (1947; repr., New York: Dover, 1978), 13-16.   **9.** Johnston, *Writing and Illuminating*, 140.   **10.** Hunter, *Papermaking*, 50-52.
11. *Ency. Brit.*, 1910-11, 20:725-26, s.v. "paper"; Hunter, *Papermaking*, 60.   **12.** Theophilus, *On Divers Arts*, 29-30 n. 2; Hunter, *Papermaking*, 60, 472; *Ency. Brit.*, 1910-11, 20:726, s.v. "paper."   **13.** Hunter, *Papermaking*, 473-75.   **14.** Ibid., 477; *Ency. Brit.*, 1910-11, 20:726, s.v. "paper."   **15.** Ibid.
16. Hunter, *Papermaking*, 483.   **17.** Ibid., 247.
18. Thomas L. Gravell and George Miller, *A Catalogue of American Watermarks, 1690-1835.* (New York: Garland, 1979), xiv. The 1810 figures are from Isaiah Thomas, *The History of Printing in America*, cited in Hunter, *Papermaking*, 532-33. For an interesting discussion of Revolutionary War paper shortages, see *The Story of Paper-Making* (Chicago: J.W. Butler Paper Co., 1901), 36-39.   **19.** Joe Nickell, "Vintage Watermarks: Clues to the Origins of Paper on the Kentucky Frontier," *Journal of Kentucky Studies* (Sept. 1987), 108.   **20.** Ibid., 109-15.
21. Hunter, *Papermaking*, 519-21.   **22.** Gravell and Miller, *Catalogue of American Watermarks*, xvi; John W. Oliver, *History of American Technology* (New York: Ronald Press, 1956), 211.
23. Oliver, *History of American Technology*, 211.   **24.** Hunter, *Papermaking*, 535.   **25.** Benjamin, *Autographs*, 147.
26. Hunter, *Papermaking*, 247.   **27.** *Ency. Brit.*, 1960, 17:237, s.v. "paper."   **28.** Hunter, *Papermaking*, 84-88, 114-19.   **29.** Ibid., 125-28.   **30.** Ibid., 225-26.
31. Ibid., 5.   **32.** Ibid., 311.   **33.** *Story of Paper-Making*, 35; Hunter, *Papermaking*, 309-10.   **34.** *Kentucky Gazette*, Dec. 19, 1795.   **35.** Gravell and Miller, *Catalogue of American Watermarks*, 98.
36. *Story of Paper-Making*, 50-51, 56-65; Hunter, *Papermaking*, 154-63.   **37.** *Kentucky Gazette*, Nov. 8, 1794.   **38.** Hunter, *Papermaking*, 170-202; *Story of Paper-Making*, 49-54. For instructions for making paper see "The Age-Old Craft of Papermaking," *Decorating and Craft Ideas*, Aug. 1983, 9, 78-82.
40. Nicholas-Louis Robert, from a description of his invention written in late 1798, quoted in Hunter, *Papermaking*, 346.
41. Hunter, *Papermaking*, 350-51.   **42.** Gravell and Miller, *Catalogue of American Watermarks*, 178.   **43.** Hunter, *Paper-*

making, 361-62. **44.** Ibid., 349-56; *Ency. Brit.*, 1960, 17:235, s.v. "paper." **45.** Grant, *Books and Documents*, 27.

46. *Story of Paper-Making*, 77, 81. **47.** Hunter, *Papermaking*, 400-401; Hunter credits John Marshall with inventing the dandy roll in 1826, yet in a note acknowledges the 1825 patent of the Phippses. **48.** Ibid., 348. **49.** Ibid., 374.
50. Ibid., 374-95, 454-55, 552-75; *Ency. Brit.*, 1960, 17:231-34, s.v. "paper"; Grant, *Books and Documents*, 101-103; Philip Gaskell, *A New Introduction to Bibliography* (New York: Oxford Univ. Press, 1972), 221-23. **51.** Grant, *Books and Documents*, 18; Hunter, *Papermaking*, 482-532.

9: Watermarks

1. Grant, *Books and Documents*, 29. **2.** Hunter, *Papermaking*, 120-23, with illustrations of "antique" and "modern" laid paper. **3.** The term used by Gaskell, *New Introduction to Bibliography*, 214. **4.** Hunter, *Papermaking*, 131. **5.** Ibid., 128.
6. Elizabeth H. Thompson, *A.L.A. Glossary of Library Terms* (Chicago: American Library Association, 1943), 148.
7. *OED*, 1961, 12:176, s.v. "watermark"; the definition reads: "A distinguishing mark or device impressed in the substance of a sheet of paper during manufacture, usually barely noticeable except when the sheet is held against strong light." **8.** Hunter, *Papermaking*, 124. **9.** Ibid., 401-405, 264. **10.** Grant, *Books and Documents*, 4, 30 (with drawing of the earliest known watermark).
11. Ibid., 30 (illus.). **12.** Ibid., 30-31 (not illus.); Hunter, *Papermaking*, 474. **13.** Hunter, *Papermaking*, 259.
14. Gaskell, *New Introduction to Bibliography*, 61. **15.** Grant, *Books and Documents*, 30.
16. Gaskell, *New Introduction to Bibliography*, 61.
17. Ibid., 61-62. **18.** Ibid., 62; Thompson, *A.L.A. Glossary*, 40. **19.** Gaskell, *New Introduction to Bibliography*, 73-75, gives an extensive table correlating size of sheet, date, watermark, and name; Hunter, *Papermaking*, 136-38, provides further details; Grant, *Books and Documents*, 31. **20.** *OED*, 1961, 4:400, s.v. "fool's-cap"; Gaskell, *New Introduction to Bibliography*, 74-75; Briquet, *Les filigranes*, 2:780-94, and illus. nos. 15720-752 in vol. 4; Hamilton, *Great Forgers*, 266.
21. Grant, *Books and Documents*, 31. The legend is likewise given in *Story of Paper-making*, 96. **22.** *OED*, 1961, 4:400, s.v. "fool's-cap." **23.** Hunter, *Papermaking*, 16n. **24.** Gravell and Miller, *Catalogue of American Watermarks*, 201; Hunter, *Papermaking*, 274. **25.** Gravell and Miller, *Catalogue of American Watermarks*, xvii.
26. Ibid., 198-99, 208. **27.** *Boston Weekly Register*, Jan. 22, 1812, and Aug. 5, 1820, cited in Hunter, *Papermaking*, 278-29. **28.** Hunter, *Papermaking*, 252-53; Gravell and Miller, *Catalogue of American Watermarks*, 24, 152 (showing photographs of the Washington watermarks), 210. **29.** Gravell and Miller, *Catalogue of American Watermarks*. **30.** Ibid., xxi.
31. Hunter, *Papermaking*, 282; Hunter also mentions other such liquid preparations. **32.** I have adapted this method of making watermarks from a means of producing "invisible writing" given in Martin Gardner, *Codes, Ciphers, and Secret Writing* (New York: Pocket Books, 1972), 86. **33.** Hunter, *Papermaking*, 416-25. **34.** Ibid., 282-83. **35.** Ibid., 283-95.
36. Ibid., 297-308; *Ency. Brit.*, 1960, 23:424, s.v. "watermarks." **37.** Hunter, *Papermaking*, 425-27.

10: Stationery and Seals

1. *Ency. Brit.*, 1960, 17:229, s.v. "paper"; Hunter, *Papermak-*

ing, 476; printing is discussed in chap. 11. **2.** Hunter, *Papermaking*, 62. **3.** Ibid., 194. **4.** Quoted from *The Instructor; or American Young Man's best Companion* (1794) by Nash, *American Penmanship*, 26. Edward Cocker, in his 1703 text (quoted in Whalley, *Writing Implements*, 22), recommended "well gum'd Paper," by which one assumes he meant paper prepared with gum sandarac. **5.** Grant, *Books and Documents*, 18; Whalley, *Writing Implements*, 73, gives "the late fourteenth century" for the first use of tub sizing; Hunter, *Papermaking*, 194.
6. Grant, *Books and Documents*, 18-19. **7.** See the three-page chart representing paper from the fourteenth to the eighteenth centuries in Gaskell, *New Introduction to Bibliography*, 73-75. **8.** Ibid. **9.** *Story of Paper-Making*, 122. **10.** Dickens, *Pickwick Papers*, 564.
11. Benjamin, *Autographs*, 146. **12.** Grant, *Books and Documents*, 27, 69-70; Hunter, *Papermaking*, 575; *Story of Paper-Making*, 112; *OED*, 1961, 7:470, s.v. "parchment." After "parchmentizing," the acid was neutralized. **13.** *OED*, 1972 Supplement, vol. A-G, 320, s.v. "Bond paper." **14.** Gaskell, *New Introduction to Bibliography*, 59. **15.** *Ency. Brit.*, 1960, 20:243, s.v. "sealing wax"; D.V. Thompson, *Materials of Medieval Painting*, 102-6. In levigation of pigments, the powdered material is placed in water, the heavy particles are allowed to settle, and the finely suspended particles are siphoned off with the water, which is then evaporated.
16. Prof. Thomas Shippey (Univ. of Leeds), lecture at the University of Kentucky, Apr. 28, 1988. **17.** Black sealing wax for sealing mourning envelopes is recommended in S.A. Frost, *Frost's Original Letter-Writer* (New York: Dick and Fitzgerald, 1867), 32. Black wax is also mentioned as part of the "ritual of mourning," by Whalley, *Writing Implements*, 77. The mere use of black wax, however (as on a business letter of 1824 in my own collection), may not necessarily signal mourning; it is often difficult to know in such instances, since mourning letters—later usually edged in black—refer not to their content but simply to their use by one in mourning. **19.** Dickens, *Pickwick Papers*, 564. **19.** Armstrong, *Hill's Educator*, 447. The dark brown wax was used for three seals on an 1890 envelope of the Adams Express Company in my collection. It would have been cheaper than wax made with the expensive pigment vermilion.
20. Neumann, *Early American*, 337, describes a brass wax jack or taper jack of about 1780: "An English stand that had a candlelike wax taper coiled around its post; when lighted, the end . . . dripped the sealing wax." Also, a "sealing wax ladle" is mentioned in Pauline Agius, "Collecting Silver and Silver Substitutes in the Seventies," *Antique Dealer and Collector's Guide*, Apr. 1972, 82.
21. Whalley, *Writing Implements*, 94; Rivera and Rivera, *Inkstands and Inkwells*, 105. **22.** *Ency. Brit.*, 1960, 20:243-44, s.v. "seals." **23.** Ibid. A reference to a king's "lettres isealed" dates from 1225 (*OED*, 1961, 9:325, s.v. "seal"). **24.** The figural seals mentioned are illustrated in Ball, "Writing Tools," 17. Watch-fob seals are illustrated in Anthony Curtis, *The Lyle Price Guide to Collectibles and Memorabilia* (New York: Putnam, 1988), 417. For the use of a thimble as a seal, see *OED*, 1961, 9:325, s.v. "seal"; for the use of a door key, see Dickens, *Pickwick Papers*, 564-65. **25.** Neumann, *Early American*, 328.
26. Robert L. Oakley, "Collecting Wax Sealers," *Antiques Journal*, Feb. 1973, 10-12. **27.** An aqua wafer in my collection was used to seal an 1852 envelope. Black wafers were among those sold at the printing office at Williamsburg, Va., in 1750; Williamsburg merchants advertised "Vermilion Wafers," "Dutch Sealing Wafers," and just "Wafers" (Rivera and Rivera, *Inkstands and Inkwells*, 199). **28.** Prof. Daniel Lyons, ed., *The American Dictionary of the English Language, Based on the Latest*

Conclusions of the Most Emminent Philologists . . . (New York: Peter Fenelon Collier, 1898), 472.   **29.** Ibid.   **30.** In a letter, Dante Gabriel Rossetti wrote: "The thick red sky has a thin red sun stuck in the middle of it, like the specimen wafer stuck outside the box of them. Even if you turned back the lid, there would be nothing behind it, be sure, but a jumble of such flat dead suns" (in *Letters of Dante Rossetti to William Allingham: 1854-1870,* ed. George Birkbeck Hill [London: T.F. Unwin, 1897], 206).

31. Ball, "Writing Tools," 17.   **32.** The paste-and-paper seal dates back to at least 1542 in Spain, and possibly much earlier. One of that date was the earliest found in a large collection: "Manuscript Documents from Spain Dating from the 12th through the 18th Centuries," accession no. 73M33, doc. no. 888, Special Collections, Margaret I. King Library, University of Kentucky. One of the affixed pieces of paper was cut—possibly after first being symmetrically folded—into a four-pointed design, somewhat resembling a compass rose; it was on doc. no. 217, dated 1775. Most of the earlier documents were on vellum and lacked any seals.   **33.** Whalley, *Writing Implements,* 75-76.   **34.** Hattie Nevada, "The Letter Edged in Black," in *Everybody's Favorite Songs of the Gay Nineties* (New York: AMSCO Music Publishing Co., 1943), 185-87. My grandmother, Golden Murphy Nickell (1895–1990), recalled that this song was popular when she was a schoolgirl and that she used to play it herself on the organ. My mother, Ella Turner Nickell (b. 1918), recalls her own mother singing the song when she was about ten years old.   **35.** Harvey Green, *The Light of the Home: An Intimate View of the Lives of Women in Victorian America* (New York: Pantheon Books, 1983), 173.

36. "Mourning Goods" in an advertisement of Jordan, Marsh and Co., *Boston Daily Evening Transcript,* Nov. 25, 1864; the advertisement does not specify the items. Whalley, *Writing Implements,* 77.   **37.** John Lewis, *Printed Ephemera* (Ipswich, England: W.S. Cowell, 1962), 149.   **38.** For example, a letter from Mrs. Roosevelt to Harry Truman, dated Sept. 11, 1945, has a narrow black border and is accompanied by a matching envelope. It is in the "President's Secretary's File" at the Harry S. Truman Library, Independence, Mo. The most recent example of European mourning stationery in my collection is French, dated 1953.   **39.** Polley, *Everyday Things,* 135-36.   **40.** *OED,* 1961, 3:229, s.v. "envelope."   **41.** Ibid.   **42.** Arthur Blair, *The World of Stamps and Stamp Collecting* (London: Hamlyn, 1972), 10, 16; the ancient Persian, Greek, and Roman postal systems existed for government, rather than public, use. Polley, *Everyday Things,* 136; Harry M. Konwiser, *The American Stamp Collector's Dictionary* (New York: Tudor, 1949), 177.   **43.** Blair, *World of Stamps,* 16.   **49.** Polley, *Everyday Things,* 136.   **45.** Blair, *World of Stamps,* 88.   **46.** Ibid., 16.   **47.** Ibid., 20, 24, 30; Samuel Grossman, *Stamp Collector's Handbook* (New York: Longacre, 1957), 49.   **48.** Grossman, *Stamp Collector's Handbook,* 10-11; Blair, *World of Stamps,* 88, 90; *Ency. Brit.,* 1960, 15:946, s.v. "Mulready, William."   **49.** Elena Marzulla, ed., *United States Stamps and Stories* (n.p.: Scott Pub. Co., 1973), 6-7; Blair, *World of Stamps,* 62-66.   **50.** Konwiser, *American Stamp Collector's Dictionary,* 63, 88, 141, 177, 274.   **51.** Mathew J. Bowyer, "Postmarks," *Antiques Journal,* Apr. 1974, 45; Blair, *World of Stamps,* 11, 99. The earliest marks for London (1661), New York (1758), and other places are illustrated in Blair, *World of Stamps,* 11.   **52.** Konwiser, *American Stamp Collector's Dictionary,* 77; Kane, *Famous First Facts,* 249.   **53.** In my collection. This was among the papers in the document box illustrated in fig. 7.2.   **54.** Mrs. E.B. Duffey, *The Ladies' and Gentlemen's Etiquette* (Philadelphia: Porter and Coates, 1877),

121.   **55.** U.S. patent no. 131,184, Sept. 10, 1872. Examples of patented envelopes include one with an inserted piece of cord to provide a zip-open feature (U.S. pat. no. 20,087, Apr. 27, 1858), and another which "consists in so shaping the pattern that when one piece is cut from the roller or continuous sheet the end of the sheet is left in the right form to use; and also in making the adhering parts that close the ends or sides to consist of narrow folds or laps that shall come inside or between the face and back" (no. 22,405, Dec. 28, 1858).

56. U.S. patent no. 6,055, issued Jan. 23, 1849, to Jesse K. Park and Cornelius S. Watson of New York City. This patent was followed by many others, including no. 16,576, issued Feb. 10, 1857, to Theodore Bergner.   **57.** Window envelope: patent no. 701,839, June 10, 1902; it was manufactured the following month by the U.S. Envelope Company, Springfield, Mass. (Kane, *Famous First Facts,* 249). Blair, *World of Stamps,* 33; *Scott 1986 Standard Postage Stamp Catalog* (Sidney, Ohio: Scott Publishing, 1986), 1:81; Konwiser, *American Stamp Collector's Dictionary,* 78.   **58.** Blair, *World of Stamps,* 88; illus. of "Fores's Musical Envelope," 111.   **59.** Grossman, *Stamp Collector's Handbook,* 91.   **60.** Ibid., 89, 166; Blair, *World of Stamps,* 88-89; Marzulla, *United States Stamps,* 217. For interested collectors, there is a *Scott 1988 U.S. First Day Cover Catalog and Checklist* (Sidney, Ohio: Scott Publishing Co., 1987).   **61.** *World Book Encyclopedia,* 1985, 15:583-84, s.v. "Pony Express." A later "last trip" on Nov. 20, 1861, is reported (Konwiser, *American Stamp Collector's Dictionary,* 189), but the date is only that of a San Francisco newspaper listing letters received via Pony Express.   **62.** The postmarks are illustrated in Konwiser, *American Stamp Collector's Dictionary,* 188, and Grossman, *Stamp Collector's Handbook,* 169.   **63.** See "Postal Scales" in Curtis, *Lyle Price Guide,* 358. See also Whalley, *Writing Implements,* 94-96.   **64.** Various advertisements in my collection, e.g., an advertisement for "Stationers' Specialties" that listed visiting cards (City Directory, Louisville, Ky., 1890); also an English advertising envelope, "A. Clare, Fancy Goods, Stationery, and Picture Post Card Depot," n.d.   **65.** *Shorter Oxford English Dictionary,* 1973, 1:284, s.v. "card."   **66.** Hunter, *Papermaking,* 480.   **67.** Ibid., 541.   **68.** *Ency. Brit.,* 1960, 23:215, s.v. "visiting cards." Thomas Jefferson's calling card, used when he was minister to the court of Louis XVI, is exhibited at the Thomas Jefferson Visitors' Center, located about two miles west of Monticello, near Charlottesville, Va. The card measures approximately 2¼ inches by 3½ inches wide and appears to have been printed by copperplate engraving. It reads: "Mr. Jefferson / Ministere Plenipotentaire / des Etats Unis de' Amerique."   **69.** Quotations from Thomas E. Hill, *Hill's Manual of Social and Business Forms* (Chicago: Moses Warren, 1875), 137-38. Duffey, *Etiquette,* 196; Curtis, *Lyle Price Guide,* 105.   **70.** Duffey, *Etiquette,* 174-75.   **71.** Advertisement for "hidden name" and "envelope" cards, *Happy Hours* (tabloid), Nov. 1911, 11.   **72.** John H. Young, *Our Deportment,* 1882; quoted in Polley, *Everyday Things,* 134-35.   **73.** For example, according to Duffey, *Etiquette,* 175, it signified "that the visit was intended for two or more members of the family."   **74.** Curtis, *Lyle Price Guide,* 103.   **75.** J. Willis Westlake, *How to Write Letters: A Manual of Correspondence* (Philadelphia: Sower, Potts, 1883), 163.   **76.** In my collection. The card bears the printed name "Miss M. Edith Merker."   **77.** Suzanne Wylie, "Valentines: Alluring Notes of Romance," in *Encyclopedia of Collectibles,* vol. TW, p. 17.   **78.** Martin Hoffman, ed., *Americana Treasures* (New York: Dodd, Mead & Co., 1983), 208.   **79.** Marian Klamkin, *Collectibles: A Compendium* (Garden City, N.Y.: Doubleday, 1981), 249.   **80.** Hoffman, *Americana Treasures,* 208; Wylie, "Valentines," 17.

81. Carroll Alton Means, "Greeting Cards: A Gallery of Best Wishes," in *Encyclopedia of Collectibles*, vol. FH, illus. p. 77. **82.** Hoffman, *Americana Treasures*, 208. **83.** Means, "Greeting Cards," 69. Some sources (e.g., *Ency. Brit.*, 1960, 5:644, s.v. "Christmas cards") cite a card of 1842 by William Maw Egley, but in fact that date is uncertain. I am indebted to Sharron Uhler, Curator of Hallmark Historical Collection, Hallmark Cards, Kansas City, Mo., for clarifying this question and providing other helpful information. **84.** Means, "Greeting Cards," 69. **85.** A small card (1³⁄₁₆ inches by 3½ inches wide)—printed with "Christmas Greetings" and holly in green and with "1910" in red—is in my collection, the latest-dated specimen of its kind there.

86. *Ency. Brit.*, 1960, 5:644A, s.v. "Christmas cards." **87.** In my collection: Easter cards dated 1883, 1905; New Year's card copyrighted 1876 (but penciled on back, "Jan. 1st, 1883"), 1⅞ inches by 3⅜ inches wide. See also Means, "Greeting Cards," 71. **88.** All Fools' card and temperance card are in my collection; related are various motto cards, religious cards, etc.; Westlake, *How to Write Letters*, 163, includes an illustration of a memorial card for Abraham Lincoln. **89.** Means, "Greeting Cards," 69; Thomas E. Hudgeons III, ed., *The Official 1984 Price Guide to Paper Collectibles*, 3d ed. (Orlando, Fla.: House of Collectibles, 1983), 311. **90.** Means, "Greeting Cards," 69-70; interview with Sharron Uhler, July 28, 1988.

91. Westlake, *How to Write Letters*, 135-37, 165. **92.** James C. Simmons, "Picture (Postcard) Perfect," *Sky*, April 1990, 33; Andress Brown, "Postcards: Pictures for Personal Messages," *Encyclopedia of Collectibles*, vol. P-Q, p. 79. **93.** Westlake, *How to Write Letters*, 13. **94.** Brown, "Postcards," 76; *Ency. Brit.*, 1960, 18:316, s.v. "post cards." **95.** Brown, "Postcards," 76.

96. Ibid., 76-79. **97.** Klamkin, *Collectibles*, 183. **98.** Brown, "Postcards," 84. **99.** Klamkin, *Collectibles*, 183-84. **100.** Brown, "Postcards," 76.

101. Hudgeons, *1984 Price Guide*, 472. **102.** This method is still used; see Margaret L. Hodgson, "Skins, Papers, Pounces," in Lamb, *Calligrapher's Handbook*, 93; Whalley, *Writing Implements*, 127-28. **103.** Gaskell, *New Introduction to Bibliography*, 80-87. **104.** Thomas Jefferson's ivory paper knife, exhibited at the Thomas Jefferson Visitors' Center (see n. 68), measures about ⅝ by 5 inches. **105.** A study of pre-envelope letters shows that many were torn as described. Sometimes the paper would simply pull free from a paste wafer.

106. Polley, *Everyday Things*, 240. **107.** Quotation in Polley, *Everyday Things*, 326; Gaskell, *New Introduction to Bibliography*, 234. **108.** Polley, *Everyday Things*, 240. **109.** Ibid., 157; Jackson, *Story of Writing*, 22. **110.** Advertisement in *Literary Digest*, June 28, 1919, 70. Mucilage is a product made from vegetable gum (such as gum arabic).

111. Kane, *Famous First Facts*, 158-59. The Carrithers catalog of ca. 1925 features the "transparent gummed tissue" tape (p. 194) along with ordinary gummed-paper and gummed-cloth tapes (pp. 120, 144). Cellophane tape (e.g., Scotch-brand tape) is a later product. **112.** *Godey's Lady's Book and Magazine* 86 (1873): 81, 273. **113.** "Temporary Binder," U.S. patent no. 1,104,394. The invention was filed Dec. 26, 1908, but was not patented until July 21, 1914. **114.** Judith Miller and Martin Miller, *Miller's Pocket Antiques Fact File* (New York: Viking, 1988), 184; Curtis, *Lyle Price Guide*, 326-27; Klamkin *Collectibles*, 174-77; Rivera and Rivera, *Inkstands and Inkwells*, 91-96; Whalley, *Writing Implements*, 127. **115.** Rivera and Rivera, *Inkstands and Inkwells*, 91-96; Elizabeth Oliver, *American Antique Glass* (New York: Golden Press, 1977), 143.

11: History of Written Forms

1. Alexander Nesbitt, *The History and Technique of Lettering* (New York: Dover, 1957), 1-8; Diana J. Rendell, "The Development of Writing," in Berkeley, *Autographs and Manuscripts*, 3-5; Ogg, *26 Letters*, 22-41; Jackson, *Story of Writing*, 14-18; Benjamin, *Autographs*, 3. **2.** Ibid. **3.** Ibid. **4.** Rodger, *Official Guide to Old Books*, 66. **5.** Although the term *script* is now often used loosely to refer to *cursive* handwriting (wherein the letters are tied together with ligatures or connecting strokes), in this book it is employed in the original sense of any handwritten or hand-printed mode of writing.

6. D. Rendell, "Development of Writing," 5-13; *Ency. Brit.*, 1973, s.v. "hieroglyphs" (from which is adapted the chart, fig. 11.6); Leo Deuel, *Testaments of Time: The Search for Lost Manuscripts and Records* (New York: Knopf, 1965). **7.** D. Rendell, "Development of Writing," 5-13; Nesbitt, *History and Technique*, 6-8; *New Standard Encyclopedia*, 1982, s.v. "alphabet"; *World Book Encyclopedia*, 1985, 1:367, s.v. "alphabet." **8.** Ogg, *26 Letters*, 88-89. **9.** Ibid., 106. **10.** Illustrations of examples from wax tablets from Pompeii, 53 and 54 A.D., and other examples from the second and sixth centuries are shown in Herman Degering, *Lettering: Modes of Writing in Western Europe from Antiquity to the End of the 18th Century* (New York: Pentalic Corp., 1965), 7-9. See also Nesbitt, *History and Technique*, 13; D. Rendell, "Development of Writing," 21.

11. Nesbitt, *History and Technique*, 9-18; Ogg, *26 Letters*, 102-63; D. Rendell, "Development of Writing," 16-21; Jackson, *Story of Writing*, 38-49. **12.** Joyce Irene Whalley, *The Student's Guide to Western Calligraphy: An Illustrated Survey* (Boulder, Colo.: Shambhala, 1984), illus. facing p. 1. **13.** Nesbitt, *History and Technique*, 9-18; Ogg, *26 Letters*, 102-63; D. Rendell, "Development of Writing," 16-21; Jackson, *Story of Writing*, 38-49. **14.** Jackson, *Story of Writing*, 62-73; Ogg, *26 Letters*, 164-74; Nesbitt, *History and Technique*, 27-32. **15.** Ogg, *26 Letters*, 174-85; Jackson, *Story of Writing*, 76; Nesbitt, *History and Technique*, 35-63. Gaskell, *New Introduction to Bibliography*, 17-19, discusses the Gothic forms in terms of their influence on printing type.

16. *Ency. Brit.*, 1960, 3:872-73, s.v. "books" (parts 3 and 4). **17.** Joseph Gies and Frances Gies, *Life in a Medieval City* (1969; repr., New York: Harper Colophon Books, 1981), 171. In his twelfth-century treatise, Theophilus, 30-31, mentions as burnishers "the tooth of a beaver, a bear, or a boar" and again "a tooth or a stone." **18.** Janet Backhouse, *The Illuminated Manuscript* (Oxford: Phaidon, 1979), 8. **19.** Gies and Gies, *Life in a Medieval City*, 171; *Ency. Brit.*, 1960, 3:872-73, s.v. "books"; Jackson, *Story of Writing*, 80-86. **20.** Gies and Gies, *Life in a Medieval City*, 175.

21. Rodger, *Official Guide to Old Books*, 159; Jackson, *Story of Writing*, 85. **22.** *Ency. Brit.*, 1980, 5:304, s.v. "illumination." See also Margaret Shepherd, *Learning Calligraphy* (New York: Collier Books, 1977), 64. **23.** Rodger, *Official Guide to Old Books*, 100. But according to Norma Levarie, *The History of Books* (New York: Da Capo Press, 1968), 23: "Illumination differed from illustration in that its essential purpose was not to clarify or exemplify the text, but to adorn it." **24.** *Shorter Oxford English Dictionary*, 1973, 1:1021, s.v. "illumination." **25.** See color illustrations in Jackson, *Story of Writing*, 51, 59.

26. Shepherd, *Learning Calligraphy*, 64. **27.** Jackson, *Story of Writing*, 82-93. **28.** Ibid.; Levarie, *History of Books*, 22. **29.** Backhouse, *Illuminated Manuscript*, 7-12; *Ency. Brit.*, 1960, 5:873, s.v. "books"; Jackson, *Story of Writing*, 76-97. **30.** Nesbitt, *History and Technique*, 64-68; Levarie, *History of Books*, 63-64. For illustrations see Levarie, 64, and Whalley, *Student's Guide*, 36-37.

31. Nesbitt, *History and Technique*, 65; D. Rendell, "Development of Writing," 23. 32. Nesbitt, *History and Technique*, 68; Whalley, *Student's Guide*, 22. 33. Whalley, *Student's Guide*, 22. 34. Ogg, *26 Letters*, 184. 35. D. Rendell, "Development of Writing," 27.

36. *Ency. Brit.*, 1960, 23:813-14, s.v. "writing." 37. Nesbitt, *History and Technique*, 107-108. 38. Illustrated in Joyce Irene Whalley, *English Handwriting, 1540-1853* (London: Her Majesty's Stationery Office, 1969), plate 7. The quotation is from *Twelfth Night*, 3.4.30. 39. D. Rendell, "Development of Writing," 27. There was also an English "court hand" (illus. in app. 1), which was an engrossers' script used in deeds, charters, and other legal documents. It was descended from Gothic and thus related to secretary. According to Benjamin, *Autographs*, 155, it "was in vogue in England about the seventeenth century. This, due both to the unusual method of shaping characters and to the practice of abbreviating extensively, could not even be read by the people as a whole. Scriveners, it was alleged, made something of a racket of it. In any event, its use was made illegal in 1735." Benjamin cites *English Law Reports*, 5th Geo. II, c. 27, and 6th Geo. II, c. 14. 40. Whalley, *Student's Guide*, 53.

41. Jackson, *Story of Writing*, 118-19. 42. Osborn, *Questioned Documents*, 167. 43. Marvin Morgan, "Handwriting Systems and Penmanship," *Identification News*, July 1985, 2. 44. Ibid., 173, fig. 103. 45. Osborn, *Questioned Documents*, 184 n. 1; "Platt Rogers Spencer," in *The National Cyclopaedia of American Biography* (1924; repr., Ann Arbor: University Microfilms, 1967), 8:11. 46. Osborn, *Questioned Documents*, 185; Morgan, "Handwriting Systems," 2. 47. Morgan, "Handwriting Systems," 2. 48. Ibid.; Osborn, *Questioned Documents*, 176-77. 49. Morgan, "Handwriting Systems," 11; Osborn, *Questioned Documents*, 179, 186. 50. Morgan, "Handwriting Systems," 11.

51. Osborn, *Questioned Documents*, 177, illus. 52. Quoted in Nash, *American Penmanship*, 47. For more on Gould, see Nash, 40ff. For a discussion of left-handed writing, see chap. 6 of Alvin and Virginia B. Silverstein, *The Left-hander's World* (Chicago: Follett, 1977), 61-69. 53. Osborn, *Questioned Documents*, 149, without specifically mentioning backhand, states that "a frequent disguise in anonymous letters is a *decided* change of slant and two writings often are essentially the same although written at a very different slant" (emphasis added). 54. Lois Harting, "The Art of Fraktur," *Early American Life*, Apr. 1977, 48-49 (see also the color illustration on the cover of that issue); *Encyclopedia of Collectibles*, 13, illus. 55. *Encyclopedia of Library and Information Science*, 1978, 24:96-97, "printers and printing, Korean."

56. Hunter, *Papermaking*, 476; Levarie, *History of Books*, 69-71. 57. Levarie, *History of Books*, 77-81; Rodger, *Official Guide to Old Books*, 93-95; Ogg, *26 Letters*, 186-205; Grant, *Books and Documents*, 41; *Ency. Brit.*, 1960, 18:500-501; s.v. "printing"; Polley, *Everyday Things*, 254-55. An earlier invention of printing from movable ceramic type, by Pi Sheng in China, between 1041 and 1049, is noted (*Ency. Brit.*, 1960, 18:500, s.v. "printing"; Polley, *Everyday Things*, 255); however, claims for a pre-Gutenberg invention by one Laurens Coster in Holland "even if real, were at best abortive" (Levarie, 80-81), and Gutenberg's total contributions, including inventing the adjustable hand mold and developing a practical press, far surpass those of any predecessor (Nesbitt, *History and Technique*, 49-50; Levarie, *History of Books*, 80-81). For a full discussion of the documentary evidence concerning Gutenberg, see Douglas C. McMurtrie, *The Gutenberg Documents* (New York: Oxford Univ. Press, 1941). 58. Levarie, *History of Books*, 77, 82. 59. *Ency. Brit.*, 1960, 18:

facing 502, s.v. "printing," caption to plate 1. 60. Ibid., 501; Rodger, *Official Guide to Old Books*, 102; Ogg, *26 Letters*, 210. Printed works *through* the year 1500 are considered incunabula.

61. Nesbitt, *History and Technique*, 66. 62. *Ency. Brit.*, 1960, 18:501-2, s.v. "printing"; Levarie, *History of Books*, 154-61; Nesbitt, *History and Technique*, 38. 63. Jackson, *Story of Writing*, 109. 64. Whalley, *Student's Guide*, 52. 65. "A Scandal in America," *Book Collector* 36 (Winter 1987): 460.

66. *Ency. Brit.*, 1960, 18:502, s.v. "printing." 67. Levarie, *History of Books*, 279. 68. John W. Oliver, *History of American Technology* (New York: Ronald Press, 1956), 440; *Ency. Brit.*, 1960, 15:824, s.v. "Morse, Samuel Finley Breese." 69. Oliver, *History of American Technology*, 440. 70. *The Story of the Typewriter, 1873-1923* (Herkimer, N.Y.: Herkimer County Historical Society, 1923), 17-18.

71. Ibid., 18. 72. Panati, *Browser's Book of Beginnings*, 84. 73. U.S. patent no. 6,085, July 23, 1829. A photograph of the patent signed by Andrew Jackson and of a reproduction of the machine are given in *Story of the Typewriter*, 19-21. 74. Ibid., 20-21. 75. Ibid., 26-27, with an engraving of the piano-like keyboard; the machine was patented by Dr. Samuel W. Francis, a New York physician, in 1857.

76. Ibid., 22-29. 77. Ibid., 30-70. 78. Ibid., 72-74. 79. Ibid., 69, 76-80. 80. Ibid., 100-105.

81. Ibid., 99. For treatment of the early typewriters as collectibles, see Curtis, *Lyle Price Guide*, 475. 82. *Story of the Typewriter*, 117. 83. James Smathers produced a working model of the electric typewriter by 1920. See *Ency. Brit.*, 1960, 22:645, "typewriter." 84. Panati, *Browser's Book of Beginnings*, 83-84; *Ency. Brit.*, 1980, 16:710-11, s.v. "shorthand." (The Stenotype machine was the invention of Ward Stone Ireland, who was an American stenographer and court reporter. 85. John Robert Gregg, *The Story of Shorthand* (New York: Gregg Pub. Co., 1941), 1-6; *Story of the Typewriter*, 12-13; *Ency. Brit.*, 1980, 16:709, s.v. "shorthand"; Panati, *Browser's Book of Beginnings*, 81.

86. Gregg, "Story of Shorthand." 87. *Story of the Typewriter*, 13; *Ency. Brit.*, 1980, 16:709, and 1960, 20:574-75, s.v. "shorthand." 88. *Ency. Brit.*, 1960, 20:576-77, and 1980, 16:709-10, s.v. "shorthand." Panati, *Browser's Book of Beginnings*, 83-84. Among later "modern abbreviated longhand systems" are Speedwriting shorthand (created about 1924 for taking down on the typewriter and in 1942 changed to a version for handwriting); Fortner Alphabet shorthand (published in 1952); Hy-Speed Longhand (a 1932 version of Graham's *Brief Longhand*, 1857); Stenoscript ABC Shorthand (the 1950 modernization of a system of 1607); and Stenospeed (developed in 1950, rev. 1951). 89. Panati, *Browser's Book of Beginnings*, 84.

12: ABC's of Penmanship

1. Philip Hofer, in an introduction to a facsimile edition of George Bickham's 1741 classic, *The Universal Penman* (New York: Dover, 1954), n.p.; Whalley, *Student's Guide*, 53; Geoffrey Ashall Glaister, *Glaister's Glossary of the Book* (Berkeley: Univ. of California Press, 1979), 18, 521. 2. Discussed earlier in chapt. 11. 3. Hofer, in Bickham, *Universal Penman;* Whalley, *Student's Guide*, 80-81, 84-85 (illus. of specimens from the books of Cocker, Seddon, and Ayers); Jackson, *Story of Writing*, 118. 4. Bickham, *Universal Penman*. 5. Katharine Morrison McClinton, *Antiques of American Childhood* (New York: Potter, 1970), 85.

6. Ray Nash, *American Writing Masters and Copybooks: History and Bibliography through Colonial Times* (Boston: Colonial Society of Massachusetts, 1959), 21. 7. McClinton, *Antiques*, 86-87; Nash, *American Writing Masters*, 23-25, 35. 8. Roon Frost,

"Early American Education," *Early American Life,* Oct. 1985, 83, 96; Susan Burrows Swan, "Appreciating American Samplers," *Early American Life,* Feb. 1984, 42-50; McClinton, *Antiques,* 84. See also *Webster's New International Dictionary,* 2d ed., s.v. "battledore." **9.** McClinton, *Antiques,* 75-78. **10.** Curtis, *Lyle Price Guide,* 113.

11. See Mara L. Pratt, *Stories of Colonial Children,* rev. ed. (Boston: Educational Pub. Co., 1908), 81. **12.** McClinton, *Antiques,* 79-82; Frost, "Early American," 83. Only the early editions of McGuffey's Readers, 1836-37, have real value to collectors, according to Ralph Kovel and Terry Kovel, *Know Your Antiques* (New York: Crown, 1973), 290-91. **13.** Swan, "Appreciating American Samplers, 41-50 (also part 2, Apr. 1984, 42-45, 72, 93); McClinton, *Antiques,* 184ff; Glee F. Frueger, *A Gallery of American Samplers* (New York: Dutton, 1978). **14.** Swan, "Appreciating American Samplers" part 1, 44. **15.** McClinton, *Antiques,* 84. **16.** Nash, *American Writing Masters,* 7. **17.** Advertisements in the *Weekly Museum* (New York), Oct. 15, 1796. **18.** Nash, *American Writing Masters,* 26-34. **19.** McClinton, *Antiques,* 87. **20.** Nash, *American Writing Masters,* 30. **21.** Benjamin Franklin Foster, *Writing and Writing Masters* (New York: Mason Brothers, 1854), 10. **22.** Ibid. **23.** Ibid., 11. **24.** Ibid. **25.** *The National Cyclopaedia of American Biography* (1924; repr., Ann Arbor, Mich.: University Microfilms, 1967), s.v. "Spencer, Platt Rogers." **26.** Ibid. **27.** Thomas E. Hill, *Hill's Manual of Social and Business Forms* (Chicago: Mose Warren, 1875), 18. **28.** The first edition of Parson's was published in 1882. **29.** G.A. Gaskell, *Gaskell's Compendium of Forms,* 45th ed. (Chicago: Fairbanks and Palmer, 1884), 88-92. **30.** *New Standard Encyclopedia,* 1982, 6:40, s.v. "handwriting"; *Webster's Biographical Dictionary,* 1st ed., s.v. "Palmer, Austin Norman." The 1888 date is given in McGuire, *Forgers,* 209.

31. The information here is based on the various Palmer items described, in my collection, including copybooks and manuals in editions from 1911 to 1931. **32.** *Business Educator* (Columbus, Ohio) 34 (June 1929); Stella H. Bloser, "The Zaner-Bloser Story of Legible Handwriting" (n.d.), typescript provided by John Marchak, Director of Communications and Advertising, Zaner-Bloser Co. **33.** *New Standard Encyclopedia,* 1982, 6:39-41, s.v. "handwriting." **34.** Letter from "A.O." to the editor of *Mechanics' Magazine* 8 (1828): 320. **35.** Quoted in Jackson, *Story of Writing,* 125.

36. Ibid. The title page of Cocker's *The Pen's Transcendencie,* 1657 (illustrated in Jackson, *Story of Writing,* 124) is outrageously adorned with pictorials of cupids, birds, and the like, all rendered in intricate curlicues. **37.** Johnston, *Writing and Illuminating,* 10; Whalley, *Writing Implements,* 18. **38.** An example is Charles Pearce, *The Little Manual of Calligraphy* (New York: Taplinger, 1981); it is limited to the use of the chisel-edged pen. **39.** *Speedball Textbook for Pen and Brush Lettering,* 20th ed. (Statesville, N.C.: Hunt Mfg. Co., 1972), 38, 44. The angle changes for some styles of lettering. **40.** Ibid., 38-41, 60-62; Charles Stoner, *Beautiful Italic Writing Made Easy* (Philadelphia: Hunt Mfg. Co., 1977), 46-48. **41.** Jackson, *Story of Writing,* 138; Nesbitt, *History and Technique,* 152. **42.** "Mordan and Co.'s Patent Oblique Pens," *Mechanics' Magazine* 17 (1832): 138-39 (illus.). **43.** Tudor Jenks, *The Century World's Fair Book for Boys and Girls* (New York: Century, 1893), 108. **44.** Larry Menser, *Learning Copperplate/ Spencerian Script* (Statesville, N.C.: Hunt Mfg. Co., 1980), 3-5. **45.** Any art store can supply the budding calligrapher with a stylographic pen (e.g., brand name Rapidograph), various calligraphic pens, and other supplies, kits, books, and the like.

46. The first quotation is from E.A. Lupfer, *Ornate Pictorial Calligraphy* (New York: Dover, 1982), back-cover blurb; this is a republication of Lupfer's *Fascinating Pen Flourishing* (Columbus, Ohio: Zaner-Bloser, 1951). Carroll Hopf, "Ornamental Pen Drawing," *Spinning Wheel,* Jan.-Feb. 1968, 14, 15; Hopf notes the term "Spencerian Work" is misleading. **47.** Hopf, *Ornamental Pen Drawing,* 14; Cocker, *The Pen's Transcendencie.* **48.** Hopf, *Ornamental Pen Drawing,* 14. **49.** Ibid. *The Penman's Paradise* was published in St. Louis by Nathaniel Knapp and Levi Rightmyer. **50.** Hill, *Hill's Manual,* 27, plate 8.

13: Written Documents

1. *Ency. Brit.,* 1910-11, 8:367, s.v. "document." **2.** Ibid., 22:958-59, s.v. "record." **3.** Thomas H. Ormsbee, *Field Guide to Early American Furniture* (New York: Bantam, 1980), 167; Walter A. Dyer, *The Lure of the Antique* (1910; repr., Toronto: Coles, 1981), 56. **4.** Russell Hawes Kettell, *The Pine Furniture of Early New England* (1929; repr., New York: Dover, 1956), 102-108 (illus.); Pauline Agius, "Furniture—What is Still Available to Furnishers and Collectors," *Antique Dealer and Collectors Guide,* Oct. 1972, 70. The earliest slant-top desks (boxes) were used in ancient Egypt and later in the medieval monastic scriptorium; one shown placed across the lap, is depicted in a thirteenth-century stone sculpture on a portal of Chartres Cathedral. See Helena Hayward, *World Furniture: An Illustrated History* (New York: McGraw-Hill, 1965), 24; see also Joseph Aronson, *The Encyclopedia of Furniture* (New York: Crown, 1938), 51-52, s.v. "desk." **5.** Ormsbee, *Field Guide,* 167.

6. Dyer, *Lure of the Antique,* 56; Kettell, *Pine Furniture,* 111-14; Albert Sack, *Fine Points of Furniture: Early American* (New York: Crown, 1950), 140-42. **7.** *Ency. Brit.,* 1960, 7:258-59, s.v. "desk"; Robert F.W. Meader, *Illustrated Guide to Shaker Furniture* (New York: Dover, 1972), 59; Alice Winchester, *How to Know American Antiques* (New York: Mentor, 1951), 41; Ralph Kovel and Terry Kovel, "Eighteenth Century Chippendale-style Desks Still Retain Popularity," *Pittsburgh Press,* Feb. 16, 1986. The distinction between "cylinder-top" and "rolltop," usually one of distinguishing between a solid piece and one of slats, is not absolute; one of the latter type, ca. 1765, is illustrated in Hayward, *World Furniture,* 118. **8.** Lester Margon, *Construction of American Furniture Treasures* (1949; repr., New York: Dover, 1956), 61. **9.** Herbert Cescinsky, *The Gentle Art of Faking Furniture* (1931; repr., New York: Dover, 1967), plate 227. A pedestal desk of ca. 1750 is illustrated in Hayward, *World Furniture.* A larger, double-sided version is known as a "partner's desk": see John Bly, "Antiques at Home, Part 2," *Antique Dealer and Collector's Guide,* May 1972, 88. Bly divides desks into "two main types"— the *escritoire* and the flat-topped, kneehole desk—as in the evolutionary chart, fig. 13.1. **10.** Klamkin, *Collectibles,* 247-48. See n.4 about a thirteenth-century depiction of a lap-type desk.

11. Of course the "schoolmaster's desk" and similar student desks in fig. 12.6 are of the same class as that of Hawthorne's mentioned earlier. **12.** Aronson, *Encyclopedia of Furniture,* 51. **13.** Shown, for example, in catalog no. 75 (1937-38), Stratton and Terstegge Co., Wholesale Hardware, Louisville, Ky., 1383-85. **14.** Yvonne Eaton, "Desks," *Courier-Journal* (Louisville, Ky.), Jan. 16, 1984. **15.** Gilbert H. Doane, *Searching for Your Ancestors,* rev. ed. (1948; repr., New York: Bantam, 1974), 36.

16. Ibid., 38-39. By tracking down distant relatives, one may be able to locate one's own family's ancestral Bible, or a copy that may be found when the original can no longer be traced. Numerous Bible records have been published, some in genealogical periodicals, others in volumes devoted to them, still others in family histories; they can be located with the assistance of local and state historical and genealogical societies. A valuable sourcebook for genealogists, listing "record sources from Colonial times to the present," is Arlene Eakle and Johni Cerny, eds., *The Source: A Guidebook of American Genealogy* (Salt Lake City: Ancestry Publishing, 1984). **17.** Doane, *Searching for Your Ancestors*, 88-97. **18.** Berkeley, *Autographs and Manuscripts*, 520; Kirkham, *Handwriting of American Records*, 102. **19.** McClinton, *Antiques*, 98-101 (illus.); see also Klamkin, *Collectibles*, 202, for additional illustrations. **20.** McClinton, *Antiques*, 125.

21. Ibid., 124-34. **22.** Ibid., 127, 130; Benjamin, *Autographs*, 9; Kenneth W. Duckett, *Modern Manuscripts* (Nashville, Tenn.: American Association for State and Local History, 1975), 15. **23.** Benjamin, *Autographs*, 56; Nathaniel E. Stein, "Autographs: Handwritten Witnesses to History," *Encyclopedia of Collectibles*, vol. AB, p. 89. Stein uses the term "clipped signatures." **24.** Berkeley, *Autographs and Manuscripts*, 519, 521. **25.** Herbert E. Klingelhofer, "Hidden Signatures," in Berkeley, *Autographs and Manuscripts*, 106-10; Benjamin, *Autographs*, 166.

26. Klingelhofer, "Hidden Signatures," 107; Benjamin, *Autographs*, 165. **27.** Berkeley, *Autographs and Manuscripts*, 518. **28.** See Charles Hamilton, *Big Name Hunting: A Beginner's Guide to Autograph Collecting* (New York: Simon and Schuster, 1973), and idem., *Collecting Autographs and Manuscripts* (Norman: Univ. of Oklahoma Press, 1961). See also Benjamin's and Berkeley's texts. **29.** Cross-writing (illus. in fig. 13.43) is discussed in Blair, *World of Stamps*, 88, and in Christopher Jarman, *Fun with Pens* (New York: Taplinger, 1970), 16. The Mary Todd Lincoln letter referred to in the caption of fig. 13.44 is in the Special Collections department, Margaret I. King Library, University of Kentucky. **30.** H.R. Verry, *Document Copying and Reproduction Processes* (London: Fountain Press, 1958), 13. Such apparatus would have developed from the cylinder seal.

31. I deduced this technique during a historical-research project (ca. 1980-86) that involved examining numerous old surveys as well as making many plat drawings from the survey "calls" (see Joe Nickell, *Morgan County: The Earliest Years* [West Liberty, Ky.: Courier, 1986], 20). The method was subsequently verified by my great-uncle, M.C. Nickell, a surveyor born in 1892, who could recall when the method had still been in use. I have personally observed the feature in Boone surveys, but how early it was employed is unknown. **32.** *Ency. Brit.*, 1910-11, 28:417, s.v. "Watt, James." **33.** *OED*, 1961, 2:980, s.v. "copying" (citing an 1882 dictionary of chemistry). **34.** Ibid., 4:325, s.v. "flimsy." Flimsy was much used by reporters, hence the term "reporters' 'copy'" (ibid.). **35.** Cited in *OED*, 1961, 2:980, s.v. "copying."

36. Gravell and Miller, *Catalogue of American Watermarks*, 210; Washington's press is exhibited at Mount Vernon and is shown on picture postcards sold there. One model of "Letter-copying press" was patented Nov. 6, 1888 (U.S. patent no. 392, 486). **37.** Thomas Jefferson, letter to C.F.C. De Volney, Feb. 8, 1805; see Andrew A. Lipscomb, ed., *The Writings of Thomas Jefferson*, vol. 11 (Washington, D.C.: Thomas Jefferson Memorial Association, 1903), 67-68. Jefferson's polygraph is exhibited at Monticello. **38.** *OED*, 1961, 2:980, s.v. "copying." Copying pencils, books, and the like are listed in the Carrithers catalog, ca. 1925. **39.** Verry, *Document Copying*, 23-25. **40.** *Ency. Brit.*, 1910-11, 7:118, s.v. "copying machines"; ibid., 1960, 16:716, s.v. "office machines"; *Webster's New International Dictionary*, 2nd ed., 1154, s.v. "hectograph."
41. *Ency. Brit.*, 1960, 16:716, s.v. "office machines."
42. Ibid., 1910-11, 7:118, s.v. "copying machines." **43.** Pat-

ents no. 180,857, Aug. 8, 1876, and no. 224,665, Feb. 17, 1880 (cited in Kane, *Famous First Facts*, 4th ed., 390-91); *Webster's*, 2d ed., s.v. "mimeograph." See also *Ency. Brit.*, 1960, 16:715-16, s.v. "office machines." **44.** De Bono, *Eureka!*, 61-62.

14: Decipherment

1. Paleography is the study of ancient modes of writing for purposes of decipherment (as in this chapter), determining age (chap. 15), or, occasionally, determining authenticity (chap. 16). **2.** Ogg, *26 Letters*, 45-49. **3.** *Ency. Brit.*, 1973, 6:898, s.v. "cuneiform." **4.** For example, Samuel A. Tannenbaum, *The Handwriting of the Renaissance* (New York: Columbia Univ. Press, 1930); L.C. Hector, *The Handwriting of English Documents* (London: Arnold, 1958); and E. Kay Kirkham, *Handwriting of American Records*. Among the texts focusing on a single script is E.A. Lowe, *English Uncial* (Oxford: Clarendon, 1960).
5. The "Hoffort" error is cited in Bill Linder, "The Early Handwriting," *How to Trace Your Family History* (New York: Fawcett, 1977), 172. See also Kirkham, *Handwriting of American Records*, 42.
6. In addition to the *abbreviation* (a shortened form of a word or phrase) and *contraction* (an omission of a letter or letters), there is the *brevigraph* (contraction of certain recurrent syllables such as *er*), *elision* (omission of a portion of a word for ease of pronunciation; e.g., "ne'er" for "never") and *curtailment* (omission of the final letter of a word); see Tannenbaum, *Handwriting of English Documents*, 119-38. **7.** Kirkham, *Handwriting of American Records*, 24-28. **8.** E.E. Thoyts, *How to Decipher and Study Old Documents*, 2d ed. (1903; repr. Detroit: Gale Research, 1974), 143. **9.** For example, in Kirkham, *Handwriting of American Records*, 24-64; Thoyts, *How to Decipher*, 142-47. **10.** Kirkham, *Handwriting of American Records*, 97-106, for an example.
11. Ibid., v. **12.** Joe Nickell and John F. Fischer, "Daniel Boone Fakelore," *Filson Club History Quarterly* 62 (Oct. 1988): 465. **13.** Thoyts, *How to Decipher*, 12. **14.** Ibid., 11.
15. The erroneous transcription appeared in Willard Rouse Jillson, *Filson's Kentucke* (Louisville, Ky.: J.P. Morgan, 1930), 179.
16. *History of Ink*. **17.** George Martin Cunha and Dorothy Grant Cunha, *Conservation of Library Materials*, 2d ed., vol. 1 (Metuchen, N.J.: Scarecrow Press, 1971), 170-71. See also Ordway Hilton, *An Evaluation of Chemical Methods for Restoring Erased Writing Ink* (London: Swindon Press, n.d.). **18.** John F. Fischer, personal communication; see also Osborn, *Questioned Documents*, 61, and Niel F. Beardsley, "The Photography of Altered and Faded Manuscripts," *Library Journal* 61 (1936): 96-99. **19.** *Applied Infrared Photography* (Rochester, N.Y.: Eastman Kodak, 1972), 51-53 (illus.). For an illustration of writing restored from a charred document, see Fred E. Inbau, Andre A. Moenssens, and Louis R. Vitullo, *Scientific Police Investigation* (New York: Chilton, 1972), 61. **20.** *Applied Infrared Photography*.
21. Ada Nisbet, *Dickens and Ellen Ternan* (Berkeley: Univ. of California Press, 1952), 55. **22.** John F. Fischer and Joe Nickell, "Laser Light: Space-age Forensics," *Law Enforcement Technology*, Sept. 1984, 27. **23.** John F. Fischer, personal communication. **24.** E. Patrick McGuire, *The Forgers* (Bernardsville, N.J.: Padric Pub., 1969), 173-74. See also Inbau, et al., *Scientific Police Investigation*, 58-60; Osborn, *Questioned Documents*, 60. All three sources provide photographs. **25.** See David Kahn, *The Codebreakers: The Story of Secret Writing* (New York: Signet, 1973); Herbert S. Zim, *Codes and Secret Writing* (New York: Scholastic Book Services, 1966), 6-10.
26. Nisbet, *Dickens and Ellen Ternan*, 54. **27.** Martin Gardner, *Codes, Ciphers, and Secret Writing* (New York: Pocket

Books, 1972), 1-31; Andrew Pennycook, *Codes and Ciphers* (New York: David McKay, 1980); Henry Lysing, *Secret Writing: An Introduction to Cryptograms, Ciphers, and Codes* (1936; repr., New York: Dover, 1974). **28.** See Zim, *Codes*, 69-72; Gardner, *Codes, Ciphers*, 1-14. The serious student should consult Helen Fouche Gaines, *Cryptanalysis: A Study of Ciphers and Their Solutions* (New York: Dover, 1956). **29.** Fletcher Pratt, *Secret and Urgent: The Story of Codes and Ciphers* (Garden City, N.Y.: Blue Ribbon Books, 1942); Gaines, *Cryptanalysis*. **30.** Sir Arthur Conan Doyle, *The Complete Sherlock Holmes* (Garden City, N.Y.: Garden City Books, n.d.), 593-612; *Edgar Allan Poe's Tales of Mystery and Imagination* (New York: Dutton, 1908), 69-101. **31.** Zim, *Codes*, 107.

15: Age Determination

1. Charles E. O'Hara, *Fundamentals of Criminal Investigation*, 3d ed. (Springfield, Ill.: C. C. Thomas, 1973), 811. **2.** Osborn, *Questioned Documents*, 571. **3.** Hamilton, *Great Forgers*, 172-84. **4.** Ibid., 29, 31. **5.** See Joe Nickell, *Inquest on the Shroud of Turin*, updated ed. (Buffalo: Prometheus, 1987), 146-47. **6.** In addition to the index, see the chronological charts, app. 2. **7.** Gaskell, *New Introduction to Bibliography*, 16ff. **8.** For example, see Glaister, *Glaister's Glossary*. For a concise discussion of printing, see Gaskell, *New Introduction to Bibliography*, 266-73; see also specific entries in Glaister, *Glaister's Glossary*. **9.** Joe Nickell, "Discovered: The Secret of Beale's Treasure," *Virginia Magazine of History and Biography* 90 (1982): 310-24. For more on linguistic analysis, see A.Q. Morton, *Literary Detection: How to Prove Authorship and Fraud in Literature and Documents* (New York: Scribner's, 1978). Morton's methodology employs a computer to compare such factors as sentence length, occurrence of certain common words as percentages of the text, occurrence of such words in certain preferred positions, and similar writing habits. **10.** Nickell and Fischer, "Daniel Boone Fakelore," 447-49. **11.** O'Hara, *Fundamentals of Criminal Investigation*, 811. **12.** Churchill, *Watermarks*, 357-58. **13.** *OED*, 1961, 7:186, s.v. "ordinance." **14.** "A Scandal in America," part 2, *Book Collector* 37 (Spring 1988): 12. **15.** Ibid., 12-18. **16.** Osborn, *Questioned Documents*, 571-72.

16: Questioned Documents

1. Osborn, *Questioned Documents*, 1. **2.** A discussion of typewriting identification is beyond the scope of this book; however, good introductions are provided by O'Hara, *Fundamentals of Criminal Investigation*, 799-805, and Paul L. Kirk, *Crime Investigation*, 2d ed., ed. John I. Thornton (New York: Wiley, 1974), 489-91; for a more extensive treatment, see Osborn, *Questioned Documents*, 581-608, and Hilton, *Scientific Examination*, 48-65. On authenticity of writing, O'Hara, *Fundamentals of Criminal Investigation*, 783. **3.** John I. Thornton and Edward F. Rhodes, "Brief History of Questioned Document Examination," *Identification News*, Jan. 1986, 7. **4.** F. Demelle, *Advis pour juger des inscriptions en faulz ou comparison descouvrir totes falsifications et saulsetz*, 1609; J. Raveneau, *Traité de inscriptions en faux et reconnoissance d'escritures et signatures pas comparison et autrement* (Paris: Chez T. Iolly, 1666); both cited in Thornton and Rhodes, "Brief History," 7, 12. **5.** Thornton and Rhodes, "Brief History," 7, 12; Ordway Hilton, "History of Questioned Document Examination in the United States," *Journal of Forensic Sciences*, JFSCA, 24, no. 4 (1979): 890-91.

6. Thornton and Rhodes, "Brief History," 7. **7.** Ibid. **8.** *Ency. Brit.*, 1960, 9:514, s.v. "forgery." **9.** Ibid., 18:662, s.v. "Psalmanazar, George." **10.** Hamilton, *Great Forgers*, 166; K. Rendell, "Great Forgers: Their Successes and Downfalls," in Berkeley, *Autographs and Manuscripts*, 92-93; *Ency. Brit.*, 1960, 5:324-25, s.v. "Chatterton, Thomas." **11.** Hamilton, *Great Forgers*, 166; K. Rendell, "Great Forgers," 92-93; *Ency. Brit.*, 1960, 12:591, s.v. "Ireland, William Henry." **12.** Hamilton, *Great Forgers*, 44-61, 88-120. **13.** Irving forgery discussed in ibid., 166-171; Robert Harris, *Selling Hitler* (New York: Penguin Books, 1987); Steven Naifeh and Gregory White Smith, *The Mormon Murders: A True Story of Greed, Forgery, Deceit, and Death* (New York: Weidenfeld and Nicolson, 1988). **14.** I had been queried by the Salt Lake City district attorney's office concerning artificial aging of iron-gallotannate ink. Subsequently I sent a letter report to that office (Joe Nickell to Gerry D'Elia, Mar. 28, 1986) pointing out anomalies seen in a photograph of the letter in question. See also Charles Hamilton, letter to editor, *Maine Antique Digest*, June 1987, 3-A. **15.** The serious student should consult such additional sources as Kenneth W. Rendell's "The Detection of Forgeries," in Berkeley, *Autographs and Manuscripts*, 73-91; Hamilton's "Thirteen Rules for Spotting Forgeries," chap. 20 of his *Great Forgers*, 261-68; Osborn's *Questioned Documents*; Hilton's *Scientific Examination of Questioned Documents*; and O'Hara's "Documentary Evidence," chap. 43 of his *Fundamentals of Criminal Investigation*, 783-832. **16.** Hamilton, *Great Forgers*, 261. **17.** Osborn, *Questioned Documents*, 167. **18.** Hamilton, *Great Forgers and Famous Fakes*, 91. **19.** Ibid., 48, 264-65. **20.** Gideon Epstein, a document expert, in testimony at the Israeli trial of the Nazi war criminal John Demjanjuk, May 5 and 11, 1987, transcript p. 5814. **21.** K. Rendell, "Detection of Forgeries," 75. **22.** Hamilton, *Great Forgers*, 264. **23.** K. Rendell, "Detection of Forgeries," 82. **24.** Ibid.; Hamilton, *Great Forgers*, 268. **25.** Ibid.; Epstein, transcript p. 5728; Osborn, *Questioned Documents*, 331-32. **26.** Osborn, *Questioned Documents*, 110-15; Hamilton, *Great Forgers*, 267-68. **27.** K. Rendell, "Detection of Forgeries," 79; Hamilton, *Great Forgers*, 100, 266-67. **28.** K. Rendell, "Detection of Forgeries," 80. **29.** Osborn, *Questioned Documents*, 521. **30.** O'Hara, *Fundamentals of Criminal Investigation*, 810-11; Osborn, *Questioned Documents*, 570; K. Rendell, "Detection of Forgeries," 84. **31.** K. Rendell, "Detection of Forgeries," 84. **32.** Robert A. Jones, "The White Salamander Murders," part 2, *Los Angeles Times Magazine*, Apr. 5, 1987, 38, 46. **33.** Roy L. Davids, quoted in Nickell, *Literary Investigation*, 146. See also Robert L. Volz, "Fair Copies and Working Copies," in Berkeley, *Autographs and Manuscripts*, 129, and Frankleyn Lenthall, "American Theater," in Berkeley, 477. **34.** Hamilton, *Great Forgers*, 265. **35.** Kirk, *Crime Investigation*, 501. **36.** O'Hara, *Fundamentals of Criminal Investigation*, 785. **37.** Ibid., 785-86. **38.** Epstein, transcript pp. 5720-21. **39.** Ibid., 5721-23. **40.** O'Hara, *Fundamentals of Criminal Investigation*, 786. For a full discussion of the subject, see Osborn, *Questioned Documents*. **41.** O'Hara, *Fundamentals of Criminal Investigation*, 796; Osborn, *Questioned Documents*, 418. **42.** Osborn, *Questioned Documents*, 418. **43.** See Inbau, Moenssens, and Vitullo, *Scientific Police Investigation*, 56. **44.** Epstein, transcript, pp. 5738, 5811. **45.** Ibid., 5811. This controversial subject requires more discussion than can be given here. For a favorable view of graphology, see the British graphologist Margaret Gullan-Whur's *The Graphology Workbook: A Complete Guide to Interpreting*

Handwriting (Wellingborough, England: Aquarian Press, 1986); for skeptical studies, see Adrian Furnham, "Write and Wrong: The Validity of Graphological Analysis," *Skeptical Inquirer* 13 (Fall 1988): 64-69, and Abraham Jansen, *Validation of Graph-*

46. Osborn, *Questioned Documents,* 249-69, 381-83.
47. Joseph E. Fields, "Confused Identities," in Berkeley, *Autographs and Manuscripts,* 111-16. See also "Confused Identities," chap. 11 of Benjamin, *Autographs,* 191-221.   **48.** Charles Hamilton, *The Book of Autographs* (New York: Simon and Schuster, 1978), 21-22.   **49.** Kenneth W. Duckett, *Modern Manuscripts* (Nashville, Tenn.: American Association for State and Local History, 1975), 304-307.   **50.** H. Keith Thompson, "The Autopen and the Signa-Signer," in Berkeley, *Autographs and Manuscripts,* 100-105. See also "HUD Scandal Verifies Collector's Warnings about the Autopen," *Manuscript Society News,* Winter 1990, 11-12.
51. Fischer and Nickell, "Laser Light," 26-27.
52. Timothy W. Sinor, et al. "Lasers and Optical Spectroscopy in Questioned Document Examination," *Journal of Forensic Sciences,* JFSCA, 31, no. 3 (July 1986): 825-39.   **53.** Joseph Sherma and Bernard Fried, "Thin-Layer and Paper Chromatography," *Analytical Chemistry* 56 (1984): 48-49.   **54.** For works on typewriter identification, see n. 2; for checkwriters, handstamps, and forged stamp impressions and cancellations, see Hilton, *Scientific Examination,* 67-73, and McGuire, *Forgers,* 192-94. For detection of erasures and other alterations, see O'Hara, *Fundamentals of Criminal Investigation,* 763-70, 815-17, 821-22; Hilton, *Scientific Examination,* 91-111; Osborn, *Questioned Documents.* For fingerprints, see O'Hara, *Fundamentals of Criminal Investigation,* 660-70; Fischer and Nickell, "Laser Light", and Hilton, *Scientific Examination,* 120-22. For various markings, stains, and foreign matter, see Hilton, *Scientific Examination,* 89; O'Hara, *Fundamentals of Criminal Investigation,* 813, 487ff., 719-26. Perusal of the *Journal of Forensic Sciences,* JFSCA, will reveal many specialized analyses relating to document examination.

APPENDIX 3: Laboratory Identification of Pens, Ink, & Papers

1. Grant, *Books and Documents,* 39.   **2.** Osborn, *Questioned Documents,* 160-61.   **3.** See ibid., 160, for an illustration.
4. Jackson, *Story of Writing,* 168.   **5.** Osborn, *Questioned Documents,* 454-55.
6. Inbau, Moenssens, and Vitullo, *Scientific Police Investigation,* 67.   **7.** Osborn, *Questioned Documents,* 453; C. Ainsworth Mitchell, *Documents and Their Scientific Investigation* (London: C. Griffin, 1935).   **8.** Cunha and Cunha, *Conservation of Library Materials,* 1:344.   **9.** Osborn, *Questioned Documents,* 458-59.
10. K. Rendell, "Detection of Forgeries," 79.
11. Osborn, *Questioned Documents,* 459-60.   **12.** Hunter, *Papermaking,* 400-406.   **13.** Berkeley, *Autographs and Manuscripts,* 38.   **14.** Hunter, *Questioned Documents,* 412. Specialized works identifying watermarks include Charles-Moise Briquet, *Les filigrantes* (1907; repr., Amsterdam: Paper Pub. Soc., 1968); W.A. Churchill, *Watermarks in Paper in Holland, France, etc. in the XVII and XVIII Centuries* (Amsterdam: M. Hertzberger, 1935); Gravell and Miller, *Catalogue of American Watermarks.* The standard treatise on paper is Hunter, *Papermaking.*   **15.** Cunha and Cunha, *Conservation,* 330.
16. Ibid., 329-33; Emil Chamot and Clyde Walter Mason, *Handbook of Chemical Microscopy,* 3d ed., vol. 1 (New York: Wiley, 1958), 170-71.   **17.** Grant, *Books and Documents,* 8-32.
18. Ibid., 72-92; McGuire, *Forgers,* 191.   **19.** Osborn, *Questioned Documents,* 479-98; Albert H. Lyter and Richard L. Brunelle, "A Systematic Approach for the Comparison of Paper Samples," *Identification News,* May 1977, 3-6.

INDEX

Joe Nickell, a former professional investigator with a world-famous detective agency, teaches business and technical writing at the University of Kentucky. His doctoral work focused on aspects of "literary investigation," including dating and authenticating written texts. A calligrapher, with an extensive collection of historical documents and antique writing materials, Dr. Nickell is a member of the Manuscript Society, the Society of Inkwell Collectors, and the International Association of Master Penmen, Engrossers, and Teachers of Handwriting. He has published many articles on various technical and investigative subjects and is the author of two books dealing with forgeries and other deceptions: *Inquest on the Shroud of Turin* (1983, 1987) and, with John F. Fischer, *Secrets of the Supernatural* (1988), both published by Prometheus Books.

Robert H. van Outer is a professional photographer in Lexington, Kentucky. He has done considerable work for document examiners, including preparation of photographic exhibits for courtroom presentation in both civil and criminal cases.

John F. Fischer is a forensic analyst in a Florida crime laboratory whose fields of expertise include microchemical and instrumental analysis. He is also president of a corporation specializing in forensic research, especially in the field of laser technology. His articles have appeared in such publications as *Identification News* and *Law Enforcement Technology.* With Joe Nickell, he is author of *Secrets of the Supernatural.* He has lectured widely on a variety of forensic subjects, including the "blood" on the Shroud of Turin and laser application to fingerprints and other trace evidence.